Second Language Acquisition and Universal Grammar

This authoritative textbook provides an overview and analysis of current second language acquisition research conducted within the generative linguistic framework. Lydia White argues that second language acquisition is constrained by principles and parameters of Universal Grammar. The book focuses on characterizing and explaining the underlying linguistic competence of second language learners in terms of these contraints. Theories as to the role of Universal Grammar and the extent of mother-tongue influence are presented and discussed, with particular consideration given to the nature of the interlanguage grammar at different points in development, from the initial state to the ultimate attainment. Throughout the book, hypotheses maintaining that second language grammars are constrained by universal principles are contrasted with claims that Universal Grammar is not implicated; relevant empirical research is presented from both sides of the debate. This textbook is essential reading for those studying second language acquisition from a linguistic perspective.

LYDIA WHITE is Professor of Linguistics at McGill University, Montréal, and Chair of the Linguistics Department. She is internationally known as a leading expert on second language acquisition. She is the author of *Universal Grammar and Second Language Acquisition* (John Benjamins, 1989) and publishes regularly in major international journals on language acquisition.

CAMBRIDGE TEXTBOOKS IN LINGUISTICS

Second Language Acquisition and Universal Grammar

In this series

P. H. MATTHEWS *Morphology* Second edition
B. COMRIE *Aspect*
R. M. KEMPSON *Semantic Theory*
T. BYNON *Historical Linguistics*
J. ALLWOOD, L.-G. ANDERSON and Ö. DAHL *Logic in Linguistics*
D. B. FRY *The Physics of Speech*
R. A. HUDSON *Sociolinguistics* Second edition
A. J. ELLIOTT *Child Language*
P. H. MATTHEWS *Syntax*
A. RADFORD *Transformational Syntax*
L. BAUER *English Word-Formation*
S. C. LEVINSON *Pragmatics*
G. BROWN and G. YULE *Discourse Analysis*
R. HUDDLESTON *Introduction to the Grammar of English*
R. LASS *Phonology*
B. COMRIE *Tense*
W. KLEIN *Second Language Acquisition*
A. J. WOODS, P. FLETCHER and A. HUGHES *Statistics in Language Studies*
D. A. CRUSE *Lexical Semantics*
A. RADFORD *Transformational Grammar*
M. GARMAN *Psycholinguistics*
W. CROFT *Typology and Universals*
G. G. CORBETT *Gender*
H. J. GIEGERICH *English Phonology*
R. CANN *Formal Semantics*
P. J. HOPPER and E. C. TRAUGOTT *Grammaticalization*
J. LAVER *Principles of Phonetics*
F. R. PALMER *Grammatical Roles and Relations*
M. A. JONES *Foundations of French Syntax*
A. RADFORD *Syntactic Theory and the Structure of English: A Minimalist Approach*
R. D. VAN VALIN, JR, and R. J. LAPOLLA *Syntax: Structure, Meaning and Function*
A. DURANTI *Linguistic Anthropology*
A. CRUTTENDEN *Intonation* Second edition
J. K. CHAMBERS and P. TRUDGILL *Dialectology* Second edition
C. LYONS *Definiteness*
R. KAGER *Optimality Theory*
J. A. HOLM *An Introduction to Pidgins and Creoles*
C. G. CORBETT *Number*
C. J. EWEN and H. VAN DER HULST *The Phonological Structure of Words*
F. R. PALMER *Mood and Modality* Second edition
B. J. BLAKE *Case* Second edition
E. GUSSMAN Phonology: Analysis and Theory
M. YIP *Tone*
W. CROFT *Typology and Universals*
F. COULMAS *Writing Systems: An Introduction to Their Linguistic Analysis*
L. WHITE *Second Language Acquisition and Universal Grammar*

Second Language Acquisition and Universal Grammar

LYDIA WHITE

McGill University, Montréal

PUBLISHED BY THE PRESS SYNDICATE OF THE UNIVERSITY OF CAMBRIDGE
The Pitt Building, Trumpington Street, Cambridge CB2 1RP, United Kingdom

CAMBRIDGE UNIVERSITY PRESS
The Edinburgh Building, Cambridge, CB2 2RU, UK
40 West 20th Street, New York, NY 10011-4211, USA
477 Williamstown Road, Port Melbourne, VIC 3207, Australia
Ruiz de Alarcón 13, 28014 Madrid, Spain
Dock House, The Waterfront, Cape Town 8001, South Africa

http://www.cambridge.org

First published 2003
Third printing 2005

Printed in the United Kingdom at the University Press, Cambridge

Typeface Times and Formata Regular 10/13 pt *System* LaTeX 2ε [TB]

A catalogue record for this book is available from the British Library

ISBN 0 521 79205 3 hardback
ISBN 0 521 79647 4 paperback

Contents

Preface

This book examines the extent to which the underlying linguistic competence of learners or speakers of a second language (L2) is constrained by the same universal principles that govern natural language in general. It is presupposed that there is an innately given Universal Grammar (UG), which constrains first language (L1) grammars, placing limits on the kinds of hypotheses that L1 acquirers entertain as to the nature of the language that they are acquiring. Assuming the correctness of this general approach, the question arises as to whether UG constrains grammars in non-primary language acquisition as well. This book will present and discuss research which investigates whether or not interlanguage grammars can be characterized in terms of principles and parameters of UG, and which explores the nature of interlanguage competence during the course of L2 acquisition, from the initial state onwards. It is hoped that the book will provide sufficient background for the reader to understand current research conducted within the framework of UG and L2 acquisition.

The generative perspective on L2 acquisition is sometimes dismissed because it has a rather circumscribed goal, namely to describe and explain the nature of interlanguage competence, defined in a technical and limited sense. Researchers whose work is discussed in this book do not seek to provide an all encompassing theory of L2 acquisition, or to account the role of performance factors, psychological processes and mechanisms, sociolinguistic variables, etc. In fact, it is doubtful whether there is any one theory that can achieve all this; certainly, no theory has succeeded so far.

It will be presupposed that the reader has some familiarity with the concepts and mechanisms assumed in current generative grammar, including the Government and Binding framework and Minimalism. The book will not be concerned with the precise technical details as to how UG principles and parameters are formulated, nor with the intricacies of current linguistic theory. Indeed, the intention is to consider the L2 issues without being tied down to a particular version of generative theory. The linguistic principles and parameters that will be discussed are those that have attracted attention in the L2 field. Out of context, these principles may sometimes seem ad hoc. It is important to understand that they are part of a system of knowledge, accounting for far more than whatever we happen to touch on in this book. A list of abbreviations and a glossary are provided which give definitions of the main linguistic and acquisition terminology used throughout the book.

This book is not intended to be a revised version of my earlier work (White 1989), which examined the first decade of research (conducted during the 1980s) on UG and L2 acquisition, looking at claims for the availability of principles and parameters of UG. There has been an enormous increase in research conducted within this general framework since that time and it is not possible to do justice to all of it. The current work takes a somewhat different perspective, a perspective which is more representative of research conducted during the 1990s. The book is organized as follows: chapter 1 provides a general introduction to UG and the logical problem of language acquisition; chapter 2 considers the logical problem of L2 language acquisition and the issue of whether principles of UG constrain interlanguage grammars; chapter 3 examines hypotheses as to the nature of the initial state (the L2 learner's earliest assumptions about the L2), including the influence of the L1 grammar; chapter 4 looks at the issue of developing grammars in the context of parameters and parameter resetting; chapter 5 considers what properties of the L2 input might stimulate grammar change; chapter 6 investigates dissociations between morphology and syntax in interlanguage grammars; chapter 7 explores the nature of argument structure and the influence of the L1 on argument structure representations; finally, in chapter 8 the nature of the ultimate attainment of L2 learners is discussed. Each chapter ends with some suggestions for general discussion, often on broader issues than those raised in the chapter in question, as well as further reading.

Throughout the book, where experiments are described, the main details of the experiment (including the languages involved, example stimuli, results, etc.) are summarized in boxes, offset from the main text. In many cases, it has been necessary to be selective in deciding which aspects of a particular experiment to focus on, in order to fit with the general themes of the book. If this has led to misrepresentation, I apologize! Readers are strongly encouraged to go to the original sources for further details, especially if they are themselves intending to pursue experimental research.

The terms *L2 learner* and *L2 speaker* are adopted as convenient cover terms for non-native acquisition or the learning of any number of languages (L2, L3, L4, Ln). No distinction will be made between second language acquisition and foreign language learning. In principle at least, any kind of non-native acquisition or learning should be subject to the same constraints, although lack of suitable input may be a major inhibiting factor in certain foreign language learning contexts.

Many people have provided helpful input on the manuscript, at various stages. For their thoughtful and detailed comments and suggestions, I would particularly like to thank: Kevin Gregg, Donna Lardiere, Dawn MacLaughlin, Bonnie Schwartz and Antonella Sorace, as well as the anonymous reviewers for Cambridge University Press. The material in this book has formed the core of my graduate seminar on L2 acquisition for several years and I would like to acknowledge the contribution of many former and current graduate students of the Linguistics Department at McGill University: their stimulating discussion and questioning of many of the issues presented here has been invaluable, as well as their ability in catching typos.

Abbreviations

Adj	adjective
AdjP	adjective phrase
A(dv)	adverb
ACC	accusative case
Agr	the functional category Agreement
AgrP	Agreement Phrase
ASP	aspect marker
Asp	the functional category Aspect
AspP	Aspect Phrase
CAUS	causative
CL	classifier
CLI	clitic
CNPC	Complex Noun Phrase Constraint
COMP	complementizer
C(omp)	the functional category Complementizer
CP	Complementizer Phrase
DAT	dative
DEC	declarative marker
D(et)	the functional category Determiner
DP	Determiner Phrase
FEM	feminine
F	finite
FP	finite phrase
GEN	genitive
GER	gerund
IMP	imperfect
INF	infinitive
I(nfl)	the functional category Inflection
IP	Inflection Phrase
MASC	masculine
n	number of subjects

#	number of stimuli
Neg	the functional category Negation
NegP	Negation Phrase
NOM	nominative case
N	noun
NP	noun phrase
ns	not significant
NS	native speaker
Num	the functional category Number
NumP	Number Phrase
O	object
PL	plural
P	preposition
PP	prepositional phrase
PASS	passive
PERF	perfective
POL	politeness marker
PRES	present
PRET	preterite
PRT	particle
PS	person
Q	question marker
S	subject
SG	singular
sig	significant
Spec	specifier
SUBJ	subjunctive
T	the functional category Tense
TP	Tense Phrase
TOP	topic marker
V	verb
VP	verb phrase
V2	verb second
V3	verb third
1	1st person
2	2nd person
3	3rd person

1 Universal Grammar and language acquisition

1.1 Introduction

This book will be concerned with characterizing and explaining the linguistic systems that second language (L2) learners develop, considering in particular the extent to which the underlying linguistic competence of L2 speakers is constrained by the same universal principles that govern natural language in general. Following Chomsky (1959, 1965, 1975, 1980, 1981a, b, 1986b, 1999), a particular perspective on linguistic universals will be adopted and certain assumptions about the nature of linguistic competence will be taken for granted. In particular, it will be presupposed that the linguistic competence of native speakers of a language can be accounted for in terms of an abstract and unconscious linguistic system, in other words, a grammar, which underlies use of language, including comprehension and production. Native-speaker grammars are constrained by built-in universal linguistic principles, known as Universal Grammar (UG).

Throughout this book, non-native grammars will be referred to as *interlanguage grammars*. The concept of interlanguage was proposed independently in the late 1960s and early 1970s by researchers such as Adjémian (1976), Corder (1967), Nemser (1971) and Selinker (1972). These researchers pointed out that L2 learner language is systematic and that the errors produced by learners do not consist of random mistakes but, rather, suggest rule-governed behaviour. Such observations led to the proposal that L2 learners, like native speakers, represent the language that they are acquiring by means of a complex linguistic system.

The current generative linguistic focus on the nature of interlanguage has its origins in the original interlanguage hypothesis. Explicit claims are made about the underlying grammars of L2 learners and L2 speakers, the issues including a consideration of the role of UG and the extent to which interlanguage grammars exhibit properties of natural language. Such questions will be explored in detail in this book. It will be suggested that the linguistic behaviour of non-native speakers can be accounted for in terms of interlanguage grammars which are constrained by principles and parameters of UG. At the same time, it will be recognized that interlanguage grammars differ in various ways from the grammars of native speakers, and some of these differences will be explored.

1.2 Universal Grammar in L1 acquisition

A major task for the first language (L1) acquirer is to arrive at a linguistic system which accounts for the input, allowing the child to build linguistic representations and to understand and produce language. UG is proposed as part of an innate biologically endowed language faculty (e.g. Chomsky 1965, 1981b; Pinker 1984, 1994), which permits the L1 acquirer to arrive at a grammar on the basis of linguistic experience (exposure to input). UG provides a *genetic blueprint*, determining in advance what grammars can (and cannot) be like. In the first place, UG places requirements on the form of grammars, providing an inventory of possible grammatical categories and features in the broadest sense, i.e. syntactic, morphological, phonological and semantic. In addition, it constrains the functioning of grammars, by determining the nature of the computational system, including the kinds of operation that can take place, as well as principles that grammars are subject to. UG includes invariant principles, that is, principles that are generally true across languages, as well as parameters which allow for variation from language to language.

Throughout this book it will be presupposed that UG constrains L1 acquisition, as well as adult native-speaker knowledge of language. That is, grammars of children and adults conform to the principles and parameters of UG. The child acquires linguistic competence in the L1. Properties of the language are mentally represented by means of an unconscious, internalized linguistic system (a grammar). As Chomsky (1980: 48) puts it, there is : 'a certain mental structure consisting of a system of rules and principles that generate and relate mental representations of various types'.[1]

UG constitutes the child's initial state (S_0), the knowledge that the child is equipped with in advance of input. The primary linguistic data (PLD) are critical in helping the child to determine the precise form that the grammar must take. As the child takes account of the input, a language-specific lexicon is built up, and parameters of UG are set to values appropriate for the language in question. The grammar (G) may be restructured over the course of time, as the child becomes responsive to different properties of the input. In due course, the child arrives at a steady state grammar for the mother tongue (S_S). This model of acquisition is schematized in figure 1.1.

As linguistic theories such as Government–Binding (Chomsky 1981a), Minimalism (Chomsky 1995) or Optimality Theory (Archangeli and Langendoen 1997)

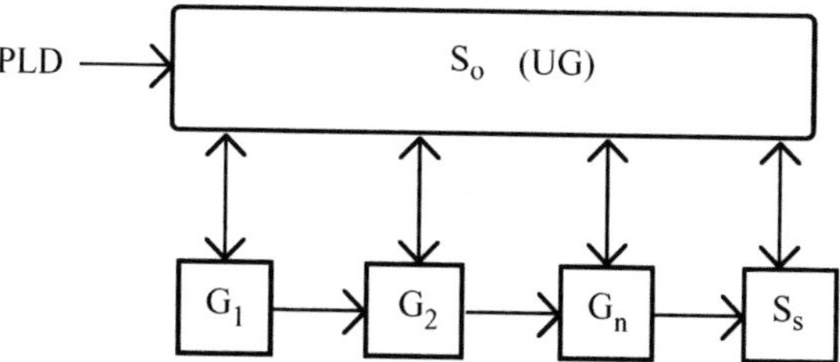

Figure 1.1 *Model of L1 acquisition*

have developed, there have been changes in how universal principles and parameters have been formalized, in other words, changes in what UG is assumed to consist of. For example, the numerous and very specific principles of the early days of generative theory, such as many of the original *Island Constraints* (Ross 1967), have been replaced with more general, invariant economy principles (e.g. Chomsky 1991), as well as computational operations, such as *Move* and *Merge* (see Marantz 1995). Parameters have gradually become more constrained, now being largely associated with the lexicon: properties of items that enter into a computation, for example, may vary in feature composition and feature strength, with associated syntactic consequences.

Such ongoing changes in the definition of UG are a reflection of development and growth within linguistic theory. Nevertheless, regardless of how UG is formalized, there remains a consensus (within the generative linguistic perspective) that certain properties of language are too abstract, subtle and complex to be acquired without assuming some innate and specifically linguistic constraints on grammars and grammar acquisition. Furthermore, there is fairly widespread agreement as to what these problematic phenomena are. This issue will be considered in more detail in the next section.

1.3 Why UG? The logical problem of language acquisition

The arguments for some sort of biological basis to L1 acquisition are well-known (e.g. Aitchison 1976; Chomsky 1959, 1965, 1981b, 1986b; O'Grady 1997; Pinker 1994): the language capacity is species specific; ability to acquire language is independent of intelligence; the pattern of acquisition is relatively uniform across different children, different languages and different cultures; language is acquired with relative ease and rapidity and without the benefit of instruction; children show creativity which goes beyond the input that they are exposed to. All of these observations point to an innate component to language acquisition. However, it is conceivable that an innate capacity for language acquisition could be general rather than domain specific and that cognitive principles not unique to language might be implicated (for relevant proposals, see O'Grady 1987, 1996, 1997, 2003). Thus, it is important to understand the arguments in favour of an innate component that is specifically linguistic in character.

UG is motivated by learnability arguments: the primary linguistic data underdetermine unconscious knowledge of language in ways which implicate specifically linguistic principles. In other words, there is a mismatch between the input (the utterances that the child is exposed to), and the output (the unconscious grammatical knowledge that the child acquires). This mismatch gives rise to what is known as the problem of the *poverty of the stimulus* or the *logical problem of language acquisition*. Given such underdetermination, the claim is that it would be impossible to account for the L1 acquirer's achievement without postulating a built-in system of universal linguistic principles and grammatical properties (Baker and McCarthy 1981; Hornstein and Lightfoot 1981). UG, then, is proposed as an explanation of how it is that language acquirers come to know, unconsciously, properties of grammar that go far beyond the input in various respects. The idea is that such properties do not have to be learned; they are part of the 'advance knowledge' that the child brings to bear on the task of acquiring a language.

The child's linguistic experience includes what is known as *positive evidence*; that is, the primary linguistic data include utterances that in some sense reveal properties of the underlying grammar (but see chapter 5). *Negative evidence*, or information about ungrammaticality, is not (reliably) available. Nevertheless, children come to know that certain sentence types are disallowed; furthermore, they acquire knowledge that certain interpretations are permitted only in certain contexts (see section 1.3.1). This kind of knowledge is acquired even though children are not taught about ungrammaticality, explicitly or implicitly.

1.3.1 An example: the Overt Pronoun Constraint

As an example of abstract knowledge which children successfully acquire despite an underdetermination problem, we consider here subtle interpretive phenomena relating to subject pronouns. It will be suggested that these properties could not be acquired solely on the basis of input; rather, a universal linguistic principle is implicated.

Languages differ as to whether or not subject pronouns must be phonetically realized, that is whether pronouns are overt or null (Chomsky 1981a; Jaeggli 1982; Rizzi 1982). In languages like English, known as [−null subject] languages, pronouns must be overtly expressed, as can be seen by comparing (1a) and (1b).

However, in *null subject* or *prodrop* languages (in other words, [+null subject] languages), pronouns may be null, taking the form of an empty category, *pro*. Typical examples are Romance languages like Spanish and Italian, as well as East Asian languages such as Chinese, Japanese and Korean. The Spanish example in (1c) and the Japanese example in (1d) illustrate this point. (Spanish examples in this section are drawn from Montalbetti (1984); Japanese examples come from Kanno (1997).)

(1) a. John believes that he is intelligent.
b. *John believes that _ is intelligent.
c. Juan cree que _ es inteligente.
John believes that is intelligent.
'John believes that (he) is intelligent.'
d. Tanaka-san wa _ kaisya de itiban da to itte-iru.
Tanaka-Mr TOP company in best is that saying-is
'Mr Tanaka says that (he) is the best in the company.'

It is not the case that null subject languages require all pronouns to be unexpressed: both overt and null subject pronouns are possible. However, as described below, overt and null pronouns do not occur in identical contexts and there are subtle restrictions on their distribution.

The particular restriction at issue here relates to pronominal subjects of embedded clauses, as in (1). There are interesting differences between [± null subject] languages in terms of what can serve as a potential antecedent for the pronoun, in other words, limitations on what the pronoun may refer to. In particular, there are restrictions on when it is possible for a pronoun to have a quantified expression (such as *everyone, someone, no one*) or a *wh*-phrase (e.g. *who, which*) as its antecedent.

In the following examples, the lower, or embedded, clause has a pronoun subject, with the main clause subject serving as a potential antecedent of that pronoun. In English, an overt pronoun in an embedded clause can be interpreted as coreferential with a referential NP in the main clause. As shown in (2), the subject of the embedded clause, *she*, refers to the matrix clause subject, *Mary*. (Where expressions are coindexed with the same subscripts, coreference is intended; different subscripts indicate disjoint reference.)

(2) [Mary_i thinks [that she_i will win]]

It is also possible for the pronoun subject of the lower clause to have a quantified phrase in the main clause as its antecedent, as in (3a), or a *wh*-phrase, as in (3b).

(3) a. [Everyone_i thinks [that she_i will win]]
b. [Who_i thinks [that she_i will win?]]

To get the relevant interpretations, imagine a room full of women about to take part in a race. In (3a), every person in the room thinks herself a likely winner: *she*, then, does not refer to a particular individual. The same thing applies in (3b): there can be many people, each of whom thinks herself a likely winner. In such cases, the pronoun is said to receive a *bound variable* interpretation.

In the examples so far, the pronoun in the embedded clause is interpreted in terms of some other NP within the same sentence, either a referential NP, as in (2), or a quantified expression or *wh*-phrase, as in (3). In addition, a pronoun can refer to some other person in the discourse altogether. This is true whether the matrix subject is a referring expression or a quantified expression, as shown in (4), where the pronoun subject of the lower clause refers to another individual, *Jane*.

(4) a. Jane_j is a great athlete. [Mary_i thinks [that she_j will win]]
b. Jane_j is a great athlete. [Everyone_i thinks [that she_j will win]]
c. Jane_j is a great athlete. [Who_i thinks [that she_j will win?]]

Note that, in principle, a sentence like *Everyone thinks that she will win* is ambiguous, with *she* being interpretable either as a variable bound to the quantifier *everyone* (as in (3a)) or as referring to a particular person, such as *Jane*, as in (4b). Similarly, *Mary thought that she would win* is ambiguous, with *she* referring to *Mary* or to some other individual. Usually, the context will favour one of the potential interpretations.

To summarize so far, embedded subject pronouns in [−null subject] languages like English can have referential or quantified NPs within the same sentence as antecedents, as well as being interpretable with discourse antecedents. In [+null subject] languages, on the other hand, it is not the case that any embedded pronominal subject can take a quantified antecedent: overt and null pronouns behave differently in this respect, as described below.

Embedded null subjects in [+null subject] languages behave very similarly to English overt subject pronouns. That is, the null subject of an embedded clause can take either a referential or a quantified expression in the main clause as its antecedent; in other words, a null pronoun can be interpreted as a bound variable.[2] This is illustrated in (5) for Spanish and in (6) for Japanese; the (a) examples show referential antecedents and the (b) examples show quantified/*wh*-phrase antecedents.

(5)	a. [Juan_i	cree	[que	pro_i	es	inteligente]]
	John_i	believes	that	(he_i)	is	intelligent
	b. [Nadie_i	cree	[que	pro_i	es	inteligente]]
	Nobody_i	believes	that	(he_i)	is	intelligent

(6) a. [Tanaka-san$_i$ wa [*pro*$_i$ kaisya de itiban da to] itte-iru]
Tanaka-Mr$_i$ TOP (he$_i$) company in best is that saying-is
'Mr Tanaka says that (he) is the best in the company.'
b. [Dare$_i$ ga [*pro*$_i$ kuruma o katta to] itta no?]
Who$_i$ NOM (he$_i$) car ACC bought that said Q
'Who said that (he) bought a car?'

Overt pronouns in [+null subject] languages, on the other hand, are more restricted than null pronouns; furthermore, they are more restricted than overt pronouns in [−null subject] languages. In particular, while an overt pronoun subject of an embedded clause in Spanish or Japanese can take a sentence-internal referential antecedent, it cannot have a quantified expression or *wh*-phrase as its antecedent. In other words, an overt pronoun cannot receive a bound variable interpretation. This contrast is shown in (7) for Spanish and in (8) for Japanese.

(7) a. Juan$_i$ cree [que él$_i$ es inteligente]
John$_i$ believes that he$_i$ is intelligent
b. *Nadie$_i$ cree [que él$_i$ es inteligente]
Nobody$_i$ believes that he$_i$ is intelligent

(8) a. Tanaka-san$_i$ wa [kare$_i$ ga kaisya de itiban da to] itte-iru
Tanaka-Mr$_i$ TOP he$_i$ NOM company in best is that saying-is
'Mr Tanaka is saying that he is the best in the company.'
b. *Dare$_i$ ga [kare$_i$ ga kuruma o katta to] itta no?
Who$_i$ NOM he$_i$ NOM car ACC bought that said Q
'Who said that he bought a car?'

In both Spanish and Japanese, overt and null pronouns can refer to someone else in the discourse, just like overt pronouns in English.[3] Thus, a sentence with a quantified expression as the main-clause subject and with a null subject in the embedded clause is potentially ambiguous; the null subject may either be bound to the quantifier, as in (5b) or (6b), or may refer to some other individual in the discourse. In contrast, a sentence with a quantified phrase as the main-clause subject and an embedded overt-pronoun subject is not ambiguous, since the bound variable interpretation is not available (see (7b) and (8b)); only an antecedent elsewhere in the discourse is possible.

The relevant differences between languages like Spanish and Japanese and languages like English are summarized in table . Crucially, overt subject pronouns in [+null subject] languages cannot take quantified antecedents, whereas null subjects can, as can overt pronouns in [−null subject] languages. In other respects, overt and null pronouns behave alike, permitting referential and discourse antecedents. Adult native speakers of [+null subject] languages unconsciously know

Table 1.1 *Antecedents for embedded subject pronouns*

	[+Null subject] languages		[−Null subject] languages
	Null pronouns	Overt pronouns	Overt pronouns
Referential antecedents	yes	yes	yes
Quantified antecedents	yes	no	yes
Discourse antecedents	yes	yes	yes

this restriction on antecedents for overt pronouns, that is, they know that overt pronouns cannot serve as bound variables.

The question then arises as to how such knowledge is acquired by native speakers of null-subject languages. This situation constitutes a learnability problem, in that there is a mismatch between the adult knowledge and the kind of data that the child is exposed to. The phenomenon in question is very subtle. The input is surely insufficient to alert the child to the relevant distinction. For one thing, utterances involving quantified antecedents are likely to be relatively infrequent. Furthermore, in many cases, overt and null pronouns permit the same kinds of antecedents (see table 1.1), so it is unlikely that the absence of overt pronouns with quantified antecedents under the relevant interpretation would be detected. A further complication is that there is nothing ungrammatical about these particular surface forms; sentences like (7b) and (8b) are grammatical on the interpretation where there is disjoint reference between the embedded pronoun subject and the main clause subject. What the child has to discover is that sentences like (7b) or (8b) are ungrammatical on the other interpretation. Negative evidence is unlikely to be available; it is implausible that L1 acquirers would produce utterances incorrectly using overt pronouns with quantified antecedents, with intended coreference, and then be provided with implicit or explicit feedback as to their ungrammaticality.

It is on grounds such as these that linguists have argued that certain properties of grammar must be innately specified. In the present case, knowledge of the distinction between overt and null pronouns is argued to be built in as a universal constraint, a principle of UG. Montalbetti (1984) proposed the Overt Pronoun Constraint in part to account for the differences described above. This constraint holds true of null-argument languages in general, including languages unrelated to each other, such as Spanish and Japanese. The Overt Pronoun Constraint is given in (9) (based on Montalbetti 1984):

(9) Overt Pronoun Constraint: overt pronouns cannot receive a bound variable interpretation (i.e. cannot have quantified or *wh*-antecedents), in situations where a null pronoun could occur.[4]

To summarize, the distinction in the behaviour of overt and null pronouns with respect to the kinds of antecedents that they permit provides an example of a poverty of the stimulus situation: the unconscious knowledge that adult native speakers have of these properties is extremely subtle. It is implausible that the child could induce such restrictions from the input alone. In consequence, it is argued that this knowledge must stem from a principle of UG, the Overt Pronoun Constraint.

This is just one example of the kind of abstract knowledge that is attributed to UG. The linguistic literature is full of many other cases, for example, constraints on the distribution of reflexives (Binding Principle A) (Chomsky 1981a), constraints on the distribution of empty categories (the Empty Category Principle) (Chomsky 1981a), and constraints on *wh*-movement (Subjacency) (Chomsky 1977). As mentioned in section 1.2, linguistic theory has developed over time and the formulation of many of the proposed principles of UG has changed. In this book, we will not be concerned with the precise technical details as to how UG principles have been formulated and reformulated. Rather, the crucial question here is the identification of linguistic knowledge that could not arise from the input alone and that requires the postulation of innate principles.

As we shall see in chapter 2, the same general issue arises in the context of L2 acquisition. That is, it appears that L2 learners are also faced with a poverty of the stimulus, namely the L2 stimulus (Schwartz and Sprouse 2000a, b; White 1985a, 1989), and that their interlanguage competence goes beyond the input that they are exposed to. Hence, the question arises as to whether interlanguage grammars are constrained by UG, an issue which will be a major focus of this book.

1.4 Parameters of Universal Grammar

In addition to universal principles, UG includes principles with a limited number of built-in options (*settings* or *values*), which allow for crosslinguistic variation. Such principles are known as *parameters*. Most parameters are assumed to be binary, that is, they have only two settings, the choices being predetermined by UG. L1 acquisition consists, in part, of setting parameters, the appropriate setting being triggered by the input that the child is exposed to. A central claim of parameter theory, as originally instantiated in the Principles and Parameters framework, is that a single parameter setting brings together a cluster of apparently disparate syntactic properties (Chomsky 1981a). This, for example, was part of the rationale for the Null Subject Parameter, which related the possibility of null subjects to other syntactic and morphological properties found in null subject languages (Chomsky 1981a; Jaeggli 1982; Rizzi 1982, amongst others). The insight behind the proposal for parameters is that they should severely reduce the acquisition task. Rather than learning a number of seemingly unrelated properties individually, the child has only to discover the appropriate setting of a parameter and a range of associated syntactic properties follows automatically. Some L1 acquisition research has provided evidence in favour of clustering, showing that properties which are argued to be consequences of a particular parameter setting emerge at about the same time (e.g. Hyams 1986; Snyder and Stromswold 1997).

Under current proposals, parametric differences between grammars are associated with properties of lexical items, particularly so-called functional categories (Borer 1984; Chomsky 1995; Ouhalla 1991; Pollock 1989). Linguistic theory distinguishes between lexical categories – verb (V), noun (N), adjective (Adj), adverb (Adv), preposition (P) – and functional categories, including complementizer (Comp or C), inflection (Infl or I) (often split into agreement (Agr) and tense (T)), negation (Neg), determiner (Det), number (Num), as well as others. Functional categories have certain formal features associated with them (such as tense, number, person, gender and case). Functional categories and features form part of the UG inventory.

There are three potential sources of crosslinguistic variation relating to functional categories:

i. Languages can differ as to which functional categories are realized in the grammar. On some accounts, for example, Japanese lacks the category Det (Fukui and Speas 1986).
ii. The features of a particular functional category can vary from language to language. For instance, French has a gender feature, while English does not.
iii. Features are said to vary in strength: a feature can be strong in one language and weak in another, with a range of syntactic consequences. For example, Infl features are strong in French and weak in English (see below), resulting in certain word-order alternations between the two languages.

The lexicons of different languages, then, vary as to which functional categories and features are instantiated and what the strength of various features may be. Such variation has a variety of syntactic effects.

1.4.1 An example: feature strength and movement

In this section, we review the role of feature strength in current accounts of syntax, and consider some examples of parametric variation which depend on feature strength. In later chapters, such variation will become relevant as we examine the nature of interlanguage grammars, and the kinds of changes that take place in the grammar during the course of L2 development.

Feature strength is an abstract property which is argued to have syntactic consequences, particularly for word order. The first example to be considered here concerns the strength of features associated with the functional category Infl. Finite verbs have tense and agreement features which have to be checked, at some point, against corresponding V(erb)-features in Infl (Chomsky 1995). Simplifying somewhat, if the V-features in Infl are strong (henceforth, strong I), there is overt movement of the finite verb, which raises from the VP to I for feature checking. If V-features are weak (henceforth, weak I), overt movement does not take place. Instead, features are checked at Logical Form (LF); this movement is not 'visible' in the syntax and is said to be covert.

This distinction between strong and weak features accounts for a number of well-known word-order differences between languages like French and English (Emonds 1978; Pollock 1989). In French, finite lexical verbs must appear to the left of the negative *pas* and to the left of VP-adjoined adverbs, as illustrated in (10). In English, on the other hand, the lexical verb remains to the right of *not* and to the right of adverbs, as shown in (11).

(10) a. Marie ne regarde pas la télévision.
Mary (ne) watches not the television
'Mary does not watch television.'
b. *Marie pas regarde la télévision.
Mary not watches the television
c. Marie regarde souvent la télévision.
Mary watches often the television
d. *Marie souvent regarde la télévision.
Mary often watches the television

(11) a. Mary does not watch television.
b. *Mary watches not television.
c. Mary often watches television.
d. *Mary watches often television.

These verb placement differences are accounted for in terms of differences in feature strength, French having strong I and English weak. At an underlying level, the two languages have the same structure (compare (12) and (13)). However, because of the difference in feature strength, finite verbs in French must raise to I for feature-checking purposes, whereas finite verbs in English remain within the VP. This is illustrated in (12) and (13).

(12)

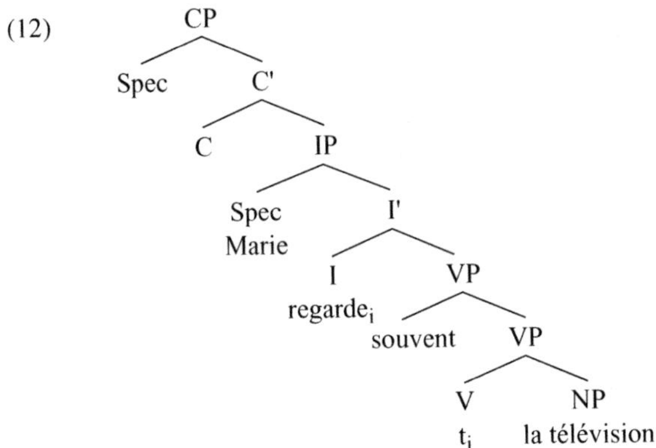

(13)

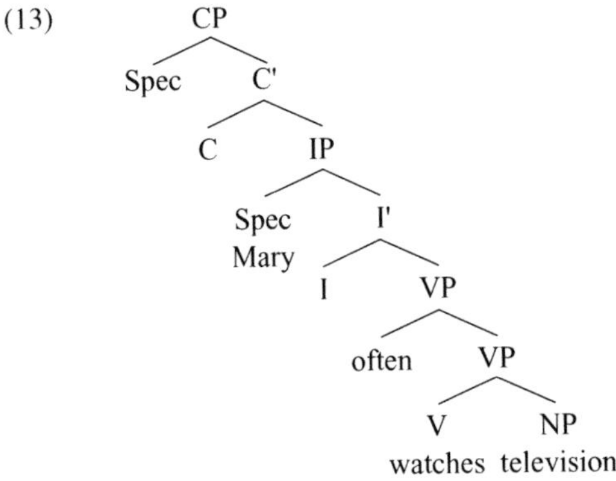

Germanic languages provide another example of crosslinguistic differences in word order which are partially explained in terms of feature strength. Languages like English and German contrast in two respects, namely the underlying position of the verb (VP initial in English, final in German), and the *verb second* (V2) phenomenon (characteristic of German but not English). Main clauses in German and English both show subject-verb-object (SVO) order when no auxiliaries or modals are present, as shown in (14a, b). In such cases, sentences with finite main verbs in final position are ungrammatical, as shown in (14c, d). However, in German main clauses containing auxiliary or modal verbs, the lexical verb appears finally (see (14e)); all verbs appear finally in embedded clauses, as in (14f). Furthermore, in German main clauses, any constituent can be fronted; when this happens, the verb must appear in the second position (V2) in the clause, as shown in (14g–j). That is, the finite verb in main clauses can only be preceded by one other constituent, which does not have to be a subject.

(14)
a. Maria trinkt Kaffee.
b. Mary drinks coffee.
c. *Maria Kaffee trinkt.
d. *Mary coffee drinks.
e. Maria möchte Kaffee trinken.
   Mary wants coffee drink-INF
f. Maria sagt, dass sie Kaffee trinken will.
   Mary says that she coffee drink-INF will
g. Kaffee trinkt Maria.
   Coffee drinks Mary
   'Mary drinks coffee.'
h. *Kaffee Maria trinkt
   coffee Mary drinks
i. Oft trinkt Maria Kaffee.
   often drinks Mary coffee
j. *Oft Maria trinkt Kaffee.
   often Mary drinks coffee

The position of the verb in German is accounted for in the following way. According to standard analyses of German, VP and IP are head final, as shown in (15) (e.g. Platzack 1986; Schwartz and Vikner 1996; Thiersch 1978).[5] Finite verbs in main clauses undergo two movements: from V to I and then from I to C, driven by strong features in C. Some other constituent (subject, object or adjunct) raises to the Spec of CP, resulting in the V2 effect. In embedded clauses, the verb cannot raise to C because this position is already filled by a complementizer, such as *dass* ('that') in (14f); consequently, embedded clauses remain V-final. This is shown in (16).

(15)

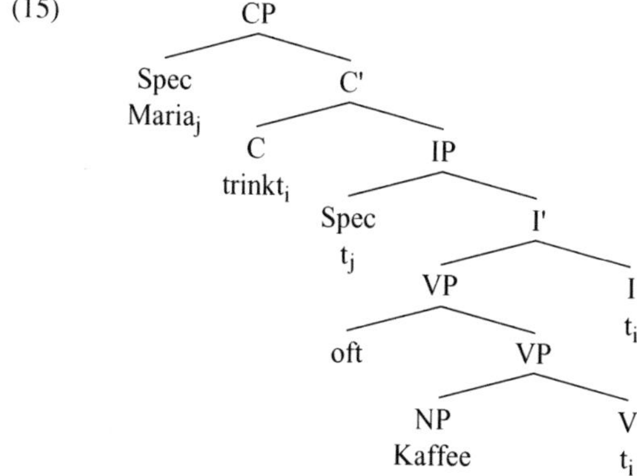

(16)

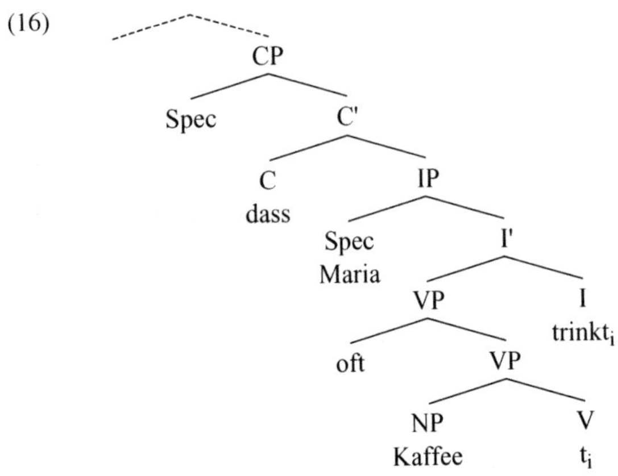

DPs provide a final example of word-order variation attributed to differences in feature strength. On many current analyses, DPs contain a functional category Num, located between D and NP, as shown in (17) (Bernstein 1993; Carstens 1991; Ritter 1991; Valois 1991). Num has number features, as well as gender features in some accounts (Ritter 1993).

(17)

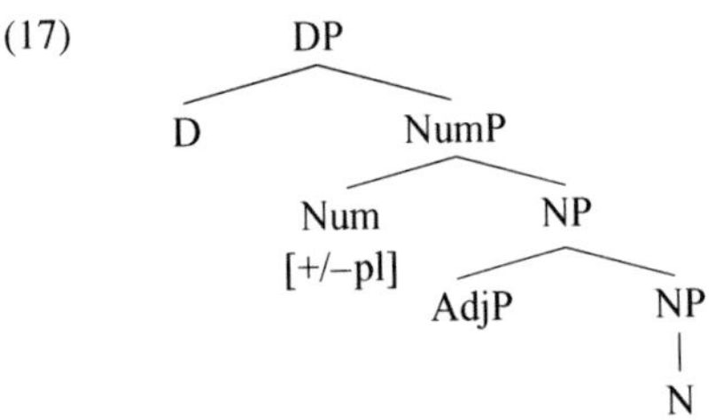

In Romance languages such as French and Spanish, number features are strong and nouns must raise overtly from N to Num for feature-checking purposes, over any adjectives that may be present. This results in the noun adjective (N Adj) order typical of Romance, as shown in the Spanish example in (18a). In English, on the other hand, Num features are weak, nouns do not raise and the word order is adjective noun (Adj N), as in (18b).

(18) a. la blusa roja
the blouse red
b. the red blouse

In other words, parallel to the situation with respect to the position of the verb in the clause, crosslinguistic differences in the position of the noun in the DP are determined by feature strength.

In summary, a variety of word-order differences are accounted for under the assumption that the strength of features in functional categories varies, being either strong or weak. Various word-order alternations between French and English (including others that have not been mentioned here) can be accounted for by one parametric difference between the two languages, namely the strength of V-related features in I. A range of differences between languages like German and English can be accounted for by two properties, the underlying position of the verb and the strength of features in C. Differences in adjective placement between Romance languages and Germanic languages can be accounted for in terms of the strength of features in Num. These parametric differences will be discussed in greater detail in later chapters, as we consider the extent to which the interlanguage grammar exemplifies parameter settings distinct from those found in the L1 grammar.

As is the case with principles of UG, the formulation of the precise mechanisms involved in feature strength and feature checking has changed over time. In this book, the issues will be presented in a way which preserves the general insights without being tied to technical details specific to any particular theory.

1.5 UG access: earlier approaches to UG and SLA

So far, we have considered UG as a system of principles and parameters which provide constraints on grammars in the course of L1 acquisition, as well as on adult native-speaker grammars. L2 learners face a task parallel to that of L1 acquirers, namely the need to arrive at a linguistic system which accounts for the L2 input, allowing the learner to understand and speak the second language. Given this apparent similarity, the question of whether UG also mediates L2 acquisition, and to what extent, has been investigated and debated since the early 1980s. The first decade of research on UG in L2 acquisition concentrated largely on the so-called *access* issue, namely, whether or not UG remains available in non-primary acquisition. (See White (1989) for an overview and discussion of the relevant literature.) This research looked for evidence that L2 learners can (or cannot) apply principles of UG, and set or reset parameters, as well as investigating the extent to which the mother tongue (L1) was involved, for example through the adoption of L1 parameter settings in interlanguage grammars. Hypotheses varied as to whether L2 learners have *no access, direct access* or *indirect access* to UG. All of these terms have turned out to be somewhat problematic.

One side of the debate, sometimes referred to as the *no access* position (for example, by Cook 1988; Cook and Newson 1996; Epstein, Flynn and Martohardjono 1996), is represented by the Fundamental Difference Hypothesis (Bley-Vroman 1990) and related claims (Clahsen and Muysken 1986; Schachter 1988). According to this view, child L1 and adult L2 acquisition differ in major respects. Proponents claim that adult L2 acquisition is not constrained by UG, or that it is only constrained by UG insofar as universal properties can be accessed via the L1 grammar. Indeed, the assumption that UG is at least partially implicated via the L1 suggests that the term *no access* is a misnomer; hence, this view is sometimes also referred to as *partial access*. Regardless of terminology, the crucial claim is that all the linguistic mechanisms available to the L1 acquirer are no longer available to the L2 learner. In support, advocates of this position tried to show that learners are 'stuck' with principles and parameter settings exemplified in the L1 (e.g. Schachter 1989) or that their grammars show no evidence for UG constraints at all (e.g. Clahsen and Muysken 1986).

On the other side of the debate is the position that L2 learners indeed have access to UG. In other words, interlanguage grammars show evidence of being constrained by UG principles; at the same time, interlanguage grammars show evidence of parameter settings other than those of the L1. Some proponents of the UG access position argued that at no stage would the interlanguage grammar actually exemplify L1 parameter settings (e.g. Flynn 1987). In other words, L2 learners arrive at relevant properties of the L2 independently of the L1 grammar. Hence, this position was often referred to as *direct access* (e.g. by Cook 1988; Cook and Newson 1996).

An alternative kind of account recognized the role of both the L1 and UG: L2 learners are indeed assumed to have access to principles and parameters of UG. However, initially at least, access would be via the L1 grammar, with the possibility of subsequent grammar restructuring and parameter resetting, in the light of exposure to L2 input (e.g. White 1985b, 1989). This position is sometimes referred to as *indirect access* (e.g. by Cook 1988; Cook and Newson 1996). However, as pointed out by Thomas (1991b, 1993), it is just as appropriate to characterize this perspective as involving direct access, since the learner is not restricted to UG principles and parameter settings exemplified in the L1 grammar.

Terms like *direct* and *indirect access* have since been replaced with *full* and *partial access* but these have proved to be equally problematic. As we shall see in chapter 3, there is still disagreement as to whether or not *full access* to UG implies absence of L1 effects on the interlanguage grammar. Epstein, Flynn and Martohardjono (1996), for example, restrict the term *full access* to the position that UG operates in interlanguage grammars independently of L1 representations. In contrast, Schwartz and Sprouse (1996) propose the Full Transfer Full Access hypothesis, arguing that there is nothing incompatible in the assumption that both UG and the L1 grammar are implicated. Since the L1 is a natural language, there is no a priori justification for assuming that a representation based on the L1 implies lack of UG constraints, or restricted access to UG.

As hypotheses about UG access developed, interest began to shift from overarching questions like 'Is UG available?' or 'What kind of UG access is there in L2?' to a closer examination of the nature of the interlanguage grammar, with particular focus on whether interlanguage grammars exhibit properties characteristic of natural language (e.g. du Plessis, Solin, Travis and White 1987; Finer and Broselow 1986; Martohardjono and Gair 1993; Schwartz and Tomaselli 1990; Thomas 1991a; White 1992c). As we shall see, this detailed focus on the grammatical properties of interlanguage grammars remains characteristic of current research.

1.6 Methodological issues: 'tapping' linguistic competence

The research to be discussed in this book seeks to establish the nature of the L2 learner's linguistic competence, addressing in particular the question of whether interlanguage grammars are UG-constrained. This raises the issue of how one can in fact discover what the unconscious linguistic system consists of. Linguistic competence is an abstraction; there is no way of directly tapping that competence. Hence, researchers must resort to various kinds of performance measures in order to determine, indirectly, the essential characteristics of mental representations. This is true whether one is interested in adult native-speaker competence, child L1 acquisition or child or adult non-native language acquisition.

A variety of methodologies have been developed over the years for investigating linguistic competence, and data have been obtained using different experimental techniques. It is, of course, the case that no methodology allows one to tap linguistic competence directly: in all cases, performance factors will be involved. Ideally, performance data from various sources will converge. When results from different tasks and different groups of learners show the same trends, this suggests that we are indeed gaining insight (indirectly) into the nature of the underlying linguistic competence.

Data can be broadly classified into three categories: *production data*, including spontaneous and elicited production; *comprehension data*, including data obtained from act-out and picture-identification tasks; and *intuitional data*, including data from grammaticality judgments and truth-value judgments (see chapter 2), as well as, more recently, a number of online techniques such as sentence matching (see chapters 3 and 4).

A myth has developed in the field of L2 acquisition that researchers working in the UG paradigm take grammaticality-judgment tasks to have some kind of privileged status, such that they provide a direct reflection of linguistic competence (e.g. Carroll and Meisel 1990: 205; Ellis 1990: 388). This is a misconception: it has always been recognized that judgment data are performance data, on a par with other data (e.g. Cook 1990: 592; White 1989: 57–8). The appropriateness of a particular task will depend on what the researcher is trying to discover. For example, grammaticality-judgment tasks provide a means of establishing whether learners know that certain forms are impossible or ungrammatical in the L2. Thus, a grammaticality-judgment task can be used to find out whether sentences which are ruled out by principles of UG are also disallowed in the interlanguage grammar. Consider, for instance, the Adjunct Island Constraint (e.g. Cinque 1990), a constraint which prohibits *wh*-phrases from being fronted out of adjunct clauses. In order to establish whether L2 learners 'know' this constraint, one could ask them whether or not sentences like those in (19) are grammatical:

(19) a. Who did you quit school because you hated?
b. What did Tom fall when he slipped on?

If interlanguage grammars are constrained by UG, then learners are expected to reject such sentences (while accepting corresponding grammatical ones).

Although grammaticality-judgment tasks suffer from a number of well-known problems (see, for example, Birdsong (1989) and Schütze (1996)), in cases like the above example they have advantages over other sources of data, such as spontaneous production. If L2 learners never produce sentences like (19), it would seem, on the face of things, to provide support for the claim that interlanguage grammars are UG-constrained. Unfortunately, however, failure to find certain sentence types in production data is no guarantee that such sentences are in fact disallowed by the grammar. There may be independent reasons why they fail to show up. The use of methodologies such as grammaticality-judgment tasks, then, allows the experimenter to investigate aspects of interlanguage competence which may not otherwise be amenable to inspection.

It is important to recognize that there is no one methodology that is appropriate for investigating all aspects of linguistic competence. For example, if questions of interpretation are being investigated, grammaticality judgments will often be totally uninformative. Consider the Overt Pronoun Constraint, as discussed in section 1.3.1. As we have seen, certain Spanish and Japanese sentences involving overt-pronoun subjects in embedded clauses and quantified phrases as main clauses subjects are ungrammatical under a bound variable interpretation, as in (7b) and (8b). This contrasts with English, where the interpretation in question is possible. If a researcher wanted to determine whether or not Spanish-speaking learners of English know that a sentence like (3a), repeated here as (20), is possible, a traditional grammaticality-judgment task would not be appropriate.

(20) Everyone thinks that she will win.

The problem is that this sentence is ambiguous for native speakers of English, being grammatical on two different interpretations (i.e. with *she* taking *everyone* as its antecedent or with a discourse referent as its antecedent). If learners respond that such sentences are grammatical, it would be impossible to tell which interpretation of the sentence was being judged. In other words, one could not tell whether the learner had acquired unconscious knowledge of the difference between Spanish and English with respect to this property. In such cases, alternative methodologies are called for, which match sentences with potential interpretations. This is often achieved by means of so-called *truth-value-judgment tasks* which require the learner to assess the appropriateness of a sentence in relation to some context (see chapter 2).

For such reasons, it is essential for the researcher to construct tasks that are appropriate for the issue being investigated. Various different methodologies will be described in greater detail in later chapters, including a consideration of their appropriateness, as well as their advantages and disadvantages.

1.7 Conclusion

In conclusion, UG is proposed as a (partial) answer to questions such as: What are natural language grammars like? What is the nature of linguistic competence? How is it acquired? As far as the first language is concerned, the assumption is that language acquisition would be impossible in the absence of innate and specifically linguistic principles which place constraints on grammars, thus restricting the 'hypothesis space' by severely limiting the range of possibilities that the language acquirer has to entertain. In subsequent chapters, we will explore the extent to which interlanguage grammars are similarly constrained. Research will be considered which examines in detail the nature of interlanguage representations. As we shall see, claims are made for early grammars (the initial state), for grammars during the course of development, as well as for the nature of the steady state. We will contrast claims that interlanguage grammars are in some sense defective (hence, not UG-constrained) with positions that argue that interlanguage grammars are not impaired, showing, rather, properties characteristic of natural languages constrained by UG.

Topics for discussion

- A number of researchers have suggested that negative evidence is in fact available in L1 acquisition. For example, Hirsh-Pasek, Treiman and Schneiderman (1984) report that mothers of 2-year-olds are significantly more likely to repeat (and sometimes rephrase) children's ill-formed utterances than their well-formed utterances. Does the availability of such feedback in fact solve the logical problem of language acquisition?

- The claim that there are domain-specific universal linguistic principles constraining grammars is, of course, contested. For example, O'Grady (1987, 1996, 1997, 2003) proposes that language acquisition should be accounted for in terms of more general cognitive principles which are not unique to language. Others place far greater emphasis on statistical properties of the input, in some cases downplaying or denying a role for innate constraints, for example, connectionist models such as Parallel Distributed Processing (Rumelhart and McClelland 1987) or the Competition Model (Bates and MacWhinney 1987). (For an overview of recent research which assumes a major role for statistical learning as well as innate constraints, see Newport and Aslin (2000).) How can one choose between these very different kinds of account (i.e. what kinds of argumentation and data are relevant)? For relevant discussion in the L2 context, see Gregg (2003).
- To what extent are functional categories universally realized and what are the implications for theories of L2 acquisition? There is considerable disagreement as to whether or not languages differ in the functional categories that they instantiate. See Bobaljik and Thráinsson (1998), Thráinsson (1996) and Webelhuth (1995) for useful discussion.
- The problem of teleology. The task of the language acquirer (L1 or L2) is to 'construct' a grammar that accommodates the linguistic input, allowing the learner to provide structural representations to utterances. The task should *not* be seen as having to acquire a grammar that matches the grammar of adult speakers of the language in question. Why is it important to make such a distinction?

Suggestions for additional reading

- It will be presupposed that the reader has some familiarity with the concepts and mechanisms assumed in current generative grammar. The Government and Binding framework is presented in Haegeman (1991), Minimalism in Radford (1997). Papers in Webelhuth (1995) provide a useful overview of both frameworks and the connections between them.
- Arguments for an innate and specifically linguistic basis to first language acquisition can be found in Chomsky (1999), Crain and Thornton (1998), Pinker (1994), amongst others. Useful overviews of L1 acquisition

theories and findings within this framework can be found in Goodluck (1991) and O'Grady (1997), as well as in several of the chapters in Bloom (1994) and in Ritchie and Bhatia (1999).

- For detailed presentation of methodologies appropriate for research on first language acquisition, see Crain and Thornton (1998) and McDaniel, McKee and Cairns (1996). For detailed discussion of the pros and cons of grammaticality-judgment tasks, see Birdsong (1989) and Schütze (1996).
- Other recent books looking at L2 acquisition can be seen as complementary to this book. Hawkins (2001a) provides an excellent introduction to L2 acquisition of syntax and morphology within a generative linguistic perspective. Herschensohn (2000) adopts a more technical Minimalist approach to L2 acquisition.

2

Principles of Universal Grammar in L2 acquisition

2.1 UG and the logical problem of L2 acquisition

As discussed in chapter 1, UG is motivated on learnability grounds: the subtle and abstract knowledge attained by native speakers goes far beyond the input that they receive as young children. In L2 acquisition, learners are faced with a similar task to that of L1 acquirers, namely the need to arrive at a system accounting for L2 input. In addition, L2 learners are also faced, at least potentially, with a logical problem of language acquisition, in that there are abstract, complex and subtle properties of grammar that are underdetermined by the L2 input (Schwartz and Sprouse 2000a, b; White 1985a, 1989). If it turns out that the L2 learner acquires abstract properties that could not have been induced from the input, this is strongly indicative that principles of UG constrain interlanguage grammars, parallel to the situation in L1 acquisition. This is true even if the linguistic competence of L2 learners differs from the linguistic competence of native speakers. In other words, it is not necessary for L2 learners to acquire the same knowledge as native speakers in order to demonstrate a poverty-of-the-stimulus situation in L2 acquisition; it is sufficient to show that L2 learners acquire complex and subtle properties of language that could not have been induced from the L2 input.

However, L2 learners already have a means of representing language, namely the grammar of the mother tongue. Thus, it might be that there is, in fact, no underdetermination problem: if L2 learners demonstrate the relevant kind of unconscious knowledge, it might be the case that they are drawing on the L1 grammar, rather than on UG itself, as argued, for example, by Bley-Vroman (1990) and Schachter (1990).

Thus, the strongest case for the operation of principles of UG in interlanguage grammars can be made if learners demonstrate knowledge of subtle and abstract linguistic properties which could neither have been learned from L2 input alone nor derived from the grammar of the mother tongue. In other words, there should be underdetermination not only with respect to L2 input but also with respect to the L1 grammar. Furthermore, one must also be able to rule out the possibility of learning on the basis of explicit instruction or by means of general learning principles (not specifically linguistic). For such reasons, L2 researchers try to identify situations involving a poverty of the L2 stimulus, where the available L2 input together with existing grammatical knowledge cannot account for acquisition unless one assumes that interlanguage grammars are constrained by UG (Schwartz and Sprouse 2000a, b; White 1989, 1990).

In summary, to demonstrate convincingly that interlanguage grammars are constrained by principles of UG, the following conditions should hold:

i. The phenomenon being investigated must be underdetermined by the L2 input. That is, it must not be something that could be acquired by observation of the L2 input, including statistical inferencing based on frequency of occurrence, on the basis of analogy, or on the basis of instruction.

ii. The phenomenon should work differently in the L1 and the L2. That is, it must be underdetermined by the L1 grammar as well. In this way, transfer of surface properties can be ruled out as an explanation of any knowledge that L2 learners attain.

2.1.1 The Overt Pronoun Constraint in L2

Let us reconsider the Overt Pronoun Constraint (Montalbetti 1984) (see chapter 1, section 1.3.1) in the context of L2 acquisition. Recall that, in [+null subject] languages, overt pronoun subjects of embedded clauses cannot receive a bound variable interpretation, hence cannot take quantified expressions or *wh*-phrases as antecedents, in contrast to null pronoun subjects. The sentences in (1) to (2) (repeated from chapter 1) illustrate the contrast in question. In the Spanish sentence in (1a), the overt pronoun *él* cannot have the quantifier *nadie* as its antecedent, whereas this interpretation is possible with the null pronoun in (1b). Similar facts obtain for the Japanese sentences in (2).

(1) a. *Nadie$_i$ cree [que él$_i$ es inteligente]
Nobody$_i$ believes that he$_i$ is intelligent
b. Nadie$_i$ cree [que *pro*$_i$ es inteligente]
Nobody$_i$ believes that (he$_i$) is intelligent

(2) a. *Dare$_i$ ga [kare$_i$ ga kuruma o katta to] itta no?
Who$_i$ NOM he$_i$ NOM car ACC bought that said Q
'Who said that he bought a car?'
b. Dare$_i$ ga [*pro*$_i$ kuruma o katta to] itta no?
Who$_i$ NOM (he$_i$) car ACC bought that said Q
'Who said that (he) bought a car?'

Is there a logical problem for the L2 learner of a null subject language like Spanish or Japanese with respect to this interpretive restriction on embedded pronominal subjects? Consider first the L2 input. Discovering the restriction on the basis of input represents as much of a challenge for the L2 learner as it does for the L1 learner. In general, overt and null pronouns appear in similar or overlapping contexts (see chapter 1, table 1.1), they take similar antecedents, and there appears to be nothing in the L2 input to signal the difference between them as far as bound variable status is concerned. Thus, frequency of occurrence in the input is unlikely to provide any useful clue as to when pronouns may occur and under which interpretations. The L2 learner, like the L1 learner, somehow has to discover that, in a restricted and rather uncommon set of sentence types, an overt pronoun cannot appear with a particular interpretation (as a bound variable), even though it can appear with another interpretation (with a referential antecedent). In addition, classroom input does not appear to be helpful in this respect. According to Pérez-Leroux and Glass (1997), this issue is not discussed in L2 Spanish textbooks or taught in L2 classrooms; Kanno (1997) makes the same observations for L2 Japanese. In other words, knowledge of the interpretative restriction on overt pronouns is underdetermined by the L2 input, satisfying the first of the two conditions described in section 2.1.

As for attaining such knowledge on the basis of the mother tongue, if L2 learners are native speakers of a [−null subject] language, such as English, nothing in the L1 grammar would allow them to arrive at the appropriate distinction, since overt pronouns in English are not restricted in the same way. Thus, an investigation of the acquisition of Spanish or Japanese by native speakers of English would also meet the second requirement outlined in section 2.1.

Acquiring the interpretive constraint on overt pronouns in L2, then, constitutes a classic learnability problem. If L2 learners are successful in this domain, it would strongly support the claim that interlanguage grammars are UG-constrained. Recently, researchers have conducted experiments to investigate whether adult learners observe the Overt Pronoun Constraint. Pérez-Leroux and Glass (1997, 1999) have examined L2 Spanish, while Kanno (1997, 1998b) has investigated L2 Japanese. In both cases, the L2 learners are native speakers of English. Thus, both conditions for investigating whether the interlanguage grammar is UG-constrained are met: the L2 input underdetermines the phenomenon being investigated and the L1 is not a potential source of information about restrictions on overt pronouns. The issue, then, is whether L2 learners in fact behave in ways that are consistent with this constraint. If they do, UG is implicated since other potential sources of such behaviour have effectively been eliminated.

In Pérez-Leroux and Glass (1999) (see box 2.1), L2 learners of Spanish at different levels of proficiency were tested by means of a task which involved translating biclausal sentences from the L1 English into the L2 Spanish, following written contexts (in the L1) which strongly favoured either a quantified antecedent

Box 2.1 Overt Pronoun Constraint (Perez-Léroux and Glass 1999)

Languages: L1 = English, L2 = Spanish.
Task: Translation from English into Spanish. Each sentence preceded by a paragraph (in English) to provide a context.
Sample stimuli:

Bound variable context	Referential context
The court charged that some journalists had been in contact with the jurors. Several of them were questioned by the judge.	In the O.J. Simpson trial, it is clear that the press has a negative bias against the defendant in their reporting. Some journalist said that he was a wife-beater.
To translate: No journalist admitted that he had talked to the jurors.	To translate: But no journalist said that he is guilty.

Results:

Table 2.1.1 *Production of null and overt pronouns (in %)*

		Bound variable stories (# = 4)		Referential stories (# = 4)	
		Null	Overt	Null	Overt
L2 groups	Elementary (n = 39)	57.7	34	21.2	67.9
	Intermediate (n = 21)	73.8	26.2	35.7	59.5
	Advanced (n = 18)	93.1	0	58.3	31.9
Native speakers (n = 20)		85	13.7	31.3	67.5

n = number of subjects
# = number of stimuli

(within the same sentence) or a discourse-based referential antecedent (external to the sentence) for the embedded subject pronoun. If the interlanguage grammar is constrained by the Overt Pronoun Constraint, translations should disfavour overt pronouns and favour null subjects where the antecedent is quantified, since overt pronouns are prohibited in this context. In the case of the referential stories, on the other hand, either kind of pronoun is grammatical. As can be seen in table 2.1.1, production of overt pronouns is significantly lower in bound-variable contexts than in referential contexts and this is true of all groups. Correspondingly, the use of null pronouns is significantly higher following bound variable contexts than referential contexts.[1] These results suggest that L2 learners, like native speakers, distinguish between referential and bound variable interpretations of pronouns, largely disallowing overt pronouns in the latter context, compared with their use in other contexts. Thus, the results are supportive of the claim that interlanguage grammars are constrained by the Overt Pronoun Constraint, even at the elementary level.

However, ideally, it would seem that the incidence of overt pronouns in bound variable contexts ought to be 0%, a result achieved only by the advanced group. Pérez-Leroux and Glass attribute the incidence of overt pronouns in the elementary and intermediate groups to a tendency to overuse overt pronouns in general (based on the L1). In many cases of L2 (and native speaker) performance, there will be such additional factors that come into play. Indeed, what is important here is not the absolute figures but rather the fact that there are significant differences in performance across different sentence types. The issue is whether the interlanguage grammar shows evidence of certain distinctions (in this case in the incidence of overt subjects with referential as opposed to quantified antecedents). If learner performance on one sentence type differs significantly from performance on another, this suggests that the interlanguage grammar represents the relevant distinction (whatever it may be). If these sentence types were represented in the same way in the interlanguage grammar, such differences would be unexpected; instead, the sentences should be treated the same. (See Grimshaw and Rosen (1990) for related discussion relevant to L1 acquisition and Martohardjono (1993, 1998) for L2.)

Turning now to L2 Japanese, Kanno (1997, 1998b) investigates whether adult learners know the prohibition on quantified and *wh* antecedents for overt pronouns. (See box 2.2.) Her task was a coreference-judgment task, quite different from the task used by Pérez-Leroux and Glass. Subjects were presented with biclausal sentences with quantified and referential main-clause subjects and overt or null embedded pronoun subjects; they had to indicate whether or not the embedded pronoun could refer to the subject of the main clause.

Kanno found that native speakers and L2 learners alike differentiated in their treatment of overt pronouns depending on the type of antecedent involved (quantified or referential) (see table 2.2.1). Native speakers overwhelmingly rejected the interpretation where an overt pronoun took a quantified antecedent, responding instead that the overt pronoun must take a sentence-external referent. This was not due to a general prohibition against quantified antecedents, since these were accepted in the case of null subjects. Nor was it due to any general dislike of sentence-internal antecedents, since referential antecedents within the same sentence were accepted. The L2 learners showed a remarkably similar pattern of results; their performance was not significantly different from the controls. Both native speakers and L2 learners, then, appeared to be following the Overt Pronoun Constraint, disallowing quantified antecedents for overt pronouns. Furthermore, Kanno took the precaution of including a control group of native speakers of

Box 2.2 Overt Pronoun Constraint (Kanno 1997)

Languages: L1 = English, L2 = Japanese.
Task: Corereference judgments. Japanese biclausal sentences, each followed by a question asking who was performing the action described in the embedded clause.
Sample stimuli:

Null pronoun with quantified/*wh* antecedent	Null pronoun with referential antecedent
Dare ga asita uti ni iru to itteiru n desu ka. *(Who says that (he) is going to stay home tomorrow?)* Q: Who do you suppose is going to stay home tomorrow? (a) same as *dare* (b) another person	Tanaka-san wa raisyuu Kyooto e iku to itteimasita yo. *(Mr Tanaka was saying that (he) is going to Kyoto next week.)* Q: Who do you suppose is going to Kyoto next week? (a) Tanaka (b) someone other than Tanaka
Overt pronoun with quantified/*wh* antecedent	**Overt pronoun with referential antecedent**
Dare ga kyoo kare ga uti ni iru to itteiru n desu ka. *(Who says that he is going to stay home today?)* Q: Who do you suppose is going to stay home today? (a) same as *dare* (b) another person	Tanaka-san wa raisyuu kare ga Tokyoo e iku to iimasita yo. *(Mr. Tanaka said that he would go to Tokyo next week.)* Q: Who do you suppose will go to Tokyo next week? (a) Tanaka (b) someone other than Tanaka

Results:

Table 2.2.1 *Acceptances of antecedents for null and overt pronouns (in %)*

	Quantified antecedents (# = 10)		Referential antecedents (# = 10)	
	Null	Overt	Null	Overt
L2 learners (n = 28)	78.5	13	81.5	42
Native speakers (n = 20)	83	2	100	47

English who judged equivalent sentences in English (with overt pronouns in the lower clause). This group allowed quantified antecedents and referential antecedents for overt pronouns to an equal (and high) extent, suggesting that the L1 English is not the source of the L2 learners' behaviour in Japanese.

There are a number of differences between these two sets of experiments, both in the methodology and in the results. In Pérez-Leroux and Glass's experiments, the task was a production task, involving translation; in Kanno's studies, learners had to make coreference judgments. In Pérez-Leroux and Glass's task, the subject of the main clause was always a quantified NP; referential antecedents had to be found elsewhere within the discourse provided by the story. In contrast, Kanno varied the nature of the main-clause subject (quantified/*wh* expression versus a referential NP), such that the referential antecedent was always within the same sentence as the embedded pronoun. There is one obvious difference in the results of the two sets of studies which may be attributed to these task differences. In the case of most groups, Pérez-Leroux and Glass found that translations of the sentences following a referential context tended to disfavour null subjects; overt pronouns were used instead (see table 2.1.1). Kanno, on the other hand, found that referential antecedents were accepted for null subjects (see table 2.2.1). Montalbetti (1984) suggests that an overt pronoun is preferred when its referential antecedent is not within the same sentence; this would account for the preference observed by Pérez-Leroux and Glass.

Despite this difference in the treatment of null pronouns and their antecedents, the crucial issue concerns treatment of overt pronouns with quantified antecedents. Here, results from the two studies are consistent with each other: L2 learners of Spanish and Japanese alike show significantly lower use or acceptance of overt pronouns with quantified antecedents, as do native speakers. Thus, taken together, the experiments of Pérez-Leroux and Glass (1999) and Kanno (1997) provide evidence for Overt Pronoun Constraint effects in different L2s, with learners at different levels of proficiency and with different methodologies being employed.

While these results are compelling, we should bear in mind that we are interested in the grammars of individual speakers rather than groups. The Overt Pronoun Constraint, as a principle of UG, should constrain the grammar of each individual learner. Group results that suggest UG-consistent behaviour on the part of L2 learners may in fact conceal potentially problematic individual variation. While Pérez-Leroux and Glass do not provide analyses of results from individuals, Kanno does. Kanno found that 100% of the native-speaker controls and 86% of the L2 learners demonstrated consistent behaviour with respect to overt pronouns with quantified antecedents, where consistency is defined as the rejection of quantified antecedents for overt pronouns in 4 or 5 cases out of 5. This level of consistent rejections by individuals suggests that the group results are indeed an accurate reflection of individual linguistic competence.

However, in another study, Kanno (1998a, b) found greater variability in individual results. A different group of English-speaking intermediate-level learners of Japanese was tested at two different points in time, with a twelve-week interval between the two sessions. The task was the same as the one in the previously described experiment. At both test sessions, there was a significant difference between coreference judgments involving a quantified antecedent, depending on whether the embedded pronoun subject was null or overt. In the latter case, acceptance of coreference was significantly lower, consistent with the Overt Pronoun Constraint. There were no differences in group performance across the two test sessions. At the individual level, however, with consistency defined as above, Kanno found that only 9 of 29 L2 learners consistently excluded quantified antecedents for overt pronouns in both test sessions. A further 15 subjects showed consistent rejection in one session or the other. Thus, at the individual level, operation of the Overt Pronoun Constraint was not consistent across subjects or over time.

Kanno (1998b) suggests that, while the Overt Pronoun Constraint does constrain interlanguage grammars, it cannot always be accessed in performance, perhaps because it has not been activated, due to insufficient exposure to suitable input. However, there is something unsatisfactory about this explanation, in that lack of relevant input is precisely the motivation for principles like the Overt Pronoun Constraint in the first place. Once the L2 learner discovers that Japanese is a null-subject language allowing both null and overt pronouns, the Overt Pronoun Constraint ought to come into effect.

For the sake of the argument, however, let us grant that there may be individual variability of the kind suggested by Kanno. What would it mean for the claim that UG constrains interlanguage grammars if individual learners do not in fact observe a particular constraint consistently? Grimshaw and Rosen (1990) consider apparently problematic results in L1 acquisition where children appear to accept violations of another principle of UG, namely, Principle B of the Binding Theory. Grimshaw and Rosen point out that a number of performance factors may intervene to conceal underlying competence. They suggest that L1 acquirers may 'know' UG principles (unconsciously) but nevertheless fail to observe or 'obey' them in certain circumstances. In other words, competence and performance will sometimes diverge, such that sentences that are ruled out as ungrammatical violations of some principle of UG are nevertheless accepted in certain cases. According to Grimshaw and Rosen, even when this happens, it is nevertheless possible to show that children know the principle in question. If the child's grammar were not constrained by some principle, one would expect grammatical and ungrammatical sentences to be treated alike, since the principle ruling out the ungrammatical sentences would not be available. Therefore, if children treat grammatical and ungrammatical sentences differently (accepting significantly more of the former than the latter), this is sufficient to show that the two sentence types are not the same in the child grammar and that the principle in question must be operating, even if children do not perform with a high degree of accuracy on the ungrammatical sentences. Linguistic competence accounts for the distinction between grammatical and ungrammatical sentences; performance factors account for the failure to observe the distinction absolutely.

Let us apply this logic to the Overt Pronoun Constraint results from individual learners in Kanno's study. Looking only at the sentences involving overt pronouns and quantified antecedents, Kanno found that some subjects, at both testing sessions, failed to consistently exclude the ungrammatical interpretation, leading her to conclude that the Overt Pronoun Constraint (hence, UG in general) is not consistently accessible. Following Grimshaw and Rosen's proposal, however, it would be more appropriate to compare each learner's acceptance of antecedents for overt pronouns, i.e. referential (grammatical) with quantified (ungrammatical). (In other words, the comparison that Kanno makes at a group level should also be made at the individual level.) If interlanguage grammars are constrained by the Overt Pronoun Constraint, then we expect each subject to show a significant difference in acceptance of grammatical versus ungrammatical interpretations. This should be so even if performance on particular ungrammatical sentences is somewhat variable. While Kanno does not provide data to allow one to check this point, she does show that the L2 learners were much more consistent in their coreference judgments involving grammatical interpretations, which suggests that, individually, they are in fact distinguishing between licit and illicit interpretations.

To summarize the findings relating to the Overt Pronoun Constraint, Pérez-Leroux and Glass (1997, 1999) and Kanno (1997, 1998a, b) have shown that learners of different L2s, at different proficiency levels, tested by means of different tasks, show significant differences in their treatment of overt pronouns with quantified antecedents (illicit) versus null pronouns with quantified antecedents or overt or null pronouns with referential antecedents (licit). Group and individual results suggest that L2 learners are making the relevant distinctions, distinctions which could not have been derived from the L1 grammar or the L2 input alone, supporting the claim that interlanguage grammars are subject to the Overt Pronoun Constraint.

2.1.2 Process versus result nominals in L2 French

The previous section discussed L2 knowledge of a principle of UG which restricts the distribution and interpretation of embedded pronominal subjects. We turn now to an examination of another aspect of grammar involving an interplay between syntactic and interpretive factors, namely the distinction between two types of nominals, known as *process* and *result* nominals. The research described below addresses the question of whether there is a learnability problem relating to the syntax–semantics interface, a relatively new field of inquiry in the L2 context. Again, the underlying assumption is that knowledge of the property in question must have its origin in UG, the issue being whether L2 learners reveal unconscious knowledge of subtle distinctions between the two types of nominals, distinctions which are unlikely to be derivable from the L2 input alone or from the L1.

Dekydtspotter, Sprouse and Anderson (1997) look at whether L2 learners are sensitive to differences between process and result nominals in L2 French. A process nominal describes an event or something ongoing; a result nominal names the 'output of a process or an element associated with a process' (Grimshaw 1990: 49). The English nominal *destruction* illustrates the distinction. In (3a), *destruction* refers to the process of destroying the city; *the enemy* brings about the destruction (i.e. it is the agent), while *the city* undergoes the destruction (i.e. it is the theme). In (3b), on the other hand, *destruction* refers to the outcome, the result of the destroying. (Examples from Grimshaw 1990: 52.)

(3) a. The enemy's destruction of the city was awful to watch. (process)
b. The destruction was awful to see. (result)

Dekydtspotter et al. (1997) investigate dyadic process and result nominals in L2 French, that is nominals taking an agent and a theme argument (as in (3a)). There are restrictions on the arguments of such nominals, in particular, restrictions on the form of the agent. Consider the sentences in (4) (a result nominal) and (5) (a process nominal). In both cases, the theme is expressed in a phrase introduced by *de* ('of'), while the agent can be introduced by *par* ('by'). In (4a), *la 9e* is the theme and *Karajan* is the agent; in (5), *Tokyo* is the theme, while *Godzilla* is the agent. So far, then, result and process nominals pattern alike.

(4) Result nominal
a. la version de la 9e par Karajan
the version of the 9th by Karajan
'Karajan's version of the Ninth symphony'
b. la version de la 9e de Karajan
the version of the 9th of Karajan

(5) Process nominal
a. la destruction de Tokyo par Godzilla
the destruction of Tokyo by Godzilla
'Godzilla's destruction of Tokyo'
b. *la destruction de Tokyo de Godzilla
the destruction of Tokyo of Godzilla

The two kinds of nominals differ, however, in that result nominals also permit the agent to be introduced by *de*, as in (4b). In process nominals, on the other hand, this is not possible, as shown by the ungrammaticality of (5b). Thus, result nominals permit multiple phrases introduced by *de* (namely, both theme and agent), occurring in either order, whereas process nominals do not. (Nevertheless, native speakers have a preference for the agent of a result nominal to be introduced by *par* rather than *de*.)

This difference between result and process nominals within French (as well as other languages) stems from independent restrictions on argument structure and event structure originating in UG. In particular, in process nominals with multiple *de* arguments there are problems in assigning the agent role, violating the principle of Full Interpretation, which requires that arguments be interpretable at LF. (Unfortunately, Dekydspotter et al. give little detail on precisely how this constraint is played out in the case of the different types of nominals that they investigate.[2]) In consequence of an independent parametric difference between French and English, the distinction between these nominals is partially obscured in English. English disallows multiple *of* phrases in these contexts, as can be seen by looking at the literal glosses for (4b) and (5b). Instead, the agent appears as a prenominal genitive, whether the nominal is process or result, as can be seen by the translations of (4a), where the agent is expressed as *Karajan's*, and (5a) where it appears as *Godzilla's*. (Alternatively, English can express the agent in a *by*-phrase, equivalent to the *par*-phrases in French: *the destruction of Tokyo by Godzilla; the version of the 9th by Karajan* – again, there is no distinction between the two types of nominal in this respect.)

Dekydtspotter et al., following Carstens (1991), attribute this crosslinguistic difference (namely, the possibility of multiple *de* arguments in French and the impossibility of multiple *of* arguments in English) to a parametric difference between the two languages. As described in chapter 1, section 1.4.1, nouns in French raise from N to the head of a functional projection, Num (Bernstein 1993; Carstens 1991; Valois 1991). When a nominal raises to Num, it governs both its arguments and case is assigned under government (via *de*-insertion) to both theme and agent. In languages like English, in contrast, nouns do not raise to Num; in consequence, a nominal will never govern its agent and case assignment to the agent via *of* insertion is ruled out, case assignment being achieved, instead, by an alternative mechanism (Spec–head agreement).

Turning to the L2 logical problem for English-speaking learners of French, at issue is whether they will acquire the distinction between process and result nominals, with respect to the possibility of multiple *de*-phrases. It is unlikely that the L2 input is sufficient to signal this difference, since what has to be acquired is knowledge that sentences like (5b) are ungrammatical, whereas sentences like (4b) are possible. Since both types of nominal allow the agent to be introduced by *par* (as in (4a) and (5a)), the potential for overgeneralization is considerable. Nor is this a topic that is specifically taught in L2 French classrooms (though contrasts between *de* and *par* in other contexts may be).

It also seems highly unlikely that properties of the L1 English would be sufficient to allow learners to arrive at the relevant distinction in the L2. Although there are subtle distinctions between process and result nominals in English, these are not manifested in the same way. Because English does not have N-raising, it does not allow multiple *of*-phrases. There is no distinction in how the agent is realized in process and result nominals; in both cases, the agent is found either as a prenominal genitive (*Godzilla's destruction*; *Karajan's version*) or in a postnominal *by*-phrase (*the destruction by Godzilla*; *the version by Karajan*). Thus, the L2 acquisition of the distinction between process and result nominals with respect to multiple *de*-phrases constitutes a learnability problem. If English-speaking learners of French show knowledge of the distinction, this would suggest that UG constrains the interlanguage grammar in this domain.

Dekydtspotter et al. tested for knowledge of the process/result distinction with respect to multiple *de*-phrases in an experiment involving English-speaking adults learning French. (See box 2.3.) The task was an acceptability judgment task, with written scenarios providing a context (i.e. somewhat similar to the procedure adopted by Pérez-Leroux and Glass (1997, 1999), except that Pérez-Leroux and Glass asked for translations not judgments). Since the context is crucial to establish the interpretation of the nominal as either process or result, the scenarios were presented in the L1 (again, like Pérez-Leroux and Glass), in order to ensure that the L2 learners would make their judgments on the basis of the appropriate interpretation. The test sentences to be judged were presented in French.

Native speakers of French distinguished sharply and significantly between the two types of nominals, accepting multiple *de*-arguments in result nominals to a significantly greater extent than in process nominals, where they were largely rejected. (See table 2.3.1.) The relatively low rate of acceptance even in result nominals reflects the fact that *par* is the preferred way of realizing the agent. The L2 learners at all levels showed the same distinction between process and result nominals, with the advanced learners not being significantly different from the controls. The beginners and intermediate subjects in general showed a much higher acceptance rate of multiple *de* phrases with both types of nominals; nevertheless there is a significant difference between the two sentence types, in the expected direction, suggesting that the distinction is represented in the grammar; this is true both at the group level and at the individual level.

Box 2.3 Process and result nominals (Dekydtspotter et al. 1997)

Languages: L1 = English, L2 = French.
Task: Acceptability judgments of sentences containing both a theme and an agent introduced by *de*. Each sentence preceded by a paragraph (in English) to provide a context.
Sample stimuli:

Result nominals (grammatical)	Process nominals (ungrammatical)
Jean loves nineteenth-century train stations. La Gare du Nord, Paris's northern train station, still has some of that feel, even though the steam engines are long gone. Whenever Jean looks at a catalogue of Monet's works (in particular the work entitled *La Gare du Nord*), he gets a feel for what it would have been like to be there. Not surprisingly, Jean adore la peinture de la Gare du Nord de Monet. Feels possible in the context? Yes No Cannot decide	Shocking and disturbing, yes, but nonetheless true! The executioner's wife was having an affair, and the only time she could meet with her lover was when her husband the executioner was on the job. She read in the newspaper that a couple of traitors had been sentenced to death on Friday, so she sent a note to her lover, saying: Viens chez moi vendredi pendant l'éxécution de mon mari des traitres Feels possible in the context? Yes No Cannot decide

Results:

Table 2.3.1 *Acceptances of multiple* de *arguments (in %)*

		Result nominals (# = 10)	Process nominals (# = 10)
L2 groups	Beginners (n = 38)	69.21	53.51
	Intermediate (n = 32)	71.56	48.96
	Advanced (n = 20)	63.5	24.17
Native speakers	French (n = 48)	50.42	15.65
	English (n = 24)	22.08	10.53

In summary, L2 learners at all levels of proficiency showed an asymmetry in their acceptance of multiple phrases introduced by *de* in result and process nominals. The results suggest that the interlanguage grammar is constrained by UG, since the distinction between process and result nominals appears to come neither from the L1 nor from the L2 input.

Nevertheless, a caveat is in order. Like Kanno (1997), Dekydtspotter et al. included a group of native speakers of the L1 who judged English translations of the French test items, all of which are ungrammatical in English, in order to see whether learners might simply be judging L2 sentences on the basis of their mother tongue. Overall, multiple *of*-phrases were rejected in both types of nominal in contrast to the L2 results, suggesting that the L1 grammar is unlikely to be the source of knowledge of the distinction with respect to the L2 sentences. Nevertheless, the difference in their judgments on the two sentence types in the L1 was significant; in other words, even though both sentence types were considered fully ungrammatical, the process nominals with two *of*-phrases were even less likely to be accepted than the result nominals. Thus, one cannot totally exclude the possibility that the distinction shown by the L2 learners was in some way based on the L1 grammar.

2.1.3 Principles of UG in early interlanguage grammars: the ECP

So far, the experimental research that we have considered has mainly targeted intermediate or advanced learners, a tacit assumption being made that if some UG principle can be shown to constrain later interlanguage grammars, it would also have constrained the grammars of earlier stages. Indeed, if interlanguage grammars are UG-constrained, this should be so from the earliest stages of L2 acquisition.[3] In other words, we expect to find evidence of UG principles functioning in the interlanguage grammars of beginners or low-proficiency L2 learners, all other things being equal. However, a methodological problem arises in this context. UG principles are proposed as an explanation of very subtle and abstract linguistic phenomena, as we have seen; in many cases, these principles relate to properties exemplified in complex sentences. In consequence, some of the sentence types that are typically investigated by linguists and acquisition researchers are, for reasons independent of the UG issue, too difficult for beginner-level L2 learners to deal with.

Kanno (1996) has shown that Japanese *case drop*, a phenomenon that occurs in simple sentences, can be used to investigate whether the interlanguage grammars of beginners and low-proficiency learners are constrained by UG. Japanese has case particles, including nominative /-ga/ and accusative /-o/, as shown in (6a) (examples from Kanno). When an object is marked with accusative case, the particle may be dropped in informal spoken language, as in (6b); however, it is ungrammatical to drop the nominative particle marking the subject, as in (6c). Thus, there is an asymmetry here, with respect to the type of particle that can be dropped.

(6) a. John ga sono hon o yonda.
John NOM that book ACC read-PAST
'John read that book'
b. John ga sono hon yonda.
John NOM that book read-PAST
c. *John sono hon o yonda.
John that book ACC read-PAST

Japanese case drop meets the criteria discussed above with respect to learnability considerations. Firstly, the relevant generalization (that accusative particles may be dropped while nominative may not) is not derivable on the basis of the L1, assuming an L1 without case particles, such as English. Secondly, it does not appear that this property could be acquired on the basis of L2 input alone, since the input underdetermines the case drop property. If the learner were to try and make the relevant generalization on the basis of 'noticing' dropped particles in the input, the potential for overgeneralization is considerable. In addition to permitting accusative case drop, Japanese has a topic marker /-wa/ which can be dropped (Kuno 1973), as shown in (7a), where the topic marker is present, and (7b), where it has been omitted.[4]

(7) a. John_i wa Hanako ga *pro*$_i$ sono hon o yonda to itta.
John_i TOP Hanako NOM (he_i) that book ACC read-PAST that said
'Speaking of John, Hanako said that he (= John) read that book.'
b. John_i Hanako ga *pro*$_i$ sono hon o yonda to itta.
John_i Hanako NOM (he_i) that book ACC read-PAST that said
'Speaking of John, Hanako said that he (= John) read that book.'

Since subjects can be topicalized and /-wa/ can be omitted from a topicalized subject, it would not be unreasonable to assume that any particle marking a subject can be dropped. In addition, the nominative /-ga/ can be dropped when it occurs on the complement of a stative verb or when it marks the subject of an unaccusative verb.[5] Furthermore, case drop is apparently not taught in Japanese L2 classrooms, although it is, presumably, exemplified in classroom input.

Fukuda (1993) attributes the asymmetry in case particle deletion (nominative prohibited, accusative permissible) to the Empty Category Principle (ECP) (Chomsky 1981), a principle which accounts for a variety of subject–object asymmetries across languages. The ECP requires nonpronominal empty categories (i.e. *traces* or *variables*) to be *properly governed*. An empty category in object position is properly governed by the verb, whereas an empty category in subject position is not properly governed. Hence, in a number of different situations, empty categories are permitted in object position but not subject position. Assuming that null case particles are empty categories of the relevant sort, it is permissible to omit an accusative case particle because the empty particle is properly governed by

Box 2.4 Case-particle deletion (ECP) (Kanno 1996)

Languages: L1 = English, L2 = Japanese.
Task: Grammaticality judgments. The naturalness of sentences is assessed on a scale of 1 (unnatural) to 3 (natural).
Sample stimuli:

Missing accusative particle in sentences with 2 overt arguments (grammatical)	Missing accusative particle in sentences with 1 overt argument (grammatical)
Suzuki-san wa dono biiru nomimasita ka? *(Which beer did Mr(s) Suzuki drink?)*	Dono biiru nomimasita ka? *(Which beer did (s/he) drink?)*
Missing nominative particle in sentences with 2 overt arguments (ungrammatical)	**Missing nominative particle in sentences with 1 overt argument (ungrammatical)**
Dono gakusee biiru o nomimasita ka? *(Which student drank beer?)*	Dono gakusee nomimasita ka? *(Which student drank (it)?)*

Results:

Table 2.4.1 *Case drop: mean naturalness scores (from 1 to 3)*

	2 overt arguments (# = 8)		1 overt argument (# = 8)	
	ACC	NOM	ACC	NOM
L2 learners (n = 26)	2.4	1.76	2.58	1.64
Native speakers (n = 20)	2.6	1.36	2.86	1.31

the verb.[6] In contrast, a null nominative particle would not be properly governed, hence nominative particles must be overt.

Kanno (1996) investigated whether beginners learning Japanese are sensitive to this asymmetry in case-particle deletion, that is, whether they distinguish between grammatical sentences with dropped accusative particles like (6b) and ungrammatical sentences with dropped nominative particles like (6c). Subjects were tested on a grammaticality-judgment task in which they had to assess the naturalness of sentences, like those in (6), with and without case particles. (See box 2.4.)

Results revealed significantly greater acceptance of accusative case drop over nominative case drop, and no significant differences between L2 learners and native speakers. This is true for sentences with one or two arguments expressed overtly. (See table 2.4.1.) These results, then, are consistent with the proposal that a UG principle (the ECP) functions in the early interlanguage grammar. Kanno was able to establish this without having to resort to the kinds of complex sentences that have previously been used to investigate knowledge of the ECP in L2 English (e.g. Bley-Vroman, Felix and Ioup 1988; White 1988) or L2 German (Felix 1988).

If the interlanguage grammars of beginners show evidence of being constrained by the ECP, one expects the same in the case of more advanced learners. In a subsequent study, Kanno (1998a) reports results which largely confirm the original findings. The second study involved intermediate-level learners of Japanese. Group results again revealed significant differences between acceptance of missing nominative and accusative case particles, consistent with the operation of the ECP. In this follow-up study, Kanno also looked at individual results and found that most individuals exhibited the relevant contrast, although not necessarily as strongly as native speakers.

In contrast, Kellerman, van Ijzendoorn and Takashima (1999), testing Dutch-speaking L2 learners, were unable to replicate Kanno's finding of a sensitivity to the subject–object asymmetry in case-particle deletion. This attempted replication, however, is somewhat problematic, in that it involved teaching a miniature artificial language to students not previously exposed to Japanese, in a single session. This artificial language had the following characteristics: it was SOV, subjects and objects could be omitted (in other words, it was a prodrop language), and overt subjects and objects were always case-marked. Students were explicitly taught these properties, by means of translation; they had no exposure to input involving missing case particles and they were not taught that case markers could be dropped. Immediately after the teaching phase, they were explicitly told that there was one rule of this language which they had not been taught and which they were to try to discover. Test sentences manipulated dropped nominative or accusative case particles, the idea being that, if interlanguage grammars are constrained by the ECP, dropping accusative case would be permissible, while dropping nominative would not. Learners showed some acceptance of dropped case marking, both nominative and accusative. A second study modified properties of the artificial language (using real Japanese lexical items instead of invented ones) and the test instructions, as well as involving somewhat older subjects; it was otherwise similar to the first study. Again, results showed no subject–object asymmetry in acceptance of case particle deletion.

Kellerman et al. claim that these results cast doubts on Kanno's conclusion that early L2 grammars are constrained by the ECP. However, there are a number of problems with these two studies which in turn cast doubts on their own conclusions. The 'L2' was artificial (the learners knew this – they were told that they were dealing with an extra-terrestrial language); learners were taught just three explicit rules, via translation. Exposure to the 'L2' was extremely brief. It seems very likely that learners simply treated the whole thing as a problem-solving exercise, rather than as a genuine language-learning situation, in which case the ECP is simply irrelevant, since it is a constraint on natural language systems, not on systems arrived at by other means.[7] Hence, the absence of ECP effects in Kellerman et al.'s study is hardly surprising, leaving Kanno's results unchallenged. (Indeed, even if Kellerman et al.'s results had supported Kanno's, one would still have to question their validity.)

Potentially more problematic for Kanno's claim that L2 learners observe the ECP is an additional experiment by Kellerman and Yoshioka (1999). This experiment involved genuine L2 acquisition, testing Dutch-speaking learners of Japanese. The task was a grammaticality-judgment task. Whereas each of Kanno's test sentences contained one dropped case particle, either nominative or accusative (as well as a case-marked NP in those sentences which contained two overt arguments), Kellerman and Yoshioka included additional sentence types, to provide a greater variety of overt and null case-marking combinations. Their reason for doing so was the incorrect and unmotivated assumption that the ECP predicts a hierarchy of acceptability, as follows (where + means overt case marking and −means no case marking):

(8) +NOM+ACC ≥ +NOM−ACC > −NOM+ACC > −NOM−ACC

Kellerman and Yoshioka's results show no evidence for this hierarchy; hence, they conclude that the ECP does not constrain the interlanguage grammar of these learners. In fact, as pointed out by Kanno (1999), no such hierarchy is predicted by the ECP, which simply says that nominative case particles in subject position should not be deleted. The ECP is neutral as to whether accusative case particle deletion will take place at all (the ECP certainly does not require this) and whether overt accusative marking is preferable to null. As Kanno points out, if one holds the accusative case markers constant (comparing +NOM+ACC to −NOM+ACC or +NOM−ACC to −NOM−ACC), Kellerman and Yoshioka's subjects do show a significant difference in their acceptance of sentences with and without nominative case particles, in favour of the former, as predicted by the ECP account.

2.2 The logical problem of L2 revisited: alternative accounts

So far, we have considered three different linguistic properties assumed to stem from UG: (i) differences between overt and null pronouns (attributed to the Overt Pronoun Constraint); (ii) the distinction between process and result nominals (attributed, indirectly, to restrictions on argument structure); (iii) subject–object asymmetries in case-particle deletion (a consequence of the ECP). In each case, the claim has been that there is a learnability problem, the L2 input alone (whether naturalistic input or classroom input including instruction) being insufficient to allow the learner to arrive at the relevant distinctions. The assumption has also been that the relevant properties could not have been arrived at on the basis of the L1: in the case of the studies involving the Overt Pronoun Constraint, learners were chosen whose L1s do not permit null subjects, with overt pronouns behaving quite differently in the two languages; in the case of process and result nominals, the L1 and L2 differed in terms of how arguments of these nominals are realized; in the case of case particle deletion, the L1 was a language without case particles at all. In all the studies described above, L2 learners showed behaviour which revealed unconscious knowledge of subtle properties of the L2, consistent with the claim that their grammars are UG-constrained.

In this section, we consider attempts to provide alternative accounts of L2 learners' successes in acquiring the kinds of subtle distinctions discussed above. Certain researchers deny that there is an underdetermination problem in such cases; hence, they claim, there is no need to assume that interlanguage grammars are UG-constrained. Two different lines of argument have been advanced. The first questions the poverty-of-the-stimulus claim, by trying to show that the L2 input is in fact sufficient to allow the relevant contrasts to be induced without recourse to principles of UG. The second accepts that the L2 input underdetermines the unconscious knowledge that L2 learners attain but maintains that this knowledge derives from the L1 grammar rather than UG.

2.2.1 L2 input

Kellerman and colleagues take the position that properties of the L2 input are sufficient to explain L2 learners' differential treatment of nominative and accusative case drop. While they failed to find a subject–object asymmetry in case-particle deletion in their three studies, they accept the validity of Kanno's (1996) finding of a robust difference between acceptances of deleted accusative versus nominative particles.

Kellerman and Yoshioka (1999) and Kellerman et al. (1999) account for the differences in their results and Kanno's in terms of differences in the L2 input. They suggest that case-particle drop would be relatively easy to formulate as a pedagogical rule and would be easy to learn on the basis of instruction. However, as neither their subjects nor Kanno's had received such instruction, this is a moot point. They also suggest that naturalistic input may show a statistical bias in favour of dropped object particles and that L2 learners in Hawaii (where Kanno's subjects were tested) are likely to have been exposed to such input. Their performance, then, could be explained in terms of properties of the L2 input and, in their view, in terms of the input alone. But this begs the original question: while input with dropped accusative case particles is certainly necessary to motivate case drop in the first place, this does not mean that it is sufficient to account for the knowledge that L2 learners acquire. The input will exemplify object NPs with and without case markers, subject topics with and without topic markers, as well as nominative markers missing on subjects of a subclass of verbs. The potential to overgeneralize, thus dropping nominative case markers on subjects in general, remains even if there is a preponderance of accusative particle drop in the input. It is important to understand that the UG approach does not deny the importance of input. But the claim is that input alone is not enough.

However, suppose, for the sake of the argument, that one could somehow demonstrate that a particular phenomenon (in this case, dropping of accusative particles) could successfully be acquired on the basis of statistical frequency in the input. While this might show that case-particle drop does not constitute a genuine learnability problem, it would not dispose of the learnability problem in general. The fact that there may not be a logical problem of L2 acquisition with respect to one phenomenon does not mean that there is never a logical problem of L2 acquisition.

2.2.2 *The L1 grammar as the source of knowledge of UG principles*

According to another approach which argues against the need to invoke UG, the complexity of the mental representations achieved by L2 learners is acknowledged, as well as the fact that input alone cannot account for such complexity. Instead, the unconscious knowledge attained by L2 learners is claimed to derive from the L1 grammar (Bley-Vroman 1990; Clahsen and Muysken 1989; Schachter 1989, 1990). For example, there are a number of subject–object asymmetries in English which do not involve case particles but which do implicate the ECP. The L2 learner of Japanese, then, may have been able to arrive at the relevant properties of case drop in Japanese on the basis of very different properties of English which are subject to the same constraint. Similarly, in the case of process and result nominals, there are a number of subtle differences between them in English (e.g. Grimshaw 1990), which might somehow explain the results obtained by Dekydtspotter et al. (1997) for L2 French. Thus, it might be argued that knowledge of the properties described in this chapter (as well as other principles discussed in the literature) stems from the mother tongue and, hence, fails to provide evidence that interlanguage grammars are UG-constrained independently of the L1 grammar.

Indeed, for many principles of UG, it appears that the L1 can never be completely ruled out as a source of the L2 learner's unconscious knowledge. Since the L1 is a natural language and since many UG principles manifest themselves in the L1 in some form or other, it will often be hard or impossible to disentangle the two (Hale 1996).[8] Nevertheless, the results described so far suggest that L2 learners are able to apply UG principles to totally new domains, including data that do not occur in the L1. As we have seen, L2 learners observe UG constraints even when they apply to very different phenomena in the L2 (restrictions on arguments of process nominals; ECP and case-particle drop), ruling out surface transfer as an explanation. Thus, it appears that there is considerable flexibility in the system; UG constraints can be applied to new data, and to situations that are entirely different from what pertains in the L1. It is not clear that this would be the case if UG principles were only somehow being 'reconstructed' on the basis of how they operate in the L1. Furthermore, as will be discussed in chapter 4, where parameters of UG are concerned, it is a relatively straightforward matter to distinguish between L1 parameter settings and other settings, hence to discover whether or not L2 learners are restricted to options realized in the L1.

In any case, an approach which sees the issue as an either/or matter (UG *or* the L1) is misconceived. This is a false dichotomy. It is inappropriate to contrast UG with the L1 as the source of UG-like knowledge; rather, both appear to be involved. This issue will be considered in greater detail in chapters 3 and 4.

2.3 Problems for the UG claim: wild interlanguage grammars

So far, results from the studies discussed in this chapter are consistent with the claim that UG constrains interlanguage grammars. L2 learners demonstrate unconscious knowledge of subtle contrasts which are by no means transparent in the L2 input and which are not realized in any obvious way in the L1. This unconscious knowledge is unexpected if interlanguage grammars are not UG-constrained. While the source of this knowledge may, at least in some cases, be UG as instantiated in the L1, it is clear that the constraints are applied to completely new data and to phenomena that do not exist in the L1. Learner grammars, then, conform with UG.

There is another way of exploring whether or not UG constrains interlanguage grammars. UG defines what a grammar is, determining what mental representations can and cannot be like. Natural language grammars fall within a range sanctioned by UG. L1 acquirers are limited by the hypothesis space provided by UG, which reduces the number of logical possibilities that have to be entertained in order to arrive at a grammar for the language being acquired. Developing L1 grammars, in other words, are 'possible' grammars (White 1982). At least with respect to the properties we have considered so far, the same appears to be true of interlanguage grammars, in the sense that they fall within the range sanctioned by UG. Interlanguage grammars, then, exhibit characteristics typical of natural language.

Grammars that do not conform to principles of UG have been variously described as *impossible* (White 1982, 1988), *rogue* (Thomas 1991a), *illicit* (Hamilton 1998) or *wild* (Goodluck 1991; Klein 1995a); the latter term will be adopted here. If interlanguage grammars are UG-constrained, wild grammars are predicted not to occur in L2 acquisition. In other words, interlanguage grammars should be restricted to properties found in the L1 and/or the L2, and/or natural languages in general. If it can be shown that interlanguage grammars do not conform to properties of natural language, this would suggest that the operation of UG is in some way impaired.

Recently, there have been proposals that interlanguage grammars are in fact sometimes wild. Two phenomena will be considered in this context: reflexives (Christie and Lantolf 1998) and null prepositions (Klein 1993b, 1995a). In both cases, it has been suggested that the interlanguage grammar shows a cluster of properties that is illicit, hence that the grammar is not sanctioned by UG.

2.3.1 Reflexive binding

There has been considerable research which investigates whether reflexives in interlanguage grammars are constrained by Principle A of the Binding Theory. Binding Theory places constraints on coreference between various kinds of NPs, Principle A being concerned with properties of anaphors, such as reflexives (*himself*, *herself*, etc.) (Chomsky 1981a). According to Principle A, an anaphor must be bound in its governing category; effectively, it must take an antecedent in a local domain (usually the same clause), as shown in (9). In (9a), coreference is possible between the reflexive, *herself*, and the subject, *Mary*, because they are within the same clause. In (9b), on the other hand, *herself* cannot refer to the subject of the higher clause, *Mary*, but it can refer to the subject of the lower clause, namely *Susan*.

(9) a. Mary_i blamed herself_i
b. Mary_i thought that Susan_j blamed $\text{herself}^{*}{}_{i/j}$

As is well known, reflexives differ crosslinguistically as to the domain in which they must be bound. While English reflexives require their antecedents to be within the same clause (i.e. local), there are many languages, such as Japanese, which permit the antecedent to be in a different clause. The Japanese sentence in (10) is ambiguous, with *zibun* ('self') able to have either the local subject, *Susan*, or the main-clause subject, *Mary*, as its antecedent. When the antecedent is in a different clause from the reflexive, this is referred to as *non-local* or *long-distance* binding.

(10) Mary$_i$ ga Susan$_j$ ga zibun$_{i/j}$ o semeta to omotta.
Mary NOM Susan NOM self ACC blamed that thought
'Mary thought that Susan blamed herself.'

In addition to domain (locality), orientation is also important, that is, whether the antecedent is a subject or not. Again, languages differ in this respect. An English reflexive can take a subject or a non-subject as its antecedent, whereas Japanese reflexives are restricted to subject antecedents. An English sentence like (11a) is potentially ambiguous, with either the subject or the object available as the antecedent, though context will usually favour one interpretation over the other. The Japanese sentence in (11b), on the other hand, only has one interpretation, where the subject, *kanja-ga*, is the antecedent.

(11) a. The patient$_i$ asked the nurse$_j$ about herself$_{i/j}$
b. Kanja$_i$ ga kangofu$_j$ ni zibun$_{i/*j}$ no koto nitsuite tazuneta.
patient NOM nurse DAT self GEN matter about asked
'The patient asked the nurse about herself.'

Much of the earlier L2 research on reflexives was conducted within the framework of Manzini and Wexler (1987) and Wexler and Manzini (1987). They proposed two parameters to handle crosslinguistic differences in how Principle A operates: the Governing Category Parameter, which dealt with domain, and the Proper Antecedent Parameter, dealing with orientation. Explicit discussion of the possibility of wild interlanguage grammars first arose in this context (Eckman 1994; Thomas 1991a). However, most of the L2 research conducted on the Governing Category Parameter and the Proper Antecedent Parameter was not directed at the issue of wild grammars but rather to the question of whether L2 learners can reset parameters and whether or not they observe the Subset Principle (Finer 1991; Finer and Broselow 1986; Hirakawa 1990; Thomas 1991b). (See White (1989) for review.)

According to subsequent linguistic analyses, parameterization of this kind is not involved. Instead, two different types of anaphors are assumed, with differing properties. Each anaphor type has a cluster of properties associated with it, as shown in (12).

(12) a. X^{max} (phrasal) reflexives. These are morphologically complex, require local antecedents and allow subjects and (in some languages) non-subjects as antecedents, e.g. *himself*, *herself* in English; *taziji* ('himself') in Chinese; *kare-zisin, kanojo-zisin* ('himself', 'herself') in Japanese.
b. X^0 (head) reflexives. These are monomorphemic, allow non-local antecedents (as well as local), and require the antecedent to be a subject, e.g. *ziji* in Chinese; *zibun* in Japanese.

While accounts differ in their details, they share the central insight that both phrasal and head anaphors undergo LF movement (Cole, Hermon and Sung 1990;

Katada 1991; Pica 1987; Reinhart and Reuland 1993, amongst others). Differences in domain and orientation fall out from the categorial differences between the reflexives: X^0 reflexives raise by head movement to Infl (itself a head). In complex sentences, they can move out of the clause in which they originate, raising from one Infl to another. In consequence, they can be interpreted with a long-distance antecedent in a higher clause; this antecedent must be a subject because only a subject will c-command the reflexive in Infl. X^{max} reflexives, on the other hand, are maximal projections which can adjoin only to the nearest maximal projection, namely the VP in which they originate. There they remain in the binding domain of either a local subject or a local object. In general, then, current accounts of reflexives agree on the following properties:

(13) a. Long-distance anaphors must be subject-oriented
b. Anaphors which allow non-subject antecedents must be local

It is in this context that there has been extensive consideration of what would constitute a wild grammar (Christie and Lantolf 1998; Hamilton 1998; Thomas 1995; White, Hirakawa and Kawasaki 1996; Yuan 1998). Christie and Lantolf (1998) hypothesize that a UG-constrained grammar will show a correlation between domain and orientation: if the interlanguage grammar allows long-distance reflexives, then reflexives will be subject-oriented; if the interlanguage grammar has local reflexives, then non-subject antecedents will be permitted. If interlanguage grammars are not UG-constrained, on the other hand, there will be a breakdown in these relationships.

Christie and Lantolf (1998) investigate the acquisition of reflexives in L2 Chinese (which has a long-distance reflexive, *ziji*) and L2 English.[9] (See box 2.5.) In the case of L2 Chinese, the learners are speakers of English, a language which only allows local reflexives. In the case of L2 English, learners are native speakers of Chinese or Korean, both of which have long-distance reflexives. (These languages also have phrasal reflexives which behave like English *himself/herself*.)

In order to understand what might be going on in the case of reflexives, it is necessary to establish how L2 learners interpret certain sentences, whether, for example, an English sentence such as (9b), repeated here as (14), has only one possible interpretation in the interlanguage grammar (with *Susan* as the antecedent of *herself*), as is the case in English, or whether it is ambiguous (with either *Mary* or *Susan* as the antecedent of *herself*), as it would be in Japanese or Chinese.

(14) Mary thought that Susan blamed herself.

Christie and Lantolf developed a truth-value-judgment task for this purpose. In a truth-value-judgment task, a particular sentence is paired with a particular context which is provided by a story, a picture, or a scenario acted out in front of the subjects (on video, for example). Subjects have to indicate whether the sentence

Box 2.5 Reflexives (Christie and Lantolf 1998)

Languages: L1 = English, L2 = Chinese and L1 = Chinese/Korean, L2 = English.
Task: Truth-value judgments. Subjects indicate whether a sentence provides a true statement about what is going on in an accompanying picture.
Sample stimuli:

Local domain (true)	Non-local domain (false)
(Picture showing Grover hitting Grover) Bert says that Grover is hitting himself on the head.	(Picture showing Grover hitting Bert) Bert says that Grover is hitting himself on the head.
Subject-oriented (true)	**Object-oriented (true)**
(Picture showing a book about Big Bird) Big Bird is giving Oscar a book about himself.	(Picture showing a book about Oscar) Big Bird is giving Oscar a book about himself.

is true in the context provided. In Christie and Lantolf's tasks, pictures were used (see box 2.5 for example stimuli). The advantage of such tasks is that subjects are not being asked to make explicit grammaticality judgments as to the form of the sentences. Indeed, all sentences in a truth-value-judgment task are generally grammatical under some interpretation. Rather, subjects are ostensibly being asked something about the meaning of the sentence. Nevertheless, their judgments reveal something about the form of the grammar, in this case the range of interpretations the grammar permits for reflexives.

As Christie and Lantolf recognize, the crucial issue is the grammar of the individual; in other words, for any particular individual, is the grammar UG-consistent or is it wild? (For related discussion, see also Eckman 1994; Thomas 1995; White et al. 1996.) Results were analysed using cluster analysis, to see whether there is a correlation between domain and orientation in individual grammars. Christie and Lantolf found no evidence for such clustering in the case of either L2. Somewhat surprisingly (given their assumptions), the control groups (Chinese and English native speakers) also failed to show evidence of clustering. It is hard to argue that L2 learners do (or do not) have wild grammars if even native speakers behave in a way that suggests their grammars are wild, a problem that Christie and Lantolf recognize.

Furthermore, Christie and Lantolf's assumption about clustering of domain and orientation is questionable. As Thomas (1995, 1998) points out, the properties described in (13) only carry a one-way implication. That is, while long-distance anaphors must be subject-oriented, it is not the case that all subject-oriented anaphors must allow long-distance antecedents. There are languages with subject-oriented anaphors which are bound only in a local domain, for example, Japanese *zibun-zisin* (Katada 1991) and the French reflexive clitic *se* (Pica 1987). There is nothing in the LF movement account to prohibit this. Similarly, while a non-subject antecedent implies a locally bound reflexive, there is no requirement that all locally bound reflexives permit object antecedents.

As Thomas discusses, Christie and Lantolf incorrectly presuppose a two-way implication between domain and orientation. They assume that a local binding domain necessarily implies the possibility of non-subject antecedents, leading them to the conclusion that L2 learners had arrived at illicit grammars. However, this is not in fact the case. Consider, for example, L2 learners of English who permit only local antecedents for reflexives like *himself* and *herself*, thus having the domain right, but also reject object antecedents, thus having orientation wrong. Such a grammar would fail to show the clustering relationship that Christie and Lantolf expected. Nevertheless, the grammar would in fact be perfectly legitimate, although not the appropriate grammar for English – this is precisely how Japanese *zibun-zisin* behaves, for example.

In addition, as Thomas points out, numerous investigations of the acquisition of English reflexives have found that learners and native speakers have a strong preference for subject antecedents even where object antecedents are possible. For example, given a sentence like *John showed Bill a picture of himself*, native speakers are more likely to interpret *John* (the subject) as the antecedent of the reflexive. In certain contexts, L2 learners and native speakers may reject interpretations which their grammars in fact permit. This makes the results of the cluster analysis even harder to interpret, since such preferences may conceal the full extent of grammatical knowledge.[10]

Indeed, Thomas (1995) suggests that languages which do not have long-distance reflexives, such as English, should not be used for investigating whether domain and orientation are correlated. Instead, one should concentrate on L2s with long-distance reflexives, such as Chinese or Japanese. But here, too, determining whether learners arrive at wild grammars is not as straightforward as Christie and Lantolf imply. If learners accept long-distance antecedents for reflexives, thus getting the domain right, and also accept objects as antecedents, this is not necessarily indicative of a wild grammar. It depends crucially on whether the object antecedent is found within a local domain or whether it is a long-distance object. In other words, there is an important distinction between (15a), where the object antecedent is in a local domain, and (15b), a biclausal sentence, where the reflexive is construed as having a non-subject antecedent outside the clause in which it appears.

(15) a. The nurse asked the patient$_i$ about herself$_i$

b. *Black-san ga White$_i$-san ni [Grey-san ga zibun$_i$ o
Black-Mr NOM White-Mr DAT Grey-Mr NOM self ACC
mita to] iimashita
saw that said
'Mr Black said to Mr White that Mr Grey saw himself.'

Long-distance reflexives in some languages (Icelandic *sig* or Serbo-Croatian *sebe*) can take a local subject or object as antecedent; non-local antecedents must always be subjects, however. In other words, equivalents of (15a) are grammatical, while interpretations like (15b) are never possible. Evidence for a wild grammar, then, would be provided if non-local non-subjects were considered acceptable antecedents for a reflexive, in other words if sentences equivalent to (15b) were permitted. In this case, there would be a violation of the requirement that the antecedent of the reflexive must c-command the reflexive at LF.

In their cluster analysis, Christie and Lantolf compare the possibility of local object antecedents (such as Chinese equivalents of (15a)) with long-distance subject antecedents (such as Chinese equivalents of (10)). Finding that both are accepted, they conclude, incorrectly, that the grammar is wild. (Eckman (1994) does the same, and draws the same conclusion.) In fact, Christie and Lantolf only had one test item relevant to the issue of long-distance objects, i.e. only one item similar to (15b). Some learners accepted the long-distance non-subject antecedent in this case, which makes it appear that their interlanguage grammars might indeed not be UG-constrained. However, given the fact that only one sentence was involved, there is considerable doubt as to the validity and generalizability of this result.[11]

Thomas (1995) overcomes these shortcomings by investigating the L2 acquisition of the Japanese reflexive *zibun*, by learners at low and high levels of proficiency. Again, the task was a truth-value-judgment task (see box 2.6). Crucially, stimuli included four biclausal sentences with long-distance objects as potential antecedents, similar to (15b).

Table 2.6.1 presents group results, where it can be seen that long-distance object antecedents are indeed accepted by low-proficiency learners, to about the same extent that local object antecedents are accepted. The results on local objects, though inappropriate for Japanese, do not provide evidence of a wild grammar but the acceptance of long-distance object antecedents is problematic. Thomas provides a further analysis in terms of individual performance, since it is properties of the individual grammar that are at issue. Using a criterion of three or four responses (out of four) to determine individual consistency,[12] Thomas concentrates on the twenty-three learners who consistently accept non-local antecedents for *zibun*, excluding from consideration those who treat *zibun* only as a locally bound

Box 2.6 Reflexives (Thomas 1995)

Languages: L1 = English, L2 = Japanese.
Task: Truth-value judgments. Contexts provided by written scenarios (3–5 sentences), illustrated by pictures. Each scenario is followed by a statement. Subjects indicate whether the statement is true.
Sample stimuli:

Biclausal: LD subject (true)	Biclausal: LD object (false)
Scenario: B hits A A wa B ga zibun o butta to iimasita *(A said that B hit self)*	Scenario: A likes B's book C wa B ni A ga zibun no hon ga suki da to iimasita *(C told B that A likes self's book)*
Monoclausal: local subject (true)	**Monoclausal: local object (false)**
Scenario: A describes A's problems to B A wa B ni zibun no mondai ni tuite hanasimasita *(A spoke with B about self's problems)*	Scenario: A asks B questions about B A wa B ni zibun no koto ni tuite iroiro na situmon o simasita *(A asked B various questions concerning self)*

Results:

Table 2.6.1 *Responses of* true *(in %)*

	LD subject (# = 4)	*LD object (# = 4)	Local subject (# = 4)	*Local object (# = 4)
L2 groups				
Low (n = 34)	55	54	85	47
Advanced (n = 24)	57	14	96	17
Native speakers (n = 34)	89	18	93	13

reflexive. The question, then, is whether these learners have unconscious knowledge of the requirement for non-local antecedents to be subjects. While the majority (70%) showed appropriate orientation, 30% of the learners (six in the low-proficiency group and one advanced) consistently allowed long-distance object antecedents (accepting interpretations like (15b)), a property not permitted in natural language.

Other researchers have also reported acceptance of binding to long-distance objects by L2 learners and controls, though to a much lesser extent. White et al. (1996) report for L2 Japanese that one learner (out of thirteen) consistently accepted long-distance object antecedents, as did one native speaker (out of ten). Thomas (1995) also found that 10% of her Japanese native speaker controls showed the same 'wild' behaviour. For L2 Chinese, Yuan (1998) found that three learners out of fifty consistently accepted long-distance objects, while no controls did so.

It is not unreasonable to assume a certain amount of 'noise' in the data; performance at 100% accuracy is unusual in any experimental attempts to get at linguistic competence. Investigation of binding principles is no exception. However, while performance factors may provide a reasonable explanation of the occasional native speaker or L2 learner who deviates from expected behaviour, it is unlikely that noisy data can provide an adequate account of the performance of Thomas's subjects, where 30% of those who have a long-distance reflexive in L2 Japanese also allow its antecedent to be a non-local object. Thomas herself assumes that there is a competence issue here; she suggests that these subjects have misanalysed *zibun* as a pronoun rather than a reflexive.[13] As such, it can take any non-local antecedent. In other words, these L2 learners adopt an alternative analysis, which happens to be inappropriate for the L2, such that their grammars nevertheless fall within the bounds of UG.

This solution in turn raises the issue of falsifiability. By changing the analysis of *zibun* from anaphor to pronoun, the prospect of a wild interlanguage grammar has been avoided. Does this mean that one can always change the analysis in order to avoid such problems? It is important to understand that the alternative proposal itself makes testable predictions. In order to explore further the possibility that *zibun* is a pronoun in the interlanguage grammar of at least some learners, one would have to include additional sentence types which investigate how learners treat pronouns in L2 Japanese. Hyams and Sigurjonsdottir (1990) raised a similar possibility for L1 acquisition of Icelandic, namely that children treat the reflexive *sig* as a pronoun; they rejected this possibility precisely because there turned out to be differences in the way children treated other pronouns and *sig*.

Another possibility is suggested by Hamilton (1998), who argues that English-speaking learners of Japanese may be treating reflexives as logophoric, i.e. anaphors which are exempt from binding principles and which can be bound non-locally within the discourse (e.g. *A picture of myself would be nice on that wall*). (See Reinhart and Reuland (1993) for a recent treatment of logophoricity, including constraints on when an anaphor can be logophoric.) Again, this would mean that these interlanguage grammars are in fact licit. And, again, this would have to be demonstrated independently with relevant stimuli, as Hamilton (1998) tries to do for L2 English.

To sum up, as far as reflexive binding is concerned, it has been suggested by Christie and Lantolf (1998) that L2 learners arrive at grammars where domain and orientation fail to cluster, with a result that their grammars may be wild rather than UG-constrained. Thomas (1995) notes, however, that this claim rests on a misconception of what the permissible and impermissible grammars are. Controlling for this by examining only the issue of whether a long-distance reflexive permits a non-local non-subject antecedent (which is illicit), Thomas finds that the majority of learners have UG-constrained grammars of anaphora. However, a minority appears to have a wild grammar. Thomas (1995) and Hamilton (1998) offer alternative analyses of this behaviour which suggest that the interlanguage is, after all, UG-constrained, though not the appropriate grammar for Japanese.

2.3.2 *Null prep*

Another example of a purported wild interlanguage grammar is provided by Klein (1993b, 1995a). Klein investigates a phenomenon which she calls *null prep*, whereby L2 learners of English omit prepositions in obligatory contexts. English has a number of prepositional verbs (verbs taking PP complements), where the preposition cannot be deleted, as shown in (16a, b). The preposition also appears in questions, as in (16c, d), as well as relatives (16e, f), whether these involve preposition stranding (16c, e) or the more formal pied-piping (16d, f). It is not possible to omit the preposition in such contexts, as shown in (17). It is omission of the kind illustrated in (17) which Klein terms *null prep*.

(16) a. The student is worrying about the exam.
b. *The student is worrying the exam.
c. Which exam is the student worrying about?
d. About which exam is the student worrying?
e. Here's the exam that the student is worrying about.
f. Here's the exam about which the student is worrying.

(17) a. *Which exam is the student worrying?
b. *Here's the exam that the student is worrying.

Although null prep is not possible in English, it is found in certain languages, such as Brazilian Portuguese, several dialects of Spanish and French, as well as Haitian Creole. However, it is relatively rare and, according to Klein's (1993b) review of a number of languages that exhibit null prep, it is found only in relative clauses (equivalents of (17b)), being prohibited in *wh*-questions (equivalents of (17a)). The examples in (18), from Haitian Creole (Klein 1995a) illustrate this point:

(18) a. Twa zanmi-yo ap pale de sinema sa a.
three friend-P are talking about movie this TOP
'The three friends are talking about this movie.'
b. Men sinema que twa zanmi-yo ap pale a.
here movie that three friend-P are talking TOP
'Here is the movie that the three friends are talking (about)'
c. *Ki sinema twa zanmi-yo ap pale a?
what movie three friend-P are talking TOP?
What movie are the three friends talking (about)?

Klein observes that relative clauses in languages allowing null prep show characteristics which suggest that they are not derived by syntactic movement: (i) in lieu of a null prep, relative clauses can contain an overt resumptive PP, consisting of a pronoun with a preposition cliticized to it, as shown in (19a) (from a dialect of Greek) – resumptives in general are characteristic of lack of movement (Sells 1984); (ii) relative clauses are introduced by complementizers rather than relative pronouns, as shown in (19b, c), from Brazilian Portuguese – relative pronouns are characteristic of movement.

(19) a. to rafio pou douleve (s'afto) ine mikro.
the office that he-works (in-it) it-is small
'The office that he works (in) is small.'
b. a mô que eu falei
the girl that I spoke
'The girl that I spoke (to)'
c. *a mô quem eu falei
the girl who I spoke
'The girl who I spoke (to)'

Klein analyses null-prep relatives as containing a null resumptive PP, which alternates with an overt resumptive PP.[14] Null prep is not permitted in *wh*-questions or relative clauses derived by movement (as in English), on the other hand, because this would constitute an ECP violation: the null preposition would be unable to properly govern the empty category resulting from *wh*-movement.

Given such restrictions, if null prep were to be found in interlanguage grammars either in relative clauses derived by movement or in *wh*-questions, this would constitute evidence of a wild grammar, violating the ECP. Previous research has reported sporadic use of null prep in L2 (Bardovi-Harlig 1987; Mazurkewich 1984a). Klein devised a series of experiments to investigate whether null prep is in fact a robust phenomenon in interlanguage grammars, and whether it occurs illicitly, i.e. in movement contexts.

Klein (1993b, 1995a) tested adult learners of English from a variety of language backgrounds and at different levels of proficiency. Learners were asked to judge the grammaticality of sentences lacking prepositions and to correct them if they

Box 2.7 Null prep (Klein 1995a)

Languages: L1s = various, L2 = English.
Task: Grammaticality judgments and corrections.
Sample stimuli (ungrammatical):
Declarative: The delivery boy applied a new job last week
Relative: This is the job which/that/Ø the delivery boy applied last week
Question: Which job did the delivery boy apply last week?
Results:

Table 2.7.1 *Acceptances of null prep in questions and relatives (in %)*

		Questions (# = 9)	Relatives (# = 9)
L2 groups	Beginners (n = 55)	69	78
	Intermediate (n = 66)	52	57
	Advanced (n = 75)	30	35
Native speakers (n = 40)		1	2

considered them to be wrong. (See box 2.7.) In other words, they were expected to insert the missing preposition. As Klein points out, it is crucial to establish learners' knowledge of the subcategorization properties of the verbs in question. For example, if a learner does not know that the verb *worry* requires a PP complement introduced by *about*, absence of the preposition does not constitute a case of the null prep phenomenon but simply indicates a lack of knowledge of the subcategorization requirements of this particular verb. For this reason, the first step in Klein's analysis of the results was to concentrate on those declaratives which learners identified as ungrammatical and corrected by the insertion of a preposition. Such corrections indicate that learners are aware that the verbs in question require a PP complement. Where the declarative was correctly identified as requiring a preposition, Klein then looked at whether learners know that the preposition is also obligatory in the corresponding questions and relatives. If questions and/or relatives with missing prepositions are accepted while the corresponding declaratives are rejected, this is taken to be evidence of illicit null prep.

Results show extensive acceptance of null prep forms in both *wh*-questions and relative clauses, even at the highest proficiency level (see table 2.7.1); all groups are significantly different from each other and from the controls. There is a decline in acceptance of null prep with increasing level of proficiency. Klein's other studies (Klein 1993a, 1995b) suggest that null prep is systematic, occurring across different age groups and L1s (including L1s with and without null prep), in both relatives and *wh*-questions.

While null prep is permissible in relative clauses in certain languages, Klein argues that it is always illicit in *wh*-questions. Since the learners she studied accepted null prep in *wh*-questions, and since her methodology rules out the possibility that this is just a general subcategorization error, the results appear to suggest a wild interlanguage grammar, violating the ECP, even in the case of those of advanced proficiency. In addition, if relative clauses are derived by movement, their grammars are wild in this respect as well, since null prep is not permitted in such cases (compare (18b and c)). However, Dekydtspotter, Sprouse and Andersen (1998) have challenged Klein's assumption that null prep is prohibited in the case of structures involving *wh*-movement. They show that null prep is found in *wh*-questions in Yoruba, as well as in popular French. Dekydtspotter et al. propose an alternative account of the null prep phenomenon in terms of preposition incorporation, arguing that it obeys general constraints on incorporation, hence suggesting that a null prep interlanguage grammar is not wild after all. (See Klein (2001) for counter-arguments.)

2.4 Methodological issues

The experiments described in this chapter have used a variety of different methodologies to try to determine the nature of the interlanguage grammar. Tasks have included elicited production (translation), grammaticality and acceptability judgments, coreference judgments, and truth-value judgments. The judgment tasks fall into two distinct types, some concentrating on the form of sentences (for example, Kanno's (1996) study of case drop – see section 2.1.3) and some concentrating on interpretation (for instance, the studies by Christie and Lantolf (1998) and Thomas (1995) on reflexives – section 2.3.1). In the case of judgments designed to probe learners' interpretations of particular sentence types, we have seen that it is crucial to provide some kind of context for the interpretation in question. Even within the judgments directed at interpretation, some tasks are more metalinguistic than others. For example, Kanno (1997, 1998b) requires subjects to choose explicitly between potential antecedents for pronouns; Dekydtspotter et al. (1997) ask learners whether a sentence 'sounds possible' in a given context. In contrast, truth-value-judgment tasks merely require the learner to indicate whether or not a particular sentence is true in a particular context. (However, see White, Bruhn-Garavito, Kawasaki, Pater and Prévost (1997) for discussion of problems associated with such tasks: even with this methodology, the effects of preferences for certain interpretations over others cannot be fully eliminated.)

Another welcome trend is the move towards analysing data in terms of the performance of individual subjects. Although group results can be quite informative, they can also be misleading, concealing properties of individual grammars. For example, if a given group of L2 learners shows a 50% acceptance rate for some structure, this could be due to half the subjects accepting all sentences and half rejecting all, or it could be the result of all subjects accepting half of the sentences. Since the claim that the interlanguage grammar is (or is not) UG-constrained is a claim about individual linguistic competence, it is crucial to determine what is going on at the individual level.

A further methodological advance concerns the use of control groups. It has been fairly standard for many years to include native speakers of the L2 as controls. Research described in this chapter has also included a more recent development, namely the use of native speakers of the L1 (e.g. Dekydtspotter et al. 1997 – see section 2.1.2; Kanno 1998b – see section 2.1.1). This allows the experimenter to determine whether or not interlanguage performance could be accounted for in terms of properties of the L1 grammar.

However, the use of native-speaker control groups, whether they are speakers of the L1 or L2, raises the issue of the so-called *comparative fallacy* (Bley-Vroman 1983). Bley-Vroman remarked that 'the learner's system is worthy of study in its own right, not just as a degenerate form of the target system' (1983: 4). A number of researchers have emphasized the need to consider interlanguage grammars in their own right with respect to principles and parameters of UG (e.g. du Plessis, Solin, Travis and White 1987; Finer and Broselow 1986; Martohardjono and Gair 1993; Schwartz and Sprouse 1994; White 1992c; Lakshmanan and Selinker 2001). As Birdsong points out with respect to grammaticality-judgment data: 'the relevant data are learners' judgments – not their similarity to or deviance from natives' judgments' (1989: 119). This focus on the interlanguage grammar remains the current perspective: much of the research described in this chapter (as well as later in the book) is committed to this position. That is, the crucial question is whether or not interlanguage grammars are UG-constrained, rather than whether or not they are native-like.

Nevertheless, avoiding the comparative fallacy does not require the experimenter to exclude native-speaker controls altogether. First of all, control groups are necessary simply to ensure: (i) that the tasks devised by the experimenter in fact are successful in testing what they are supposed to test; and (ii) that the facts in question are indeed as the experimenter supposes them to be (or as claimed in the theoretical linguistics literature). For example, in Christie and Lantolf's study (section 2.3.1), the performance of the native speakers was unexpected, given the researchers' assumptions about what properties of reflexives should cluster. Secondly, there are legitimate reasons for asking whether the learner in fact shows unconscious knowledge of principles and parameters relevant to the L2. What is problematic is when certain conclusions are drawn on the basis of failure to perform like native speakers. Failure to acquire L2 properties may nevertheless involve acquiring properties different from the L1, properties of other natural languages, properties that are underdetermined by the L2 input. Such failure does not necessarily imply lack of UG, as we have seen.

A related problem is how to interpret significant differences between native speaker and L2 learner performance on some task. Consider, for example, the results of the study by Dekydtspotter et al. (1997) on process and result nominals (section 2.1.2.). Their beginner and intermediate subjects showed a significantly higher acceptance rate of multiple *de*-phrases with process nominals (ungrammatical in French). Thus, it might be claimed that their grammars are not constrained by the relevant principles governing argument structure. It has been suggested in this chapter that a more appropriate comparison is to look at whether certain sentence types are treated significantly differently from other sentence types by the same group of learners (c.f. Grimshaw and Rosen 1990). If such distinctions are found, this suggests that the interlanguage grammar represents the relevant distinction (whatever it may be), even if the degree to which they observe it differs from native speakers. This was in fact the case in Dekydtspotter et al.'s study: all groups distinguished between process and result nominals in terms of acceptability of multiple *de*-phrases.

2.5 Conclusion

In conclusion, this chapter has considered evidence that interlanguage grammars are constrained by principles of UG. While earlier research on UG and L2 acquisition concentrated largely (though certainly not exclusively) on L2 English, many other L2s are now being investigated, including, in the experiments described here, L2 Spanish, Japanese, French and Chinese. Results from several experiments suggest that learners of a variety of L2s demonstrate unconscious knowledge of subtle distinctions that are unlikely to have come from the L2 input (including instruction) or from the L1, consistent with the claim that principles of UG constrain interlanguage grammars. The claim that interlanguage grammars are sometimes wild (hence, not falling within the bounds laid down by UG) has also been considered. We have seen that analyses adopted by L2 learners may in fact be true of natural language, even if they happen not to be appropriate for the L1 or L2 of the learners in question. Of course, the reason why L2 learners should arrive at such alternative analyses still requires explanation.

In the next chapter, a different issue is discussed, namely the nature of the initial state in L2 acquisition. We will consider the extent to which the L1 grammar determines properties of the early interlanguage grammar, and whether or not UG constitutes the initial state, as in L1 acquisition (see chapter 1).

Topics for discussion

- Is it ever possible to eliminate the L1 as a source of knowledge of principles of UG or is this a non-issue? According to Dekydtspotter et al. (1997), if one adopts the Minimalist Program whereby computational principles are universally the same and invariant, it no longer makes sense to distinguish between direct access to UG or indirect access via the L1.
- According to Schwartz and Sprouse (2000a, b), too much current L2 research uses linguistic theory to provide relatively sophisticated and detailed analyses of interlanguage data, without considering the logical problem of L2 acquisition. They suggest that such research does not help us to understand the nature of L2 acquisition or interlanguage competence. In contrast, Hawkins (2001b) argues that many researchers are overly preoccupied with the logical problem of L2 acquisition. Instead, he suggests, a better way to reach an understanding of L2 acquisition is to focus on differences between native speaker and L2 learner grammars (described in terms of current linguistic constructs). Are these positions incompatible?
- In this chapter we have seen several examples where problematic interlanguage data are reanalysed in terms of some other theory. To what extent does this render the claim that UG constrains interlanguage grammars unfalsifiable?
- Linguistic theory is constantly changing and undergoing development; proposals as to the precise nature of UG have changed considerably over the years. What are the implications for L2 acquisition research, and particularly for theories that assume a role for UG? (See Schwartz and Sprouse (2000b) and White (1995a) for discussion.)
- Davies and Kaplan (1998) and Lantolf (1990) advocate group grammaticality judgments, where learners (in pairs or groups) discuss test items together, in order to arrive at decisions about their grammaticality. Why is this approach problematic?

Suggestions for additional reading

- For more detailed discussion of the logical problem of L2 acquisition, see Bley-Vroman (1990), White (1989: chapter 2) and Schwartz and Sprouse (2000a, b).

3 The initial state

3.1 What is the initial state?

In chapter 2, it was argued that there is a logical problem of L2 acquisition. Experimental evidence was reviewed which suggests that interlanguage grammars allow the representation of subtle and abstract distinctions whose source could not be the L1 grammar or the L2 input, hence must be UG. In other words, interlanguage representations are constrained by UG, conforming to principles such as the Overt Pronoun Constraint and the ECP. While some researchers have proposed that interlanguage grammars are 'wild', hence not fully UG-constrained, there are alternative analyses of the phenomena in question which can accommodate the potentially problematic data.

In this chapter, we turn to a different (though related) issue, namely the nature of the initial state in L2 acquisition. The term *initial state* is variously used to mean the kind of unconscious linguistic knowledge that the L2 learner starts out with in advance of the L2 input and/or to refer to characteristics of the earliest grammar. As Schwartz and Eubank (1996) point out, the interlanguage initial state was a neglected topic until the mid 1990s. In earlier work on UG in L2 acquisition, assumptions about the initial state were usually implicit. Even where they were explicit, the initial state was not the main focus of research. For example, White (1985b) proposed that L2 learners start out with L1 parameter settings. Although not presented as such at the time, this is clearly an initial state claim, since it presupposes that at least part of the L1 grammar (namely, L1 parameter settings) determines how the learner initially approaches the L2 data. Rather than focusing on the initial state, early research explored the question of whether different stages of interlanguage development could be characterized as exemplifying different parameter settings and whether the L2 learner could achieve settings which differ from the L1 settings. In other words, research addressed the question of whether parameters can be reset and under what conditions; initial grammars as such were rarely considered. More recently, a number of explicit hypotheses have been advanced as to the nature of the initial state in L2 acquisition, which also

Figure 3.1 *L2 acquisition without UG*

make claims about the kind of development (or lack thereof) that can be expected subsequently.

In L1 acquisition, UG is the initial state (Chomsky 1981b), determining, in advance, the form and the functioning of language-particular grammars (see chapter 1, section 1.2). While UG is the initial state (or S_0), it is not entirely clear what happens subsequently, that is, whether UG somehow 'turns into' a particular steady-state grammar (S_S) in the course of language acquisition or whether it remains distinct from specific instantiations. Possibly because this matter is of little consequence for researchers interested in L1 acquisition or in native speaker competence, the issue has been relatively little discussed; where it is discussed, the former assumption is often adopted. As DeGraff (1999: 15) puts it: 'L1A is the process by which exposure to PLD transforms the innately specified experience-independent *faculté de langage* into a language-particular grammar by assigning fixed values to parameter arrays specified by UG.'

In the context of L2 acquisition, the question of whether UG becomes a particular grammar or remains distinct from particular grammars is central. If UG is transformed into a grammar which may subsequently be modified during the course of acquisition (S_0.... S_1.... S_S) then only the particular steady-state instantiation of UG would remain available in non-primary language acquisition. Perhaps the first person to raise this issue in the L2 context was Bley-Vroman (1990: 18–19), who suggested the following computer analogy:

> It is as if an application program came with an installation-configuration program, with which you set parameters to customize the application to your computer and your tastes. You use this installation program just once, it sets up the application to operate properly, often stripping it down, removing options your machine cannot implement. You never use the installation program again. The application program is now a particular program for your machine.

In other words, UG survives only as the language-specific mother-tongue grammar. Bley-Vroman's Fundamental Difference Hypothesis rests on the assumption that UG as a distinct 'entity' does not survive L1 acquisition.[1] On this view, the initial state of L2 acquisition is, necessarily, the L1 grammar (L1 S_S), as schematized in figure 3.1. Subsequently, there may be development away from the L1 grammar, until a steady state interlanguage grammar is attained (IL S_S).

Arguing against the position that UG becomes a language-specific grammar and in favour of the position that UG remains constant and distinct from any particular grammar, Flynn and Martohardjono (1994) and Epstein et al. (1996) point out that bilingual first language acquisition would be hard to account for on the former view, given that the two languages that a bilingual child is acquiring will often require contradictory parameter settings. Since bilingual children are known to acquire two distinct grammars (Meisel 1989; Müller and Hulk 2000; Paradis and Genesee 1996), this suggests that UG must be distinct from both grammars and that it constrains both grammars. (See Schwartz (1987) and Cook (1991) for related observations.)

All the initial-state proposals to be considered in this chapter presuppose the following: UG is constant (that is, unchanged as a result of L1 acquisition); UG is distinct from the learner's L1 grammar; UG constrains the L2 learner's interlanguage grammars. In spite of this common ground, there is considerable disagreement over the nature of the interlanguage initial state.

Two logical possibilities will be considered here: the grammar of the mother tongue (the L1) is the initial state or UG is the initial state. (It is of course conceivable that neither UG nor the L1 constitutes the interlanguage initial state, an alternative which will not be discussed.) It may be useful to think of the issue by asking what unconscious preconceptions the learner has about the nature of the L2. In advance of input, does the learner start out with a language-specific grammar, namely, the L1 grammar? Alternatively, does the learner start with no preconceptions other than the 'blueprint' provided by UG?

We first consider proposals that the initial state is indeed a specific grammar. In particular, the L2 learner is assumed to start out with grammatical representations derived from the L1 grammar, in whole or in part. Falling into this category are the Full Transfer Full Access Hypothesis of Schwartz and Sprouse (1994, 1996), the Minimal Trees Hypothesis of Vainikka and Young-Scholten (1994, 1996a, b) and the Valueless Features Hypothesis of Eubank (1993/1994, 1994, 1996). These proposals contrast with others where the interlanguage initial state is argued not to be a particular grammar but rather UG itself, similar to the situation in L1 acquisition. Falling into this latter category are the Initial Hypothesis of Syntax (Platzack 1996), where this claim is explicit, and the Full Access Hypothesis of Epstein et al. (1996, 1998), where it is implicit. It is important to understand that all the hypotheses to be considered here presuppose that UG constrains interlanguage grammars, although some accounts imply an impairment to certain UG-related domains, as we shall see. In other words, the fact that the L2 learner may start off by adopting a particular grammatical representation (based on the L1) does not preclude UG-constrained changes in response to properties of the L2 input.

3.2 A grammar as the initial state

3.2.1 *The Full Transfer Full Access Hypothesis*

We begin with an examination of the Full Transfer Full Access Hypothesis of Schwartz and Sprouse (1994, 1996), according to which the initial state in L2 acquisition is a particular grammar. Faced with accounting for L2 input, learners adopt the grammar that they already have, the steady-state grammar of the mother tongue. In contrast to other researchers who argue for less than total involvement of the L1 (see sections 3.2.2 and 3.2.3), Schwartz and Sprouse propose *full transfer*: the entire L1 grammar (in the sense of all abstract properties but excluding specific lexical items) constitutes the initial state. Furthermore, it is hypothesized that changes to the initial grammar can take place; in other words, the learner is not 'stuck' with representations based on the L1 steady state. When the L1 grammar is unable to accommodate properties of the L2 input, the learner has recourse to UG options not instantiated in the L1, including new parameter settings, functional categories and feature values, in order to arrive at an analysis more appropriate to the L2 input, although this may turn out not to be the same analysis as that found in the native-speaker grammar. The resulting interlanguage grammars are UG-constrained, hence, the term *full access*. Full transfer, then, is Schwartz and Sprouse's claim about the initial state; full access is their claim about subsequent grammar restructuring during the course of development. Full Transfer Full Access is schematized in figure 3.2 (adapted from White (2000)).

3.2.1.1 Full Transfer Full Access: evidence

Two kinds of evidence serve to support the claims of Full Transfer Full Access: (i) evidence of L1 properties in the interlanguage grammar; (ii) evidence of restructuring away from the L1 grammar. A case study by Haznedar (1997) supports Full Transfer Full Access, providing evidence of an L1-based initial state, as well as subsequent changes to the interlanguage grammar. Haznedar examines spontaneous production data gathered from a Turkish-speaking child, named

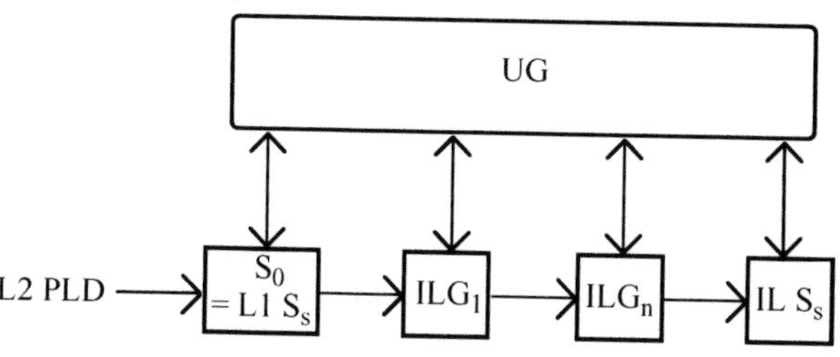

Figure 3.2 *Full Transfer Full Access*

Erdem, who was learning English. Erdem was initially interviewed at the age of 4, after three months in England. For the first two months he had been almost entirely in a Turkish-speaking environment at home; thereafter, he spent a month in an English nursery school. Thus, the data that Haznedar reports are relevant to the initial state.

Turkish and English differ as to word order, particularly headedness of both lexical (in this case, VP) and functional (NegP) projections: Turkish is verb final while English is verb initial and Turkish is Neg final while English is Neg initial. Haznedar reports that, for the first three months of recording, Erdem consistently (almost 100%) produced head-final word order, suggesting transfer of Turkish headedness. For example, he would produce utterances like (1a) (head-final VP) and (1b) (head-final NegP). In the fourth month, Erdem switched headedness of both VP and NegP to their English values, now consistently producing head-initial utterances like (1c) and (1d).

(1) a. I something eating.
b. Finish no.
c. You eating apple.
d. I not eat cornflake.

Although the data are somewhat limited, due to the fact that there were relatively few relevant utterances in the first three months of recording, they are nevertheless highly suggestive, supporting both components of Full Transfer Full Access: Erdem's initial grammar clearly exhibits Turkish word order but he also successfully switches to English order.

Haznedar's (1997) study is a case study, involving spontaneous production data.[2] Case studies have the advantage of following an individual or individuals over time, so that changes in the interlanguage grammar can be observed. However, there are disadvantages to relying on case studies and there are disadvantages to relying on production data alone. Firstly, one cannot be sure that case studies are representative of anything more than the behaviour of the individuals in question. Secondly, it is not clear to what extent spontaneous production data accurately reflect properties of the underlying grammar. In particular, if certain forms are absent in spontaneous production, this does not necessarily reflect absence of some corresponding abstract grammatical category, a point that will be considered in more detail in section 3.2.2.2, as well as in chapter 6. However, in these data from Erdem, this problem does not arise since he did initially produce word orders clearly based on his L1 rather than on the L2; in other words, nothing is being inferred about the grammar based on absence of some phenomenon.

Experimental data provide another way of exploring the claims of the Full Transfer Full Access Hypothesis. One possibility is to conduct experiments with learners of a particular L1, looking for evidence of properties of that L1 in the interlanguage grammar. But more compelling evidence can be provided by considering learners of different L1s acquiring the same L2 (Schwartz and Sprouse 1996, 2000b). Such learners are predicted to behave differently, reflecting different initial states. Indeed, some of the earliest experimental research on L2 parameter setting is relevant in this context. White (1985b, 1986), for example, showed that French-speaking and Spanish-speaking learners of English behaved differently with respect to null subjects in English. In grammaticality-judgment tasks, Spanish speakers were significantly more likely to accept null subjects in English than French speakers were. This differential behaviour based on properties of the L1 (Spanish but not French being a null subject language) supports Full Transfer Full Access. That is, the difference in behaviour with respect to null subjects reflects different L2 initial states (and, as yet, no subsequent restructuring).

More recent examples of experimental research supporting Full Transfer Full Access are provided by Yuan (1998) and Slabakova (2000). In both these studies, learners of different L1s show distinctly different behaviour with respect to the linguistic properties under investigation, suggesting different representations, by inference due to different initial states.

Yuan (1998) investigated acquisition of the long-distance reflexive *ziji* in L2 Chinese, considering both domain (long-distance versus local antecedents) and orientation (subject versus object antecedents) (see chapter 2, section 2.3.1). Here we focus on domain only. (See box 3.1.)

Box 3.1 Full Transfer Full Access – Reflexives (Yuan 1998)

Languages: L1s = English/Japanese, L2 = Chinese.
Task: Coreference judgments. Following each test item, subjects select from a list of potential antecedents for the reflexive *ziji*.
Sample stimulus (favouring long-distance binding):

Wang Ming bu gaoxing de shuo Li Dong jingchang bu xiangxin ziji.
(*Wang Ming said unhappily that Li Dong often does not trust self*.)

Results:

Table 3.1.1 *Acceptances of long-distance antecedents from embedded finite clauses (in %)*

L2 groups	L1 Japanese (n = 24)	92
	L1 English – intermediate (n = 32)	53
	L1 English – advanced (n = 25)	71
Native speakers (n = 24)		94

Yuan found that English-speaking and Japanese-speaking learners of Chinese at the same level of proficiency (intermediate, as determined by a proficiency test) behaved quite differently with respect to their treatment of *ziji*. Japanese, like Chinese, has a long-distance reflexive, whereas English does not. The Japanese speakers recognized the long-distance nature of *ziji* and their performance did not differ significantly from that of the native speakers of Chinese. The English speakers, on the other hand, were much less likely to accept long-distance antecedents for the reflexive (especially in finite contexts), even when a long-distance interpretation was pragmatically favoured; their judgments differed significantly from those of the Japanese-speaking group and from the native speakers of Chinese. These results, then, suggest that the two intermediate-level L2 groups are treating long-distance reflexives very differently, reflecting properties of these anaphors in their respective L1s, thus supporting Full Transfer. The advanced English-speaking group showed evidence of acquiring the long-distance properties of *ziji*, suggesting that L2 learners are not confined to L1 properties, in support of Full Access.

One might question why results from learners of intermediate proficiency should be relevant to the initial state. While Full Transfer Full Access predicts evidence of L1-based properties in early interlanguage, it crucially does not make any predictions about how long L1 influence should last. It is not the case that restructuring of the initial-state grammar necessarily takes place early on, nor is it the case that the whole grammar must be changed at once. In the case of the initially adopted Turkish word order (discussed in section 3.2.1.1), very basic properties of the English input reveal that head final is an inappropriate analysis. This, presumably, is why the L1-based initial state lasted only a short while. There was an early reanalysis (within the first three months) to the head-initial categories appropriate for the L2. But in other situations, the L2 input to motivate change may be more obscure or even lacking altogether. In the case of reflexives, Yuan's study suggests that intermediate-level learners with English as a mother tongue still have problems in recognizing the long-distance nature of Chinese *ziji*. The situation regarding reflexives is quite different from the situation regarding word order. Since Chinese also has a local reflexive (*taziji*) and since the long-distance reflexive *ziji* can take both local or long-distance antecedents, the L2 input is more ambiguous and it may be insufficient to lead the learner to postulate a long-distance reflexive for the L2. In other words, an L2 learner who always *produces* reflexives restricted to local antecedents will not be wrong; any confusion, then, is likely to arise in *interpreting* long-distance reflexives used by other people. Even if misinterpretation results, the alternative local interpretation will not be ungrammatical though it may be inappropriate at times.

Another experiment whose results support Full Transfer Full Access was conducted by Slabakova (2000). Slabakova investigates a crosslinguistic aspectual contrast in telicity. A clause is telic if the situation it describes includes a natural endpoint; it is atelic if there is no such endpoint. For example, in (2a), the activity is understood as having been completed, whereas (2b) does not necessarily imply completion.

(2) a. Angela made a cake.
b. Angela made cakes.

Telicity can be realized in different ways. In languages like English and Spanish, there is no special verbal morphology to indicate whether an event is telic or atelic.[3] Rather, in clauses involving transitive verbs, like those in (2), telicity depends on properties of the direct object: an event is telic if the object has specified cardinality, as in (2a), that is, if it can be exhaustively counted or measured, as is the case for DPs with determiners (*an apple, three apples, the apple(s)*); an event is atelic if the object is of unspecified cardinality, i.e. if it lacks a determiner (*apples, cake*), as in (2b). In Slavic languages such as Bulgarian, on the other hand, telicity is generally indicated by means of verbal morphology, telic events being marked with a preverb and atelic unmarked, while the cardinality of the object is irrelevant to the aspectual interpretation. Slabakova (2001) argues that the difference between Slavic languages and languages like English is a consequence of a parametric difference relating to a functional category, Aspect. (See also Smith (1991) and Snyder (1995a).)

Turning to L2 acquisition, Slabakova investigates the acquisition of English by native speakers of Bulgarian, a language whose setting of the aspectual parameter differs from English, and by native speakers of Spanish, a language with the same setting as English. If the L1 grammar forms the interlanguage initial state, differences are expected, with respect to aspectual interpretation, between these two groups of learners.

Determining aspectual interpretations is not a simple matter, since both telic and atelic sentences are grammatical. However, there are contexts where one or other interpretation is more natural. Slabakova took advantage of such contextual differences to devise an aspectual interpretation task. In the test sentences, the context (provided by the first clause) is held constant, as well as the form of the verb in the second clause. (See examples in box 3.2.) The only thing that varies is the cardinality of the direct object in the second clause; in other words, there are no other aspectual cues. To native speakers of English and Spanish, the presence or absence of a determiner in the object DP in these sentences is sufficient to determine the telicity of the second clause and hence the naturalness of the sentence as a whole. Given a first clause which sets up the expectation of a habitual, non-completed event, an atelic second clause sounds more natural than a telic one. In Bulgarian, however, presence or absence of the determiner has no effect on aspectual interpretation.

Box 3.2 Full Transfer Full Access – Aspect (Slabakova 2000)

Languages: L1s = Bulgarian/Spanish, L2 = English.
Task: Aspectual interpretation task. Test sentences contain two clauses. Subjects judge (on a scale from −3 to +3) how well the two clauses go together.
Sample stimuli:

1st clause habitual, 2nd clause telic
Antonia worked in a bakery and made a cake.
1st clause habitual, 2nd clause atelic
Antonia worked in a bakery and made cakes.

Results:

Table 3.2.1 *Aspectual interpretation: mean ratings (from −3 to +3)*

		Telic (# = 6)	Atelic (# = 6)
L2 groups	L1 Bulgarian (n = 22)	1.44	1.95
	L1 Spanish (n = 21)	0.55	2.04
Native speakers	American English (n = 16)	0.19	2.09
	British English (n = 16)	0.81	2.41

If Bulgarian-speaking learners of English initially represent telicity as it is represented in the L1, they should have particular difficulties, since English verbal morphology provides no indication of aspect. Slabakova found that native speakers of English and Spanish-speaking learners of English distinguished sharply between the two sentence types, finding the ones with an atelic second clause significantly more natural than those with a telic second clause. (Both possibilities are grammatical, so the issue is naturalness rather than grammaticality.) The Bulgarian speakers, on the other hand, showed a non-significant difference between the two sentence types. (See table 3.2.1.) Looking only at the telic sentences, there were highly significant differences between the groups, attributable solely to the performance of the Bulgarian speakers. There were no significant differences between the groups on the atelic sentences. Slabakova suggests that the Bulgarian speakers are relatively accurate on the atelic sentences because these, in Bulgarian, would not carry overt aspectual morphology. Hence, these sentences are interpreted as atelic and are considered natural in the L2 English; in consequence the Bulgarian speakers' judgments pattern with those of the Spanish speakers and the native speakers of English. In the case of the telic sentences, on the other hand, the Bulgarian speakers are misled by the lack of aspectual morphology in the L2 and treat these as sometimes telic, sometimes atelic, being unaware of the significance of the cardinality of the object.

3.2.1.2 Full Transfer Full Access: conceptual issues

So far we have considered evidence that suggests that the L1 grammar is implicated in the interlanguage initial state. It is important to remember that, according to the Full Transfer Full Access Hypothesis, the L1 grammar in its entirety is involved. The studies that we have considered have not, however, looked at the initial state as a whole; indeed, it is unrealistic to expect anyone to do so. Rather, particular properties have been investigated and, in the case of the ones we have considered so far, there is indeed evidence of L1 properties in the interlanguage grammar; furthermore, learners of different L1s behave differently with respect to the same L2, consistent with the assumption that the L1 is the initial state.

It is also necessary to consider what might constitute counter-evidence to the claim that there is full transfer in the initial state. That is, what would demonstrate that the L1 grammar in its entirety is *not* the initial state? One kind of potential counter-evidence can be dismissed immediately. If at some point L2 learners *fail* to show evidence of L1 effects, or if L2 learners of different L1s behave in the *same* way with respect to some particular phenomenon in the L2, this does not automatically disconfirm the hypothesis. Since Full Transfer Full Access crucially assumes that the interlanguage grammar will be restructured in response to properties of the L2 input interacting with UG, it is conceivable that the grammars of L2 learners of different L1s will at some point converge on the relevant properties of the L2 (or that they will converge on some non-L1, non-L2 properties).

Such a possibility raises the general issue of falsifiability: in the absence of L1 effects, proponents of Full Transfer Full Access can maintain that learners are already beyond the full transfer stage. How, then, could one ever show that this hypothesis might be wrong? In fact, there are situations which are predicted by Full Transfer Full Access not to occur, thus rendering the hypothesis falsifiable. If learners of different L1s learning the same L2 can be shown to have the same initial state and the same early stages of development, despite differences in how the two L1s treat the linguistic phenomenon being investigated, this would constitute counter-evidence. Experimental evidence of precisely this kind is provided by Yuan (2001), who shows that French-speaking and English-speaking learners of Chinese treat verb placement in exactly the same way from the earliest stage of L2 acquisition, even though French and English differ in the relevant respects. We will postpone discussion of this evidence until section 3.2.3.1.

3.2.1.3 Full Transfer Full Access: summary

To summarize, the Full Transfer Full Access Hypothesis makes claims about the initial state, about grammars during development and about the steady state:

a. The initial state in L2 acquisition is the L1 steady state grammar in its entirety. One needs to think of this as in some sense a copy (or clone) of the L1 grammar, a copy which can be modified without affecting the original. Although Full Transfer Full Access presupposes that the L2 learner restructures the interlanguage grammar, the mother tongue grammar does not (usually) get altered in response to L2 input (but see Sorace (2000) for cases where the L2 may indeed have effects on the L1 grammar.)

b. The L2 learner is not limited to L1-based representations. If the L1-based analysis fails for some reason, restructuring of the grammar will occur; in other words, L2 input will trigger grammar change. L2 development is UG-constrained, with interlanguage grammars falling within the range sanctioned by UG. (See chapter 4.)

c. Final outcome – convergence on a grammar identical to that of a native speaker is not guaranteed, because properties of the L1 grammar or subsequent interlanguage grammars may lead to analyses of the input that differ from those of native speakers. (See chapter 8.)

3.2.2 The Minimal Trees Hypothesis

In this section, we examine another perspective on the interlanguage initial state, namely the Minimal Trees Hypothesis of Vainikka and Young-Scholten (1994, 1996a, b), which also proposes that the initial state is a grammar, with early representations based on the L1. However, in contrast to Full Transfer Full Access, only part of the L1 grammar is seen as constituting the initial state. Under this approach, the initial grammar is claimed to lack functional categories altogether, hence, L1 functional categories will not be present, nor will functional categories from any other source (such as UG).

Vainikka and Young-Scholten claim that grammars in the earliest stage of development are different from later grammars, lacking certain properties which subsequently emerge. This claim is made in the context of the Weak Continuity Hypothesis for L1 acquisition (Clahsen, Eisenbeiss and Penke 1996; Clahsen, Eisenbeiss and Vainikka 1994; Clahsen, Penke and Parodi 1993/1994; Vainikka 1993/1994). According to this hypothesis, while functional categories are available in the UG inventory, initial grammars lack the full complement of functional categories, containing lexical categories and their projections (NP, VP, PP, AP), and possibly one underspecified functional projection, FP (Clahsen 1990/1991). Det, Infl and Comp and associated projections (IP, CP and DP) emerge gradually, triggered by input.

It is this conception of early grammars that Vainikka and Young-Scholten develop in the context of L2 acquisition. According to their proposal, the initial state in L2 acquisition consists of a grammar partly based on the L1: the lexical categories of the mother tongue are found in the initial interlanguage grammar, together with associated L1 properties, in particular, headedness. Functional categories, however, are lacking. Although functional categories are not realized in the initial grammar, the full UG inventory of functional categories remains available. L2 learners gradually add functional categories to the interlanguage grammar, on the basis of L2 input, and are eventually able to project the associated projections (IP, CP, DP, etc.). The claim is that functional categories are added 'bottom up', in discrete stages, so that there is an IP stage before CP. In other words, presence of CP in the grammar implicates IP: one can have IP without CP but not CP without IP. Thus, although the emergence of functional categories is claimed to be triggered by input, there must presumably be some kind of built-in sequence that dictates this order. After all, there seems to be no reason in principle why a learner should not 'notice' properties in the L2 input which would motivate a CP before properties which would motivate IP.

On the Minimal Trees account, the initial states of learners of different L1s will differ, depending on the headedness characteristics of lexical categories in the L1s in question. Vainikka and Young-Scholten (1996a) claim that headedness of lexical categories will be reset to the value appropriate for the L2 before the appearance of any functional categories. Emergence of functional categories, on the other hand, in no way depends on properties of the L1 grammar; in other words, there is predicted to be no transfer in this domain, no stage or grammar in which properties of the mother-tongue functional categories are found, an assumption which differs from Full Transfer Full Access. Rather, the L2 learner acquires L2 functional categories, with L2 properties. Thus, L1 and L2 acquisition of any particular language are generally assumed to be identical with respect to functional categories and projections. (Vainikka and Young-Scholten (1998) do propose one difference, relating to what properties of the input trigger the emergence of functional categories, namely bound morphology in L1 acquisition versus free morphemes in L2.)

3.2.2.1 Minimal Trees: evidence

In a series of papers, Vainikka and Young-Scholten (1994, 1996a, b, 1998) examine spontaneous and elicited production data from adult learners of German, immigrants to Germany who had had no formal instruction in the L2. A variety of L1s are represented in their studies, including Turkish and Korean, which, like German, have head-final VPs, as well as Spanish and Italian, which are head initial. Some of the data are longitudinal (following the same learners over time), some cross-sectional (drawn from different learners who are hypothesized, post hoc, to be at different stages of development).

As described above, the early interlanguage grammar, according to Vainikka and Young-Scholten, has: (a) lexical categories with headedness characteristics from the L1; (b) no functional categories. In other words, in the initial state of a Korean-speaking or Turkish-speaking learner of German, sentences would be represented as in (3a), whereas in the case of a Spanish speaker or Italian speaker the representation would look like (3b). Sentences are represented as VPs, because there are as yet no higher functional projections like IP or CP; VPs accord with the headedness of the VP in the L1.

(3) Stage 1 – the lexical stage

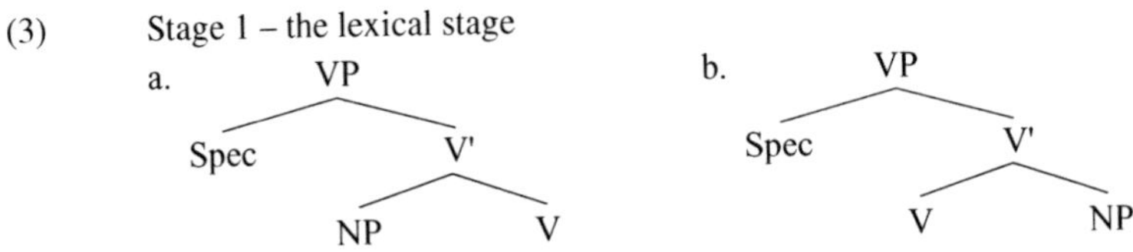

Evidence for L1-based headedness of VPs in the early grammar is quite robust. Vainikka and Young-Scholten (1994) found that over 95% of VPs were head final in the case of the three least advanced Turkish and Korean speakers. (Unfortunately, no independent measure of proficiency is provided. Stages of development are determined in terms of performance on the syntactic and morphological properties being investigated, which is somewhat circular.) These L2 learners produced utterances like those in (4) (from Vainikka and Young-Scholten 1994). Such sentences are ungrammatical in German, where main clauses require a finite verb in second position.

(4) a. Oya Zigarette trinken.
Oya cigarette drink-INF
'Oya smokes cigarettes.'
a. Eine Katze Fisch alle essen.
a cat fish all eat-INF
'A cat ate the entire fish.'

Data from speakers of head-initial languages show something quite different. Four Romance speakers at a similar stage of development show predominantly head-initial VPs. Typical productions are shown in (5) (from Vainikka and Young-Scholten (1996a)):

(5) a. Trinke de orange oder?
drink the orange or?
'(She's) drinking the orange (juice), right?
a. De esse de fis.
she eat the fish
'She's eating the fish'

Although the VP in German is head final, finite verbs must move to second position in main clauses; this is known as verb second (V2) (see chapter 1, section 1.4.1). The data from the Turkish and Korean speakers considered alone might be taken simply as evidence of acquisition of the verb-final nature of the L2, rather than as evidence of L1 headedness. The data from the Romance speakers considered alone might be taken as evidence of acquisition of V2 in the L2, rather than as evidence of L1 headedness. But taken together, the data are highly suggestive: the least advanced learners of different L1s adopt different word orders in the early interlanguage grammar, consistent with the claim that the initial state includes L1 lexical categories and their headedness.

But the crucial question is whether the early grammar is restricted to lexical categories, which is, after all, the central proposal of the Minimal Trees Hypothesis. Let us consider what kind of evidence is advanced to support the claim that functional categories are initially lacking. Vainikka and Young-Scholten assume that spontaneous production data provide a relatively direct and reliable window onto the underlying grammar: if some form is absent in production, the underlying category associated with it is absent from the grammar. In the situation considered here, absence of particular lexical items (function words and inflectional morphology) is taken to imply absence of corresponding functional categories. Thus, Vainikka and Young-Scholten look at a number of morphological and lexical properties to determine whether or not functional categories are present in the interlanguage. At the morphological level, they look for presence or absence of an agreement paradigm, productive person and/or number morphology implicating at least IP. At the lexical level, they look for presence/absence of auxiliary and modal verbs, since these are assumed to be generated in Infl.

Vainikka and Young-Scholten argue that the language of the least advanced Turkish/Korean speakers and the least advanced Romance speakers has the following characteristics: (a) incidence of correct subject – verb agreement is low; instead, where a finite verb with agreement should be found, infinitives or bare stems or default suffixes predominate; and (b) modals and auxiliaries are almost non-existent. Another kind of evidence that Vainikka and Young-Scholten adduce is syntactic: according to them there is no evidence that the verb raises out of the VP. These characteristics suggest the lack of IP. In addition, there are no *wh*-questions or subordinate clauses introduced by complementizers, suggesting lack of CP.

On this account, the lexical (VP) stage constitutes the initial state. The next stage, according to Vainikka and Young-Scholten, is characterized by the emergence of a functional category which does not exist in adult German (or in any other language). They call this projection FP (finite phrase), following Clahsen (1990/1991). At this stage, a German sentence will be represented as in (6), regardless of L1. In other words, where necessary, headedness of lexical categories has been restructured to accord with L2 headedness (Vainikka and Young-Scholten 1996b).

(6) FP stage

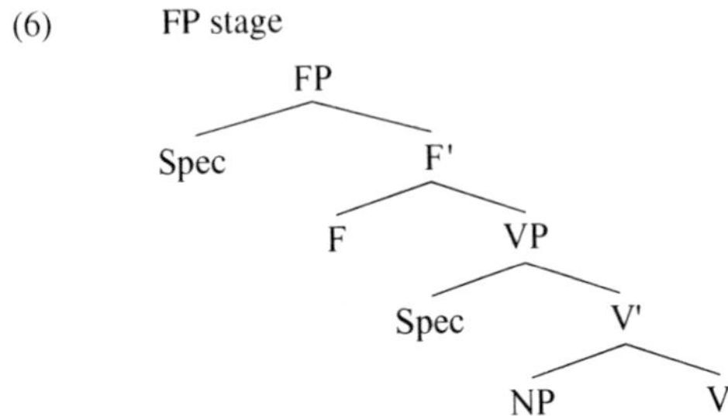

Their reason for postulating an FP as opposed to an IP is that some learners showed evidence of properties that are characteristic of the presence of IP; at the same time, these properties were not consistently present. This group of learners produced an increasing number of auxiliaries and modals; they also produced sentences where the main verb had raised out of the VP, as well as verb-final utterances, giving the impression that verb raising is optional. At the same time, subject–verb agreement was still largely absent, nor were there any complementizers. Examples of utterances at this stage (from a speaker of Turkish) are given in (7) (from Vainikka and Young-Scholten 1994). In (7a), the verb appears to the left of the object, suggesting that it has moved out of the VP. At the same time, it is not inflected. In (7b), the uninflected verb is still within the VP, in final position.

(7) a. Ich sehen Schleier.
I see-INF veil
'I see the veil'
b. Immer jeden Tag fünfhundert Stück machen.
always every day 500 unit make-INF
'(I) always make 500 units every day'

Verb raising implicates a functional projection higher than the VP for the verb to move to; lack of overt agreement morphology suggests to Vainikka and Young-Scholten that this projection is somehow different from IP. They resolve the conflict occasioned by presence of verb raising but lack of accurate inflectional morphology by proposing a category F, to which the verb moves. F is underspecified (lacking agreement features); FP is head initial.

In the next stage (represented by yet another group of L2 learners), raising of finite verbs becomes obligatory and the correct agreement paradigm is present, as shown in the examples in (8), suggesting that agreement features are now available. Vainikka and Young-Scholten propose that IP has been added (replacing FP) and that it is head initial (see (9)). According to them, CP is not yet motivated because embedded clauses introduced by complementizers are still lacking (see (8)).

(8) a. Er hat gesagt, nimmst du Lokomotive?
he has-3SG said take-2SG you train
'He said, will you take the train?'

b. Ich kaufe dich Eis.
I buy-1SG you ice-cream
'I will buy you some ice-cream'

(9) IP stage

```
IP
├── Spec
└── I'
    ├── I
    └── VP
        ├── Spec
        └── V'
            ├── NP
            └── V
```

The final stage would involve the acquisition of CP. However, Vainikka and Young-Scholten report that none of their subjects show evidence of reaching this stage.

There are data from a number of different studies which are inconsistent with the Minimal Trees Hypothesis. According to Minimal Trees, there are no functional categories in the initial state. To argue against this view, it is sufficient to show that at least some functional categories are in fact present from the beginning. As Haznedar (1997) points out, the data from Erdem's early productions (see section 3.2.1.1) are clearly inconsistent with the Minimal Trees Hypothesis: at least one functional category (NegP) is present initially. Indeed, Vainikka and Young-Scholten themselves provide evidence of a functional category in the early stage data: the examples in (4) and (5) include definite and indefinite articles, suggesting that the functional category Det must be present. Other evidence against Minimal Trees is provided by Grondin and White (1996) who show that two English-speaking children learning French have determiners firmly in place from the earliest recordings. In addition, they report a number of reflexes of IP; for example, finite verbs appear to the left of negative *pas*, suggesting that they have raised out of the VP. Lakshmanan (1993/1994) shows that a 4-year-old Spanish-speaking child learning English has IP early on, as evidenced by extensive use of the copula *be* in spontaneous production.

As for CP, Lakshmanan and Selinker (1994) report that the same Spanish-speaking child, as well as a French-speaking child of the same age, produced tensed embedded clauses early on (in the third interviews), with null complementizers (which are, of course, permitted and preferred in English), while infinitival complements are found from the second interview. Examples are given in (10).

(10) a. I think it's for me.
b. I don't want to play with you.

Gavruseva and Lardiere (1996) find evidence for CP in the first transcripts of spontaneous production data from Dasha, an 8-year-old Russian-speaking child learning English, two months after her initial exposure to the L2. Dasha produces subject auxiliary inversion in yes/no and *wh*-questions, as shown in (11a) and (11b), consistent with movement of auxiliaries to C, with the *wh*-phrase in (11b) in Spec CP; embedded clauses are found from the third recording session onwards (after less than three months of exposure to the L2), as shown in (11c).

(11) a. Can I see please?
b. What are we going to do?
c. Mama know that we go outside.

Furthermore, as Gavruseva and Lardiere point out, while there is robust evidence for CP in the early interlanguage grammar, IP must be considered to be absent if Vainikka and Young-Scholten's criterion for determining presence of a category is adopted. As will be discussed in section 3.2.2.2, Vainikka and Young-Scholten define a category as being present in the grammar only if lexical items/inflectional morphology associated with it occur in 60% or more of obligatory contexts. Gavruseva and Lardiere found that incidence of CP-related phenomena, such as subject – auxiliary inversion in questions, was 100%. At the same time, suppliance of subject – verb agreement in obligatory contexts was less than 40%, while production of modals and auxiliaries generally fell below 52%. As the example in (11c) shows, although CP is implicated because of the presence of the complementizer *that*, verbal inflection is lacking (*know* rather than *knows*). Since the Minimal Trees Hypothesis claims that IP emerges before CP and that IP is not present until its reflexes are found in 60% of obligatory contexts, these findings are contradictory and cannot be accounted for. On the other hand, if it is recognized that a functional category can be present in the abstract, even though not consistently realized lexically, there is no such contradiction; we return to this point below (and in chapter 6).

Data that suggest the influence of the L1 grammar in the functional domain can also be used to argue against the Minimal Trees Hypothesis. Recall that Minimal Trees expects transfer of lexical categories only. When functional categories emerge, they will exhibit properties relevant to the L2 (triggered by L2 input), not properties derived from the L1. But, as Schwartz and Sprouse (1996) point out, there is evidence for L1 effects in the functional domain. For example, as described above, Erdem's NegP has the headedness of NegP in the L1 Turkish. Furthermore, in a series of studies conducted by White and colleagues (Trahey and White 1993; White 1990/1991, 1991a, 1992a), French-speaking children (aged 10–12) learning English allow lexical verbs to appear to the right of adverbs, as shown in

(12), suggesting that the verb has raised to I and that I has strong features, a characteristic of French but not English (see chapter 1, section 1.4.1). (These studies will be discussed in more detail in chapters 4 and 5.)

(12) a. Susan plays often the piano.
b. Susan plays$_i$ [often [$_{VP}$ t$_i$ the piano]]

One possible response might be that the data implicating functional categories, as discussed so far, are drawn from child L2 acquisition. Could the Minimal Trees Hypothesis be recast as a claim only about adult L2 acquisition? Although Vainikka and Young-Scholten do advance the hypothesis in the adult context, the logic of their argument implies that it applies equally to child L2 acquisition. The Minimal Trees Hypothesis is a hypothesis about initial-state grammars in general; Vainikka and Young-Scholten motivate it on the basis of similar proposals for child L1 acquisition. Thus, child L2 acquisition can hardly be excluded. Any data, whether from child or adult L2 learners, that suggests the presence of functional material in the initial state, or emergence of CP before IP, or L1 effects on functional categories, is problematic for the Minimal Trees Hypothesis.

Vainikka and Young-Scholten (1996b) counter some of the problematic data which seem to suggest the initial presence of functional categories by questioning whether such data are genuinely relevant to the initial state. For example, they point out, correctly, that the data discussed in Grondin and White (1996) may not in fact be relevant, since the children had been exposed to French for some months before they were first recorded (even though they did not speak any French during that time). They also question the data discussed by Lakshmanan and Selinker (1994), since evidence for CP is scanty until the fifth and sixth recordings, at which point the children could be deemed to be beyond the initial state. Recognizing that the majority of adults in their own studies do not appear to have grammars totally lacking functional categories, they suggest that they may already have passed the no functional category stage (Vainikka and Young-Scholten 1994).

This again raises the issue of falsifiability – how early is early enough? If researchers can resort to the claim that an earlier stage lacking functional categories would have been found had data elicitation started early enough or that a 'silent period' preceding L2 production would have had no functional categories, it renders the Minimal Trees Hypothesis unfalsifiable. Indeed, to investigate the possibility that there might be a stage prior to the emergence of L2 speech in which functional categories are lacking, we need methodologies that do not rely on production data. Comprehension tasks where functional properties are manipulated are not easy to construct.

It should be noted, however, that the falsifiability problem is by no means unique to the Minimal Trees Hypothesis. As discussed in section 3.2.1.2, in the absence of evidence of transfer, the proponents of the Full Transfer Full Access Hypothesis could resort to the same appeal: there would have been transfer if an earlier stage had been examined. We return to this general issue in section 3.4.

3.2.2.2 Minimal Trees: conceptual issues

In addition to empirical evidence suggesting that the Minimal Trees Hypothesis is misconceived, there have been a number of objections on conceptual grounds. Regardless of whether one accepts the Weak Continuity Hypothesis for L1 acquisition, there are problems with the claim that the initial state of L2 learners is limited to lexical categories. Given a steady-state grammar (the L1) with functional categories, as well as UG with an inventory of functional categories, why should these be totally absent in the interlanguage initial state, indeed how could they be? As Schwartz and Sprouse (1996: 66) point out, 'It is difficult to imagine what sort of cognitive mechanism would be involved in extracting a proper subpart of the L1 grammar and using that proper subsystem as the basis for a new cognitive state.'

We have seen above that Vainikka and Young-Scholten postulate two stages involving a head-initial functional category, first FP, then IP. In both cases, this is different from German. On most analyses of German, VP and IP are head final, while CP is head initial (see chapter 1, section 1.4.1); this is the analysis that Vainikka and Young-Scholten adopt for the grammars of native speakers. Finite verbs in main clauses raise from V to I and then to C. Some other phrase (the subject, the object or an adjunct) moves to the Spec of CP, yielding the V2 effect. In other words, the position of the finite verb in main clauses depends on there being a functional head (C) to the left of the VP, as shown in (13).

(13)

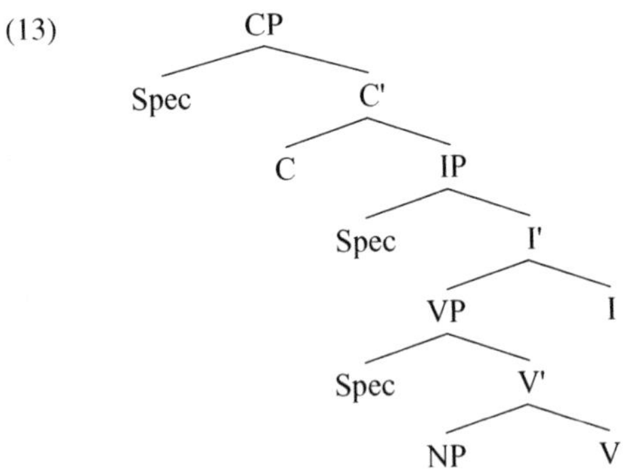

The L2 learners who are described by Vainikka and Young-Scholten as being beyond the initial state show clear (though not necessarily consistent) evidence of verb movement out of the VP. And as the verb is found following the subject, a fairly obvious analysis would be that these learners in fact have the representation in (13), namely a full CP (Epstein et al. 1996; Schwartz 1998a; Schwartz and Sprouse 1994), with the verb in C and the subject in Spec of CP. Since Vainikka and Young-Scholten assume that there is no CP at this stage, they are forced to assume that FP and IP are head initial in order to account for the observed word order; if FP and IP were head final, finite verbs should remain at the end of the sentence, contrary to fact.

What, then, drives Vainikka and Young-Scholten's hypothesis that CP is absent, even given the presence of data consistent with a CP projection (namely finite verbs occurring outside the VP near the front of the clause)? Recall that Vainikka and Young-Scholten crucially assume that absence of some form in production data means absence of the corresponding abstract category. In the case of CP, they fail to find evidence of overt complementizers and conclude that there is no C, hence no CP. Similarly, they conclude that, in the absence of an overt verbal agreement paradigm, there is no IP.

In making these assumptions, Vainikka and Young-Scholten are adopting a form of 'morphological bootstrapping' (Clahsen et al. 1996), the idea being that the learner's acquisition of functional categories is a consequence of having already acquired regular inflectional paradigms, with overt morphology acting as a trigger for projecting functional structure. In other words, in the absence of overt morphology or other lexical items associated with functional categories (such as modals and complementizers), the associated syntactic positions are assumed not to be in place.

A number of researchers have questioned the assumption that, if a form is absent in production data (or used inaccurately or with variability), the associated functional category must necessarily be lacking. There is a difference between 'knowing' abstract functional properties and knowing how these happen to be lexically realized in a particular language; problems with the latter do not necessarily indicate problems with the former (Epstein et al. 1996; Grondin and White 1996; Haznedar and Schwartz 1997; Lardiere 1998a, b, 2000; Prévost and White 2000a, b; Schwartz 1991; Schwartz and Sprouse 1996). If learners show evidence of syntactic properties associated with functional categories, this suggests that the categories are present, even in the absence of particular lexical items or morphology. This issue will be discussed in more detail in chapter 6.

Another problem with Vainikka and Young-Scholten's account is that presence and absence are defined in an arbitrary, and apparently unmotivated, way. A category is defined as present in the grammar if lexical items associated with it are produced in 60% or more of obligatory contexts; otherwise, it is assumed to be absent. In other words, the criterion for acquisition is an accuracy level of 60%. In earlier L1 acquisition research, as well as in early L2 research that investigated acquisition orders relating to function words and morphology (Bailey, Madden and

Krashen 1974; Dulay and Burt 1974), a criterion of 90% accuracy was adopted (Brown 1973). This is, of course, equally arbitrary and is the result of equating performance (almost totally accurate use of inflectional morphology) with acquisition. Vainikka and Young-Scholten recognize that the 90% criterion is too high but it is not clear what a criterion of 60% achieves. Indeed, it would be more appropriate to take evidence of emergence of some property as evidence of acquisition (Meisel, Clahsen and Pienemann 1981; Stromswold 1996).

3.2.2.3 Minimal Trees: summary

In summary, according to the Minimal Trees Hypothesis:

a. The interlanguage initial state is a grammar containing lexical categories (drawn from the L1 grammar) but no functional categories.
b. Developmental stages involve the addition of functional categories (available from UG), which emerge gradually, triggered by L2 input. Functional categories are added to the representation from the bottom up (i.e. CP could not be acquired before IP).
c. Final outcome – L2 learners should, presumably, converge on the L2 grammar, at least as far as functional projections and their consequences are concerned, since L2 data triggering the relevant properties are available.

3.2.3 *The Valueless Features Hypothesis*

We turn now to a third hypothesis concerning the interlanguage initial state, the Valueless Features Hypothesis of Eubank (1993/1994, 1994, 1996). Like Full Transfer Full Access and Minimal Trees, the Valueless Features Hypothesis claims that the initial state is a grammar. Eubank argues for 'weak' transfer, maintaining that the L1 grammar largely – but not entirely – determines the interlanguage initial state. Like Full Transfer Full Access and unlike Minimal Trees, the Valueless Features Hypothesis claims that L1 lexical and functional categories are present in the earliest interlanguage grammar. However, although L1 functional categories are available, their feature values are claimed not to be. That is, feature strength does not transfer. Instead of being either strong or weak, features are valueless or 'inert' in the initial state.

As described in chapter 1, section 1.4.1, feature strength has consequences for word order. In a language like English, where I has weak V-features, finite verbs remain within the VP. In languages like French, where I is strong, the verb raises to I to check its features. In other words, finite lexical verbs either must raise (as in French) or may not raise (as in English).

On the Valueless Features Hypothesis, feature values are neither weak nor strong. According to Eubank, this has the following consequence: when features are not specified for strength, finite verbs can alternate between raising or not raising. In other words, if the L2 learner is acquiring a language with strong features like French, both the word orders in (14) are expected in early stages, the grammatical (14a), where the finite verb has raised out of the VP, and the ungrammatical (14b), where the verb has not raised. The predictions are identical for an L2 with weak features, like English. That is, both of the word orders in (15) are predicted to occur because, in the absence of a specification of feature strength, the verb can 'choose' to raise or not, as the case may be.

(14) a. Marie regarde_i [souvent [$_{VP}$ t_i la télévision]]
b. Marie [souvent [$_{VP}$ regarde la télévision]]

(15) a. Mary [often [$_{VP}$ watches television]]
b. Mary watches_i [often [$_{VP}$ t_i television]]

The assumption that valueless features implies optional verb raising is a stipulation whose justification is unclear; we return to this point in section 3.2.3.2.

3.2.3.1 Valueless Features: evidence

In support of the hypothesis, Eubank examines data from a variety of sources. In earlier work on adverb placement, White (1990/1991, 1991a) showed that French-speaking learners of English produce and accept both the word orders in (15). She suggested that (15b) is the result of transfer of the strong feature value from French. Eubank argues that White's data in fact support the Valueless Features Hypothesis, given the fact that the order in (15a), without verb raising, was also found. On a strong transfer account, this order should be impossible, since the strong feature should force verb raising. (See chapters 4 and 5 for more detailed presentation of these data and their implications.)

A problem for the Valueless Features account is that verbs should raise optionally over negatives as well. That is, a French-speaking learner of English would be expected to produce both preverbal and postverbal negation, as in (16).

(16) a. The children like_i [not [$_{VP}$ t_i spinach]]
b. The children (do) [not [$_{VP}$ like spinach]]

However, such variability has not been reported. In other words, there is less variability here than expected under the inert features proposal. White (1992a) found that French-speaking learners of English consistently reject sentences like (16a) where *not* follows the lexical verb. (See chapter 4, section 4.5.2.1.) In addition, Eubank (1993/1994) examines spontaneous production data (from Gerbault (1978) and Tiphine (undated)) and finds the same thing: French-speaking children learning English produce negatives like (16b) but not like (16a). Eubank accounts for the absence of optional verb raising over negation in terms of the interaction of inert features in Tense and weak features in Agr. But the lack of sentences like (16a) is in fact consistent with these learners having acquired the relevant feature value of English, namely weak agreement.[4]

Experimental evidence that goes against the Valueless Features Hypothesis is provided by Yuan (2001). Yuan examines the L2 acquisition of Chinese, a language with weak features, hence lacking verb movement. In Chinese, sentences like (17a) are grammatical, whereas (17b) is not.

(17)	a. Zhangsan	changchang	kan	dianshi.
	Zhangsan	often	watch	television
	b. *Zhangsan	kan	changchang	dianshi.
	Zhangsan	watch	often	television

Subjects were adult native speakers of French and English, learning Chinese; they were at various levels of proficiency, including beginners. (See box 3.3.) The L1 of one group (English) shares the property of weak feature strength with the L2 Chinese, while the L1 of the other group (French) has the opposite strength. According to the Valueless Features Hypothesis, both groups should initially behave in the same way, regardless of L1 feature strength, permitting optional verb placement in Chinese. However, subjects at the lowest level of proficiency (who had studied Chinese for less than six months) showed no evidence of optional verb placement. This was true of both the French speakers and the English speakers. In two different tasks, production and acceptance of the grammatical order, as in (17a), were very high, while production and acceptance of the ungrammatical order, where the verb has raised, as in (17b), were correspondingly low, as shown in table 3.3.1.

Not only are these results inconsistent with the Valueless Features Hypothesis, since they provide no evidence for optional verb raising, they also appear to be inconsistent with the Full Transfer Full Access Hypothesis, since there is no evidence that I is initially strong in the grammars of the French speakers. (However, proponents of both the Valueless Features Hypothesis and Full Transfer Full Access could argue that the two first-year groups had already had sufficient exposure to the L2 to acquire the weak feature strength appropriate for Chinese, once again raising the question of falsifiability.)

What happens beyond the initial state? According to the Valueless Features Hypothesis as originally propounded by Eubank, inertness is a temporary phenomenon, characteristic only of the early interlanguage grammar. Subsequent acquisition of feature strength (strong or weak) is claimed to depend on the emergence of inflectional morphology. Eubank follows Rohrbacher (1994) in assuming that feature strength is determined by the nature of morphological

Box 3.3 Parameter setting – features (Yuan 2001)

Languages: L1s = English/French, L2 = Chinese.
Tasks:

i. Oral production.
ii. Grammaticality judgments. Pairs of sentences differing only as to verb position. Subjects indicate whether or not both sentences are acceptable.

Sample stimuli:

a. Wo gege he pingchang Deguo jiu.
b. Wo gege pingchang he Deguo jiu.

(*My brother drinks usually German wine.*
My brother usually drinks German wine.)

Results:

Table 3.3.1 *Production and judgments of grammatical and ungrammatical word orders*

		Production			Grammaticality judgments		
		SAVO	*SVAO	Other	SAVO	*SVAO	Both
L2 groups (L1 English)	Level 1 (n = 24)	223 (93%)	9	8	136 (95%)	3	4
	Level 2 (n = 15)	140 (100%)	0	0	88 (98%)	0	2
	Level 3 (n = 16)	160 (100%)	0	0	91 (96%)	0	4
	Level 4 (n = 12)	120 (100%)	0	0	63 (88%)	1	8
L2 groups (L1 French)	Level 1 (n = 15)	148 (99%)	0	2	70 (91%)	5	2
	Level 2 (n = 16)	141 (88%)	0	19	93 (97%)	2	0
	Level 3 (n = 17)	167 (98%)	0	3	98 (99%)	0	1
Native speakers	(n = 10)	92 (92%)	0	8	60 (100%)	0	0

paradigms: Infl is strong if and only if inflectional morphology is rich, a term that is variously defined but which essentially means that verbs show distinct person and/or number morphology. In other words, strong I will be triggered by rich morphology, weak I otherwise. (Arguments against this claim will be discussed in chapter 6.)

On the assumption that morphology and feature strength are correlated in this way, the following predictions can be made for L2 acquisition: learners who have not yet acquired overt agreement should show variability in verb placement (characteristic of inertness in the initial state), whereas learners who have acquired agreement should consistently raise or fail to raise the verb, depending on the L2 in question. Eubank and Grace (1998) and Eubank, Bischof, Huffstutler, Leek and West (1997) conducted experiments testing these predictions. In both studies, the L1 (Chinese) and L2 (English) share the same feature strength, namely weak. As we have seen, the Valueless Features Hypothesis predicts optional verb raising even in such cases. Thus, Chinese-speaking learners of English who have not yet acquired English third-person-singular agreement should sometimes raise the main verb over an adverb, a possibility not permitted in either language, whereas learners who have acquired third-person-singular agreement should not do so.

Both studies included an oral translation task to determine whether or not third-person-singular agreement morphology had been acquired, as well as another task to determine whether or not learners permit verb raising. Eubank and Grace (1998) use a sentence-matching task for the latter purpose, while Eubank et al. (1997) use a truth-value-judgment task.

The sentence-matching methodology (Freedman and Forster 1985) involves presenting pairs of sentences on a computer screen. Subjects have to press a response key indicating whether the two sentences are the same (matched) or different (unmatched). It has been established that native speakers respond significantly faster to matched grammatical pairs than matched ungrammatical pairs, for a range of constructions. Thus, response times can be used as a diagnostic of grammaticality, even though subjects are not making explicit grammaticality judgments. The sentence-matching methodology has recently received considerable attention in L2 acquisition research, the rationale being that it may also provide a diagnostic of grammaticality in interlanguage grammars (Beck 1998a; Bley-Vroman and Masterson 1989; Clahsen and Hong 1995; Duffield and White 1999; Duffield, White, Bruhn de Garavito, Montrul and Prévost 2002; Eubank 1993). (For a recent critique of the use of sentence-matching tasks in L2 acquisition research, see Gass (2001).)

To test verb raising, Eubank and Grace include pairs of sentences like (15a) and other pairs like (15b), repeated here as (18). (See box 3.4.)

(18) a. Mary often watches television.
b. Mary watches often television.

If feature values are inert, verb raising will be permitted but not required and both sentence types will be grammatical. In other words, there should be no difference in

Box 3.4 Valueless Features Hypothesis (Eubank and Grace 1998)

Languages: L1 = Chinese, L2 = English.
Task: Sentence-matching. Pairs of sentences presented on computer screen. Subjects decide whether the two sentences are the same or different.
Sample stimuli:

Grammatical (No V-raising)	Ungrammatical (V-raising)
The woman often loses her books	The boy takes often the flowers
The woman often loses her books	The boy takes often the flowers

Results:

Table 3.4.1 *Mean response times in ms.*

		V-raising (ungram)	No raising (gram)	
L2 groups	No agreement (n = 14)	3038	2841	sig
	Agreement (n = 18)	2594	2618	ns
Native speakers (n = 36)		1546	1491	sig

response times to pairs like (18a) compared to pairs like (18b). On the other hand, if the L2 learners have a grammar where the weak value has been established, the pairs involving verb raising, like (18b), will be ungrammatical. Hence, it should take significantly longer to respond to this type than to grammatical pairs like (18a).

Native speakers of English behaved as predicted, responding significantly more slowly to the ungrammatical pairs with the raised verbs. (See table 3.4.1.) The L2 learners were divided into two groups on the basis of the translation task: (i) a *no agreement* group whose suppliance of agreement was inconsistent – this group is assumed still to be in the initial state; and (ii) an *agreement* group, who consistently produced third-person-singular morphology – by hypothesis, this group is beyond the initial state. In the case of the no agreement group, no significant difference is predicted between the two types of sentence pairs, since they are both grammatical in a grammar that tolerates but does not require verb raising because of inert features. The agreement group, in contrast, is expected to show the same contrast as native speakers, that is, to take significantly longer to respond to the pairs involving verb raising, which are ungrammatical in a grammar with weak agreement. However, the results showed the reverse: the no agreement group responded significantly more slowly to the ungrammatical pairs (like the native speakers), whereas the agreement group did not.

Box 3.5 Valueless Features Hypothesis (Eubank et al. 1997)

Languages: L1 = Chinese, L2 = English.
Task: Truth-value judgments. Short narratives, each followed by a sentence. Subjects indicate whether the sentence is true or false in the context of the narrative.
Sample stimulus:

> Tom loves to draw pictures of monkeys in the zoo. Tom likes his pictures to be perfect, so he always draws them very slowly and carefully. All the monkeys always jump up and down really fast.
> Tom draws slowly jumping monkeys.
> True False

Results:

Table 3.5.1 *Responses to V-raising items (in %)*

		False	True
L2 groups	No agreement (n = 14)	69.5	30.4
	Agreement (n = 18)	81.7	18.3
Native speakers (n = 28)		91	9

Eubank et al. (1997) examined the same issues, using a modified truth-value-judgment task, to determine whether the unexpected results from the sentence-matching task are attributable to the methodology rather than being a reflection of grammatical knowledge. The rationale, assumptions and predictions were the same as for Eubank and Grace but different subjects were tested. (See box 3.5.) Their truth-value-judgment task centres on test sentences which are ambiguous in the case of a grammar that allows optional verb raising (thus permitting a response of *true* or *false*) but unambiguous in a grammar that does not (allowing only *false*). In the example in box 3.5, the sentence *Tom draws slowly jumping monkeys* is false if *slowly* is construed as modifying *jumping*, that is, if it is analysed as in (19a). In contrast, the sentence is true if it is interpreted with raising of the verb over the adverb, with the structure in (19b), where *slowly* is understood as modifying the verb *draws*.

(19) a. Tom draws [$_{NP}$ [slowly jumping] monkeys]
b. Tom draws$_i$ [slowly [$_{VP}$ t$_i$ jumping monkeys]]

In a grammar which prohibits verb raising, only the former interpretation, involving modification within the NP, is possible (but see below). The prediction, then, is that native speakers of English and learners with agreement (as defined above) will respond in the same manner, treating all such items as false. The no agreement group, on the other hand, is expected to alternate between responses, reflecting the ambiguity of these sentences in a grammar with optional verb raising.

Contrary to predictions, Eubank et al. found that all three groups differ significantly from each other in their responses; that is, the agreement group did not perform exactly like the native speakers. (See table 3.5.1.) Nevertheless, it is clear from the results that the response patterns of the three groups are in fact quite similar: all groups, including the native speakers, give some responses of *true*, and, for all groups, including the no agreement group, responses of *false* predominate. If verb raising truly were optional in interlanguage grammars, one might expect a much higher proportion of *true* responses. In several of the crucial scenarios, the test sentence is extremely odd if the verb has not raised, involving NPs like *slowly jumping monkeys* and *quietly toasted bread*. If the grammar really sanctions verb raising, one might expect the more natural verb-raised interpretation to be adopted (leading to a higher number of responses of *true*). An alternative possibility is that subjects resorted to interpretations involving verb raising even though their grammars prohibit it, precisely because the alternatives were pragmatically so odd.[5] Also, one cannot exclude the possibility that subjects read the sentences with the adverb 'in parentheses' (e.g. *Tom draws, slowly, jumping monkeys*), in which case a response of *true* would be given and yet the verb has not raised over the adverb.

There are a number of respects in which Eubank et al.'s task departed from more standard truth-value-judgment tasks. In the first place, the test items should all be grammatical; appropriateness is then determined on the basis of the story (or picture) which supplies the context. (See examples testing knowledge of reflexives, chapter 2, boxes 2.5 and 2.6.) However, in Eubank et al.'s task, English sentences with raised verbs are ungrammatical for native speakers and for learners who have acquired the weak English feature value. Furthermore, they are ungrammatical but appropriate, given the contexts. It really is not clear that there is any prediction as to what subjects (native speakers or otherwise) should do in such circumstances. Eubank et al. appear to assume that the interpretation where the adverb modifies the verb simply will not come to mind (because the sentences are ungrammatical) but this has not been demonstrated, and clearly it does come to mind some of the time.

A related problem is that each context in Eubank et al.'s task sets one interpretation off against the other, for example, there is something slow going on in the story as well as something fast (see box 3.5). Again, this diverges from the usual practice (see chapter 2, boxes 2.5 and 2.6), where the context describes just one situation and subjects have to judge whether or not the test sentence is true of that situation. Because there is no difference in interpretation depending solely on the position of the verb (*slowly draws* versus *draws slowly*), it is in fact impossible to match contexts with interpretations without introducing such additional complications. The truth-value-judgment methodology is simply unsuitable for testing issues relating to feature strength.

To sum up, neither the sentence-matching experiment nor the truth-value-judgment experiment bears out the predictions of the Valueless Features Hypothesis. In both studies, the results from the group who had passed the criterion for acquiring inflection are particularly problematic, since these learners have overt morphological inflection but are still, ostensibly, permitting verb raising. In consequence, Eubank et al. (1997) and Eubank and Grace (1998), following Beck (1998a), interpret their results as providing evidence of an even stronger version of the Valueless Features Hypothesis, whereby inert features are a permanent property of interlanguage grammars, rather than just being found in the initial state. This position, the Local Impairment Hypothesis, will be discussed in chapter 4.

In addition, setting aside the methodological problems discussed above, there are problematic inconsistencies in the results from the two tasks as regards the no agreement groups. If both groups have grammars with inert features, why are they behaving differently? In the sentence-matching task, the no agreement group performed like native speakers, taking significantly longer to respond to ungrammatical sentences, suggesting absence of verb raising. In the truth-value-judgment task, the no agreement group gave more responses of *true* than other groups (although responses of *false* predominated), interpreted by Eubank et al. as indicating that verb raising is permitted. To accommodate the former finding, Eubank and Grace suggest that the Minimal Trees Hypothesis must be the correct account of the initial state (which is then followed by a grammar with inert features): in the sentence-matching task, the results from the no agreement group are consistent with an initial grammar with only a VP projection, in which case the sentences with raised verbs would be ungrammatical, because there would be no functional category for the verb to raise to. Unfortunately for this proposal, the results from the truth-value-judgment task do not support such an account: if the no agreement subjects had only a VP, verb raising would be impossible and their responses should have been exclusively *false*, contrary to fact.

3.2.3.2 Valueless Features: conceptual issues

Such difficulties reflect deeper problems with the Valueless Features Hypothesis, at the conceptual level. It really is not clear what it means for feature strength to be inert, or what motivates this proposal. Nor is it clear whether inertness is confined to features of Infl or why this should be so. Eubank suggests that inertness is somewhat similar to underspecification of functional categories proposed for the grammars of L1 acquirers (e.g. Wexler 1994). However, proposals for underspecification in L1 acquisition are, in fact, quite different: underspecified

Tense, for example, results in variability (in verb-raising languages) between finite and non-finite verbs. Finite verbs always raise, whereas non-finite verbs (*optional infinitives*) do not. On Eubank's account, on the other hand, it is finite verbs that show variability. Again, it is not clear what this claim follows from. Indeed, one might just as well predict that variability should *not* occur, as noted by Schwartz (1998b) and by Robertson and Sorace (1999): in the absence of a strong feature forcing raising, the verb should not move at all, since it is the strong feature value that motivates movement. Since inert implies not strong, all verbs should remain within the VP. Even if inertness could somehow be rendered less stipulative, it is, in any case, not obvious why feature strength should be inert in interlanguage grammars. As Schwartz and Sprouse (1996) point out, why should all properties of the L1 grammar be found in the initial state with the exception of feature strength?

3.2.3.3 Valueless Features: summary

To summarize, the claims of the Valueless Features Hypothesis are as follows:

a. The interlanguage initial state is a grammar containing lexical and functional categories, as well as features, drawn from the L1 grammar. Feature strength is inert.
b. L2 feature strength will be acquired during the course of development, when morphological paradigms are acquired.
c. Final outcome – ultimately, L2 learners should converge on the L2 grammar.

3.3 UG as the initial state

The three hypotheses considered so far (Full Transfer Full Access, Minimal Trees and Valueless Features) agree that the L1 grammar forms the interlanguage initial state, although they disagree on whether the whole L1 grammar is implicated. We turn now to two hypotheses which reject the possibility that any properties of the L1 grammar are involved in the interlanguage initial state. Instead, something quite different is proposed, namely that the L2 learner starts out with UG rather than with any particular grammar.

3.3.1 The Initial Hypothesis of Syntax

According to Platzack's (1996) Initial Hypothesis of Syntax, the initial states of L1 and L2 acquisition are identical. The initial state is UG; it includes functional categories with all features set at default or unmarked strength, namely weak. Weak is claimed to be the default value, on the grounds that overt movement (motivated by strong features) is costly (Chomsky 1993, 1995). All learners (L1 or L2), then, will initially assume weak features. In the case of L2 acquisition, this is claimed to be so even if the L1 grammar has strong feature values. Subsequently, the learner has to work out which features should in fact be set to strong, on the basis of L2 input (such as input showing evidence of overt movement). The Initial Hypothesis of Syntax represents an updated version of earlier markedness proposals, whereby L2 learners were argued to resort to unmarked options made available by UG regardless of the situation in the L1 (Liceras 1986; Mazurkewich 1984a).

The Initial Hypothesis of Syntax has not, as yet, been pursued with any degree of detail in the L2 context. There is, however, experimental evidence that casts doubts on such claims. As mentioned above, results from White (1990/1991, 1991a) suggest that L2 learners do not start off with all features set at weak values: French-speaking learners of English transfer strong features from the L1, hence allowing verb movement over adverbs in the L2. On the other hand, the results of Yuan (2001) could be seen as offering support, since French-speaking learners of Chinese, whose L1 has strong I, do not at any stage permit verb raising in the L2.

Sprouse (1997) and Schwartz (1997) question the claim that L2 learners start off with weak features. The Initial Hypothesis of Syntax presupposes Kayne's (1994) antisymmetry hypothesis, whereby all languages are underlyingly SVO. SOV word order is the result of a strong object feature which must be checked in AgrO, causing the object to raise over the verb. The Initial Hypothesis of Syntax, then, predicts that all L2 learners will start off with SVO order because object features are initially weak, so that no object movement is possible. This prediction holds regardless of what the L2 word order is and regardless of feature strength and word order in the L1: thus, learners whose mother tongue is SOV are predicted to have an initial SVO stage, even if the L2 is also SOV. As we have already seen, this prediction is false. Turkish- and Korean-speaking learners of German initially assume that German is SOV (Schwartz and Sprouse 1994; Vainikka and Young-Scholten 1994), as do Turkish-speaking learners of English (Haznedar 1997).

3.3.2 *Full Access (without Transfer)*

The final proposal to be considered in this chapter is the Full Access Hypothesis of Flynn and Martohardjono (1994), Flynn (1996), and Epstein et al. (1996, 1998). According to Epstein et al. (1996: 750), the Full Access Hypothesis is not, strictly speaking a hypothesis about the initial state. Nevertheless, although not proposed as an explicit initial-state hypothesis, in fact it has clear implications for the nature of the initial state, as we shall see. Furthermore, this hypothesis implies, like the Initial Hypothesis of Syntax, that UG must constitute the initial state in L2 acquisition.

What is meant by the Full Access Hypothesis? Epstein et al. argue that the interlanguage grammar is UG-constrained at all stages; grammars conform to the principles of UG and learners are limited to the hypothesis space allowed by UG. In other words, UG remains accessible in non-primary acquisition. So far, the assumptions are identical to those advanced by proponents of Full Transfer Full Access; in other words, the *full access* of Full Transfer Full Access is the *full access* of Epstein et al. Furthermore, this assumption is shared by Vainikka and Young-Scholten, who argue that all of UG is available in L2 acquisition, although some properties (functional categories) emerge after others. The Valueless Features Hypothesis was also originally intended as a full access theory, interlanguage grammars being constrained by UG, with inertness of features only a temporary property.

What, then, makes Epstein et al.'s Full Access Hypothesis different from the positions considered so far? In contrast to the first three initial-state proposals, Epstein et al. (1996: 751) specifically reject the possibility that the L1 grammar forms the initial state. For this reason, I will sometimes refer to their position as Full Access without Transfer. In spite of this rejection, they do recognize the presence of L1 effects in interlanguage grammars. But if these effects are not due to L1-based initial representations, then it is difficult to understand just what they have in mind.[6]

If the initial state is not the L1 grammar, what is it? The (implicit) logic of Epstein et al.'s argumentation necessitates that it is not a grammar at all but rather UG. In other words, the initial state in L2 acquisition is the same as the initial state in L1. In fact, however, Epstein et al. (1996: 751) reject this possibility as well, stating that the initial state in L2 is not S_0, so presumably not UG itself. It is hard to conceive what the initial state could possibly be, if it is neither at least partially the L1 grammar nor UG. I will continue to interpret their hypothesis as implying that UG must be the initial state, although they fail to recognize that this is the logical outcome of their position.

To understand how it is that Epstein et al.'s position implicates UG as the initial state, consider that they specifically argue in favour of the Strong Continuity or Full Competence Hypothesis as the correct account of functional categories in L2 grammars and against the Minimal Trees Hypothesis of Vainikka and Young-Scholten. According to the Strong Continuity Hypothesis, all functional categories are present in L1 grammars from the beginning (Borer and Rohrbacher 1997; Hyams 1992; Lust 1994; Wexler 1998). In contrast, as discussed in section 3.2.2, the Minimal Trees Hypothesis claims that initially no functional categories are present and that they emerge gradually. Since the Minimal Trees Hypothesis is a

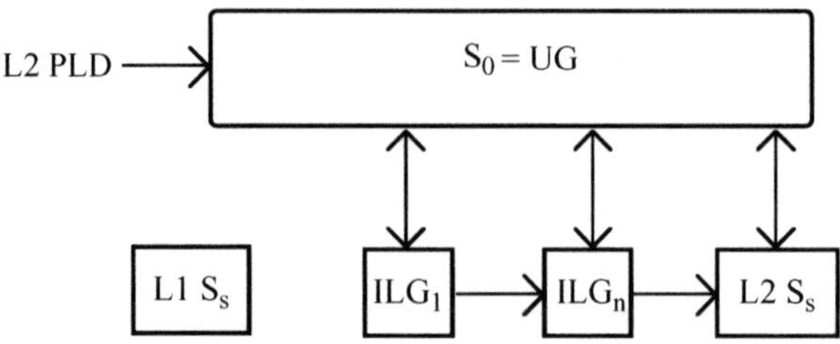

Figure 3.3 *Full Access (without transfer)*

claim about the nature of the interlanguage initial state, Epstein et al.'s refutation necessarily involves an alternative initial-state claim, in particular the claim that the earliest interlanguage grammar will contain a full complement of functional categories. And, since they reject the possibility that the L1 grammar forms the initial state, the source of functional categories in the early interlanguage grammar can only be UG itself.

Hence, whether they recognize it or not, the clear implication of Epstein et al.'s Full Access Hypothesis is that UG is the initial state in L2 as well as in L1. The Full Access Hypothesis is illustrated in figure 3.3 (adapted from White 2000), which shows the L1 grammar dissociated from the interlanguage grammars, in other words, Full Access without Transfer. (Figure 3.3 applies equally to the Initial Hypothesis of Syntax.)

The logical outcome of this position is that interlanguage grammars of learners of different L1s will be the same, because of the influence of UG, with no effects attributable to the L1, since the L1 does not form the initial state. In fact, Epstein et al. do not exclude the possibility of L1-effects and differences between learners of different L1s, although, as already mentioned, it is not at all clear how the L1 fits into their scheme of things. As to the final state achievable in L2 acquisition, this should in principle be a representation identical to that of native speakers of the L2 (Flynn 1996: 150).

3.3.2.1 Full Access: evidence

Epstein et al. (1996) conducted an experiment with child and adult Japanese-speaking learners of English which, they argue, provides evidence against the Minimal Trees Hypothesis and in favour of Strong Continuity and Full Access. In addition, they claim that the results demonstrate lack of L1 influence in the early grammar. By implication, then, this experiment should be relevant to the initial state, since the Minimal Trees Hypothesis involves claims about the initial state, as does Full Transfer Full Access.

The experiment involved an elicited imitation task. Stimuli were designed with the intention of testing knowledge of various morphological and syntactic

Box 3.6 Full Access (Epstein et al. 1996)

Languages: L1 = Japanese, L2 = English.
Task: Elicited imitation.
Sample stimuli:
Items testing for IP

The nervous doctor wanted a new lawyer in the office. (past tense)
The happy janitor does not want the new television. (neg/*do* support)
The little girl can see a tiny flower in the picture. (modal)

Items testing for CP

Which secret message does the young girl find in the basket? (*wh*-question)
Breakfast, the wealthy business man prepares in the kitchen. (topicalization)
The lawyer slices the vegetables which the father eats. (relative clause)

Results:

Table 3.6.1 *Accurate imitations (in %)*

		IP (# = 12)	CP (# = 12)
L2 groups	Children (n = 33)	69	50
	Adults (n = 18)	68	45

properties associated with the functional projections IP and CP. (See box 3.6.) The rationale behind this choice of methodology is the assumption that learners (L1 or L2) can only successfully imitate sentences that are analysable by the current grammar (Lust, Flynn and Foley 1996). If so, L2 learners should not be able to imitate sentences exemplifying grammatical properties normally analysed in terms of functional categories unless those categories are present in the grammar. For example, if learners can imitate sentences containing verbs marked for third-person-singular agreement, then they are assumed to have the functional category that hosts agreement, namely IP.

Results showed no significant differences between child and adult learners of English in their imitation abilities. (See table 3.6.1.) Both groups were more accurate at imitating sentences testing for presence of IP than those testing for CP. (Epstein et al. suggest that the lower performance on CPs is not due to absence of a CP projection but rather to processing problems associated with long-distance movement, compounded by the lack of syntactic *wh*-movement in the L1 grammar, leading to problems with *wh*-movement sentences in the L2. This explanation provides a good example of their somewhat ambivalent attitude to the role of the

L1: here the L1 is used to explain away problems with the data; yet at the same time they deny a role to the L1 as far as representation of such sentences is concerned.)

Let us consider (a) whether their experiment in fact tells us anything about the initial state; and (b) what it shows more generally about Full Access. These results do not provide evidence against Minimal Trees or against Full Transfer Full Access, despite claims to the contrary by Epstein et al., because they tell us nothing about the presence or absence of functional categories in the initial state. Epstein et al.'s adult subjects were of low-intermediate proficiency, with an average of one year of exposure to English in an English-speaking country, as well as seven years of instruction in the L2. The children, whose proficiency level is not reported, had lived in the USA for an average of three years, with an average of three years of formal instruction in English. Thus, these learners must be well beyond an initial-state grammar. Strong Continuity (argued for by Epstein et al.) and Minimal Trees (advocated by Vainikka and Young-Scholten) differ only in their claims about the presence of functional categories at the outset of L2 acquisition. None of the theories we have considered claims that intermediate level learners will have grammars totally lacking functional categories. Epstein et al.'s results are irrelevant as far as the Minimal Trees Hypothesis is concerned; these intermediate learners could simply be past the lexical stage. Similarly, the results are irrelevant as an argument against Full Transfer Full Access. Epstein et al. claim that the fact that their subjects show evidence of L2 functional categories argues against an early L1-based grammar, on the assumption that Japanese lacks functional categories (Fukui and Speas 1986). But Full Transfer Full Access is not just a full transfer theory; it is also a full access theory. So the fact that intermediate-level learners show evidence of L2 categories is not an argument against an L1-based initial state. The data are neutral on this point.

Clearly, Epstein et al.'s results are irrelevant to the initial state. In what sense do they otherwise support Full Access? All the initial-state hypotheses included in this chapter presuppose that UG constrains interlanguage grammars. All assume that L2 functional categories will be attainable. In other words, they are all full access theories. So, in so far as Epstein et al.'s data could provide evidence of full access, they are neutral between a number of different full access theories.

However, evidence for full access on the basis of this study is weak, at best. Epstein et al. fail to demonstrate that there is a poverty of the stimulus with respect to learning English inflectional morphology and function words (Schwartz and Sprouse 2000a); thus, it is not clear in what sense UG is implicated at all. Even if it is, there is a problem with their use of elicited imitation. Setting aside general questions as to the suitability of elicited imitation for investigating the nature of linguistic competence (see Bley-Vroman and Chaudron (1994) and the commentaries on Epstein et al. (1996)), their task included no ungrammatical sentences.

If learners can only imitate sentences that fall within their current grammatical competence, then, given ungrammatical sentences to imitate (for example, lacking inflection or with incorrect inflection), they should not imitate these but rather correct them in accordance with their current grammar. In the absence of ungrammatical stimuli, the data are uninterpretable: successful imitation could indicate a reflection of grammatical properties or simply an ability to imitate whatever stimuli are presented.

3.3.2.2 Full Access: conceptual issues

The Initial Hypothesis of Syntax is underdeveloped in the L2 context. This leaves the Full Access Hypothesis of Epstein et al. as the only version of Full Access without Transfer that has been explored in any detail. In principle, Full Access without Transfer is a perfectly coherent position. Unfortunately, Epstein et al.'s proposal suffers from several problems, including equivocation over the role of the L1, which makes it almost impossible to establish precisely what their predictions are for the initial-state or subsequent grammars.

With these caveats in mind, let us consider whether Full Transfer Full Access and Full Access without Transfer are irreconcilable. Epstein et al. recognize the existence of L1 effects but are reluctant to attribute these to an initial representation based on the L1, partly, perhaps, because they feel that there is less L1 influence than might be expected on a Full Transfer account, as well as considerable commonalities between learners of different L1s. But suppose that initial representations are in fact based on the L1 but that for some properties L1-based representations are fleeting, with almost immediate triggering of L2 properties, based on L2 input and drawing on UG. Indeed, we have seen that some L1 word-order effects are quite short-lived. Thus, it might appear that there are L1 effects in some areas of the grammar but not others, whereas in fact there are short-lived and long-lived effects. In that case, one needs an account of why some L1 characteristics are easily overridden, while others have lasting effects in the interlanguage representation. A theory of triggering can perhaps contribute to such an explanation (see chapter 5).

3.3.2.3 Full Access: summary

In summary, the implications of the Initial Hypothesis of Syntax and the Full Access Hypothesis are as follows:

a. The L2 initial state is not the L1 grammar. UG is the initial state.
b. L2 development is UG-constrained, with interlanguage grammars falling within the range sanctioned by UG.

Table 3.1 *Initial state and beyond: hypotheses compared*

	Full Transfer Full Access	Minimal Trees	Valueless Features	Full Access (without Transfer)
Initial state	L1 lexical and functional categories, features and feature strength	No functional categories L1 lexical categories	L1 lexical and functional categories; (some) inert features.	Full complement of lexical and functional categories, features and feature strength
Development	Different path for learners of different L1s, at least initially. Restructuring of functional properties in response to L2 input	Emergence of functional categories in stages, in response to L2 input	Inert features replaced by L2 feature strength	No development required in abstract properties of functional categories
Steady state	L_n (L2-like grammar possible but not inevitable)	L2-like grammar	L2-like grammar	L2-like grammar

c. Final outcome – the linguistic competence of L2 learners will be effectively identical to that of native speakers (Flynn 1996), any apparent differences being attributable to performance factors.

3.4 Assessing initial-state hypotheses: similarities and differences

It can be seen that there is considerable overlap in the various initial-state proposals that we have considered. In consequence, there is also an overlap in their predictions, sometimes making it hard to find suitable evidence to distinguish between them. Full Transfer Full Access, Minimal Trees and the Valueless Features Hypothesis share the assumption that L1 properties are implicated. Full Transfer Full Access, the Valueless Features Hypothesis and Full Access without Transfer coincide in assuming a full complement of functional categories in the initial state. All of the theories assume that L2 functional properties will be present in later grammars. All hypotheses assume that interlanguage grammars will be UG-constrained in the course of development. The implication of all hypotheses except Full Transfer Full Access is that the steady-state grammar of an L2 speaker will, in principle at least, converge on L2 functional properties (setting aside the possibility that L2 learners may not get adequate input). In the case of Full Transfer Full Access, convergence is possible but not guaranteed, depending on the L1s and L2s in question. (See chapter 8 for further discussion.) In table 3.1, the four major proposals are summarized in terms of what they have to say about the initial state, development and the final state.

What kind of evidence is needed to distinguish between the various claims, as well as to resolve the falsifiability problem? As we have seen, where data do not support a particular hypothesis, there has been a tendency to resort to the claim that the data do not, in fact, come from initial-state learners and that earlier data, if found, would support the hypothesis in question. This would appear to render several of the hypotheses untestable but in fact it is possible to get round this problem, at least in certain cases.

a. Absence of functional categories. The Minimal Trees Hypothesis is the only proposal to argue for absence of functional categories in the initial state. Thus, a demonstration of the presence of functional categories in the earliest stages is in principle sufficient to show that Minimal Trees does not obtain. Here, however, we run into the problem of falsifiability: if evidence for functional categories is found in some group of learners, it is always possible to claim that their grammars were not, after all, in the initial state.

b. Feature strength. Evidence of strong or weak feature values in the initial state is evidence against Valueless Features. (Evidence for strong feature values in earliest stages is also evidence against the Initial Hypothesis of Syntax.) Again, in the face of data suggesting that features are not inert, it is always possible to claim that learners were not in the initial stage.

c. L1 effects. The presence of L1 functional categories, features or feature strength (or other L1-based properties) at any point (in the initial state, during the course of development, or at the endstate) would provide evidence against Full Access without Transfer, as well as the Minimal Trees Hypothesis, since both of these proposals claim that L1-based properties will never be found in the functional domain. On the other hand, absence of L1 properties at some point does not necessarily argue against Full Transfer Full Access, since this hypothesis assumes the possibility of restructuring away from the L1-based initial state, after which L1 effects should disappear. Again, this raises the question of falsifiability: in the absence of L1 effects, how can one tell what an earlier grammar would have looked like?

d. Developmental sequences. The Full Transfer Full Access Hypothesis predicts differences between learners of different L1s learning the same L2, in particular, different initial states. It is also the only hypothesis to predict different development paths for learners of different L1s (at least until the learners converge on the relevant L2 properties). Thus, if learners of different L1s learning the same L2 can be shown to have the same initial state and the same early stages of development, this would be counter-evidence to Full Transfer Full Access and would constitute evidence in favour of Full Access without Transfer. (Even here, unfortunately, one could still resort to the claim that some supposed initial state was not in fact the initial state.)

3.5 Interlanguage representation: defective or not?

Hypotheses about the interlanguage initial state can be broadly classified into two types, as described above. On the one hand are proposals that the initial state is a grammar, the L1 grammar, in whole or in part. This contrasts with the position that the initial state is not yet a language-specific grammar but, rather, UG itself. All the hypotheses that we have considered in this chapter agree that L2 learners can acquire functional categories and feature values not instantiated in the L1, though not necessarily immediately. Despite their differences over the nature of the initial state, all these positions agree that interlanguage representations are constrained by UG. Indeed, all these hypotheses are full access theories in some sense.

Nevertheless, although UG availability is assumed, the various hypotheses differ quite radically in terms of their assumptions about the nature of an interlanguage grammar. There is disagreement over: (a) whether or not a full complement of functional categories is initially available; (b) whether or not L1 functional categories and feature values are found in the initial state; (c) whether or not default feature values or inert feature values occur. There is another area of disagreement, which is the logical outcome of these different views on the nature of the grammar, which relates to the issue of 'completeness'. On the one hand are theories that presuppose that any particular interlanguage grammar will be complete, in the sense that it will manifest a full complement of lexical and functional categories, features and feature strength. In other words, the interlanguage grammar is a grammar with all the properties of natural languages (though not necessarily the L2) and interlanguage grammars are not wild (in the sense discussed in chapter 2). The Full Transfer Full Access Hypothesis falls into this category, since the initial state is the L1 representation, a natural-language grammar, manifesting L1 functional categories, features and feature values. When the grammar is subsequently restructured, it remains a natural-language grammar. Similarly, Full Access without Transfer is of this type, as is the Initial Hypothesis of Syntax; the interlanguage representation is always a fully fledged, UG-constrained grammar, including functional categories, features and feature values (though these are not seen as stemming from the L1).

In contrast, the Minimal Trees Hypothesis and the Valueless Features Hypothesis imply that an interlanguage grammar in early stages is in some sense temporarily defective or impaired, in that it lacks properties that are assumed to be given by UG and that are found in the grammars of adult native speakers. As we have seen, the Minimal Trees Hypothesis assumes that functional categories are initially lacking; in other words, not all UG properties are available at once. The Valueless Features Hypothesis assumes that feature strength is initially inert. In both cases, the idea is that these properties will eventually be acquired.

This view of early grammars as temporarily lacking certain characteristics contrasts with yet another position, whereby the interlanguage grammar is said to suffer from permanent impairment. Beck (1998a) argues for the Local Impairment Hypothesis, whereby inert features are not just a property of early grammars; rather, feature strength is never acquirable, on this view. As a result, the interlanguage grammar is different in nature from the L1 grammar, from the L2 grammar, and from natural-language grammars in general. In other words, the interlanguage representation is never fully UG-constrained. This impairment is considered to be quite local, confined to feature strength (possibly only strength of Infl-related features). Others argue that interlanguage grammars suffer from more global impairment, being quite different from natural languages, and not being UG-constrained at all (Meisel 1997). Whether the impairment is local or global, interlanguage grammars are effectively wild on these views. We will consider these views and their implications in more detail in chapter 4.

3.6 Conclusion

In this chapter, we have considered claims about the initial state, comparing several hypotheses that have focused on the nature and role of functional categories and their features in early interlanguage grammars. Full Access without Transfer and Full Transfer Full Access would seem to represent the most logical possibilities, at least in principle: either UG is the initial state or the L1 grammar is the initial state. The Minimal Trees Hypothesis and the Valueless Features Hypothesis fall somewhere in between: neither UG in its entirety nor the L1 in its entirety constitute the initial state. These two proposals are influenced by corresponding hypotheses for L1 acquisition, Minimal Trees by the Weak Continuity Hypothesis and Valueless Features by the hypothesis that features can be underspecified in L1 acquisition (Wexler 1994). Even if such hypotheses are correct for L1 acquisition (and this is much debated), the motivation for assuming that they apply to L2 grammars is not strong.

While many of the hypotheses considered in this chapter are directed specifically at the initial state, they also make predictions for later development and ultimate attainment, topics that will be considered in later chapters.

Topics for discussion

- The initial-state proposals discussed in this chapter crucially depend on the assumption that UG is not transformed into a particular grammar in the course of L1 acquisition. If UG does turn into a language-specific grammar, what are the implications for theories of L2 acquisition?
- Several L1 acquisition theories assume that early grammars are in some sense defective (even though this is not always recognized). For example, underspecified Tense (Wexler 1994) or underspecified number (Hoekstra and Hyams 1998) appear to be characteristic only of grammars in the course of acquisition. Does this mean that grammars in L1 acquisition can, after all, be wild? What are the implications?
- According to Lakshmanan and Selinker (2001), theories that argue for transfer (whether full or partial) are in danger of incurring the comparative

fallacy. That is, if interlanguage data are to be assessed in their own right, then it is as much of a problem to try and explain them in terms of the L1 grammar as it is to compare the interlanguage grammar with the L2 grammar. Do you agree?

- Design a series of 'thought experiments' to show how one might falsify each of the hypotheses discussed in this chapter.

Suggestions for additional reading

- A special issue of *Second Language Research* (vol. 12.1, 1996), edited by Schwartz and Eubank, is devoted to the initial state, containing some of the papers discussed in this chapter.
- Hawkins (2001a) proposes a combination of Minimal Trees and Full Transfer. He concurs with Vainikka and Young-Scholten that the initial state has only lexical categories. However, when functional categories emerge, his assumption is that they show L1 characteristics. Hawkins argues against Full Access in the functional domain (see chapter 4).

4

Grammars beyond the initial state: parameters and functional categories

4.1 Introduction

In the previous chapter, a variety of hypotheses were considered as to the nature of the grammatical representations adopted by learners in the earliest stages of L2 acquisition. In this chapter, we examine developing interlanguage grammars, exploring the issue of whether grammars change over time and, if so, in what respects. We will consider whether interlanguage grammars can be characterized in terms of parameters of UG, concentrating particularly on the situation that obtains when the L1 and L2 differ in parameter values.

As discussed in chapter 2, there is considerable evidence to suggest that interlanguage grammars are constrained by invariant principles of UG, since learners are sensitive to subtle properties of the L2 that are underdetermined by the input. L2 learners successfully acquire highly abstract unconscious knowledge, despite a poverty of the L2 stimulus, suggesting that this knowledge must originate from UG. Nevertheless, in some cases one cannot totally eliminate the L1 as the source of such abstract knowledge: even where languages differ considerably at the surface level, the same universal principles may apply at a more abstract level. For this reason, the issue of parameters and parameter resetting is of crucial importance in assessing the role of UG in L2 acquisition. If the L1 and L2 differ in their parameter settings and if the learner's linguistic behaviour is consistent with parameter values appropriate for the L2, this strongly supports the position that UG constrains interlanguage grammars. Conversely, failure to achieve L2 parameter settings is often taken as clear evidence against a role for UG. However, it will be suggested in this chapter (and subsequently) that failure to acquire L2 parameter settings does not necessarily indicate failure of UG.

4.2 Parameters in interlanguage grammars

In this chapter, we will consider two general positions, as well as two subcategories within each, on the status of parameters in interlanguage grammars.

The first position argues for a breakdown in parametric systems, either global or local. The implication of global breakdown is that there are no parameters at all in interlanguage grammars; claims for more local breakdown, on the other hand, assume that parameters are found in interlanguage grammars but that some of them are defective.

Proponents of global breakdown in the parameter system include Clahsen and Hong (1995) and Neeleman and Weerman (1997), who argue that interlanguage grammars are construction specific, hence very different from UG-constrained grammars. Their claim is that, in L2 acquisition, each construction theoretically associated with a given parameter has to be learned separately, on a construction-by-construction basis. According to some researchers, this is achieved by means of what is often called *pattern matching*: the learner concentrates on surface properties, unconsciously taking account of similarities and differences across various linguistic forms (Bley-Vroman 1997). Such proposals are characteristic of the Fundamental Difference Hypothesis (Bley-Vroman 1990), according to which UG does not constrain interlanguage grammars (or does so only weakly, by means of properties that can be 'reconstructed' via the L1).

Claims for a more local breakdown in interlanguage parameters are made in the context of feature strength. Extending the Valueless Features Hypothesis (see chapter 3, section 3.2.3), Beck (1998a) argues that 'inert' feature values are a permanent property of interlanguage grammars. In consequence, some parameters are never set, neither the L1 value nor the L2 value being realized in the interlanguage grammar.

Breakdown (whether global or local) implies that there will be impairment to grammatical representations: interlanguage grammars are not fully UG-constrained and may demonstrate properties which are not otherwise characteristic of natural language. In other words, they are in some sense defective or 'wild' (see chapter 2, section 2.3).

The alternative perspective maintains that interlanguage grammars are unimpaired: they can be characterized in terms of UG parameters and in general exhibit properties of natural language. Again, there are two types of account which fall into this category. The first is the No Parameter Resetting Hypothesis, according to which only L1 parameter settings are exemplified in interlanguage grammars (Hawkins 1998; Hawkins and Chan 1997). Since the L1 is a natural language, interlanguage grammars can indeed be described in terms of UG parameters. However, the range of parametric options is totally restricted, 'new' parameter settings being unavailable.

The No Parameter Resetting Hypothesis contrasts with the hypothesis that parameters can be reset. That is, interlanguage grammars can realize parameter values distinct from those found in the L1; these values may either be appropriate for the

L2 or they may be settings found in other languages. Thus, full access to UG is assumed, with new parameter values being, in principle, achievable. Most of the initial-state hypotheses considered in chapter 3 adopt this view. According to the Full Transfer Full Access Hypothesis, parameters in interlanguage grammars will initially be set at the values that obtain in the L1 (i.e. full transfer). In response to L2 input, parameters can be reset to values more appropriate to the L2 (i.e. full access). On this kind of account, developing grammars will be characterized by parameter resetting, from the L1 value to some other value. According to Full Access without Transfer, on the other hand, L1 settings are never adopted; rather, appropriate L2 settings are, in principle, effective immediately.[1] On this view, then, there is parameter setting (as in L1 acquisition) but there is no need for resetting.

To sum up, in the rest of this chapter four perspectives on parameters in interlanguage grammars will be considered: (i) global impairment, implying no parameters at all; (ii) local impairment, or breakdown in the case of some parameters; (iii) no parameter resetting, according to which only L1 settings are available; (iv) parameter resetting, which assumes the possibility of acquiring parameter settings distinct from those found in the L1. Under the first two views, interlanguage grammars fail to conform to properties of natural language. Under the two latter perspectives, interlanguage grammars are natural-language systems in which parameters are instantiated.

4.3 Global impairment

If interlanguage grammars are constrained by UG, syntactic and morphological properties related by a single parameter should cluster together. In other words, characteristics typical of either the L1 parameter setting or the L2 setting should be exemplified. Given a range of phenomena which are associated together under a particular parameter setting, these same phenomena should be characteristic of the interlanguage grammar and should, ideally, be acquired at more or less the same time. Consequently, researchers who argue against parameters in L2 acquisition seek to support their position by demonstrating the absence of clustering effects in interlanguage grammars.

4.3.1 *Breakdown of the Null Subject Parameter*

One such case is advanced by Clahsen and Hong (1995: 59), who put forward what they call the 'weak UG' view. On this view, while the grammars of adult learners are constrained by UG principles (via the L1), access to parameters has been lost. In other words, there is a total breakdown in the domain of parameters only; principles remain intact (or intact in so far as they are found in the L1 grammar). Clahsen and Hong's hypothesis is that properties that would 'co-vary' (i.e. cluster) under some parameter setting in L1 acquisition no longer do so in L2 acquisition.

In order to investigate this hypothesis, Clahsen and Hong look at adult L2 acquisition of German by speakers of Korean, in the context of the Null Subject Parameter. (See chapter 1, section 1.4.) Korean is a [+null subject] language, permitting empty subjects in a variety of contexts. German, in contrast, is a [–null subject] language; subjects must be overt, with a few limited exceptions. Examples in (1) and (2), from Korean and German respectively, illustrate the relevant properties (Clahsen and Hong's (4)). As can be seen by comparing (2) and (3), subject pronouns must be overt in German.

(1) Peter-ka Inge-lul sarangha-n-tako malha-n-ta.
Peter-NOM Inge-ACC love-PRES-that say-PRES-DEC
'Peter says that (he) loves Inge.'

(2) *Peter sagt, dass Inge liebt.
Peter says that Inge loves
'Peter says that (he) loves Inge.'

(3) Peter sagt, dass er Inge liebt.
Peter says that he Inge loves
'Peter says that he loves Inge.'

Clahsen and Hong adopt an account that attributes the distribution of null subjects to two independent but interacting parameters (Jaeggli and Safir 1989; Rizzi 1986). On the one hand, null subjects must be *licensed*. That is, there must be some property that permits null subjects in principle. Licensing is a necessary but not a sufficient condition. In addition to being licensed, a null subject must be *identified*. In order to interpret a missing argument, one must be able to work out what it refers to; there must be some way of recovering the content of the null subject from other properties of the sentence. Various types of identification have been proposed in the literature. Rich verbal agreement (formalized in terms of so-called *phi-features* in Agr) allows null subjects to be identified in Romance languages such as Italian and Spanish (see Jaeggli and Safir 1989 for an overview). In languages lacking agreement, such as Chinese, Japanese and Korean, a preceding topic in the discourse provides the means to identify a null element (Huang 1984).

Null subjects are in fact licensed in German as well as Korean. (Hence, German permits null expletives, which do not need to be identified, since they are non-referential.) Thus, the licensing parameter value is the same in both languages. The two languages differ, however, as to identification. Null subjects are identified in Korean by a preceding topic. German, on the other hand, is a language with

Table 4.1 *Licensing and identification of null subjects*

	Korean	German	Italian
Licensed	Yes	Yes	Yes
Identified	Yes, via topics	No	Yes
		Agr = [−pronominal]	Agr = [+pronominal]

relatively rich verbal agreement. Even so, null subjects cannot be identified. This is because Agr lacks the feature [+pronominal], required for identification purposes. In Romance null subject languages, on the other hand, Agr is [+pronominal] and null subjects can be identified. These differences are summarized in table 4.1 (adapted from Clahsen and Hong's (5)).

In the case of German L2 acquisition, Korean speakers have to reset the parameter that determines how null subjects are identified. They have to establish two things: (i) German is a language with agreement; (ii) Agr is non-pronominal. According to Clahsen and Hong, in the L1 acquisition of German, these two properties co-vary. That is, children allow null subjects in L1 German until they acquire the agreement paradigm (Clahsen 1990/1991; Clahsen and Penke 1992). Once subject-verb agreement is acquired, subjects are used systematically. In other words, when agreement emerges in L1 German, the child recognizes that Agr is [−pronominal] and null subjects are eliminated from the grammar.[2]

According to Clahsen and Hong (1995), if properties have been shown to co-vary in L1 acquisition, in this case, presence of agreement (non-pronominal Agr) with absence of null subjects, then one expects the same to obtain in L2 acquisition if parameters are unimpaired. If such clustering fails to occur, this demonstrates that interlanguage grammars cannot be characterized in terms of UG parameters. Clahsen and Hong test for evidence of clustering, using the sentence-matching procedure, which requires subjects to identify pairs of sentences as the same or different (see chapter 3, section 3.2.3.1). Recall that it takes native speakers longer to recognize ungrammatical sentence pairs as being the same (Freedman and Forster 1985). Clahsen and Hong hypothesize that, if L2 learners have successfully acquired the German value of the identification parameter, it should take longer to recognize ungrammatical sentence pairs involving incorrect agreement than grammatical pairs with correct agreement; at the same time, ungrammatical pairs with null subjects should take longer than grammatical pairs with lexical subjects. (See box 4.1 for examples of the stimuli.)

As a group, the native speakers showed significant differences in response times to grammatical and ungrammatical sentence pairs, being slower on the ungrammatical sentences, as expected. This was true of sentences testing for ± agreement,

Box 4.1 Global impairment – null subjects (Clahsen and Hong 1995)

Languages: L1 = Korean, L2 = German.
Task: Sentence matching.
Sample stimuli:

Grammatical (+agreement)	Grammatical (−null subjects)
Peter und Inge wohnen in Düsseldorf Peter und Inge wohnen in Düsseldorf (*Peter and Inge live-3PL in Düsseldorf*)	Maria sagt, dass sie die Zeitung liest Maria sagt, dass sie die Zeitung liest (*Maria says that she the newspaper reads*)
Ungrammatical (−agreement)	**Ungrammatical (+null subjects)**
Peter und Inge wohnt in Düsseldorf Peter und Inge wohnt in Düsseldorf (*Peter and Inge lives-3SG in Düsseldorf*)	Maria sagt, dass oft die Zeitung liest Maria sagt, dass oft die Zeitung liest (*Maria says that often the newspaper reads*)

Results:

Table 4.1.1 *Numbers of subjects whose grammars show clustering*

L2 learners (n = 33)		−agreement	+agreement
	+null subject	2	5
	−null subject	13	13
Native speakers (n = 20)			
	+null subject	0	1
	−null subject	1	18

as well as sentences testing for ±null subjects. In order to determine whether these properties do or do not co-vary in the grammars of individuals, Clahsen and Hong present results in terms of how individuals behave with respect to the two properties in question. (See table 4.1.1.) Native speakers are predicted to respond faster to grammatical pairs with overt subjects, showing that they know that German is not a null-subject language [–null subject], as well as to grammatical agreement pairs, showing that they know that German is a language with overt agreement [+agreement]; 18 out of 20 native speakers behaved as predicted. In other words, almost all native speakers recognized the necessity of agreement in German at the same time as recognizing the impossibility of null subjects.

The L2 learners presented a more varied picture. (See table 4.1.1.) Thirteen out of 33 of the Korean speakers showed the same response pattern as the controls, namely slower responses to the ungrammatical sentences of both types, suggesting that they had successfully reset the parameter, recognizing that German requires overt subjects and agreement. Clahsen and Hong suggest that these learners may simply have acquired the two properties independently but this, of course, is also true of the native speakers. When looking at properties of a grammar at a particular point in time, one cannot tell what the grammar might have been like at an earlier stage. This requires comparing subjects at different stages of development or following the same subjects over an extended period of time.

Two subjects failed to distinguish in their response times between grammatical and ungrammatical sentences in either condition. This behaviour, in fact, is consistent with operating under the L1 value of the parameter: they have not yet acquired the fact that German requires agreement and overt subjects, treating it, rather, as a null subject language without agreement, like Korean. Of more interest are the subjects whose response latencies show a significant grammaticality effect for only one of the two properties (±agreement or ±null subjects). Five subjects failed to distinguish in their response times between overt and null subject sentences, suggesting that the interlanguage is [+null subject]. At the same time, they did distinguish in their response times between sentences with correct and incorrect agreement, suggesting that the interlanguage is [+agreement]. Thirteen subjects showed the reverse pattern; in their interlanguage grammars, German is not a null subject language but it also does not have overt agreement. In these cases, the two properties fail to co-vary, which is taken by Clahsen and Hong as evidence of a failure of parameters; the presence of agreement is presumed to be the trigger for loss of null subjects, so one should not be able to have one without the other.

However, an alternative account is possible. Clahsen and Hong's assumption about the co-varying of agreement and the requirement for overt subjects is clearly incorrect for languages like Italian, where rich agreement and null subjects coincide because Agr is [+pronominal] (see table 4.1). Indeed, the results of the five Korean speakers who distinguished in response latencies between the ungrammatical and grammatical agreement pairs but not between pairs with or without null subjects are consistent with the Italian value of the identification parameter. While it may be true that these Korean speakers may not have acquired the German parameter value, they appear to have acquired a value other than the Korean one, treating German like Italian, a null subject language with rich agreement. If learners of German acquire rich agreement while also treating Agr as [+pronominal], this is precisely the result one would expect. On such an analysis, null subjects are grammatical and agreement is grammatical, hence learners show response latency differences in the case of the ±agreement sentences but not in the case of the ±null subject sentences.

Assuming this reanalysis of Clahsen and Hong's results, 20 of their 33 subjects demonstrated behaviour consistent with some value of the identification parameter (Korean value, German value or Italian value). On the other hand, the results from the remaining 13 subjects who took longer on the sentence pairs involving null subjects but did not distinguish between grammatical and ungrammatical agreement pairs are, ostensibly, more supportive of Clahsen and Hong's claim that there are no parameters in interlanguage grammars.

Even here it is not necessarily the case that the results are as problematic as Clahsen and Hong suggest. Like Vainikka and Young-Scholten (1994, 1996a, b) and Eubank (1993/1994, 1994, 1996), Clahsen and Hong equate acquisition of abstract agreement with accuracy in surface morphology. However, as will be discussed in greater detail in chapter 6, there is a difference between having abstract features or categories (in this case, agreement) realized in the grammar and knowing the particular surface morphology associated with them. L2 learners might know that German has agreement at an abstract level, and that this is non-pronominal. At the same time, they might not yet have fully acquired the morphology by which agreement is realized on the surface, thus failing to recognize deviant morphology in some cases. If so, the failure to show differences in response times between grammatical and ungrammatical sentence pairs testing agreement is relatively uninformative. We simply cannot tell what the status of abstract agreement is in these grammars, hence we cannot conclude anything about this group of subjects. (In later chapters, we will address in more detail the question of how one can show that some property is present at an abstract level in the absence of appropriate morphology.) In contrast, in the case of learners who do distinguish between sentence pairs involving grammatical and ungrammatical agreement morphology, it seems reasonable to conclude that they have both the relevant abstract representation and the appropriate surface realization.

A methodological issue with the sentence-matching procedure is worth mentioning here, relating to the sentence pairs contrasting overt and null subjects. At issue is whether learners distinguish between grammatical pairs of sentences like (3) and ungrammatical pairs like (2). The sentence-matching methodology requires that grammatical and ungrammatical pairs be of equivalent length, so that grammaticality is the only difference between them. Since a sentence with an overt subject is longer than one without an explicit subject, Clahsen and Hong insert adverbs in the null subject sentences (see examples in box 4.1). This means that the grammatical and ungrammatical pairs differ in two ways, presence versus absence of an overt subject and presence versus absence of an adverb. Thus, it is not clear that the sentence-matching procedure is in fact successful in isolating the relevant property, making the results harder to interpret.

4.3.2 Breakdown of a word-order parameter

Using the Null Subject Parameter as a particular example, Clahsen and Hong (1995) argue that there are no parameters in L2 acquisition, based on presumed absence of clustering. In this section, we will continue to pursue this issue, considering another parameter, the OV/VO parameter (Neeleman and Weerman 1997). If interlanguage representations do not conform to UG parameter settings, the issue arises as to the nature of the interlanguage grammatical system in the absence of parameters. Learners must nevertheless come up with analyses of the L2 input; they must be able to interpret and produce L2 sentences. A number of researchers have proposed that interlanguage grammars differ from native-speaker grammars in being 'construction specific' (Bley-Vroman 1996, 1997).

One explicit proposal for a construction-specific interlanguage grammar is advanced by Neeleman and Weerman (1997) who maintain that the grammars of L1 acquirers (and adult native speakers) are constrained by a word-order parameter which is lacking in the interlanguage grammars of L2 learners. The parameter that they propose is the OV/VO parameter, which accounts for head-final or head-initial word order crosslinguistically.[3] Dutch and English, the languages under investigation, differ as to the values of this parameter that they instantiate. The settings of the parameter, as Neeleman and Weerman conceive it, have a range of associated consequences, namely: (i) whether or not scrambling is permitted (that is, whether the direct object can appear distant from the verb which assigns case to it); (ii) the distribution of particles; (iii) the possibility of extraction of objects from particle constructions; and (iv) exceptional case marking (ECM) (that is, the ability of some verbs to case mark an embedded subject). The properties in question are listed in table 4.2.

Examples are given in (4) to (8) (from Neeleman and Weerman 1997). The sentences in (4) show the basic word-order difference between Dutch, where VPs are head final, and English, where VPs are head initial. In (5), we see that the direct object in Dutch can be scrambled; that is, it does not have to occur adjacent to the verb, in contrast to English. The sentences in (6) show that particles like *up* in English can appear before or after the direct object, whereas in Dutch the particle must be adjacent to the verb. A further property of particle constructions is illustrated in (7): in both languages, extraction of a phrase from within the object of

Table 4.2 *The OV/VO parameter*

Word order	OV	VO
Scrambling	+	–
	O adverb V	* V adverb O
Particles	Prt V	V (X) Prt
	Always adjacent	May be separated
Extraction from object of particle verb	+	+/–
ECM	–	+

a verb-particle construction is possible if the verb and particle are adjacent. Where the verb and particle are separated (only possible in English), such extraction is not permitted. Finally, (8) illustrates contrasts in exceptional case marking, where the subject of a non-finite embedded clause receives accusative case from the verb in a higher clause. This is not possible in Dutch (except to a very limited extent) but is possible in English.

(4) OV vs. VO
a. Ik heb de poes gezien.
I have the cat seen
b. I have seen the cat.

(5) Scrambling vs. case adjacency (O adv V/*V adv O)
a. ... dat Jan langzaam het boek las.
... that John slowly the book read
b. ... dat Jan het boek longzaam las.
... that John the book slowly read
c. John read the book slowly.
d. *John read slowly the book.

(6) Particles
a. ... dat Jan Marie geregeld uit lacht.
... that John Mary regularly out laughs
b. ... *dat Jan Marie uit geregeld lacht.
... that John Mary out regularly laughs
c. John looks up the information.
d. John looks the information up.

(7) Extraction from object of a verb particle construction
a. Waar heeft Jan informatie over op gezocht?
what has John information about up looked
b. What did John look up information about?
c. *What did John look information about up?

(8) ECM

a. *dat Jan Marie verwacht Shakespeare te lezen.
   that John Mary expects Shakespeare to read

b. John expects Mary to read Shakespeare.

The question arises as to how to determine whether a set of syntactic properties is indeed unified under some parameter setting in L1 acquisition. If structures which have been independently identified on linguistic grounds as likely to fall under some parameter emerge at about the same time, this is usually considered to provide strong support for the claim that they are indeed associated under some parameter setting (Hyams 1986; Snyder 1995a; Snyder and Stromswold 1997). Because other factors, such as sentence complexity, may come into play, Neeleman and Weerman make the questionable assumption that the crucial issue is not that the properties in question should be acquired together but that they be acquired in an error-free manner. However, this proposal is problematic: there are many things that children acquire in an error-free manner which should not be included in this particular parameter. Furthermore, there are properties associated with parameters in L1 acquisition that are not acquired in an error-free manner. (For example, according to the analysis of null subjects offered by Clahsen and Hong (section 4.3.1), German-speaking children initially mistakenly assume that German is a null subject language, with topic identification of null subjects.)

Using spontaneous production data available on the CHILDES database (MacWhinney 1995), as well as from other sources, Neeleman and Weerman show that basic word-order acquisition is error free for both Dutch and English acquired as first languages. As for scrambling, violations of case adjacency by children learning English are non-existent. Rather, verbs and direct objects are found together and are never interrupted by some other constituent such as an adverb. In L1 Dutch, on the other hand, both scrambled and non-scrambled word orders are found. (In fact, Neeleman and Weerman are incorrect in stating that acquisition of scrambling is error free in L1 Dutch. Schaeffer (2000) shows that Dutch 2-year-olds fail to scramble in contexts where scrambling is obligatory for adults.) ECM constructions are common in L1 English and infrequent in L1 Dutch, where they are limited to the subset of contexts in which they can occur in that language. In the case of verb-particle constructions, in the Dutch L1 data, the particle is always adjacent to the verb, whereas in English it appears either adjacent or separated. Neeleman and Weerman offer no data on extraction of objects from verb-particle constructions on the grounds that the relevant constructions do not occur in early L1 data from either language. To summarize, the L1 data suggest early acquisition of word order (OV/VO) and somewhat later acquisition of the associated properties, while for one of them there is no relevant evidence.

strength is considered to be permanently impaired. Thus, there is predicted to be no development in this domain; even the grammars of advanced interlanguage speakers are assumed to suffer from this impairment. The second difference is that Beck does not assume a causal relationship between overt morphology and feature strength. Even if learners show evidence of development in the domain of morphology, this is not expected to have effects on verb raising: interlanguage feature strength will remain impaired even if inflectional morphology is totally accurate.

4.4.1 *Local impairment: evidence*

Beck tests the Local Impairment Hypothesis in the context of the adult L2 acquisition of German by speakers of English. As discussed in chapter 1 (section 1.4.1), VP and IP in German are underlyingly head final. In main clauses, the finite verb moves to C (via I), in order to check strong features. Some other constituent raises to the Spec of CP, resulting in verb second (V2). In the case of a grammatical sentence like (9a), the verb has raised to C, while the subject, *Maria*, has moved to Spec CP. In (9b), it is the adverb which has moved to Spec CP; consequently the subject remains in Spec IP. The sentence in (9c) is ungrammatical because the verb has failed to raise from final position.

(9)
a. [$_{CP}$ Maria$_j$ trinkt$_i$ [$_{IP}$ t$_j$ [oft [$_{VP}$ Kaffee t$_i$] t$_i$]]
   Maria drinks often coffee
b. [$_{CP}$ Jetzt$_j$ trinkt$_i$ [$_{IP}$ Maria [t$_j$ [$_{VP}$ Kaffee t$_i$] t$_i$]]
   Now drinks Maria coffee
c. *[Maria [oft [$_{VP}$ Kaffee trinkt]]]
   Maria often coffee drinks

According to the Local Impairment Hypothesis, feature strength in interlanguage grammars is impaired. In the absence of strong or weak features, placement of the finite verb in simple clauses is expected to be optional, such that it sometimes remains in the VP (unraised) and sometimes occurs in the V2 position (raised to C).[4]

Beck used a translation task (English to German) to establish whether learners ever produce raised verbs; correct translations of three of the sentences would require the verb to precede the subject, as in (9b), demonstrating unambiguously that it must have moved out of the VP into C. On the basis of this task, Beck divided subjects into two groups, an 'inversion' group who demonstrated evidence of verb raising to C (although three test items are hardly sufficient to establish this point), and a 'no inversion' group who failed to do so. The implication appears to be that the former are more proficient than the latter.

Box 4.3 Local Impairment Hypothesis (Beck 1998a)

Languages: L1 = English, L2 = German.
Task: Sentence matching.
Sample stimuli:

Grammatical (V-raising – SVAO)	Ungrammatical (No raising – SAVO)
Der Nachbar kauft bald das Bier. Der Nachbar kauft bald das Bier. *(The neighbour buys soon the beer.)*	Der Lehrer erst kauft einen Saft. Der Lehrer erst kauft einen Saft. *(The teacher first buys a juice.)*

Results:

Table 4.3.1 *Mean response times (z-scores)*

		V-raising (# = 15)	No raising (# = 15)	
L2 groups	No inversion (n = 21)	−0.0878	0.0878	sig
	Inversion (n = 26)	−0.0316	0.0175	ns
Native speakers (n = 27)		−0.1385	0.1403	sig

The main task was a sentence-matching task. Test sentences consisted of grammatical pairs like (9a) as well as ungrammatical pairs like (10). (See box 4.3.)

(10) *Maria oft trinkt Kaffee.
Mary often drinks coffee

One might question why Beck's ungrammatical sentences do not take the form of (9c), namely, SOV order without verb raising. This is because she assumes, along with Full Transfer Full Access, Minimal Trees and Valueless Features, that the initial-state grammar of English-speaking learners of German will have SVO as the basic word order, this being the order found in the L1. Thus, in her experiment, L2 learners are being assessed on whether or not the English order in (10) is grammatical for them as well as the German order in (9a).

According to the Local Impairment Hypothesis, verb raising is predicted to be optional regardless of acquisition stage, because feature strength is impaired in initial and subsequent grammars. This predicts the following for both groups of L2 learners: regardless of how they performed on the translation task, there will be no differences in response latencies in the sentence-matching task to sentence pairs with raised or unraised verbs, since they are both presumed to be grammatical in grammars with impaired feature strength. For native speakers of German, on the other hand, response latencies to sentence pairs like (10) should be significantly slower than to pairs where the verb has raised, as in (9a).

Controls responded as predicted, that is, their response times to the grammatical sentence pairs were significantly faster than to the ungrammatical pairs. (See table 4.3.1.) L2 learners, on the other hand, did not behave as expected. The 'no inversion' group, like the native speakers, showed a significant difference between grammatical and ungrammatical pairs, taking longer to respond to the latter. This is unexpected on the Local Impairment Hypothesis; this group should have treated both sentence types alike if their grammars are characterized by optionality. The 'inversion' group's results are consistent with the hypothesis: their response latencies to the two sentence types were not significantly different, apparently supportive of the claim for optional verb raising.

However, these results are problematic for the Local Impairment Hypothesis as well. Beck does not in fact establish what the underlying interlanguage word order is for any of her subjects. Even if she is correct in assuming that some subjects still treat German as underlyingly SVO, one would expect more proficient learners (as the 'inversion' group presumably are) no longer to adopt the L1 English SVO order but, rather, to have restructured to SOV. (See du Plessis et al. (1987) and Vainikka and Young-Scholten (1994) for evidence of restructuring from SVO to SOV in L2 German.) Recall that Beck's ungrammatical test pairs do not include sentences with unraised verbs in final position (such as (9c)). Yet, for a grammar with appropriate SOV order, it is precisely such sentences that should have been compared to the grammatical sentences like (9a). In the absence of the relevant data, it is hard to accept that this group has optional verb raising in German.

In summary, the experimental evidence for impaired features as a permanent property of interlanguage grammars is not compelling. Beck's results are problematic for the Local Impairment Hypothesis. The 'no inversion' group behaved like native speakers on the sentence-matching task, distinguishing between grammatical and ungrammatical sentences, contrary to expectations. Although the 'inversion' group failed to make this distinction, it is not clear that the sentence types being tested were in fact appropriate.

4.4.2 Local Impairment: assessment

The Local Impairment Hypothesis suffers from the same conceptual problems as the Valueless Features Hypothesis. The claim that features are inert or impaired, and that the consequence of this impairment is variability in verb placement, is stipulative. It does not follow from any theory of the effects of feature strength on grammars. Nor is it clear why impairment should be confined to strength of features in I and C. As noted in chapter 3 (section 3.2.3.2), in the absence of strong features, there should be no raising at all, rather than optional verb raising (Robertson and Sorace 1999; Schwartz 1998b; Schwartz and Sprouse 2000b).

There is also a question of plausibility: what are the grounds (theoretical or empirical) for claiming that impairment is permanent? The Local Impairment Hypothesis would seem to predict that interlanguage grammars never recover from variability in verb placement. Beck (1997) recognizes that this is not in fact the case. In other words, advanced L2 speakers do not demonstrate the predicted variability. In consequence, Beck (1997) suggests that where L2 learners appear to perform in a manner appropriate for the L2, this is achieved not on the basis of the grammar itself but is due to the operation of additional, agrammatical, explicitly learned mechanisms that lead to superficially correct L2 performance. Such a proposal is only of interest if it can be demonstrated that there are in fact empirical differences between a grammar that has the relevant L2 properties and a grammar that lacks those properties but that can resort to additional 'patch up' mechanisms. Otherwise, it renders the Local Impairment Hypothesis unfalsifiable: in the event of 'success' in the acquisition of L2 word order (i.e. lack of variability), it can always be claimed that learners achieve the same surface performance as native speakers by radically different means.

4.5 UG-constrained grammars and parameter setting

So far, we have considered proposals that interlanguage grammars cannot be characterized in terms of parameter settings, instead being impaired either globally or locally, such that no parameters are instantiated at all or at least some parameters have broken down. The implication of impairment is that interlanguage grammars are not fully UG-constrained; rather, they demonstrate properties which are not characteristic of natural language in general. We now turn to the alternative, namely that interlanguage grammars can be characterized in terms of parameter settings. As we shall see, some researchers maintain that interlanguage grammars exemplify only L1 settings, others that only L2 settings are to be found, yet others argue for development and change in the form of parameter resetting, from the L1 value to the L2 value or to settings found in other languages. Regardless of these differences, these proposals share the intuition that interlanguage representations are unimpaired, in that they conform to possible parameter settings.

4.6 No parameter resetting

The first hypothesis to be considered in this context is the No Parameter Resetting Hypothesis. Although this position was not discussed in the context of initial-state proposals in chapter 3, it nevertheless carries an implicit initial-state claim, as well as an explicit claim about the kind of grammar development that can or cannot be expected. The interlanguage grammar is assumed to have recourse *only* to those parameter settings realized in the L1. Thus, this hypothesis differs from Full Transfer Full Access in claiming that there is no subsequent parameter resetting in response to L2 input – new parameter values cannot be acquired. Hence, representations like those of native speakers of the L2 will necessarily be unattainable whenever the L1 and L2 differ in parameter values. On this account, then, there is full transfer but not full access.

According to the No Parameter Resetting Hypothesis, the L1 grammar constitutes the learner's representation of the L2 initially and subsequently. Unlike the proposals discussed earlier in this chapter, parameters as such are not assumed to break down. Rather, the problem lies in resetting, which is considered to be impossible. However, some proponents of this hypothesis argue that the interlanguage grammar (with L1 settings) is able to accommodate L2 data that differ considerably from L1 data, imposing an analysis which is UG-constrained and L1-based, even though it has no exact parallel in the L1 (e.g. Tsimpli and Roussou 1991). Others argue that the effect of being restricted to L1 parameter settings is that learners have to resort to ad hoc local fixes to their grammars (Liceras 1997).

Smith and Tsimpli (1995: 24), advancing a version of the No-Parameter Resetting Hypothesis that emphasizes parameterization of functional categories, make the following claim:

> We will maintain that the set of functional categories constitutes a sub-module of UG, namely the UG lexicon. Each functional category is associated with an entry specified for relevant functional features . . . Parameterization is then defined in terms of a finite set of alternative values that a functional category can be associated with. Cross-linguistic variation is thus restricted to differences in the parametric values of functional categories . . . Moreover, if we assume that the critical period hypothesis is correct, maturational constraints on the functional module can be interpreted as entailing its complete inaccessibility after the end of this period . . . UG may still be available but parameter-setting cannot be.

It is not entirely clear from the above quotation whether 'values' refers to features of functional categories or to their strength. Here it will be assumed that both are intended. The implication of the claim for a functional module which becomes inaccessible is that no new functional categories, features or feature strength can be acquired by adult L2 learners.

4.6.1 No parameter setting: evidence

Following this line of reasoning, Hawkins and Chan (1997) propose the Failed Functional Features Hypothesis, according to which adult L2 learners are unable to acquire features differing from the those found in the L1. In spite of being restricted to L1 parameter values, the interlanguage grammar is able to generate representations that account for the L2 data and that fall within the general constraints of UG.

As described in chapter 1 (section 1.4.1), verbal features within C motivate verb raising in German, from V to I to C. Here, we consider another feature characteristic of the CP domain, namely a feature relevant to *wh*-movement. Hawkins and Chan investigate the acquisition of English restrictive relative clauses by native speakers of Cantonese. They assume a parametric difference between Chinese and English relating to presence or absence of a [± wh] feature in C.

In English, relative clauses can be introduced by a *wh*-phrase, by the complementizer *that*, or without any explicit indicator, as shown in (11a, b, c). The complementizer *that* cannot co-occur with an overt *wh*-phrase, as in (11d). Resumptive pronouns are not possible, as shown in (11e). (Examples in this section come from Hawkins and Chan (1997).)

(11) a. The girl who you like
b. The girl that you like
c. The girl you like
d. *The girl who that you like
e. *The girl who you like her

English relative clauses are derived by operator movement. An overt operator, such as a *wh*-phrase, or a null operator moves to the Spec of CP, leaving a variable (or trace) *t*. In English, C has a [± wh] feature (Rizzi 1990). It is this feature which motivates operator movement, in relative clauses as well as in *wh*-questions. The [wh] feature in English is strong. As a result, in relative clauses a *wh*-phrase has to move overtly into the Spec of CP to check the [+wh] feature in the head C (by Spec–head agreement); a null operator has to move if the feature is [–wh], again for feature checking purposes. The complementizer *that* is the lexical realization of [–wh] in C, hence it cannot co-occur with a *wh*-phrase in Spec CP because this would result in a feature clash ([–wh] in C but [+wh] in Spec). The structure of the relative clause is shown in (12); *wh*-movement is shown in (12a), corresponding to (11a), and null operator movement in (12b), corresponding to (11b) and (11c).

(12)

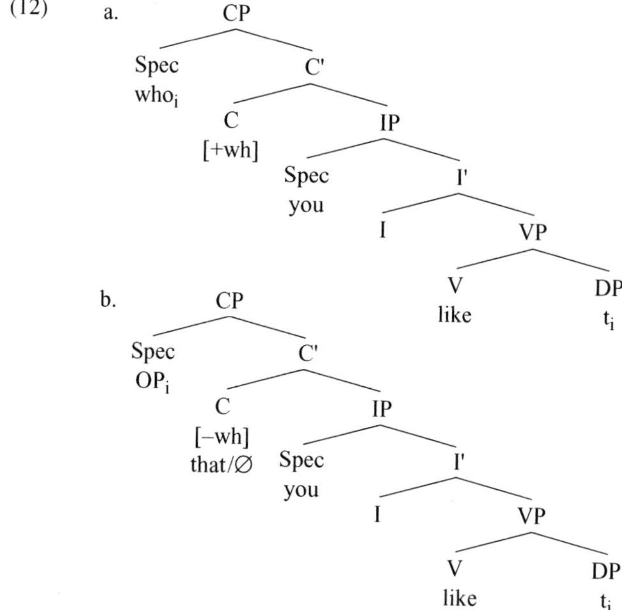

One other property of relative clauses is relevant. *Wh*-movement is constrained by a principle of UG known as Subjacency (Chomsky 1981a, b, 1986a), which prevents a *wh*-phrase from moving 'too far' from its original position. The specific formulation of Subjacency has changed over the years. In Government and Binding theory it was couched in terms of bounding nodes (Chomsky 1981a); subsequently, the constraint was expressed in terms of barriers (Chomsky 1986a). In either case, the idea is that a phrase which moves, such as a fronted *wh*-phrase occurring in questions or relative clauses, may not cross more than one bounding node or barrier at a time, where DP and IP are bounding nodes in English. In the relative clause in (13), *who* has crossed a contiguous DP and IP and the sentence is ungrammatical:

(13) *This is the boy [$_{CP}$ who$_i$ [$_{IP}$ Mary described [$_{DP}$ the way [$_{CP}$ t$_i$ that [$_{IP}$ Bill attacked t$_i$]]]]]

Relative clauses in Chinese are somewhat different from English; Mandarin and Cantonese are alike in the relevant respects. DPs containing relative clauses are head final. Relative clauses are introduced by complementizers (*ge* in Cantonese; *de* in Mandarin) rather than by *wh*-phrases. Resumptive pronouns are found where there would be an empty category in English. As can be seen in the Mandarin examples below, the resumptive pronoun can be overt, as in (14a), or it can be null, as in (14b). Where it is null, the assumption is that the empty category is *pro*, rather than a variable bound to a moved operator (Huang 1984; Xu and Langendoen 1985).

(14) a. Wo xihuan ta de neige nuhai.
I like her COMP that girl
'the girl that I like'
b. Wo xihuan de neige nuhai.
I like COMP that girl
'the girl that I like'

Chinese C, in contrast to English, is assumed to lack the [$\pm$wh] feature. As a result, there is no motivation for operator movement, since there is no strong feature in C requiring a *wh*-phrase or operator to move to Spec CP for feature checking. In consequence, there can be no variable within the relative clause in Chinese; instead, the relative clause contains either an overt resumptive pronoun or a null pronoun, *pro*, bound to a null topic, base-generated in the Spec of CP. This has consequences for Subjacency, as we shall see below. The structure of the Chinese relative clause is shown in (15), corresponding to (14):

(15)

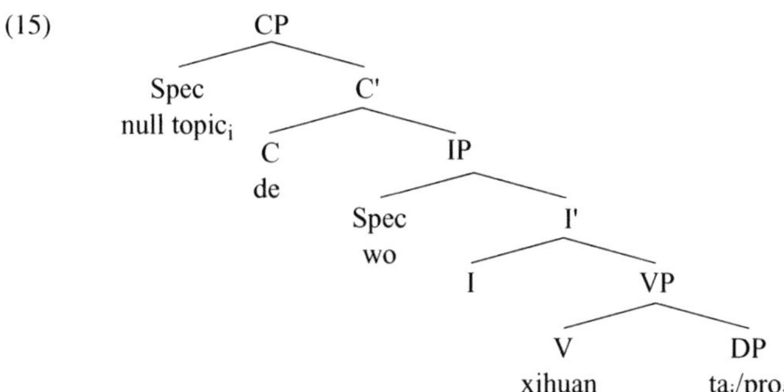

As far as Subjacency is concerned, Chinese sentences which superficially would appear to violate Subjacency are in fact grammatical, as the example in (16) shows (from Xu and Langendoen 1985).

(16) zheben shu$_i$ [$_{NP}$ [$_{IP}$ du guo *pro*$_i$ de] ren] bu duo
this book$_i$ read ASP *pro*$_i$ COMP man not many
'This book, the people who read (it) aren't many.'

Here, the topicalized DP (*this book*) is associated with an empty category within the relative clause, with a contiguous IP and NP intervening. Such structures are licit because the relationship between *pro* (a null resumptive pronoun) and the fronted phrase is not one of movement; rather, it is the same as the relationship between any pronoun and its antecedent, a relationship which is not subject to

Subjacency. Thus, the topic and *pro* can have two or more bounding nodes intervening between them.

Hawkins and Chan (1997) maintain that L2 learners have access only to those functional features instantiated in the L1. Since C in Chinese lacks a [wh] feature, the same will be true of C in the interlanguage grammar. Learners will be able to acquire the complementizer *that* but this will not be a lexical realization of [–wh]; rather, like *ge* in Cantonese or *de* in Mandarin, it will have no [wh] feature at all. The Failed Functional Features Hypothesis predicts that Cantonese speakers will not be able to derive English relative clauses by means of operator movement, hence that they will have particular difficulties in recognizing that resumptive pronouns and Subjacency violations are ungrammatical in English. In contrast, learners of English whose L1 also has a [wh] feature, such as French, should experience no such difficulties.

To test the predictions of the Failed Functional Features Hypothesis, an experiment was conducted. (See box 4.4.) Subjects were post-puberty learners of English (adolescents and young adults), with Cantonese or French as their mother tongue, at three different levels of L2 proficiency. If L2 learners have acquired the [wh] feature of English, they should acquire the associated properties of relative clauses, including knowledge of the grammaticality of sentences with fronted *wh*-phrases and a gap within the relative clause, as well as the prohibition against doubly filled comps (**who that*), resumptive pronouns and Subjacency violations. It is predicted that Chinese speakers will fail to acquire this knowledge, because of the lack of a [wh] feature in the L1, in contrast to French speakers.

These predictions were tested by means of a grammaticality-judgment task, which included a variety of grammatical and ungrammatical relative clauses. Results showed significant differences due to L1, with the French speakers at all levels of proficiency outperforming the Chinese on all aspects tested. (See table 4.4.1.) The advanced French speakers did not differ from the native-speaker controls and neither did the intermediate and elementary French speakers on some of the sentence types. There was significant improvement with increasing proficiency for both L1 groups, which would seem to argue against the Failed Functional Features Hypothesis. Although not attaining the level of performance of the French speakers, the Chinese speakers do show increasing accuracy on most aspects of English relative clauses. The advanced Chinese group appears to be quite successful in acquiring most properties of English relatives, such as fronting of *wh*-pronouns and the impossibility of resumptive pronouns.

According to Hawkins and Chan, these appearances are deceptive. They maintain that, in the interlanguage grammars of the Chinese speakers, relative clauses are not derived by operator movement. Instead, an L1-based analysis is adopted:

Box 4.4 No parameter resetting (Hawkins and Chan 1997)

Languages: L1 = Cantonese/French, L2 = English.
Task: Grammaticality judgments.
Sample stimuli:
Grammatical:

The boy who I hit broke the window.
The lady that I met yesterday was my former teacher.
The girl John likes is studying at the university.

Doubly filled CP: *The dog which that hurt a child ran away.
Resumptive pronoun: *The patient that I visited him was very sick.
Subjacency (CNPC): *This is the boy who Mary described the way that Bill attacked.

Results:

Table 4.4.1 *Accurate judgments (in %)*

		Grammatical sentences	Ungrammatical sentences		
			Double CP	Resumptives	Subjacency
L2 groups	Elementary (n = 47)	56	50	38	71
(L1 Chinese)	Intermediate (n = 46)	67	68	55	61
	Advanced (n = 54)	79	83	90	38
L2 groups	Elementary (n = 33)	81	91	81	72
(L1 French)	Intermediate (n = 40)	88	95	90	79
	Advanced (n = 40)	92	98	96	90
Native speakers (n = 32)		96	99	98	85

wh-phrases are base-generated as topics in Spec CP, binding a null resumptive *pro*, an analysis which falls within the bounds of UG (for similar proposals, see Martohardjono and Gair 1993; White 1992c). Evidence in favour of this analysis is as follows. If one looks at the results on relative clauses containing resumptive pronouns, the lower-proficiency Chinese speakers accept these to a considerable extent, in contrast to the advanced group who reject them with a high degree of accuracy. (See table 4.4.1.) At the same time, subjects at lower proficiency levels are significantly more likely to reject Subjacency violations than the advanced group. Hawkins and Chan suggest that what is going on here is a change from a requirement for overt resumptive pronouns (based on properties of the L1) to the recognition that English does not permit overt resumptives (based, presumably, on observations of the L2 data). The lower-proficiency learners accept overt resumptives in general; they reject Subjacency violations not because of Subjacency but because they are expecting an overt pronoun within the relative clause. The advanced group recognizes that English does not permit overt resumptives and instead assumes that the gap in a relative clause is a null resumptive *pro*. Hence, they accept apparent Subjacency violations, which are not in fact violations in their grammars, since no movement has taken place.

Hawkins and Chan's data show clear differences based on L1. French shares with English the property of having a [wh] feature, hence *wh*-movement in relatives. French speakers outperform Chinese speakers at every level of proficiency. While these results are taken as evidence of failed features in the interlanguage grammar, Hawkins and Chan nevertheless maintain that the Chinese speakers have shown evidence of accommodating L2 input in a way that is not simply the result of surface transfer, and in a way that is UG-consistent. Fronted *wh*-phrases, which would not be encountered in Chinese relative clauses, are interpreted as topics (an option available and much used in Chinese). However, there does seem to be something very odd about a grammar which permits null resumptives and disallows lexical ones; it is not clear that this is in fact a possibility realized elsewhere.

4.6.2 No parameter resetting: assessment

The No Parameter Resetting Hypothesis, including the Failed Functional Features Hypothesis, which is a particular version of the more general hypothesis, predicts that interlanguage grammars will be confined to L1 feature values, even if there is ample positive evidence to motivate resetting. Triggers for parameter setting in the input (see chapter 5) will be ignored, or can no longer function as triggers. Even though there appears to be ample positive evidence that English is a language with *wh*-movement, it is claimed that Chinese speakers are never able to acquire the [wh] feature because this is unrealized in the L1.

However, there are other results that suggest, contra Hawkins and Chan, that Chinese speakers are not confined to an interlanguage lacking a [wh] feature. If so, this would suggest that interlanguage grammars are not restricted to L1 feature values, even if these are initially adopted. While Hawkins and Chan are by no means alone in finding that speakers of East Asian languages have problems in recognizing Subjacency violations (e.g. Johnson and Newport 1991; Schachter 1989, 1990), there is evidence to show that high-proficiency Chinese speakers do acquire the relevant properties of English, at least with respect to *wh*-movement in questions. White and Juffs (1998) show that a group of Chinese-speaking learners of English who were immersed in English as adults in China performed extremely accurately on a timed grammaticality-judgment task involving Subjacency violations. These subjects did not differ significantly from the native-speaker controls in their rejections of ungrammatical sentences. These results are quite different from those reported by Hawkins and Chan (1997) and suggest that the [wh]feature had been acquired. (Most studies of Subjacency other than Hawkins and Chan have concentrated on *wh*-questions. *Wh*-questions in Chinese do involve a [+wh] feature but it is weak (i.e. there is no overt movement). Hawkins and Chan do not appear to take this into account.)

Another point is relevant, which again suggests that Chinese speakers cannot be limited to representations lacking a [± wh] feature. A distinction has been made between strong and weak violations of Subjacency (Chomsky 1986a; Cinque 1990). Some violations are relatively worse than others, in consequence of the number and types of barriers or bounding nodes that are crossed. For example, many people consider (17a), involving *wh*-movement from within the lower relative clause, to be worse than (17b), where extraction is from a complex NP.

(17) a. *This is the book which$_i$ John met a friend who had read t$_i$
 b. *?This is the book which$_i$ John heard a rumour that you had read t$_i$

If relative clauses (and other *wh*-structures) are not derived by movement but by base-generated topics associated with null resumptive pronouns, L2 learners should not treat strong and weak violations differently, since all 'violations' would be grammatical. However, several studies have shown that L2 learners of English whose L1s lack *wh*-movement nevertheless judge certain kinds of Subjacency violations as being worse than others (Epstein et al. 1996; Martohardjono 1993; Pérez-Leroux and Li 1998). Given an L1 without *wh*-movement, hence with no basis to make a distinction between strong and weak violations, such sensitivity goes beyond what could be established via the L1 grammar alone.

Finally, although Hawkins and Chan do not discuss this, the Failed Functional Features Hypothesis appears to predict that English-speaking learners of languages without syntactic *wh*-movement, such as Chinese, Japanese or Korean, will mistakenly assume *wh*-movement to be possible, in relative clauses and elsewhere. That is, they should be unable to lose the [± wh] feature in C, leading to the converse of the behaviour reported above. Even advanced learners of Chinese should presumably reject resumptive pronouns in Chinese relative clauses; they should front *wh*-phrases (and reject *wh*-in-situ questions); they should reject sentences which are ungrammatical Subjacency violations in English but grammatical in Chinese. While I am not aware of relevant research on this point, it seems unlikely that English speakers would continue to impose a movement analysis in such circumstances.

According to the No Parameter Resetting Hypothesis, the interlanguage grammar is UG-constrained because it has the same properties as the L1 grammar. But while the grammar itself is not impaired, no development is possible, in the sense of grammar restructuring. Full Transfer Full Access appears to fare better at accounting for the combined results of various studies on *wh*-movement in interlanguage grammars, since it assumes a major role for transfer, hence, predicting L1-based analyses in interlanguage grammars, while also allowing for the possibility of eventual parameter resetting.

Hawkins and Chan (1997) discuss No Parameter Resetting only in terms of features, but logically it would seem that the hypothesis should apply to feature strength as well, that is, L2 learners should not be able to reset strength from strong to weak or vice versa (see Hawkins 2001a: 254). In other words, there does not appear to be any principled reason for the hypothesis to distinguish between features and feature strength. However, as will be discussed in the following sections, learners are able to acquire L2 word orders that differ from L1 order and that depend on feature strength, providing further counter-evidence to the No Parameter Resetting Hypothesis.

4.7 Parameter setting and resetting

According to the claims discussed so far in this chapter, interlanguage grammars suffer from a breakdown of parameters (globally or locally) or are restricted to L1 parameter values. In the remaining sections, we consider proposals that interlanguage grammars are not limited to the parameter settings realized in the L1 grammar. Rather, functional categories, features and feature values absent from the L1 grammar are instantiated in the interlanguage representation. This is the position adopted by the various full access hypotheses discussed in chapter 3 (e.g. Epstein et al. 1996; Schwartz and Sprouse 1996). The interlanguage grammar is fully UG-constrained in the functional domain, such that the grammar can draw on the full range of functional categories, features and feature strength; hence, parameter resetting is possible.

Chapter 3 surveyed a variety of hypotheses about the interlanguage initial state, including Full Transfer Full Access, which maintains that the L1 grammar constitutes the initial state but that there will be subsequent restructuring in response to properties of the L2 input (Schwartz and Sprouse 1994, 1996). In the case of parameters, then, these will be initially set at their L1 values but will subsequently be reset. That is to say, parameter resetting is in principle possible. The alternative full access approach, Full Access without Transfer, maintains that the L1 is not implicated in the interlanguage representation, initially or subsequently (Epstein et al. 1996; Flynn 1996). Rather, parameters are set to L2 values, on the basis of UG interacting with L2 input, without a prior stage of L1 settings. Thus, these approaches agree that L2 parameter values are attainable; they differ over whether L1 settings are ever found. At issue is whether or not there are changes in interlanguage parameter settings during the course of development: on the first view there are, while on the second view there are not.

As discussed in chapter 1 (section 1.4), there are three potential sources of crosslinguistic variation as far as functional projections are concerned: the categories themselves, their features and the strength of those features. In subsequent sections, we will review studies which suggest that L2 learners can indeed acquire functional categories, features and feature strength which differ from those found in the L1. We will also consider whether or not successful attainment of L2 functional projections is preceded by a stage implicating L1 categories and features, and whether this is always the case. Finally, we will consider whether L2 learners sometimes arrive at interlanguage grammars exhibiting parameter settings (or combinations of parameter settings) which are found in neither the L1 nor the L2 but which are present in some other language. We will examine these issues by considering research on clausal (IP) and nominal (DP) projections.

4.7.1 The Verb Movement Parameter: acquiring new feature strength

A major source of parametric variation is provided by differences in feature strength (Chomsky 1995). Hence, if L2 learners can be shown to acquire L2 feature strength where this differs from L1 feature strength, this constitutes evidence in favour of parameter resetting and against global or local impairment or the No Parameter Resetting Hypothesis. In this section, we consider whether or not L2 learners can reset a parameter which depends on feature strength, namely, the Verb Movement or Verb Raising Parameter, which accounts for differences in the placement of lexical verbs in a variety of languages. In this case, the languages under consideration are English and French.

As discussed in chapter 1 (section 1.4.1), whether or not a finite verb raises overtly is determined by strength of features in higher functional categories. Pollock (1989) (building on earlier work by Emonds (1978)) attributes a variety of word-order differences between French and English to a parametric difference in feature strength, French having strong I and English weak. While simple declarative word order looks identical in the two languages, the difference between them is revealed in a range of constructions, including, but not limited to, negatives,

Table 4.3 *Verb placement differences between French and English*

	Strong I (V in I) (French)	Weak I (V in VP) (English)
Declaratives	Les chats attrapent les souris.	Cats catch mice.
Negation (V neg vs. neg V)	Les chats (n')attrapent (V) pas (neg) les chiens.	Cats do not (neg) catch (V) dogs.
	*Les chats pas attrapent les chiens.	*Cats catch not dogs.
Adverbs (SVAO vs. SAVO)	Les chats attrapent (V) souvent (A) les souris.	Cats often (A) catch (V) mice.
	*Les chats souvent attrapent les souris.	*Cats catch often mice.
Questions (VS vs. SV)	Attrapent (V) -ils (S) les souris?	Do they (S) catch (V) mice? *Catch they mice?

adverb placement, and questions, as summarized in table 4.3. In French, finite lexical verbs move to I; hence, they appear to the left of negation and adverbs and they may appear to the left of the subject in questions. (This is because, once the verb has left the VP, it can move from I to C.) In English, on the other hand, the lexical verb does not move; hence, it appears to the right of negation, adverbs and subjects. In other words, there is a cluster of seemingly disparate constructions where the position of the verb can be attributed to just one parametric difference between the two languages.

In chapter 3, a study by Yuan (2001) was presented (see chapter 3, box 3.3) which demonstrates that L2 learners can set features of I to the value appropriate for the L2. In Yuan's study, the L2 was Chinese, which has weak I. Hence, verb raising is not possible. The L1s in question were French (with strong I) and English (with weak I). The French speakers and the English speakers, regardless of proficiency level, recognized the impossibility of verb raising in Chinese. That is, they neither accepted nor produced ungrammatical sentences like (18b), whereas they did accept and produce grammatical sentences like (18a).

(18) a. Zhangsan changchang kan dianshi. (SAVO)
Zhangsan often watch television
b. *Zhangsan kan changchang dianshi. (SVAO)
Zhangsan watch often television

Both groups of learners behaved in the same way: there were no effects of the strong feature value of French in the interlanguage grammar, even in the group that had only been learning Chinese for a few months. In other words, the results are consistent with Full Access without Transfer.

Box 4.5 Verb Movement Parameter (White 1992)

Languages: L1 = French, L2 = English.
Tasks: (i) Elicited production; (ii) Preference task. Subjects read pairs of sentences and decide whether or not one of the sentences is better than the other.
Sample stimuli (preference task):

Questions	Negatives	Adverbs
Like you pepperoni pizza?	The boys like not the girls.	Linda takes always the metro.
Do you like pepperoni pizza?	The boys do not like the girls.	Linda always takes the metro.

Results:

Table 4.5.1 *Production of questions by L2 learners*

Total questions produced	1171
Total with main verb raising	2 (0.17%)

Table 4.5.2 *Preference task. Rejections of main verb raising (in %)*

	Questions	Negatives	Adverbs
L2 learners (n = 72)	86	85	23
Native speakers (n = 29)	97	98	95

Yuan's results contrast with results from White (1992a), who investigated the L2 acquisition of English by native speakers of French. Whereas Yuan (2001) only investigated whether verbs in Chinese interlanguage raise over VP initial adverbs, White investigated all three constructions listed in table 4.3, namely question formation, negative placement and adverb placement. According to Full Access Full Transfer, French-speaking learners of English will start out with the L1 parameter setting (strong I); this value must be reset to weak, if the relevant L2 properties are to be acquired. Before resetting, it is predicted that verb raising will be possible in all three constructions; once the parameter is reset, there should be verb raising in none of them. According to Full Access without Transfer, on the other hand, there should be no stage implicating verb raising. The results, ostensibly at least, are consistent with neither hypothesis, as we shall see.

Subjects were children in intensive English as a Second Language programmes, beginners at the time of testing. (See box 4.5.)[5] Data on one of the three properties, namely question formation, were gathered by means of an elicited oral production task. In addition, there was a preference-judgment task involving all three sentence types.

Results from the oral production task show that lexical verbs were never raised in questions (see table 4.5.1); that is, questions of the form in (19a) were not produced.

(19) a. Like you pepperoni pizza?
b. The boys like not the girls.
c. Linda takes always the metro.

Results from the preference task showed that questions and negatives patterned together: sentences with verbs raised in questions, as in (19a), or in negatives, as in (19b), were rejected with a high degree of accuracy. (See table 4.5.2.) At the same time, judgments on adverb placement were quite different. Sentences like (19c) were accepted to a considerable extent, being judged to be as good as or better than the sentences they were paired with in the preference task. Thus, in the case of negation and questions, the learners seem to have discovered that English has weak I whereas in the case of adverbs they have not.

White's solution to this apparent contradiction is to account for the results in terms of the split-Infl hypothesis of Pollock (1989). That is, rather than one category, Infl, there are in fact two, namely, Tense and Agr, as shown in (20).[6]

(20)

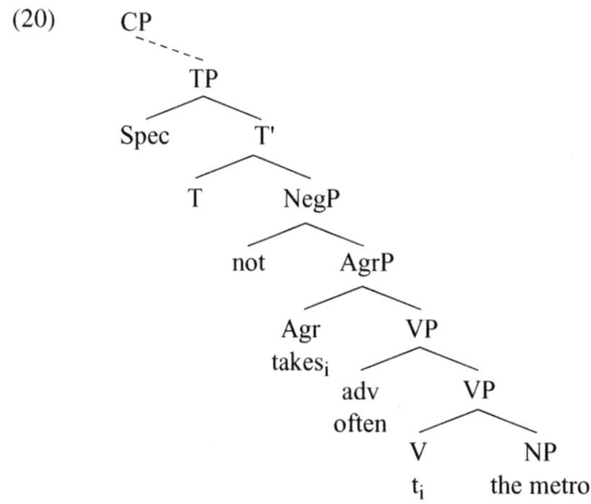

The French-speaking learners of English, then, have reset the strength of features in T to weak. Hence, the lexical verb cannot raise as far as T and so verbs never

Table 4.4 *DP differences between French and English*

	Romance (e.g. French)	English
Adjective placement (N Adj vs. Adj N)	le livre (N) anglais (Adj)	the English (Adj) book (N)
± Gender	le livre (MASC) la bière (FEM)	the book the beer
Agreement	le (MASCSG) livre (MASCSG) anglais (MASCSG) la (FEMSG) bière (FEMSG) anglaise (FEMSG)	the English book the English beer

appear before negation and they do not invert with the subject in questions. These same learners, on the other hand, have not reset the strength of Agr. Because it is still strong, the lexical verb can raise out of the VP, but only as far as Agr, accounting for the Verb Adverb order found in the interlanguage. It is not clear, however, why feature strength of different categories should be reset at different times. Possibly, the presence of *do*-support in questions and negatives provides a trigger for resetting the strength of T (see chapter 5). Another problem is that verbs do not raise consistently over adverbs in the grammars of these learners; there is variability here, which is unexpected if Agr is strong.[7]

In conclusion, these data suggest successful setting of the strength of T to the L2 value. (Indeed, they provide no evidence as to whether the L1 value of T was ever adopted.) At the same time, the data are consistent with the adoption of L1 strength of Agr and failure to reset, at this point in development. In chapter 5, we will consider what kind of evidence might lead to resetting of the Verb Movement Parameter.

4.7.2 Nominal projections: feature strength, features and categories

Characteristics of DPs in interlanguage grammars provide additional evidence that parameters can be reset. As described in chapter 1 (section 1.4.1), many current analyses of the DP include a functional category Num, whose N-features are strong in Romance languages like Spanish and French (Bernstein 1993; Ritter 1992; Valois 1991), in contrast to Germanic languages like English and German where they are weak. This difference in feature strength accounts for differences in word order within the DP (parallel to the account for word-order differences within IP): nouns raise overtly to Num in Romance, yielding the order N Adj, as shown in (21a), whereas they do not do so in English, yielding the order Adj N, as shown in (21b).[8]

(21)

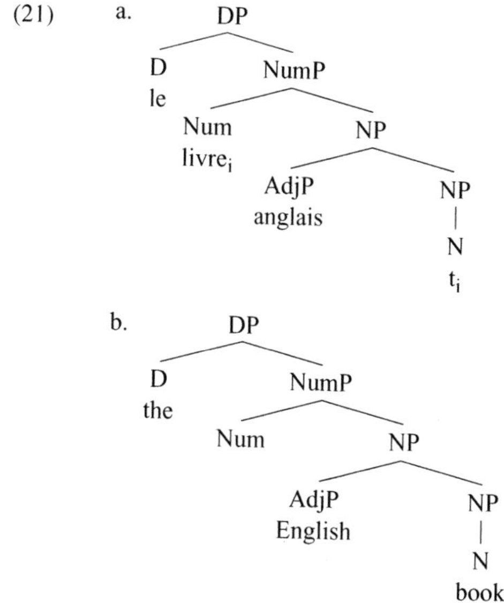

In addition, nouns in Romance languages are classified in terms of a gender feature, while determiners and adjectives show gender and number agreement with the head noun. English, on the other hand, lacks gender features and gender agreement. These differences between Romance and English are summarized in table 4.4, using examples from French. In the following sections, we consider to what extent learners of Romance languages acquire these properties and to what extent there is evidence of L1 influence. We will also consider whether or not the properties in question are attributable to the settings of a single parameter.

4.7.2.1 New feature strength

In the interlanguage grammar of an English-speaking learner of French or Spanish, Num features must be reset from weak to strong, if word order appropriate to the L2 is to be achieved. The various approaches to parameters in interlanguage grammars that we have been considering make different predictions with respect to acquisition of L2 feature strength in such circumstances. As far as the No Parameter Resetting Hypothesis is concerned, L2 learners should be confined to L1 feature strength. In other words, English-speaking learners of French should be unable to acquire N Adj order, whereas French-speaking learners of English should be unable to lose it. According to the Local Impairment Hypothesis, variable Adj N and N Adj orders are predicted to occur, even in advanced L2 speakers, parallel to claims made for the verbal domain. (Beck (1998a), Eubank and Grace (1998) and

Table 4.5 *Noun/adjective order in interlanguage DPs*

Study	Languages	Proficiency level	*Adj N	*N Adj
Hawkins 1998	L1 English, L2 French	Advanced 1 (n = 10)	5%	
		Advanced 2 (n = 10)	0	
Gess and Herschensohn 2001	L1 English, L2 French	Beginners 1 (n = 6)	66%	
		Beginners 2 (n = 8)	9%	
		Intermediate (n = 29)	7%	
		Advanced 1 (n = 14)	1%	
		Advanced 2 (n = 20)	0	
		Advanced 3 (n = 7)	0	
Bruhn de Garavito and White 2002	L1 French, L2 Spanish	Low (n = 30)	2%	
		Intermediate (n = 12)	9%	
Parodi et al. 1997	L1s Korean and Turkish, L2 German	Low/intermediate (n = 11)		0.5%
	L1s Romance, L2 German	Low/intermediate (n = 4)		20%

Eubank et al. (1997) do not, in fact, discuss nominal feature strength. However, there seems no reason not to extend their hypothesis to this area. That is, on an approach that argues for inertness, there appears to be no principled reason not to claim that *all* features are inert in interlanguage grammars.) According to Full Transfer Full Access, following a stage of L1 feature strength, L2 strength should be attainable; this predicts a stage of Adj N order prior to attaining the appropriate N Adj order. Full Access without Transfer predicts successful acquisition of N Adj order with no initial stage of Adj N order.

There are several recent studies which suggest that L2 learners of Romance languages successfully acquire N Adj order. These studies examine DPs containing adjectives in spontaneous production or by means of elicited production of such DPs. Incidence of incorrect adjective–noun (*Adj N) word order is quite low, often non-existent. Table 4.5 provides a summary of the relevant studies. As far as English-speaking learners of French are concerned, Hawkins (1998) (reported in Hawkins 2001a) found that two groups of advanced L2 proficiency showed few errors. In other words, nouns were almost always raised over adjectives in relevant contexts. Gess and Herschensohn (2001) report similar results from advanced learners, on a written sentence-completion task. However, it should be noted that Gess and Herschensohn's task is very like a classroom activity, possibly drawing on explicit learned knowledge, rather than unconscious knowledge of the L2. Even so, they find English adjective–noun order produced by beginners, suggesting an initial stage where Num features are weak. The results generally fail to support the No Parameter Resetting Hypothesis.

Is there any evidence of impaired or inert features? Recall that, according to the Local Impairment Hypothesis, feature values are inert regardless of the situation in the L1 and the L2. Even if both the L1 and the L2 have strong features, variability is predicted. Bruhn de Garavito and White (2000, 2002) show that, in the case of French-speaking learners of Spanish, there is no period of variability, contrary to the predictions of the Local Impairment Hypothesis: correct N Adj order is present and consistently used by low-proficiency learners.

Research by Parodi, Schwartz and Clahsen (1997) also suggests that there is no variability when the L1 and L2 have the same feature strength. Parodi et al. examined data from untutored L2 learners of German, whose mother tongues were Korean, Turkish, Italian and Spanish. German, like English, has weak Num, hence Adj N order is required and N Adj order is ungrammatical (*N Adj). The same is true of Korean and Turkish. Results show that raising of nouns over adjectives was totally non-existent in the German interlanguage of the Korean and Turkish speakers. In contrast to these results were those from the Romance speakers. These subjects produced *N Adj word order to varying degrees in their interlanguage German (from 0% to 37.5% of all DPs including adjectives, depending on proficiency level).

The results from the studies described above, taken together, suggest that feature strength is resettable. Furthermore, as the subjects discussed by Parodi et al. were untutored learners, one can exclude the possibility, in their case at least, that correct word order was simply an effect of instruction. At the same time, the data suggest there is a prior stage in which L1 feature strength is adopted. Thus, results appear to favour the Full Transfer Full Access Hypothesis.

Nevertheless, the data suggest some variability when L1 and L2 differ in feature strength, which is somewhat problematic for Full Transfer Full Access. It is not the case that there is a stage where only the L1 feature strength word order is found. The beginner group studied by Gess and Herschensohn (2001) produced appropriate French order at the same time as L1 order (34% N Adj versus 66% *Adj N). The Romance speakers studied by Parodi et al. produced German order at the same time as L1 order (80% Adj N versus 20% *N Adj). Furthermore, Parodi et al. show that such variability occurs at the individual level. In other words, while there is L1 influence, this is not consistent. L1 effects alternate with L2 properties.

4.7.2.2 New features

In the cases of L2 feature strength described so far, the L1 and L2 share features (V features in Infl, N features in Num), the only difference being in their

Table 4.6 *Gender agreement accuracy in L2 DPs*

Study	Languages	Proficiency level	Accurate gender agreement
Hawkins 1998	L1 English, L2 French	Advanced 1 (n = 10)	82.5%
		Advanced 2 (n = 10)	89.5%
Gess and Herschensohn 2001	L1 English, L2 French	Beginners 1 (n = 6)	0%
		Beginners 2 (n = 8)	43%
		Intermediate (n = 29)	67%
		Advanced 1 (n = 14)	91%
		Advanced 2 (n = 20)	86%
		Advanced 3 (n = 7)	98%
Bruhn de Garavito and White 2002	L1 French, L2 Spanish	Low (n = 30)	81.5%
		Intermediate (n = 12)	89%

strength. We turn now to the question of whether new features can be acquired, that is, features required in L2 representations but altogether absent from the L1, taking gender in Romance as a case in point. At issue is whether learners of languages like French and Spanish can acquire the gender feature, given an L1 such as English, where nouns are not classified according to gender and where there is no gender agreement.

In Romance languages, nouns fall into two gender classes, masculine and feminine. Gender is an inherent feature of nouns (Corbett 1991). Gender of this type, often referred to as grammatical gender, is arbitrary. This contrasts with natural or biological gender. In addition to a gender feature on nouns, gender agreement (or concord) is found on adjectives and determiners, which agree in gender with the head noun. On current accounts, this is achieved by means of feature checking (Carstens 2000).

Table 4.6 presents results from several recent studies (the same as those reported in table 4.5) which examine spontaneous and elicited production data for accuracy of gender agreement between determiners and nouns or determiners, adjectives and nouns. Hawkins (1998) (reported in Hawkins 2001a) examines data from advanced learners of French, considering gender agreement between determiners and nouns (adjectives not being included). Subjects exhibited persistent problems: (i) showing greater accuracy with gender agreement on definite determiners than on indefinite and (ii) adopting a 'default' gender on determiners (leading to overuse of one or other gender). Hawkins attributes these problems to the lack of a gender feature in the L1 English, hence supporting the Failed Functional Features Hypothesis. However, it is noteworthy that his subjects were relatively accurate on gender overall (see table 4.6). Furthermore, Bruhn de Garavito and White (2000, 2002) show that similar phenomena (that is, greater problems with agreement in the case of indefinite determiners, as well as the use of default gender) also occur in the acquisition of Spanish by French speakers. Since both languages have gender, the absence of gender in the L1 cannot be the crucial factor. (In chapter 6, the issue of incorrect or default forms will be considered in more detail.)

Gess and Herschensohn (2001) report that advanced proficiency learners of French achieved a high degree of accuracy on gender and number agreement between determiners, adjectives and nouns, again suggesting that L2 learners can acquire features which are absent in the L1. On the other hand, learners at lower proficiency levels were quite inaccurate on agreement. As Gess and Herschensohn do not separate gender and number agreement in their results, it is impossible to determine whether the problem at lower levels of proficiency is restricted to gender.

It is conceivable that failure to achieve greater accuracy in gender agreement is a problem specific to production and that it does not reflect underlying competence. In other words, L2 learners, even at low levels of proficiency, might acquire an abstract gender feature, together with the requirement for agreement, but fail to implement it all the time. (See chapter 6 for further discussion.)

This issue is investigated by White, Valenzuela, Macgregor, Leung and Ben-Ayed (2001), who devised an interpretation task in order to investigate the acquisition of gender agreement without relying on production data. The L2 was Spanish. Subjects were native speakers of French (which has gender) and English (which does not), at various levels of L2 proficiency. If L2 learners can acquire features not present in the L1, then both English and French speakers should exhibit knowledge of Spanish gender. If there are L1 effects initially, then low-proficiency learners whose mother tongue is English should perform worse than those whose mother tongue is French. Furthermore, English speakers should perform better on number features than gender, since number is present in the L1.

In order to test for unconscious knowledge of gender and number agreement, White et al. make use of a phenomenon known as N-drop, whereby Romance DPs can contain ‘null nominals’, in other words, nouns which are not overtly realized (Bernstein 1993; Snyder, Senghas and Inman, 2002). This phenomenon is very productive in Spanish. The null nominal is licensed and identified by gender and number agreement on the remaining adjectives and/or determiners (e.g. Snyder 1995a); that is, its content is recoverable from these agreement features (similar to the situation with respect to null subjects, as described in section 4.3.1). An example is given in (22). In (22a), the N, *libro*, is overt. In (22b), *libro* has been dropped; the determiner *uno* identifies the missing noun as masculine and singular. (In this particular example, the adjective *grande* is invariant in form.) The corresponding English sentence with N-drop, (11c), is ungrammatical. Instead, the pronoun *one* is required, as in (11d).

(22) a. Uno libro grande está encima de la mesa.
a-MASCSG book-MASCSG big is on-top of the table
'There is a big book on the table.'
b. Uno grande está encima de la mesa.
a-MASCSG big is on-top of the table
c. *There is a big on the table.
d. There is a big one on the table.

White et al. developed a picture-identification task, involving a story which consisted of a number of sentences, each followed by three pictures, equally plausible in the context. (See box 4.6.) Subjects had to indicate which picture was the appropriate one for any given sentence. Each test sentence contained a null nominal, as in (23).

(23) ¿Me compro este negro?
CLI buy this-MASCSG black-MASCSG
'Shall I buy this black one?'

The phrase *este negro* contains a null nominal, which is masculine and singular, as shown by the form of the determiner *este* ('this') and the adjective *negro* ('black'). This sentence is followed by pictures of a black sweater (*el suéter*, masculine), a black shirt (*la camiseta*, feminine) and a black tie (*la corbata*, feminine). Crucially, the vocabulary is not supplied. If learners have gender agreement percolating through the DP, they should pick the picture of the sweater, this being the only noun whose gender is masculine, like that of the adjective in the null nominal. Otherwise, they are expected to pick randomly. (An independent vocabulary test established whether subjects knew the lexical items and their gender in isolation. Subjects who did not pass the vocabulary test were eliminated.) Since the gender/number of the missing noun could only be established on the basis of the gender/number of the adjective and/or determiner in the test sentence, this task provides a means of determining, via comprehension rather than production, whether abstract features are present in learner grammars.

Table 4.6.1 presents the results, comparing performance on number and gender. Advanced and intermediate groups showed considerable accuracy on both features, regardless of L1, with no significant differences between them and the native speakers. Only the low-proficiency English speakers showed a significant difference in accuracy between number and gender, suggesting L1 influence at this level. These results suggest that new features can be acquired: the English speakers proved to be very accurate on gender, a feature not present in the L1.

To sum up, taking gender as a case in point, L2 learners are able to acquire gender and gender agreement, suggesting that features not present in the L1 are attainable in the interlanguage grammar At the same time, there are L1 effects in the case of learners at lowest levels of proficiency, suggesting initial transfer of

Box 4.6 Acquiring new features – gender (White et al. 2001)

Languages: L1s = English/French, L2 = Spanish.
Task: Picture identification. Sentences containing null nominals, each accompanied by 3 pictures. Subjects indicate which picture is appropriate for any given sentence.
Sample stimulus:

> Paco se prueba algunas cosas también y le pregunta a María: '¿Me compro este negro?'
> *(Paco tries on some things too and asks Maria: 'Shall I buy this black (one) ?')*

Results:

Table 4.6.1 *Mean accuracy on number and gender*

		Number (# = 14)	Gender (# = 14)
L2 groups (L1 English)	Low (n = 10)	11.5	7.4
	Intermediate (n = 7)	12.57	11.57
	Advanced (n = 7)	13.57	12.57
L2 groups (L1 French)	Low (n = 5)	11.6	10.2
	Intermediate (n = 8)	12.62	10.86
	Advanced (n = 16)	12.63	12.44
Native speakers (n = 20)		13.2	13.05

L1 features (or lack of them). Advanced learners show some problems in production but when other tasks are used to assess their interlanguage competence, the problems disappear, an issue we will return to in chapter 6.

4.7.2.3 New functional categories

The results discussed so far suggest that L2 learners can acquire feature strength which differs from the L1, as well as features which are not instantiated in

Table 4.7 *Accurate production of articles in obligatory contexts (in %)*

Contexts	L2 English Robertson 2000	L2 English Leung 2001	L3 French Leung 2001
Definite	83.2%	85%	Beginners: 60% Intermediate: 81.3%
Indefinite	77.9%	99.5%	Beginners: 99.6% Intermediate: 99.2%

the L1. We will now consider whether new functional categories can be acquired. Before pursuing this question, the issue of universality must briefly be addressed, that is, whether or not all functional categories are realized in all languages. If all categories are present in all languages, there is no such thing as a functional category not exemplified in the L1, hence the issue of grammar development in this domain does not arise. A very large set of functional categories has been argued for in the recent literature (Cinque 1999; Pollock 1997; Rizzi 1997); it seems somewhat unparsimonious to assume that these are necessarily instantiated in every grammar (Iatridou 1990). I will therefore assume, for the sake of the argument, that languages can differ in terms of the functional categories that they instantiate. (See also Bobaljik and Thráinsson (1998), Thráinsson (1996) and Webelhuth (1995).)

Even so, it is not an easy matter to determine whether or not particular categories are exemplified in particular languages. There has been a longstanding debate over whether languages like Chinese and Japanese lack functional categories (Fukui and Speas 1986); on the whole, the current consensus is that they do have functional categories, although these are not necessarily identical to the categories found in languages like English. For example, it has been suggested that Chinese lacks the functional category D. Instead, it has a functional category CL (classifier), with properties rather different from D (Cheng and Sybesma 1999). If so, this allows one to investigate whether a Chinese-speaking learner of English can acquire D (and associated features, such as ± definite) or whether an English-speaking learner of Chinese can acquire CL. The No Parameter Resetting Hypothesis presumably predicts that new categories cannot be acquired. Full Access (with or without Transfer), on the other hand, predicts that they are acquirable.

Recently, there has been some attention to the determiner system in the grammars of L2 speakers whose L1 is Chinese (Leung 2001; Robertson 2000). Table 4.7 presents production of determiners in obligatory contexts, as reported in these two studies. Robertson (2000) examined use of definite and indefinite articles in the L2 English of advanced learners whose L1 was Taiwanese and/or Mandarin. Production data were gathered by means of an elicited production task, involving collaborative problem-solving. Robertson found that suppliance of determiners was quite high. Inaccurate responses consisted of omission of articles, rather than misuse of definite for indefinite or vice versa. (Individual accuracy ranged from 67.5% to 97%.) There were pragmatic effects: echo contexts (where the speaker repeated what the previous person had said) resulted in a much higher proportion of determiner omission. Robertson shows that there are syntactic constraints on determiner omission: by and large, determiners are only dropped where the NP in question forms a chain with a preceding NP which has an overt determiner.

Leung (2001) explores the acquisition of French as a third language (L3) by Cantonese–English bilinguals, who were advanced speakers of English, having learned it in childhood. They were learning the L3, French, as adults. Results from an elicited production task (picture description) showed a much lower incidence of determiner omission than Robertson found: omission (in the case of singular count nouns) was around 6% in both L2 English and L3 French. However, article usage was not error free (see table 4.7). While use of indefinite articles in indefinite contexts was extremely accurate (almost 100%) in L2 English and L3 French regardless of proficiency level, indefinite articles were also used in contexts where definite articles were expected. The error was most extensive in the case of beginner learners of French.

Both these studies suggest that Chinese-speaking learners of English and French acquire articles, possibly implicating the functional category D, together with the associated feature ± definite. (However, suppliance is not always fully accurate, a point we will return to in chapter 6.) Nevertheless, a note of caution is in order here: one needs to eliminate the possibility that Chinese-speaking learners of English or French are categorizing L2 articles as classifiers, the functional category found in the L1. In other words, it is necessary to establish, on independent grounds, whether these forms behave like English determiners or like Chinese classifiers, something which it is not possible to do on the basis of the data reported by Robertson or by Leung.

4.8 Settings of neither L1 nor L2

So far, we have examined a variety of recent studies reporting successful acquisition of feature strength, features and functional categories not found in the L1. Since many of these studies involve adult learners, the results argue against Smith and Tsimpli's (1995) claim that the functional sub-module of UG becomes unavailable in post-puberty acquisition. Nevertheless, while resetting appears to be possible, it is by no means inevitable that L2 parameter values are achieved. Some learners do indeed seem to persist with L1 parameter settings. Furthermore,

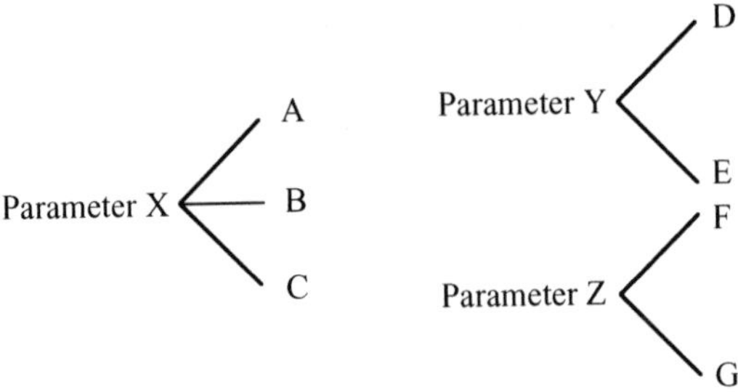

Figure 4.1 *Parameter settings of neither L1 nor L2*

there are other logical possibilities besides the ones we have considered so far. Earlier in this chapter (section 4.3.1), it was suggested that some Korean-speaking learners of German arrive at the Italian setting of the Null Subject Parameter, that is, a setting of neither the L1 nor the L2. In this section, we consider other examples of this nature.

There are two ways in which it is in principle possible for the interlanguage grammar to show parameter settings which differ from both the L1 and the L2. Consider the situation shown in figure 4.1. The left-hand side illustrates some parameter, X, which has three settings, A, B and C. It is logically possible, then, that the L1 might instantiate setting A, the L2 setting B and the interlanguage grammar setting C.

The possibility that L2 learners arrive at parameter values exemplified in neither the L1 nor the L2 was discussed in earlier research on UG and L2 acquisition, one proposal of this type being advanced by Finer and Broselow (1986) and Finer (1991). They investigated the Governing Category Parameter, a parameter accounting for crosslinguistic differences in the distribution of reflexives, which was argued to have five settings (Wexler and Manzini 1987). Finer and Broselow (1986) reported that learners of English whose mother tongue was Korean treated English reflexives neither like Korean reflexives (which freely permit long-distance antecedents) nor like English ones (which require local antecedents); instead, reflexives in the interlanguage grammar behaved as they do in Russian, in that long-distance binding was permitted but only out of non-finite clauses.

If parameters are restricted to binary values, this possibility disappears. Given binary parameters, it is no longer possible to account for parametric variation in the distribution of reflexives in terms of a multivalued Governing Category Parameter. However, parameters do not work in isolation: grammars include sets of interrelated parameters. So another way in which an interlanguage grammar might differ from either the L1 or the L2 is in having combinations of parameter settings which reflect neither the L1 nor the L2. Consider figure 4.1 again. On the right are two parameters, Y and Z, each with two settings. Imagine a situation where the L1 has setting D of parameter Y and setting F of parameter Z while the L2 has settings E and G. It is logically possible for an interlanguage grammar to instantiate combinations which together represent neither the L1 nor the L2 (D and G; E and F). If one considers more than two parameters, the range of available combinations extends accordingly.

4.8.1 Settings of neither L1 nor L2: reflexives

An example of L2 acquisition involving this situation is provided by MacLaughlin (1996, 1998), again involving the distribution of reflexives. MacLaughlin suggests that L2 learners reset parameters relating to reflexives but that they will not necessarily acquire the parameter settings appropriate for the L2. She adopts Progovac's (1992, 1993) Relativized Subject framework, which shares the following assumptions with the LF movement approach discussed in chapter 2 (section 2.3.1): crosslinguistically, reflexives can be morphologically simplex (a head, X°) or complex (phrasal, XP); long-distance binding is associated only with simplex reflexives and long-distance binding must be subject oriented.

MacLaughlin investigates the L2 acquisition of English reflexives by native speakers of Chinese and Japanese. English reflexives like *himself, herself* are polymorphemic and require local antecedents, which are not necessarily subjects. Chinese and Japanese both have simplex reflexives (*ziji* in Chinese, *zibun* in Japanese) which permit long-distance subject antecedents, as well as phrasal reflexives which require local antecedents. MacLaughlin (1998) explains the behaviour of reflexives crosslinguistically in terms of two parameters, a reflexive parameter and an Agr parameter (following Bennett 1994; Progovac 1992,1993), as given in (24):

(24) Reflexive parameter: a reflexive is monomorphemic or polymorphemic.
Agr parameter: Agr is null[9] or morphological.

These two parameters account for the crosslinguistic binding facts as follows. A reflexive must be bound to its antecedent in a domain containing a SUBJECT.[10] On Progovac's account, a head reflexive must be bound to its antecedent in the domain of a SUBJECT which is also a head (namely, Agr), whereas a phrasal reflexive must be bound within the domain of a SUBJECT which is also phrasal (namely the subject of a clause or complex NP). XP anaphors will always require local binding because the nearest XP subject will be within the same clause (or NP) as the reflexive. Head reflexives, on the other hand, must be in the domain of some Agr, not necessarily within the same clause. If Agr is morphologically overt, the reflexive must be bound within the same clause (i.e. locally). However, if Agr

Table 4.8 *Grammar types sanctioned by two parameters*

	Type 1	Type 2	Type 3
Reflexive	poly	mono	mono
Agr	overt/null	overt	null

is never realized morphologically (as in Chinese or Japanese) or is not realized in non-finite clauses (as in Russian), the reflexive can be bound in the domain of a higher Agr, thus permitting long-distance antecedents.

The reflexive parameter distinguishes between different types of reflexives. The Agr parameter, on the other hand, distinguishes between null or overt agreement morphology. It should be noted that if a reflexive is polymorphemic, the status of Agr is irrelevant, since the reflexive will always be bound within the domain of a phrasal SUBJECT, not Agr. The setting of the Agr parameter becomes crucial in the case of monomorphemic reflexives. These two parameters yield the three possibilities shown in table 4.8.

Type 1 represents the situation in English, where all reflexives are polymorphemic and only local binding of reflexives is possible, as well as the situation for phrasal reflexives in languages like Chinese and Japanese. Type 3 is found in languages like Chinese and Japanese, where long-distance binding is always possible with monomorphemic reflexives. Type 2 is characteristic of languages like Russian, where long-distance antecedents for reflexives are possible but only out of non-finite clauses. These types represent 'possible' grammars.

In MacLaughlin's experiment (see box 4.7) subjects were given various types of sentences to read, all containing reflexives, and asked whether or not the reflexive could refer to various NPs mentioned in the sentence. As well as reporting group data, MacLaughlin analyses individual performance, looking at consistency of response patterns (80% in a particular direction being considered to demonstrate consistency).

The responses of six of the subjects were restricted to local antecedents, suggesting a type 1 grammar (i.e. the parameter combination appropriate for the L2). Two subjects showed type 3 behaviour, as in the L1. There were seven subjects whose responses suggest a type 2 combination, allowing long-distance binding only out of non-finite clauses. These results confirm findings of research conducted in earlier frameworks, which showed significantly more long-distance binding out of non-finite clauses in L2 English (e.g. Finer and Broselow 1986; Hirakawa 1990). In such cases, the interlanguage grammar is like neither the L1 nor the L2 but it does represent a combination of parameter settings found in other languages.

Box 4.7 Other parameter settings (MacLaughlin 1998)

Languages: L1 = Chinese/Japanese, L2 = English.
Task: Coreference-judgment task.
Sample stimuli:

Biclausal finite
Barbara thinks that Lisa is proud of herself.

herself can be *Lisa*	Agree—	Disagree—
herself can be *Barbara*	Agree—	Disagree—

Biclausal non-finite
Michael forced Peter to help himself.

himself can be *Peter*	Agree—	Disagree—
himself can be *Michael*	Agree—	Disagree—

Results:

Table 4.7.1 *Number of subjects by response patterns*

	Type 1	Type 2	Type 3
L2 learners (n = 15)	6	7	2
Native speakers (n = 18)	18	0	0

MacLaughlin suggests that in the case of these seven subjects, the parameter relating to reflexive type has not been reset whereas the Agr parameter has been. As a result, long-distance binding is possible in principle (because the reflexive is monomorphemic) but this can only happen in the case of clauses which are non-finite (i.e. where Agr is not overtly realized).

One might legitimately ask why it is that L2 learners make this kind of misanalysis. What causes them to successfully reset the Agr parameter but to fail to reset the parameter relating to reflexive type? Acquisition involves an interaction of UG, the learner's current grammar and the L2 input. Progovac and Connell (1991) propose that, for speakers of languages like Japanese or Chinese, L2 input in the form of third-person-singular agreement provides evidence that Agr is overt in English, accounting for the resetting of the Agr parameter. However, what is not so clear is why L2 learners fail to reset the reflexive parameter: it would seem that the L2 English input provides fairly transparent evidence that reflexives are morphologically complex. (Although it might seem odd that the input fails to trigger the relevant reflexive type, it is noteworthy that this is not a problem unique to L2 acquisition. According to McDaniel, Cairns and Hsu (1990) and Thomas (1994), young children acquiring English as an L1 also initially fail to recognize that English reflexives are polymorphemic and restricted to local antecedents.)

Unfortunately, there is a circularity problem with much of the research that depends on the distinction between monomorphemic and polymorphemic reflexives, in that no independent evidence is provided to show that English reflexives are indeed monomorphemic in these interlanguage grammars (e.g. Bennett 1994; Bennett and Progovac 1998; MacLaughlin 1998). In addition, such studies also fail to provide an independent test of whether or not subjects have acquired morphological Agr in English. Most monomorphemic reflexives are deficient in person, gender and number agreement, so one might expect L2 learners to fail to use forms like *himself, herself, themselves*, etc., appropriately (i.e. to fail to make them agree with their antecedents) if such reflexives are truly monomorphemic. In fact, White (1995b) found that Japanese-speaking learners of English were quite accurate on person, gender and number agreement between reflexives and their antecedents, suggesting that English reflexives are recognized as being polymorphemic; at the same time, learners still allowed them to take long-distance antecedents, as if they were monomorphemic.

The most compelling evidence for the L1 parameter setting (type 3) would be if one could demonstrate that L2 learners of English not only fail to observe agreement between English reflexives and their antecedents but also fail to show evidence of morphological agreement on verbs, as well as allowing long-distance antecedents. The most compelling evidence for some other setting (type 2) would be provided if learners of English fail to observe agreement between English reflexives and their antecedents, show morphological agreement on finite verbs and treat reflexives as allowing long-distance antecedents. As most studies look only at domain and orientation and not at the relevant agreement phenomena, the relevant evidence is still lacking.

4.8.2 Settings of neither L1 nor L2: case checking

A somewhat different example of an interlanguage grammar with properties of neither the L1 nor the L2 is provided by Schwartz and Sprouse (1994) in their case study of an adult Turkish-speaking learner of German, known as Cevdet. Looking at production data, Schwartz and Sprouse examine Cevdet's word-order development and argue that the interlanguage grammar is restructured in a number of different respects during the course of acquisition. Initially, they hypothesize, Cevdet produced SOV order. As Turkish and German are both SOV languages, presence of SOV order in the initial stage is consistent with L1 headedness or with successful acquisition of L2 headedness. However, Turkish differs from German in not being a V2 language (see chapter 1, section 1.4.1). V2 begins to emerge in what Schwartz and Sprouse characterize as stage 2. Here, some constituent other than the subject is fronted, as shown in (25a), and the subject remains in Spec IP, giving the appearance of inversion between subject and verb. At the same time, Cevdet is still producing sentences without inversion, as shown in (25b) and (25c), which are ungrammatical in German.

(25) a. dann trinken wir bis neun Uhr.
then drink we until nine o'clock
'Then we will drink until nine o'clock.'
b. In der Türkei der Lehrer kann den Schüler schlagen.
in the Turkey the teacher can the pupils beat
'In Turkey, teachers can hit pupils.'
c. Ankara ich kenne.
Ankara I know

What is particularly interesting about this stage is that the subject of Cevdet's inverted V2 structures (where the verb precedes the subject) is almost always a personal pronoun, as in (25a). When the subject is a full DP, as in (25b), inversion is hardly ever found: 69 out of 70 examples with inversion involved a pronoun subject. In stage 3, inversion is occasionally found with non-pronominal subjects, as in (26). However, this is still not extensive, only 10.5% of post verbal subjects being full NPs.

(26) Das hat eine andere Frau gesehen.
this has an other woman seen
'Another woman saw that.'

While this distinction between DPs and pronouns with respect to inversion is not characteristic of German, such a distinction is observed in French. In the case of questions in French, pronoun subjects can invert with the verb but full DPs cannot.

Schwartz and Sprouse offer the following analysis of Cevdet's stage 2 interlanguage where pronominal subjects are treated differently from non-pronominal subjects. They propose that the issue relates to checking of case features. Every overt DP has a case feature which must be checked. UG makes available a number of different (and parameterized) mechanisms for case checking (Rizzi and Roberts 1989). In German, case features are checked by Spec–head agreement (where the subject DP raises to the Spec of AgrP, in order to check its case feature against a corresponding feature in Agr) or under government (where the verb in C governs the subject or its trace in Spec AgrP). Schwartz and Sprouse assume that only the Spec–head agreement option is available in Turkish. A third possibility is found in French, where case checking is achieved via incorporation. Subject clitics (whose case features have to be checked) are incorporated onto the verb that bears the associated case features. When acquiring V2, then, Cevdet appears to have hit upon the incorporation option, an option utilized in neither the L1 nor the L2, such that only pronominal subjects can occur in inversion contexts. If the government option were available, the verb in C should be able to govern the subject regardless of whether or not it is pronominal. In stage 3, Cevdet acquires the government option.

Once again, there is something puzzling here. This learner has arrived at an analysis that is fully compatible with UG. However, it is not at all clear what properties of the L2 German input would lead Cevdet to arrive at an analysis in terms of incorporation.

4.9 Parameter setting and resetting: assessment

To summarize, results discussed in the preceding sections suggest that developing interlanguage grammars: (i) show changes in feature strength, from strong to weak or vice versa; (ii) contain features not present in the L1 grammar; (iii) contain functional categories not present in the L1 grammar. In other words, learners can acquire L2 functional categories, features and feature values, together with their associated consequences, thus, implicating parameter resetting. These findings hold true of child and adult learners, across a variety of languages, tested by means of various methodologies. L2 learners may also arrive at parameter settings of neither the L1 nor the L2, though it is not always clear what properties of the L2 input motivate such misanalyses. Development away from the L1 grammar provides additional evidence in favour of interlanguage grammars being fully UG-constrained, in so far as these grammars exhibit properties which are not derivable from the L1 or from surface properties of the L2 input and which are consistent with natural language grammars.

In some cases, we have seen evidence for a stage where L1 values of parameters are instantiated before L2 values come into place; in other cases, the relevant L2 properties emerge very early, without any obvious stage of L1 influence. On the whole, the results are consistent with Full Transfer Full Access: learners start out with L1 functional categories, features and feature strength and are able to acquire L2 categories, features and feature strength. Nevertheless, some aspects of the results are puzzling for this view, in that effects of the L1 reveal themselves more often than not in the form of variability, with L1 and L2 properties co-occurring, rather than there being initial effects of the L1 setting alone.

More generally, results are not totally unproblematic as far as claims for parameters in interlanguage grammars are concerned. In the case of the Verb Movement Parameter, three properties assumed to be the consequence of feature strength of I did not cluster in the interlanguage grammar: White (1992a) found that French-speaking learners of English consistently prohibited verb raising in questions and negatives, as if I were weak, as it is in the L2, while at the same time permitting verb raising over adverbs, as if I were strong, as it is in the L1. If this is one parameter, then constructions related under it are not being treated in the same way. In the case of nominals, we have seen considerable success in three different areas (strength, features, categories), which might seem supportive of the claim that clusters of properties are implicated. Unfortunately, it is unclear to what extent one parameter is involved. Gess and Herschensohn (2001) attribute differences between French and English in the nominal domain to a DP parameter, which accounts for many of the differences discussed above. However, this purported parameter does not appear to be generalizable beyond Romance versus English: it seems to suggest that languages with gender and gender agreement will also have strong Num, hence N-raising over adjectives, contrary to fact. German, for example, has gender and gender agreement but no N-raising. Ultimately, theories of parameter setting in interlanguage grammars depend on convincing proposals from theoretical linguists as to the nature of parameters.

4.10 Conclusion

In this chapter, we have considered proposals for total or local breakdown in parameters, for restriction to L1 parameter values, and for successful setting of parameters to values distinct from the L1. Despite conflicting evidence and conflicting theories, results from several studies suggest that interlanguage grammars conform to parameters of UG. Nevertheless, L2 performance is by no means perfect. In particular, there is often divergence between syntactic and morphological performance, with greater accuracy on syntactic properties than on morphological ones. Variability is characteristic of the morphological domain. We address this issue in more detail in chapter 6.

Topics for discussion

- Several studies in this chapter explore word order in the DP in Romance, particularly the relative positions of nouns and adjectives, which are accounted for in terms of feature strength. Yet it might reasonably be argued that this property is something that is taught in the L2 classroom and learned prescriptively, hence that it does not constitute a genuine poverty of the L2 stimulus situation. How can one distinguish between a theory that attributes some phenomenon to 'deep' properties of an abstract grammar and a theory that says it is learned as an isolated construction?

- Can functional categories be lost in L2 acquisition? For example, in the case of Chinese versus English, the L2 learner of Chinese must acquire CL and lose Det, while the L2 learner of Chinese must do the opposite. One possibility is that the new category is acquired without the old one being lost. How could one determine this?
- Impairment. It has been assumed here that a grammar restricted to L1 settings is not impaired, in the sense that it conforms to principles and parameters of UG. On the other hand, it is impaired in the sense that true restructuring in response to L2 input is not possible.
- Clustering. Most of the studies described here assume that clustering must take place during the course of acquisition. What would it mean if one could show that certain properties cluster in the endstate and yet had not been acquired together? In other words, can there be different routes to the same endstate?
- Does parameter 'resetting' imply that the L1 grammar is also changed?
- An implication of global impairment and of the Local Impairment Hypothesis and the No Parameter Resetting Hypothesis is that it is impossible to be fully 'successful' in adult L2 acquisition. Such theories concentrate on difficulties that L2 learners have, as well as on differences between interlanguage grammars and native-speaker grammars. How can such theories account for successful L2 acquisition?

Suggestions for additional reading

- Several earlier studies examine the effects of word-order parameters in interlanguage, in the context of the debate over whether or not parameters can be reset in L2 acquisition (e.g. Clahsen and Muysken 1986; du Plessis et al. 1987; Flynn 1987; Hulk 1991; Schwartz and Tomaselli 1990).
- For additional evidence that new functional categories and feature strength can be acquired, see research on the L2 acquisition of clitics (Duffield and White 1999; Duffield et al. 2002; White 1996a).
- For arguments that gender is not represented in the same way in L2 as it is in L1, see Carroll (1999).
- For arguments that L2 grammars are UG-constrained but that the course of acquisition differs in L1 and L2, see Herschensohn (2000).

5

The transition problem, triggering and input

5.1 Introduction

As a number of researchers have pointed out, theories of language acquisition must explain both properties of linguistic representations (the form and nature of the grammar) and transition or development (how and why grammars change over time) (Carroll 1996, 2001; Felix 1986; Gregg 1996; Klein and Martohardjono 1999; Schwartz and Sprouse 1994). In other words, there is a need for a *property theory* as well as a *transition theory* (Gregg 1996). In previous chapters, discussion has centred on representational issues such as the nature of the interlanguage grammar, the degree to which the L1 grammar determines interlanguage representations, and the extent to which the interlanguage grammar falls within the class of grammars sanctioned by UG. Indeed, most research on L2 acquisition conducted within the generative framework in the last twenty years has focused on issues of representation, in other words, on a property theory of interlanguage. Clearly, however, interlanguage grammars are not static: they change over time. What remains to be considered is how development takes place, in particular, what drives transition from one stage to another.

The logical problem of language acquisition (see chapters 1 and 2) motivates a particular kind of representational account, an account that assumes built-in universal principles, in other words, UG. Felix (1986) observed that, in the case of L1 acquisition, far more had been achieved at that time in terms of explaining the logical problem than the developmental problem. In other words, property theories of L1 acquisition were well in advance of transition theories. Carroll (1996, 2001) and Gregg (1996) make similar observations in the L2 context: we are still far from a transition theory of L2 acquisition.

The lack of a developmental theory is not always recognized. Confusion has arisen because of terms like *language acquisition device* (LAD) (Chomsky 1981b) and *parameter (re)setting*, both of which seem to imply that UG is itself some kind of learning mechanism, hence accounting for development. However, as pointed out by Borer (1996), Gregg (1996) and Carroll (2001), amongst others, this is a misconception. As Borer (1996: 719) puts it:

> UG is first and foremost a set of constraints on possible natural language grammars, and only secondarily, and not according to all models, a language acquisition device (LAD). It is perfectly possible for an output grammar to be constrained by UG, although the process of acquisition is informed by an independent acquisition device . . . The Principles and Parameters Model was put forth originally as a solution to the logical problem of language acquisition, abstracting away from developmental issues altogether.

In other words, while UG accounts for native-speaker knowledge of language, and provides constraints on possible grammars (including grammars in the course of acquisition), the theory of UG is not, of itself, a theory of language development. Rather, UG is a theory as to the nature of linguistic competence. Although UG helps to explain how languages are acquired, this is in the limited sense of how it is that learners come to know properties that go beyond input, why grammars show certain characteristics, why linguistic rules are of one kind rather than another. These do not have to be learned; that is the claim. In addition to the theory of UG, there is a need for a theory of how linguistic competence is acquired (L1 or L2), as well as a theory of what drives change in grammars during the course of development. UG may be independent of an acquisition device, as Borer suggests, or it may form part of one (e.g. Hilles 1991). The LAD will also have to contain learning principles, parsing/processing mechanisms, etc.

Just as the theory of UG in general is sometimes misinterpreted as being a theory of language development, so is the concept of parameter setting. Parameter resetting certainly implies grammar change. However, this does not mean that the concept of parameter resetting as such provides a theory of the transition from one grammar to another, one parameter setting to another. Even if one looks for UG-based properties in learner grammars at various points in time, this is a question of representation rather than development. If an interlanguage grammar at time X conforms to parameter setting A and at time Y to parameter setting B, this does not explain how the change from A to B comes about. In order to account for grammar change and development, a theory of parameters requires a theory of the relationship between input and parameter settings, a theory that explains how input drives parameter setting. (See Carroll (2001) for relevant discussion.)

As discussed in chapter 4, there is considerable debate as to whether parameter setting takes place in L2 acquisition. The claim that interlanguage grammars instantiate parameter values different from the L1 implicates a transition theory, even if such a theory is not as yet well developed. If the L2 learner's grammar initially instantiates one parameter setting and subsequently another, this change must somehow be motivated. Gregg (1996) suggests that a transition theory for L2 acquisition must include the following: (i) a learning mechanism, which he equates with a parser (see below); (ii) a theory of how linguistic input brings about changes in linguistic competence. These two are closely connected.

5.2 Parsing

Speakers of a language (whether it is their L1 or their L2) must parse (or process) the input, that is, they must assign a structure to each utterance. In other words, on hearing a sentence, the current grammar must assign some structural representation to it. Parsing is required at many different levels: phonetic, phonological, morphological, syntactic and semantic.

Parsing the input, then, presupposes the existence of a grammar. But how does the learner (L1 or L2) arrive at any kind of grammar in the first place? A major parsing problem facing L1 and L2 learners in early stages is what has been called the segmentation problem (e.g. by Peters 1985); for recent discussion, see papers in Weissenborn and Höhle (2001). Initially, when listening to a foreign language, the learner has little or no idea of where the word breaks are. The learner must divide up the speech stream into words and morphemes before these can be further categorized. This is, of course, no trivial feat. In the discussion that follows, we will presuppose that this has already been achieved: the learner is able to segment the L2 input into words and categorize them into parts of speech, this information being stored in a mental lexicon. Furthermore, along the lines of many of the theories considered in the previous chapters, it will be assumed that the L2 learner adopts the L1 grammar (in whole or in part) as the initial interlanguage grammar. Hence, there is a grammar in place to parse the L2 input with. The issue, then, is what factors drive change from this point on.

Many researchers have argued that parsing plays a crucial role in grammar development, proposing that acquisition is driven by parsing failure (Berwick and Weinberg 1984; Carroll 2001; Gibson and Wexler 1994; Schwartz and Sprouse 1994, 1996; White 1987a). The idea is that the language learner attempts to parse the input on the basis of the existing grammar; if the parse is unsuccessful, or if the parse suggests the need for an analysis inconsistent with the current grammar, this signals that the grammar is in some sense inadequate, motivating restructuring.

5.3 The filtering effects of grammars

The learner's current grammar determines the extent to which the input can be parsed. In the event of parsing failure (due to input that is not amenable to analysis), restructuring may be initiated. This presupposes that the input can be sufficiently parsed for it to be possible to determine whether or not it fits the current grammar. In other words, there must be some level at which the input is perceived and partially analysed. But sometimes the current grammar prevents certain kinds of input from being perceived at all, effectively operating as a filter on the input. In certain contexts in L2 acquisition, this filtering effect may be such that it is impossible to detect parsing failures at all. As a result, no transition is possible, hence no grammar change or development.

In many respects, attempts to explore the relationship between input, representation and acquisition are better developed in the domain of L2 phonology than syntax. For example, in a series of experiments, Brown (1998, 2000) examines how the L2 learner's L1 phonological representations inhibit or facilitate perception of L2 speech sounds. Where perception is inhibited, acquisition of new phonological contrasts is impossible. Brown assumes full transfer; furthermore, the implication of her theory is that there will be circumstances where native-like phonological representations are impossible to attain.

Brown adopts the theory of feature geometry (e.g. Rice and Avery 1995), whereby phonological segments are represented in terms of distinctive features, phonemes being distinguished from each other by the presence of at least one contrastive feature. The full inventory of features is part of UG, as is the feature geometry, which constrains the hierarchical arrangement of features. While the underlying geometry is the same across languages, there are differences in terms of the features that languages instantiate. Crucial to Brown's approach is the assumption, based on infant speech perception studies (e.g. Werker and Tees 1984), that features not required in a particular language become inaccessible to the L1 acquirer within the first year of life.

Brown hypothesizes that the L2 learner's speech perception (and hence the acquisition of contrastive features not exemplified in the L1) is constrained by the L1 feature inventory. If a contrastive feature is absent in the L1, learners will be unable to perceive, hence unable to acquire, L2 contrasts that depend on this feature. Thus, they will be unable to distinguish between two L2 phonemes that depend on a distinctive feature not present in the L1. If a contrastive feature is present in the L1, learners will be able to perceive (and acquire) phonemes that contrast with respect to this feature, even if the L1 lacks the particular phonemes in question. In other words, the crucial L1 property is presence or absence of particular features, not presence or absence of particular phonemes.

To illustrate, we will consider some of the English contrasts that Brown investigates, namely /p/ vs. /f/ (which contrast in terms of the feature *continuant*), /f/ vs. /v/ (which contrast in terms of the feature *voice*), and /l/ vs. /r/ (which contrast in terms of the feature *coronal*). Brown's subjects are native speakers of Japanese and Chinese. Both of these languages have phonemes corresponding to

Table 5.1 *Feature contrasts between English, Japanese and Chinese*

English contrasts	Japanese phonemes	Chinese phonemes	Contrastive feature	Japanese	Chinese	Predictions for L2 acquisition of contrasts
/p/ vs. /f/	/p/, /f/	/p/, /f/	continuant	Yes	Yes	Japanese speakers: yes Chinese speakers: yes
/f/ vs. /v/	/f/	/f/	voice	Yes	Yes	Japanese speakers: yes Chinese speakers: yes
/l/ vs. /r/	/r/	/l/	coronal	No	Yes	Japanese speakers: no Chinese speakers: yes

/p/ and /f/ (or close equivalents), continuant being a contrastive feature. In the case of /f/ vs. /v/, neither language has a phoneme equivalent to /v/ but voice is otherwise contrastive. Finally, each language has only one of the phonemes /l/ vs. /r/, the other variant occurring as an allophone. In Japanese, the feature [± coronal] is never contrastive, whereas in Chinese it is. These facts are summarized in table 5.1.

Brown hypothesizes that, in the case of speech sounds that contrast in the L2 but are not present in the L1, the learner will be able to categorize these as distinct phonemes only if the L1 represents the relevant feature contrast. Thus, in the case of the English /p/ vs. /f/ contrast, neither Japanese nor Chinese speakers should have difficulties, since the relevant feature [± continuant] is present in the L1, as well as the phonemes in question. Furthermore, since the crucial property is hypothesized to depend on L1 features not phonemes, both groups should be able to distinguish between /f/ and /v/. Even though /v/ is lacking in Japanese and Chinese, voicing is a distinctive feature in both languages.

Finally, differences in performance on /l/ vs. /r/ are predicted on the basis of L1. In both Japanese and Chinese, these sounds are allophones; they do not contrast. On Brown's account, the acoustic signal is broken down into phonetic categories, which are then categorized by the feature geometry. In native English, /l/ and /r/ will be categorized as distinct, specified [± coronal]. When the Japanese speaker comes to categorize these sounds, the coronal feature is not available to distinguish between them, so these sounds end up categorized as the same, both being [+approximant]. In other words, in the absence of the relevant contrastive feature, the sounds cannot even be discriminated, so there is no motivation to construct a new representation. In contrast, Chinese speakers have [± coronal] in their feature inventory (which distinguishes between alveolar /s/ and retroflex /ṣ/) and they can use this feature to categorize /l/ and /r/ as being distinct, even though these particular sounds are not contrastive in Chinese.

Box 5.1 Grammars as filters (Brown 2000)

Languages: L1s = Chinese/Japanese, L2 = English.
Task: Picture selection. Subjects hear a verbal cue and indicate which picture it corresponds to.

Results:

Table 5.1.1 *Accuracy in detecting contrasts (in %)*

		/p/ vs. /f/	/f/ vs. /v/	/l/ vs. /r/
L2 groups	L1 Japanese (n = 15)	94	99	61
	L1 Chinese (n = 15)	90	96	86
Native speakers (n = 10)		100	98	96

To test these hypotheses, Brown (2000) conducted a series of experiments, involving perception of English contrasts by native speakers of Japanese and Chinese. Here we focus on a picture-selection task, where subjects heard a verbal cue (e.g. *rake* or *lake*) and had to indicate which picture (of a rake or a lake) the word corresponded to. (See box 5.1.) The rationale is that, in the event that learners cannot detect/represent a linguistic contrast, their performance should be random.

Results showed, as predicted, that the Japanese speakers were significantly less accurate than the Chinese speakers with respect to perception of the English /l/ vs. /r/ contrast. (See table 5.1.1.) The Chinese speakers did not differ from the native-speaker control group. Furthermore, the Japanese speakers performed significantly more accurately on the contrasts where the relevant distinctive feature is present in the L1. The highly accurate performance by both groups on /f/ vs. /v/ shows that it is not the presence of contrastive phonemes in the L1 which is crucial; contrastive features are enough.

Results from another experiment by Brown (2000) show that there is no change with increasing proficiency as far as the perception of the English /l/ vs. /r/ contrast is concerned. Two groups of Japanese-speaking learners of English were compared, a low-proficiency and a high-proficiency group. The groups performed identically (and poorly) on perception of /l/ vs. /r/, whereas there was significant improvement in the case of /b/ vs. /v/, another case where Japanese does not have distinct phonemes corresponding to these two sounds but does have the relevant distinctive feature.

To summarize, Brown's results suggest that there are certain cases where transition from one representation to another is not possible; there can be no development or grammar change in circumstances where the effect of the L1 representation is to prevent the L2 input from being parsed in a particular way.[1] In the situation described here, the /l/ vs. /r/ contrast is not perceived by Japanese speakers, due to absence of a coronal feature in the L1. Even though [±coronal] is a feature originally available in the UG inventory, it appears that adult L2 learners cannot retrieve it if it has not already been activated in the L1.

This account has parallels with the Failed Functional Features approach of Hawkins and Chan (1997), discussed in chapter 4 (section 4.6.1), whereby L2 learners are restricted to functional features realized in the L1 grammar, analysing the L2 input accordingly. On Brown's account, properties of the L1 representation lead to failure to perceive certain distinctions relevant to the L2. Nevertheless, L2 learners are able to acquire phonemes that are not found in the L1, provided that the features relevant to their representation are present in the L1 grammar; in other words, existing features can be used to accommodate new data.

5.4 Parameter setting: triggers and cues

Fortunately, L2 acquisition does not always involve such extreme cases of inability to process the input. We turn now to situations where the learner is, presumably, able to detect (unconsciously) a mismatch between the linguistic input and the current grammar, at least in certain cases. As Gregg (1996) points out, an adequate transition theory must account for how the linguistic input brings about grammar change. In this context, we will focus on syntactic representation and how parameter resetting might come about. The concept of *triggering* is central.

Since different languages exhibit different parameter settings, it must be the case that the input plays a crucial role in determining which option or setting is chosen. Parameters give the language acquirer advance knowledge of what the possibilities will be, that is, they severely restrict the range of choices that have to be considered. As discussed in chapters 1 and 4, these built-in options are currently thought of largely in terms of differences in feature strength, with a range of syntactic consequences depending on whether the strong or weak value of some feature is operative. A function of the input data is to *fix* one of the possible settings. In other words, the input determines the choice between the various built-in settings: some property of the input triggers a particular setting.

Consider, for example, the acquisition of word order, assuming a Head–Complement parameter which determines the position of heads with respect to their complements, i.e. head initial or head final (Chomsky 1986b). (See also chapter 4, section 4.3.2.) In the initial state of L1 acquisition, this parameter is open and waiting to be set. In the case of a language like English, various properties of the input could potentially trigger the head-initial setting, such as verb–object (VO) or P–NP order, both of which show that heads precede their complements. Conversely, in the case of a language like Japanese, the head-final setting will be triggered by OV order or the presence of postpositions, for example.

In fact, such a conception of triggering is an oversimplification. It is not the case that any utterance can serve as a trigger. Rather, input must already have been at least partially processed and must have been assigned some syntactic representation. In order to fix the appropriate setting of the Head–Complement parameter, the child must already have analysed at least the following: the sentence must have been segmented into words; syntactic categories like N and V, as well as their phrasal projections, NP and VP, must already be known; grammatical relations like subject and object must be known. In other words, an unanalysed stream of speech could not serve as a trigger for anything; it could not become *intake* to the grammar (cf. Corder 1967).

In recent years, there has been considerable discussion in the L1 learnability literature as to the precise nature of parameter setting and the role of triggers and triggering (Clark and Roberts 1993; Dresher 1999; Dresher and Kaye 1990; Fodor 1998, 1999; Gibson and Wexler 1994; Lightfoot 1989, 1999b). This research considers in detail what exactly a trigger is, what the triggering relationship might be, what properties of input act as triggers, how simple or complex a trigger must be, as well as how structured.

As these researchers have pointed out, there are many cases where input is ambiguous, consistent with more than one parameter setting or set of parameter settings, as suggested by the following example:

(1) Cats catch mice.

Assuming that the learner can parse the sentence as containing two nouns (*cats*, *mice*) and one verb (*catch*), what kind of grammar could generate a sentence like (1) and hence provide an appropriate representation? The problem is that there are too many analyses that fit the data: this sentence is consistent with all the possibilities shown in (2), as well as many others:[2]

(2)
a. SVO order and no verb raising (English): $[_{IP}$ cats $[_{VP}$ catch mice$]]$
b. SVO order and verb raising (French): $[_{IP}$ cats catch$_i$ $[_{VP}$ t_i mice$]]$
c. SOV order and V2 (German): $[_{CP}$ cats$_j$ catch$_i$ $[_{IP}$ t_j $[_{VP}$ mice $t_i]$ $t_i]]$
d. OVS (V2 and object fronting) (German): $[_{CP}$ cats$_k$ catch$_i$ $[_{IP}$ mice$_j$ $[_{VP}$ t_k $t_i]$ $t_i]]$

Suppose that, on independent grounds such as context or plausibility, the learner can establish that *mice* is the object of the verb. This eliminates only (2d) (which means *Mice catch cats*); the other analyses remain as possibilities. In particular, given a surface string like *Cats catch mice*, it is impossible to determine the underlying position of the verb.

For such reasons, it has been proposed that there must be designated, unambiguous and unique *cues* or *triggers*, consisting of partially or fully analysed structures (Dresher 1999; Dresher and Kaye 1990; Fodor 1994, 1998, 1999; Lightfoot 1999a, b; Roeper and de Villiers 1992; Roeper and Weissenborn 1990). In other words, parameters must in some sense be waiting for input of a particular kind, namely the designated structural trigger which will determine the appropriate parameter value. A parameter value is fixed only when the relevant cue is encountered; in consequence, parameter-setting to inappropriate values should not occur.[3] Cues are part of the built-in knowledge supplied by UG.

Let us reconsider the Verb Movement Parameter, discussed in chapter 4 (section 4.7.1), whereby the position of the finite verb is determined by the strength of features in Infl, verb raising being driven by strong I. At issue is the nature of the input that could serve to fix this parameter at the strong value. Returning to the examples in (2a) and (2b), the surface utterance, *Cats catch mice*, could be analysed in terms of overt verb raising (as in (2b)) or absence of raising (as in (2a)). A sentence of this type, then, cannot serve as a cue; it cannot provide unambiguous evidence as to whether I is strong or weak. The problem with the surface form is that there is no indication of where the VP boundary lies, hence one cannot tell whether or not the verb has raised.

In response to this kind of problem, Lightfoot (1999b) proposes that the trigger for strong I must be structural and syntactic, specifically that it consists of clear instances of finite lexical verbs in Infl. While sentences like (2a) and (2b) are ambiguous with respect to the position of the verb, disambiguating data do exist, as shown in the French sentences in (3), where the verb (*attrapent*) occurs to the left of the negative (*pas*), and (4), where the adverb (*souvent*) occurs to the right of the verb, indicating that the verb must have raised out of the VP.

(3) Les chats (n')attrapent pas les chiens.
[$_{IP}$ Les chats attrapent$_i$ [pas [$_{VP}$ t$_i$ les chiens]]
the cats catch not the dogs
'Cats do not catch dogs.'

(4) Les chats attrapent souvent les souris.
[$_{IP}$ Les chats attrapent$_i$ [souvent [$_{VP}$ t$_i$ les souris]]
the cats catch often the mice
'Cats often catch mice.'

For such sentences to serve as cues or triggers for strong I, it is necessary that the input has already been analysed sufficiently for the grammar to recognize verbs in general, to recognize that the verb is finite, and that negation and adverbs are generated at the left edge of the VP, hence that the verb can no longer be in the VP. In other words, once again, it cannot be the input in the form of utterances in the speech stream that serves as the trigger; rather, it must be analysed input. The grammar must also in some sense be expecting the cue, that is, waiting for evidence as to whether or not V is in I. It is important to note that although there is one cue (namely, V in I), there are a number of different sentence types in which this cue may be manifested (including, but not limited to, sentences containing negation or medial adverbs). Thus, the trigger is unique but it is not confined to any one particular sentence type.

Now consider the V2 phenomenon. Once again, as discussed in chapters 1 and 4, a parameter is implicated here, involving strength of features in C, where strong C results in the verb raising from I to C, as shown in (2c), repeated here as (5).

(5) $[_{CP}$ cats$_j$ catch$_i$ $[_{IP}$ t$_j$ $[_{VP}$ mice t$_i]$ t$_i]]$

The same triggering problem arises in this context, that is, surface strings of the form *Cats catch mice* are ambiguous with respect to the position of the verb. What, then, might be the unambiguous structural trigger for the strong value of C, hence V2? Fodor (1999) suggests that it is a [+finite] feature on C. While strings of the form *Cats catch mice* are ambiguous as to whether or not V2 is involved, declarative sentences where the finite lexical verb appears to the left of the subject show that it must have raised not only out of the VP but also out of IP, past the subject which is in Spec IP, as shown in (6).[4]

(6) Heute fängt meine Katze eine Maus.

$[_{CP}$ heute	fängt$_i$	$[_{IP}$ meine	Katze	$[_{VP}$ eine	Maus t$_i]$ t$_i]]$
today	catches	my	cat	a	mouse

'My cat will catch a mouse today.'

To summarize, the triggering problem is not trivial. Unanalysed input cannot serve as a trigger for parameter setting; cues must be structural and predetermined.

5.4.1 Morphological triggers: a digression

In the discussion so far, the cue for strong I has been assumed to be syntactic, namely, unambiguous evidence that V is in I, which is exemplified in a variety of syntactic structures. However, alternative claims have been advanced, according to which feature strength is causally dependent on the nature of the morphological paradigm. In other words, the trigger is claimed to be morphological rather than syntactic: rich morphological paradigms trigger strong feature values, while impoverished morphology results in weak feature strength (Rohrbacher 1994, 1999;

Vikner 1995, 1997). On this approach, rich morphology is seen as a necessary precursor to at least some strong features, triggering the strong value, with associated consequences for verb placement. It is claimed that the child does not determine strength of I on the basis of syntactic evidence (such as analysed input like (3) and (4)) but rather on the basis of inflectional morphology. We will refer to this proposal as the Rich Agreement Hypothesis following Bobaljik (to appear).

Rich agreement has been defined in various ways, details of which need not concern us. Suffice it to say that existence of a morphological paradigm showing a number of distinctive number and/or person markings is taken to be crucial (Rohrbacher 1994, 1999; Vikner 1995, 1997). The Rich Agreement Hypothesis makes reference to the verbal paradigm: in the absence of a rich morphological paradigm exhibiting a variety of person/number contrasts, feature strength will be weak. Hence, there will be no verb movement. On this account, in the L1 acquisition of verb-raising languages, there is expected to be a correlation between emergence of verbal agreement and emergence of verb raising. As the rich paradigm is acquired, feature strength is set to [strong], with verb raising as a consequence. Thus, it should not be possible for L1 acquirers to have acquired verb raising in the absence of a rich morphology.

However, there are theoretical and empirical grounds to question such a close relationship between overt morphology and abstract feature strength, taking into consideration data from L1 acquisition and dialect variation, as well as diachronic and synchronic data from a number of verb raising languages (Bobaljik, to appear; Lardiere 2000; Lightfoot 1999b; Sprouse 1998). In particular, while it does indeed seem to be the case that languages with rich inflection also have verb raising, it is not the case that languages with impoverished inflection necessarily lack verb raising. There are a number of languages and dialects which allow verb movement in the absence of rich morphological paradigms, for example, a dialect of Swedish spoken in Finland (Platzack and Holmberg 1989), Middle Danish (Vikner 1997), Middle English and Early Modern English (Lightfoot 1999b), Afrikaans (du Plessis et al. 1987), and Capeverdean Creole (Baptista 1997). In other words, these languages must have abstract feature strength set at the strong value (since this is what drives verb movement) and yet they lack overt morphological correlates, demonstrating that feature strength cannot have been triggered by rich agreement. Once one allows for the possibility that there are some languages where the cue for strong I cannot be overt morphology, it is impossible to maintain the argument that the trigger *must* be morphological. Furthermore, as far as L1 acquisition is concerned, Verrips and Weissenborn (1992) show that children acquiring German and French have appropriate verb placement well before the full agreement paradigm is being used. This means that feature strength must be set appropriately even in advance of the acquisition of the full agreement paradigm or even in the absence of rich agreement altogether. We will continue to assume, therefore, that the cue for strong I is syntactic. We return to the issue of rich morphology in chapter 6.

5.5 Triggers for L2 parameter resetting: more on verb movement

As discussed in chapters 3 and 4, researchers have proposed that parameters in the interlanguage grammar are initially set to the values instantiated in the L1 (Schwartz and Sprouse 1994, 1996; White 1985b, 1989). Where the L2 requires a different parameter setting from the L1, discrepancies will arise in parsing the L2 input. Assuming that grammar change is driven by parsing failures, parameter resetting should be initiated in such circumstances, with the appropriate values determined by cues in the L2 input.

In what follows, we examine potential discrepancies between L2 input and the current interlanguage grammar, and the role of cues in triggering parameter resetting, continuing with the Verb Movement Parameter as an example. Consider first, the English-speaking learner of French. In both languages, finite auxiliary verbs are positioned in I, as shown in (7).

(7) a. Mary has eaten the apple.
b. Mary [$_{IP}$ has [$_{VP}$ eaten the apple]]
c. Marie a mangé la pomme.
d. Marie [$_{IP}$ a [$_{VP}$ mangé la pomme]]

Assuming that the English-speaking learner of French has acquired the relevant vocabulary, an utterance like (7c) can successfully be parsed by the current grammar, being assigned the structure in (7d), an analysis appropriate for both the L1 and the L2.

The situation regarding lexical verbs is somewhat different. The V-features in I will initially be set to weak, the English value; in consequence, it is expected that lexical verbs remain in the VP. A sentence like (8) can be (mis)parsed by the current grammar, as shown in (8b), with the verb remaining in the VP, appropriate for the L1 English but not for the L2 French.

(8) a. Les chats attrapent les chiens.
b. [$_{IP}$ Les chats [$_{VP}$ attrapent les chiens]]

However, when the interlanguage grammar is faced with sentences like (3) and (4), repeated here as (9) and (10), a discrepancy will arise. The finite verb is external to the VP. While the learner can presumably parse such sentences by placing V in I, such an analysis is inconsistent with the current grammar. In other words, a partial parse is possible but there is a mismatch between the resulting structure and the current parameter setting. Such input, then, potentially serves as a cue for parameter resetting, showing that I must be strong in French.

(9) Les chats (n')attrapent pas les chiens.
[$_{IP}$ Les chats [$_{IP}$ attrapent$_i$ [pas [$_{VP}$ t$_i$ les chiens]]]

(10) Les chats attrapent souvent les souris.
[$_{IP}$ Les chats [$_{IP}$ attrapent$_i$ [souvent [$_{VP}$ t$_i$ les souris]]]

Turning to the opposite situation, namely the acquisition of English by French speakers, here the value of I must be reset from strong to weak, if the relevant properties of English are to be acquired. The L2 learner must somehow determine that a lexical verb is never in I in the L2, in other words that I is weak. As before, sentences containing only lexical verbs, such as (1), repeated here as (11), do not provide clear evidence as to where the VP boundary falls, hence cannot provide an unambiguous cue as to which setting is appropriate, as discussed above. They could be (mis)parsed in terms of a grammar with strong I, permitting verb raising, as shown in (2b), repeated here as (11b).

(11) a. Cats catch mice.
b. [$_{IP}$ cats catch$_i$ [$_{VP}$ t$_i$ mice]]

Similarly, while sentences containing auxiliary verbs, such as (7a), will occur in the L2 input, these can be parsed and analysed in a way that is consistent with either value of the parameter, hence cannot serve as cues to resetting.

The question then arises as to what might serve as a cue that I is not strong in the L2. There is a range of sentence types that is potentially indicative of weak I, including negatives, questions and adverb placement. Input like (12a) or (12c) contains the auxiliary *do*. One possibility is that these sentences are treated just like other sentences with auxiliaries (for example, (7a)), in which case they can successfully be parsed in terms of the L1 grammar and are unlikely to lead to parameter resetting. Alternatively, once the learner recognizes that *do* is semantically vacuous (unlike other auxiliaries and modals that appear in I), then such input might serve to indicate that lexical verbs cannot raise, since the only reason for the presence of this auxiliary is to carry tense and agreement features.

(12) a. Cats do not catch dogs.
b. Cats [$_{IP}$ do [not [$_{VP}$ catch dogs]]]
c. Do cats eat rats?
d. [$_{CP}$ Do$_i$ [$_{IP}$ cats t$_i$ [$_{VP}$ eat rats]]]
e. Cats often catch mice.
f. Cats [often [$_{VP}$ catch mice]]

In the case of (12e), the position of the adverb relative to the verb should force the sentence to be parsed with the lexical verb within the VP.[5] Such a parse is inconsistent with strong I, indicating the need for resetting.

To summarize, it is presupposed that triggers for parameter resetting appear in the positive evidence, or primary linguistic data. For example, provided the learner can do at least a preliminary parse, input like (9) shows that V is in I in French, while input like (12) suggests that lexical verbs remain within the VP in English. In other words, the learner has to detect the presence of relevant structural cues in the input. These cues motivate particular parameter settings.

5.6 A role for negative evidence in triggering?

We turn now to a consideration of negative evidence and the role, if any, it might play in L2 parameter resetting. Negative evidence consists of information about ungrammaticality. Direct negative evidence, such as correction or grammar teaching (where this deals implicitly or explicitly with what a language may and may not do), provides explicit information about what is ungrammatical, information about what sentences should not be generated by the grammar, about structures that are obligatorily absent. Since some instructed L2 learners are known to receive grammar teaching and correction, one possibility is that negative evidence might serve as a means to bring about parameter resetting. However, unlike positive evidence, negative data cannot, in principle, form part of the primary linguistic data. In the context of a theory of parameter setting driven by triggers, there is no way in which negative evidence can serve as a cue for resetting in the sense discussed above.

Consider, once again, the French-speaking learner of English. If the interlanguage grammar is characterized by L1 parameter settings, at least initially, then I will be strong and sentences like (13) can be generated. Hence, they may be produced by the learner, even though they do not occur in the L2 input.

(13) Cats catch often mice.

The issue of concern here is whether ungrammatical forms like (13) can be eliminated from the grammar (along with the strong value of I that allows them to be generated) by providing negative evidence, for instance, by correcting such utterances if produced, or by grammar instruction (in the form of rules, such as *English does not permit an adverb to appear between the verb and its object*).

The problem is that informing the learner of the ungrammaticality of sentences like (13) provides no structural cue whatsoever. Positive input like (12e) can be parsed as in (12f), hence indicating that the lexical verb is in the V position within the VP. In contrast, negative evidence contains no such cue. As pointed out by Schwartz (1993), negative evidence (as well as explicit positive evidence) contains information *about* the language; this is not the kind of data that can serve as input to a grammar. In other words, it is in principle impossible for negative evidence to bring about parameter resetting.

Nevertheless, there is, potentially, an alternative kind of negative evidence which might work in the context of a cue-based theory. This is known as *indirect negative evidence*. The idea is that the learner somehow determines that certain structures or cues are absent or non-occurring. Chomsky (1981a: 9) suggests the following:

> A not unreasonable acquisition system can be devised with the operative principle that if certain structures or rules fail to be exemplified in relatively simple expressions, where they would be expected to be found, then a(n) . . . option is selected excluding them in the grammar, so that a kind of 'negative evidence' can be available even without corrections, adverse reactions, etc.

It is important to recognize that a proposal of this kind can only work if the language learner somehow knows what to look for (i.e. has a reason for checking whether something is missing).[6] In the context of predetermined parameter settings and cues, it is conceivable that the grammar might be 'searching' for the cue for one setting to some parameter and that, in the absence of the relevant cue, the other setting would be motivated.

Lightfoot's (1999b) proposals to account for certain historical changes in English suggest a potential form of indirect negative evidence in the context of resetting the Verb Movement Parameter. Historically, English had strong features in Infl, with associated properties; hence, lexical verbs raised to I, preceding negation and adverbs, as they do in French. In subsequent stages of English, movement of lexical verbs to I became impossible. Lightfoot argues that, in order for the strong value of the parameter to be set, it is not in fact sufficient for there to be evidence of V-in-I in the input. Rather, there must be some threshold; if instances of the cue drop below this threshold, the strong value is not instantiated. In later stages of English, instances of finite lexical verbs in I dropped dramatically, due to modal auxiliaries losing their verb-like characteristics, the introduction of periphrastic *do*, etc.; the threshold was not met and a child acquiring English at that time adopted the weak value of the parameter.[7]

This historical change has parallels with the situation facing learners whose L1 has verb raising (such as French) acquiring an L2 lacking verb raising (such as English). If strong I is instantiated in the interlanguage grammar of a

French-speaking learner of English, there will in fact be few instances of V-in-I in the L2 input to confirm this. In some sense, then, failure of the L2 input to reach the necessary threshold of instances of V-in-I might constitute a form of indirect negative evidence, indicating the need to reset the strength of I from strong to weak. (The L2 situation differs from Lightfoot's account of historical change, in that children acquiring English as their mother tongue did not start off with a grammar with strong I which then changed to weak. Rather, the grammars of their parents instantiated the strong value while the children acquired only the weak value, because the input motivating strong had dropped below some threshold.)

In summary, if parameter setting depends on predetermined, structural cues, then, where such cues are available in the positive L2 input, parameter resetting should in principle be possible. That is, in the event of a parsing breakdown, or inconsistencies between a parse and the current grammar, the learner should restructure the grammar accordingly. As we have seen, in the case of the Verb Movement Parameter, such discrepancies do arise between an analysis based on L1 parameter settings and properties of the L2 input. In other words, there will be parsing inconsistencies which suggest the need for parameter resetting.

5.7 Triggering in L2: manipulating the input

It is one thing to maintain that some structural property of the input serves as a cue for parameter setting. It is quite another matter to demonstrate that this is in fact the case, since it is impossible to prove that some linguistic property acts as a trigger for some parameter setting. In L1 acquisition research, proposals for cues have been investigated indirectly, for example, by examining whether clusters of linguistic properties emerge at more or less the same time, or whether there are cascading effects, suggesting the influence of some particular cue in the input (e.g. Hyams 1986; Snyder 1995a; Snyder and Stromswold 1997). As far as historical change is concerned, researchers have considered whether a set of changes takes place at more or less the same time or, again, whether there is a cascade of effects stemming from a purported change in a cue's threshold (Lightfoot 1999b). In L2 acquisition, on the other hand, it is possible to manipulate the input more directly, ensuring, to some extent, that certain linguistic forms are supplied (or not supplied). Where linguistic theory provides some indication of potential cues, these can be isolated and manipulated in the classroom.

Issues related to triggering have occasionally been investigated in the L2 context. In particular, there have been several experimental studies of effects of classroom input on the Verb Movement Parameter. In a series of studies, White and colleagues

(Trahey 1996; Trahey and White 1993; White 1990/1991, 1991a, 1992a; White, Spada, Lightbown and Ranta 1991) investigated the L2 acquisition of English verb placement by native speakers of French. As we have seen, if the interlanguage grammar of French-speaking learners of English has I set to strong, this value must be reset to weak, if the relevant L2 properties are to be acquired. White and colleagues investigated two main issues, namely: (i) whether one can supply positive evidence (including input with suitable cues) in the classroom to bring about resetting from the French to English value; (ii) whether or not negative evidence is effective in this context.

In section 5.5, it was suggested that each setting of the Verb Movement Parameter has its own cue, namely evidence that V is in I, in the case of French, or evidence that V is in the VP, in the case of English. If so, resetting from strong I to weak should be achievable on the basis of positive evidence, or triggers in the L2 English input, such as presence of *do*-support, demonstrating that lexical verbs remain in the VP.

The particular focus of most of the studies by White and colleagues was on placement of adverbs relative to lexical verbs in finite clauses. Amongst other things, the French-speaking learner of English must come to know that sentences like (14a) with a preverbal adverb (henceforth, SAVO) are grammatical in English, whereas sentences like (14b) with the adverb appearing between the verb and its object (henceforth, SVAO) are not, the complete reverse of the facts for French:[8]

(14) a. Cats often catch mice. (SAVO)
b. *Cats catch often mice. (SVAO)

At issue is whether the appropriate value of the Verb Movement Parameter can be triggered by providing the learner with L2 input that demonstrates that lexical verbs in English remain in the VP. As we have seen, there are several different structures (see chapter 4, table 4.3) which could potentially exemplify this cue. Another issue, then, is whether input which focuses on only one of these constructions can effect changes to the other constructions as well. In other words, if the cue is provided in only one form, does it result in more general, across-the-board changes, as would be expected on a parameter setting account?

The experiment reported in White (1990/1991) was undertaken to explore some of these questions. (See box 5.2.) Subjects were elementary school children, beginners at the time of testing, who were enrolled in intensive English as a Second Language programmes where language teaching was communicative, with no form-focused or explicit instruction (other than during the experimental treatments). Subjects were divided into two groups, one of which (the *question group*) was instructed, for two weeks, on English question formation (including word

Box 5.2 Verb movement parameter (White 1990/1991)

Languages: L1 = French, L2 = English.
Task: Preference task.
Sample stimulus:

a. Linda always takes the metro.
b. Linda takes always the metro.

Only a is right Only b is right Both right Both wrong Don't know

Results:

Table 5.2.1 *Preference task: mean acceptances of SVAO and SAVO orders*

		*SVAO (# = 12)		SAVO (# = 16)	
		Pretest	Post-test	Pretest	Post-test
L2 groups	Question group (n = 56)	8.2	9	7	10
	Adverb group (n = 82)	8	1.75	6	14
Native speakers (n = 26)		0.5		15	

order in questions, the need for *do*-support, etc.) but not adverb placement, while the other (the *adverb group*) received instruction on adverb placement, including the possibility of SAVO order and the impossibility of SVAO. Instruction included error correction and rules about where to place adverbs or how to form questions, as well as a variety of classroom activities manipulating the structures in question. In other words, the input was quite explicit and included both positive and negative evidence.

Both groups were pretested for knowledge of adverb placement on a variety of tasks. One of these, a preference task, is presented in box 5.2. Results were consistent across tasks: while subjects showed some acceptance of English SAVO order, their acceptance and use of SVAO (ungrammatical in English but grammatical in French) was higher, consistent with the adoption of the L1 parameter value in the interlanguage grammar. After the teaching intervention, subjects were retested on the same tasks; results were again consistent across tasks. The adverb group showed a dramatic increase in use of SAVO order and a significant decline in use of SVAO, basically rejecting such sentences altogether, like the native speakers. The question group, on the other hand, showed a slight but significant increase in their use of SAVO but no change with respect to SVAO, which they continued to accept. (See table 5.2.1.) In other words, instruction on questions with *do*-support, which was intended to provide the cue that V must remain in the

VP in English, failed to generalize to another case where V should remain in the VP, namely after VP-initial adverbs. In contrast, providing explicit evidence about word-order possibilities concerning adverb placement did lead to changes, such that ungrammatical forms were recognized as such and grammatical forms were used appropriately. So far, then, the results are not consistent with across-the-board parameter resetting.

The instruction received by both groups was very explicit, bearing little resemblance to naturalistic input. Hence, it might be the case that the classroom input simply did not provide genuine cues for parameter resetting. In a follow-up study, Trahey and White (1993) sought to remedy this problem by providing an additional group with a 'flood' of positive evidence on English adverb placement. Materials were prepared which exposed the subjects to adverbs in a variety of syntactic contexts, including SAVO (e.g. *Cats often catch mice*). Given the impossibility of SVAO order in English, no such forms were exemplified in the input flood. There was no explicit instruction, no error correction, and no practice or exercises manipulating adverbs. Thus, this input avoided the problem of providing information *about* the language. Rather, primary linguistic data with cues to the position of the verb were provided, in that sentences like *Cats often catch mice* demonstrate that the verb must be within the VP.

Results from this experiment differed from the results of the adverb group in the earlier experiment: significant increases in acceptance and use of SAVO were found, but without a corresponding drop in acceptance and use of the ungrammatical SVAO order. Supplying many exemplars of a potential cue to the lack of verb raising (in the form of sentences like (14a)) failed to drive out forms like (14b), suggesting that resetting of the strength of I was not achieved.

5.7.1 Manipulating the input: assessment

So far, it appears that it is not possible to stimulate parameter resetting by deliberately supplying sentences that target purported cues for a particular value of a parameter, at least in this case. The subjects studied by Trahey and White (1993) received ample positive evidence (which was not explicit) for SAVO order in English, i.e. for the verb's remaining within the VP. Similarly, the subjects instructed on question formation were exposed to positive evidence (both explicit and implicit) that lexical verbs do not raise, in the form of *do*-support in English questions. In spite of this input, subjects continued to permit a word order in L2 English (SVAO) which is consistent with verb raising due to L1-based feature strength.

Negative evidence was also provided in some of the above classroom studies. That is, the children were corrected when they produced ungrammatical sentences and they were instructed as to which adverb positions were prohibited. In White (1990/1991), the adverb group was provided with just such evidence during the instructional period. As it turned out, these were the only subjects who learned that SVAO is not a possible English word order. Thus, explicit negative evidence (and only negative evidence) appeared to be successful in bringing about change, driving out the ungrammatical forms. Schwartz (1993) and Schwartz and Gubala-Ryzack (1992) question whether parameter resetting was implicated at all. Rather, they propose that the changes effected as a result of explicit negative evidence did not involve unconscious linguistic competence (the interlanguage grammar), or UG-based principles and parameters. Although negative evidence effected changes in linguistic behaviour, it did not succeed in bringing about restructuring of the interlanguage grammar, in the form of a transition from one parameter setting to another.

Schwartz (1993) and Schwartz and Gubala-Ryzack (1992) base their observations on the fact that the teaching interventions in the studies by White and colleagues had additional effects that appear to be unrelated to the parameter in question. Indeed, the learners made generalizations which appear not to be grammar-based. In particular, they rejected grammatical English sentences with intransitive verbs followed by a prepositional phrase, as in (15) (White 1990/1991).

(15) Mary walks quickly to school.

The learners had not been instructed on such sentences. In consequence of the teaching, generalizations were apparently being made on the basis of surface patterns, such that learners would not permit an adverb to be placed between the verb and any other constituent. As Schwartz and Gubala-Ryzack point out, there is no conceivable grammatical analysis that could account for this behaviour. One conclusion might be that these L2 learners have ended up with a 'wild' grammar as a result of explicit instruction. Schwartz and Gubala-Ryzack conclude, rather, that the unconscious grammatical system was not affected at all. Instead, a separate system of learned linguistic knowledge was implicated (Schwartz 1993).

Schwartz and Gubala-Ryzack offer an additional argument for this claim, based on the fact that changes in behaviour with respect to adverb placement proved to be short-term. White (1991a) reports on a follow-up study with the same subjects. One year after the classroom intervention, after no further instruction on adverb placement, the children had completely reverted to their pre-instructional behaviour, largely rejecting SAVO order and accepting SVAO. Schwartz and Gubala-Ryzack (1992) consider that the very fact that knowledge of ungrammaticality was lost is an indication that parameters were never in fact implicated.

The evidence discussed so far indicates that parameter resetting does not take place on the basis of explicit classroom input (positive or negative). (This does not imply that explicit input is ineffective in L2 acquisition, only that whatever it affects is not the system of UG-based principles and parameters.) One other consideration is whether or not indirect negative evidence might be effective, that is, whether learners somehow become sensitive to absence of certain properties in the L2 input. In the case of the Verb Movement Parameter, French-speaking learners of English would have to 'detect' the lack of exemplars of V in I in general or SVAO word order in particular. The issue of indirect negative evidence was not directly examined in the studies by White and colleagues. However, the results are not consistent with this possibility. The question group received considerable evidence of *do*-support in questions (i.e. evidence that lexical verbs remain in the VP); the input flood group received considerable evidence of SAVO word order (again showing that the lexical verb is within the VP). In consequence, potential instances of V in I were severely reduced. Nevertheless, in the interlanguage grammars of these subjects, verb raising in English continued to be permitted, at least past adverbs.

5.8 Beyond explicit teaching

The relative ineffectiveness of explicit classroom input in bringing about a transition from one parameter setting to another is not particularly surprising in the context of a cue-based theory, given that explicit instruction supplies information about the language, rather than providing primary linguistic data containing relevant cues. But classroom learners, of course, are constantly exposed to primary linguistic data as well. Indeed, outside of the experimental interventions, there was little or no explicit form-focused instruction or correction in the above studies. As White (1992a) reports, in another study involving children in the same intensive programmes (see chapter 4, box 4.5), the L2 learners did in fact show convincing evidence of knowing that V remains in the VP in English when tested on question formation and negative placement. As this knowledge was achieved prior to any explicit instruction, it presumably was effected by cues in the more naturalistic input. In other words, in terms of the split-Infl hypothesis (Pollock 1989) (see chapter 4, section 4.7.1), some property of the English input, presumably *do*-support, had indeed triggered resetting of the strength of T, even though strength of Agr had not been reset.

In addition, there is evidence to suggest that L2 learners can *override* explicit evidence about the L2. In other words, they can detect cues in the primary linguistic data, despite incomplete or misleading grammar teaching. Bruhn-Garavito (1995) discusses such a case. The L2 in question is Spanish; the property under consideration is coreference between embedded subject pronouns in subjunctive clauses and the subject of a matrix clause.

In Spanish, there is a *subjunctive rule*, which dictates that the subject of an embedded subjunctive clause is obligatorily disjoint in reference from the subject of the matrix clause. In other words, it cannot corefer with the matrix subject. In (16), the subject in both the main clause and the embedded clause is the null pronoun, *pro*. In the matrix clause, the subject is first-person singular, as can be determined by inflection on the verb. In the embedded clause, the subjunctive verb form could, in principle, be either first or third person (since the verbal morphology is the same). However, the first-person interpretation is ruled out, because this would result in coreference with the matrix subject, which is prohibited by the subjunctive rule.

(16)	[$_{CP}$ *pro*$_i$	quiero	[$_{IP}$ que	*pro*$_{*i/j}$ vaya	a	la	fiesta]]
		want-1SG	that	go-*1/3SG-SUBJ	to	the	party

'I want *me/him/her to go to the party.'

The obligatory disjoint reference follows from Principle B of the Binding Theory, which states that a pronoun must be free in its governing category, that is, that it cannot corefer with an NP within the same governing category (Chomsky 1981a). According to Rochette (1988), subjunctive clauses are IPs, not CPs. On the assumption that CP is a governing category but that IP is not, both the matrix subject and the embedded subject in sentences like (16) are contained within the same governing category (the overall CP); hence, the subjects must be disjoint in reference.

There are other cases involving the Spanish subjunctive, however, where coreference between matrix and embedded subjects is possible. This is true where there is a modal verb in the subjunctive clause or where the subjunctive clause is an adjunct. This is shown in (17).

(17)	a. [$_{CP}$ *pro*$_i$ espero	[$_{CP}$ que	*pro*$_{i/j}$ pueda	hablar	con	él	hoy]]
	hope-1SG	that	can-1/3SG	speak	with	him	today

'I hope that I/he/she will be able to speak with him today.'

	b. [$_{CP}$ *pro*$_i$ voy	a	llamarte	[$_{CP}$ cuando	*pro*$_{i/j}$ llegue]]
	am-going-1SG	to	call-you	when	arrive-1/3SG-SUBJ

'I will call you when I/he/she arrive(s).'

On Rochette's analysis, the embedded clause in (17a) is a CP, as is the adjunct clause in (17b). Hence, the embedded subject is free within that clause and can therefore corefer with a subject in another clause.

Bruhn-Garavito (1995) points out that in L2 Spanish classes it is usual to provide explicit instruction on the subjunctive rule, as well as error correction. Most grammar-based textbooks make specific mention of this restriction on the use of the subjunctive. In other words, L2 learners of Spanish are taught the facts in (16). Furthermore, they are typically not taught the exceptions, namely that adjunct clauses and subjunctive clauses containing modal verbs do not fall under this generalization, nor is this mentioned in textbooks. Indeed, teachers in Bruhn-Garavito's study reported that sentences like (17) are ungrammatical, precisely because they violate the subjunctive rule, a judgment which was not shared by Bruhn-Garavito's native-speaker control group.

If interlanguage grammars are UG-constrained, once the L2 learner discovers the nature of the embedded projection (distinguishing between embedded IPs and embedded CPs), this knowledge should trigger the relevant binding properties, with coreference possible where there is a CP boundary (as in (17)) but not where there is only an IP (as in (16)). This should be the case even though instruction is misleading, taking the form of a blanket subjunctive rule requiring disjoint reference in all cases. Since this phenomenon involves a UG principle rather than a parameter, it is not the case that parameter resetting is implicated. Nevertheless, given an L1 without the subjunctive (such as English), the learner must establish what kind of constituent the subjunctive clause is; if the clause is parsed as a CP, there are certain consequences for binding (coreference), whereas if it is parsed as an IP, there are other consequences (disjoint reference).

Bruhn-Garavito conducted an experiment on advanced, adult learners of Spanish. (See box 5.3.) Learners were tested by means of a truth-value judgment task. In cases like (16), a context was established which rendered coreference plausible. If Principle B is instantiated in the interlanguage grammar, learners should reject sentences like (16) with coreference intended between the null subject of the embedded subjunctive clause and the subject of the matrix clause, even though the context favours this. In the case of sentences like (17), on the other hand, a coreferential interpretation should be permitted. Thus, the question of interest is whether L2 learners distinguish between the sentence types, disallowing coreference with the matrix subject in the case of subjects of embedded subjunctive clauses and allowing it when the embedded subjunctive clause contains a modal or when it is an adjunct clause.

As can be seen in table 5.3.1, the native speakers of Spanish made a sharp distinction between the cases where disjoint reference is required and those where coreference is permitted. Their underlying linguistic competence, then, differed radically from the prescriptive rule presented in grammar books, according to which coreference is never possible. The L2 learners also made the relevant distinction, although not as sharply. In about 50% of responses to the standard examples of the subjunctive rule, disjoint reference was not observed. In other words, learners accepted an interpretation where the subject of the subjunctive clause was coreferent with the subject of the main clause. Nevertheless, acceptance of coreference

Box 5.3 Overcoming misleading input (Bruhn-Garavito 1995)

Languages: L1s = English/French/other, L2 = Spanish.
Task: Truth-value judgments. Short contexts, each followed by a comment. Subjects indicate whether the comment is reasonable in the context.
Sample stimulus:

Mencha cumple años el viernes. Desea recibir muchos regalos.
Mencha dice: Quiero que reciba muchos regalos.
(*It is Mencha's birthday on Friday. She wants to get a lot of presents.*
Mencha says: I want that Ø get a lot of presents.)

Results:

Table 5.3.1 *Acceptances of coreference between matrix clause and embedded subjunctive clause subjects (in %)*

	Subjunctives	Subjunctive + modal	Subjunctive adjuncts
L2 learners (n = 27)	50.75	86	87.4
Native speakers (n = 12)	2.5	85	91.66

in these cases was noticeably lower than acceptance of coreference in the other clause types. Furthermore, an analysis of individual subject data showed that the L2 learners fell into two distinct groups, with about half of them requiring disjoint reference in the case of embedded subjunctive clauses (just like the native speakers) and about half permitting coreference. The first group, then, have acquired unconscious knowledge of when coreference is permitted and when it is not, even though they were taught that coreference is *never* possible. As French is very like Spanish with respect to coreference possibilities in subjunctive clauses, it might be argued that 'successful' performance derived from the L1. However, as Bruhn-Garavito demonstrates, French speakers and English speakers did not differ to any great extent in their judgments; there were French speakers and English speakers in the group who rejected coreference in subjunctive clauses and there were French speakers and English speakers in the group who allowed coreference.

To sum up, Bruhn-Garavito's study shows that learners of Spanish can acquire a subtle contrast in the coreference possibilities for various kinds of subjunctive clauses in the L2, even though explicit instruction denies the existence of such a contrast. In the case of those learners who demonstrate knowledge of the relevant constraint, Principle B is presumably operative in the grammar and embedded subjunctive clauses are appropriately analysed as IPs. The second group, in contrast, seem to be treating embedded subjunctive clauses as CPs. What is not yet clear is what the relevant triggering data might be in such cases, that is, what property of subjunctive clauses leads to them being analysed as IPs.

5.9 Conclusion

In this chapter, the transition problem has been considered, that is, the question of how development takes place in L2 grammars. It has been suggested that grammar change in L2 acquisition, as in L1 acquisition, is driven by parsing failure (inconsistencies between a particular parse and the current grammar) and that structural properties of the L2 input act as cues to parameter resetting. When the learner's current grammar is unable to fully parse the L2 input, change is motivated. Cues in the input will be inconsistent with some parameter settings and will motivate others. Cues must be present in the primary linguistic data; negative evidence cannot play the same role because it only provides information about the language.

The precise role of classroom input in the triggering process is not yet clear. In the studies on adverb placement, explicit classroom input did not appear to supply relevant cues for parameter resetting; even implicit input was not wholly successful in this respect. On the other hand, Bruhn-Garavito's study suggests that L2 learners can work out subtle properties of the L2 even given explicit input which is actually misleading as to abstract properties of the L2.

Finally, it should be noted that the presence of suitable sentence types exemplifying certain cues does not, of course, guarantee that they are recognized as cues by the learner. In the case of L2 acquisition, it seems that the L1 parameter value may persist, even when the L2 input contains suitable cues. A similar failure to act immediately on potential cues is true of L1 acquisition as well: even if linguists can identify triggers which should force a change from one representation to another, we still do not know why change does not take place immediately, or why some parameter settings are triggered earlier and with greater ease than others.[9]

Topics for discussion

- It has been suggested here that Brown's (1998, 2000) theory of L2 phonological acquisition shows parallels with the Failed Functional Features Hypothesis. On the other hand, it might be considered to provide evidence for Full Transfer Full Access. Why?
- Assumptions about the nature and degree of change in grammars during the course of development vary considerably, depending in part on

what the initial state is assumed to be. For example, according to the Minimal Trees Hypothesis, functional categories are initially absent and are gradually added. This contrasts with Full Access accounts, whereby functional categories are present in the initial state, hence do not have to be acquired. For each of the theories described in this book, discuss the nature and type of change that is predicted to take place over time.

- According to Full Access without Transfer or the Initial Hypothesis of Syntax (chapter 3), L2 learners start off with parameters either open or set to default values, as determined by UG. Similarly, the Minimal Trees Hypothesis assumes that parameters relating to functional categories will revert to default or open settings. If these accounts are correct, to what extent (if any) does it change the assumptions about triggering that have been discussed in this chapter?
- According to Schwartz and Gubala-Ryzack (1992), failure to retain instructed knowledge over time indicates that unconscious linguistic competence was never involved. What are the implications for L1 attrition, where people 'lose' knowledge of their first language, including syntactic knowledge, as a result of extensive exposure to the L2?
- Morphological triggers. Which initial state theories discussed in chapter 2 assume a triggering role for morphology?

Suggestions for additional reading

- Carroll (2001) provides perhaps the most detailed attempt to provide a transition theory which presupposes that linguistic representation is modular and UG-constrained. Herschensohn (2000) advances what she terms *Constructionism*, an approach which provides both a representational theory of L2 which assumes UG (couched in terms of Minimalism) and a developmental theory that relies on other strategies and learning procedures.
- Earlier accounts of the role of positive and negative evidence in L1 and L2 are couched in terms of the Subset Condition and the Subset Principle. For detailed discussion of the Subset Principle in L2 acquisition and overview of related empirical research, see White (1989, chapter 6).
- For discussion about learnability, the nature of parameter setting and the role of triggers in L1 acquisition, see Clark and Roberts (1993), Dresher (1999), Dresher and Kaye (1990), Fodor (1998, 1999), Gibson and Wexler (1994), and Lightfoot (1989, 1999b).

- Many of the papers in DeGraff (1999) discuss the relationship between language acquisition, language change and creolization, as does Lightfoot (1999b).
- For extensive discussion of the issue of negative evidence in relation to parameter resetting, see Schwartz (1993), Schwartz and Gubala-Ryzack (1992) and White (1992b). Other research on manipulating classroom input in the context of UG-based theories of L2 is presented by Izumi and Lakshmanan (1998), White (1995b) and White, Hirakawa and Kawasaki (1996). For claims that classroom instruction may fail to provide sufficient input to trigger UG principles, see Felix and Weigl (1991).
- L2 parsing issues are explored in a number of studies (Juffs and Harrington 1995, 1996; Schachter and Yip 1990; White and Juffs 1998). These studies suggest that there can be divergence between online parsing and underlying syntactic knowledge, in other words, discrepancies between knowledge and use of language. For evidence that L2 learners make use of L1-based parsing strategies, see Fernández (1999, to appear).

6

Morphological variability and the morphology/syntax interface

6.1 Morphological variability: identifying the problem

In several earlier chapters (chapters 3, 4 and 5), issues have arisen with respect to the relationship between interlanguage morphology and syntax, for example, presence or absence of verbal inflection and presence or absence of null subjects or of verb movement. There is considerable disagreement over the relationship between overt inflectional morphology and more abstract functional categories and their features, following similar disagreements in the field of L1 acquisition. In this chapter, we consider the morphology/syntax interface, discussing the extent to which morphology and syntax are interdependent in grammars in general, including interlanguage grammars. In particular, the implications of morphological variability will be addressed.

It is well known that L2 learners exhibit optionality or variability in their use of verbal and nominal inflection and associated lexical items. Morphology relating to tense, agreement, number, case, gender, etc., as well as function words like determiners, auxiliaries and complementizers, are sometimes present and sometimes absent in spontaneous production data, in circumstances where they would be obligatorily produced by native speakers. Furthermore, when morphology is present, it is not necessarily appropriate; certain forms are overused, occurring in contexts where they would not be permitted in the grammar of a native speaker.

Some of the earliest research on interlanguage concentrated on properties which we now recognize as being related to functional categories. (See Zobl and Liceras (1994) for an overview.) Research on morpheme acquisition orders conducted during the 1970s (Bailey, Madden and Krashen 1974; Dulay and Burt 1974, amongst many others) suggested that certain inflectional affixes and function words are acquired in a largely invariant order. It should be noted that in these studies, acquisition is defined in terms of accuracy of suppliance in obligatory contexts, with the criterion being set at 90% accuracy (following Brown (1973) for L1). Before achieving the 90% criterion, morphology was not absent; rather, learners would produce various morphemes and function words but would not use them consistently. At the time, this was generally taken to mean lack of acquisition. Meisel, Clahsen and Pienemann (1981) presented an opposing view; these researchers argued that acquisition of underlying knowledge must be distinguished from use of such knowledge, a position similar to the one adopted in this book. In other words, the so-called order of acquisition reported in many of the morpheme studies of the 1970s reflects the order in which learners achieve almost total accuracy of usage, which is not the same as acquisition per se.

More recent studies, including those conducted within the UG framework, continue to observe the same phenomenon, that is, inconsistent use of inflectional morphology and function words. While the fact of variation is uncontroversial, there is relatively little agreement as to what it implies, in particular whether it indicates major impairment to the interlanguage grammar or whether it is indicative of something else, and, if so, what. Theories that assume full access to UG might seem to imply that L2 acquisition should be comparatively quick and error free, and successful in all respects, including morphology. Since perfect mastery of the L2 is clearly not inevitable, with L2 learners exhibiting continuing problems in the morphological domain, some researchers have taken L2 learners' difficulties with inflectional morphology as evidence against the operation of UG in L2 acquisition (Clahsen 1988; Meisel 1991). As we shall see, however, morphological variability may be attributable to ongoing problems with language use, rather than to a failure to acquire abstract morphosyntax or to an impairment in grammatical representation.

In the following sections, two radically different perspectives are presented on the morphology/syntax interface in interlanguage grammars. On the first view, variability in incidence of inflectional morphology is accounted for in terms of grammatical representation. In particular, morphological variability is argued to reflect either (i) a developmental phenomenon, whereby the interlanguage grammar lacks certain abstract categories or features in early stages, these being subsequently acquired; or (ii) some kind of permanent grammatical impairment or deficit. According to the second approach, abstract morphosyntactic features are present even in the early interlanguage grammar, and the underlying syntactic representation is unimpaired. Instead, there may sometimes be a breakdown in the relationship between one part of the grammar and another, such that the learner cannot always access the relevant morphology even when it has been acquired (Haznedar and Schwartz 1997; Lardiere 1998a, b, 2000; Lardiere and Schwartz 1997; Prévost and White 2000a, b; Robertson 2000). This position has come to be known as the Missing (Surface) Inflection Hypothesis. Hawkins (2000) refers to this kind of approach as implying a breakdown in computation, rather than representation.

Table 6.1 *Functional categories and morphosyntactic features in English*

Functional category	Abstract morphosyntactic features	Surface morphological realization in English
Infl	± tense/finite; ± past; ø features (person, number).	–s; –ed; –Ø
Comp	± wh	that; whether; Ø
Det	± definite; ± plural	a; the; Ø

6.2 Surface versus abstract morphology

In order to consider the implications of morphological variability in more detail, it is important to distinguish between abstract morphosyntax and associated surface forms. As noted by Grondin and White (1996), Hyams and Safir (1991), Lardiere (2000), Schwartz (1991), amongst others, one must distinguish between abstract features, such as Tense and Agreement, and how they are realized or spelled out morphologically. There is no one-to-one correspondence between underlying representation and surface form. While languages share abstract properties, they differ as to the forms by which these properties are spelled out. There is nothing in UG that specifies that past tense in English must be realized by a morpheme */-ed/* or that agreement must manifest itself as */-s/* in the third-person singular. Indeed, there is nothing in UG that dictates that abstract features must have any kind of overt manifestation.

Consider table 6.1, which shows functional categories like Infl, Comp and Det and some of their associated abstract features. In English, these features are realized in various ways (via inflection or function words). In some cases, there is no overt reflection of features, in which case we can think of null morphemes as being involved. For example, agreement (so-called ϕ-features) is not marked morphologically on English verbs except in the case of third-person singular in the present tense. Similarly, while regular English verbs mark past tense by means of the */-ed/* suffix, some verbs show no explicit morphology for past (*cut/cut*), while others indicate past tense by irregular forms involving internal vowel changes (*sing/sang*) or by suppletion rather than affixation (*go/went*). Nevertheless, even in the absence of explicit morphology, there is evidence for Infl and related tense and agreement features. In the case of a sentence like *I sing*, the verb carries features for person (first), number (singular) and tense (–past), which happen not to be overtly realized.[1] These abstract features are not visible in the form of overt verbal affixes. Yet we know that they must be present at some level because of a variety of agreement phenomena. For instance, the form *he sing* is ungrammatical because of a feature clash between the form of the verb (first or second person) and the pronoun (third person).

Another example concerns other lexical items associated with functional categories, namely function words as opposed to affixes: determiners are not required with all nouns in English (e.g. *I hate dogs*); nevertheless, we assume the presence of DP in English, including null determiners in some cases. Similarly, English complementizers are often optional (e.g. *I think that he will be late; I think he will be late*) but there are nevertheless grounds to believe that a CP is projected in both cases. It should be clear, then, that the fact that some functional category or set of features is represented at an underlying level does not entail that there will be a corresponding overt form. As a corollary, absence of surface morphology does not necessarily imply absence of more abstract categories and features.

A further complication, as Lardiere (2000) points out, is that one has to distinguish between null morphemes and absence of morphemes. These have very different consequences: null morphemes have corresponding positions or features in a syntactic representation (for example, English agreement as described above). In contrast, there are cases where something is simply not realized at all; the syntactic representation lacks a particular category or feature. Such would be the case for grammatical gender in English, for example, a feature which English lacks (see chapter 4, section 4.7.2.4).

The tendency in much L2 acquisition research has been to interpret absence of morphology in interlanguage production only in the second sense. That is, absence of overt morphology is taken to indicate absence of the corresponding morphosyntactic categories. In contrast, the position taken in this chapter is that, while an L2 learner's production might lack overt inflection for tense or agreement, his or her underlying grammar nevertheless represents the categories of Tense and Agreement, and their corresponding features. This must, after all, be the case for native speakers, when anything other than third-person singular is involved.

6.3 Accounts of morphological variability in L1 acquisition

Variability in the suppliance of overt morphology is not restricted to L2 acquisition, being reported in L1 acquisition as well. Furthermore, hypotheses as to what might be going on in L1 acquisition have had considerable influence on proposals for L2. Hence, some L1 perspectives will briefly be considered here. Approaches can be broadly classified into two types (as will also be the case for L2 acquisition): morphology-before-syntax versus syntax-before-morphology. The former is associated with the Rich Agreement Hypothesis (see chapter 5, section 5.4.1), the latter with the Separation Hypothesis (see below).

6.3.1 Morphology-before-syntax

Several L1 researchers have claimed that overt morphology and underlying syntax are linked in language acquisition, with a very close and direct relationship between them. In particular, absence of (consistent) overt morphology is indicative that certain grammatical categories have not yet been acquired (e.g. Clahsen, Penke and Parodi 1993/1994; Radford 1990). On many such accounts, there is assumed to be a causal connection, or triggering relationship, between the two, the acquisition of overt morphology driving the acquisition of syntax.[2]

There are two perspectives on how acquisition of morphology might trigger acquisition of syntax, one maintaining that morphology triggers categories and features, the other assuming that it is crucial for feature strength. According to the first view, exemplified by the Weak Continuity Hypothesis for L1 acquisition (Clahsen, Eisenbeiss and Vainikka 1994; Clahsen et al. 1993/1994), acquisition of overt morphological paradigms drives the acquisition of (at least some) functional categories and their features. According to the second position, acquisition of overt morphological paradigms determines acquisition of feature strength, strong features values being motivated by rich morphology.[3] This is the Rich Agreement Hypothesis (Rohrbacher 1994, 1999; Vikner 1995, 1997), as discussed in chapter 5 (section 5.4.1). In either case, the acquisition of overt morphology is claimed to be a necessary precursor to the acquisition of abstract morphosyntax. We will use the term *Rich Agreement Hypothesis* to cover both these positions, while recognizing that they are not identical.

6.3.2 Syntax-before-morphology

Other accounts of L1 acquisition adopt the Separation Hypothesis (Beard 1987, 1995; Lardiere 2000), a hypothesis that treats abstract morphosyntactic features and surface forms as distinct: morphosyntactic features can be represented in the grammar, with various syntactic consequences, in the absence of corresponding overt morphology. If anything, the syntax drives the acquisition of morphology rather than vice versa. In other words, it is only if the grammar already includes abstract categories or features like Tense and Agreement that the learner can begin to discover their precise overt morphological manifestation in the language being acquired (Borer and Rohrbacher 1997).[4]

Nevertheless, many researchers who argue for the primacy of syntax over overt morphology in L1 acquisition also assume that there are representational differences between child and adult grammars, differences that are reflected in a particular kind of morphological variability, the so-called *optional infinitive* phenomenon. There is an early stage reported for the L1 acquisition of many languages, during which the main verb in a child's utterance is sometimes finite and sometimes non-finite.[5] These non-finite forms are known as optional infinitives (Wexler 1994) or root infinitives (Rizzi 1993/1994). Variation during this stage is structurally determined, in that there is a contingency between verb form and verb position. In the acquisition of languages with verb raising, non-finite forms are found in positions typical of non-finite verbs, whereas finite forms occur in positions typical of finite verbs. In other words, non-finite verbs do not raise past negation in L1 French and are not found in the V2 position in L1 German. Non-finite forms, then, are indeed non-finite in L1 acquisition (but see Phillips (1996) for an opposing view). Furthermore, when agreement morphology is present on finite verbs, it is appropriate; *faulty* agreement is very rare (for example, third-person morphology with a second-person subject) (Hoekstra and Hyams 1998; Poeppel and Wexler 1993).

In addition to ± verb raising in L1s like French and German, there are a number of other syntactic correlates of optional infinitives: when finite verbs are produced, pronoun subjects are nominative, whereas when non-finite forms are used, pronouns occur in a default case, which is accusative in languages like English. This follows from the assumption that nominative case is assigned by Infl (or checked by Spec–head agreement within IP) – non-finite verbs do not raise to Infl, hence nominative case cannot be assigned. In the acquisition of [−null subject] languages, null subjects are frequent during the optional infinitive stage, particularly when the verb form is non-finite; they disappear when optional infinitives disappear. This is attributed to the fact that non-finite clauses in general can take null subjects, namely PRO (Hyams 1996). In other words, null subjects in optional infinitive clauses are just like null subjects in adult non-finite clauses (e.g. [*I want* [*PRO to win*]]). When the child's main verb is non-finite, PRO can occur as the subject; when the main verb is finite, it cannot.[6] When the optional infinitive stage ends, PRO subjects are no longer possible, except in dependent clauses.

On some accounts, this variability between finite and non-finite verbs reflects *underspecification* of abstract categories or features in early child grammars.[7] It is not always clear what underspecified means in this literature, that is, whether it is categories like Tense and Agreement that can optionally be omitted (Schütze and Wexler 1996; Wexler 1994, 1998) or whether the categories are present but with their features not fully specified (Hoekstra, Hyams and Becker 1999; Hyams 1996; Wexler 1994). In either case, when [+finite] Tense is present, a finite verb form is found; in languages with strong I, this verb raises to check its features. When finiteness is absent, non-finite forms are found; hence, verbs do not raise, because they have no corresponding [+finite] feature to check. On such accounts, then, functional categories and their features are represented in child grammars but differ from how they operate in adult grammars, where such underspecification does not occur. (Indeed, there is a sense in which the child grammar can be seen as suffering from a deficit here.) Nevertheless, while features are claimed to be underspecified, this is not due to absence of the relevant verbal morphology: optional infinitives and finite forms co-occur, and finite verbs, when produced, are appropriately inflected.

Rizzi (1994) and Haegeman (1995) offer a somewhat different analysis, involving *truncation*. On this account, in early L1 acquisition there is no restriction on what projection can serve as the root of a matrix declarative clause, in contrast to the adult language where roots are normally CPs. The child's structure may be truncated at any point below CP, such that root VPs, root IPs, and root NegPs are possible, in addition to CPs. Variability, then, is the consequence of different roots being projected for different utterances. Root VPs are non-finite, whereas other roots are finite. Rizzi and Haegeman both assume that early grammars possess the same set of functional categories and features as adult systems, none of them being underspecified.

To summarize, both the morphology-before-syntax and the syntax-before-morphology accounts assume that absence of morphology or optionality of morphology reflects properties of the child's syntactic representation. On the former account, absence of overt morphological paradigms is taken to indicate absence of corresponding morphosyntax, because the former are argued to trigger the latter. On the latter account, abstract morphosyntax is in place but some categories or features may be underspecified, or the child's grammar permits a wider range of root clauses than the adult's. As we shall see, while finite and non-finite forms also co-occur in adult interlanguage, there are a number of respects in which adult behaviour is quite different from child behaviour, suggesting that a different account is required. In particular, abstract features appear to be intact, rather than underspecified.

6.4 Perspectives on the morphology/syntax interface in L2

6.4.1 Morphology-before-syntax: incompleteness and deficits

Morphology-before-syntax (or Rich Agreement) proposals for L2 acquisition have also been advanced. According to these proposals, absence of consistent overt morphological paradigms is interpreted as an indication that associated syntactic properties are lacking, either temporarily or permanently, from the interlanguage grammar. As we shall see, for some researchers, L1 and L2 acquisition are considered alike: the initially absent overt morphology is eventually acquired, together with the concomitant categories and features. Other researchers argue that L1 and L2 acquisition are essentially different: in L2 acquisition there is claimed to be a breakdown in the purported triggering relationship between overt morphology and underlying syntax, with a permanent failure of the grammar in consequence.

Research that assumes a close relationship between overt morphology and interlanguage syntax has already been discussed in earlier chapters. In chapter 3, various hypotheses as to the initial state were considered, including the Minimal Trees Hypothesis of Vainikka and Young-Scholten (1994, 1996a, b) and the Valueless Features Hypothesis of Eubank (1993/1994, 1994, 1996), both of which relate emergence of functional syntax to prior morphology. In chapter 4 (section 4.3.1), Clahsen and Hong's (1995) claim for a breakdown between syntax and overt agreement in the context of the Null Subject Parameter was presented, a position we have termed the Global Impairment Hypothesis. These perspectives will briefly be reviewed again here, with a focus on their perspectives on morphological variability.

The Minimal Trees Hypothesis of Vainikka and Young-Scholten extends the Weak Continuity Hypothesis of Clahsen and colleagues to L2 acquisition. As discussed in chapter 3 (section 3.2.2), Vainikka and Young-Scholten claim that overt morphology is absent in initial grammars and that functional categories are not projected at all. Morphology is claimed to act as the trigger for acquisition of functional projections, in L2 acquisition as well as L1. However, according to Vainikka and Young-Scholten (1998), in L2 acquisition it is free functional morphemes that act as triggers instead of bound inflectional morphology (see Zobl and Liceras (1994) for a similar proposal), the idea being that modals trigger the underspecified FP projection, the copula paradigm triggers AgrP, while complementizers trigger CP. Note that this is still a morphology-driven account: the free morphemes trigger the functional projections.[8] Vainikka and Young-Scholten offer two explanations of variability in inflectional morphology, which are not mutually exclusive. On the one hand, L2 learners may produce inflected forms where they have not in fact analysed the affixes as distinct morphemes (Vainikka and Young-Scholten 1998: 101); in other words, affixes are just *noise* in the data (Hawkins 2001a: 348). On the other hand, variability in either free or bound morphology is indicative of *stage seepage* (Vainikka and Young-Scholten 1994: 296), such that properties of earlier grammars (without functional categories or related morphology) coincide with the current grammar (with functional categories and related morphology).

As discussed in chapter 3 (section 3.2.3), Eubank argues that feature strength is inert in early interlanguage grammars, meaning that features are not specified as either strong or weak. Subsequent acquisition of feature values is claimed to depend on the emergence of inflectional morphology, feature strength being determined by the nature of the morphological paradigm, in accordance with the Rich Agreement Hypothesis. On Eubank's account, morphological variability goes along with syntactic variability: in the absence of the full verbal paradigm, inflectional morphology will sometimes be present, sometimes not, and verbs will sometimes raise and sometimes not. Once the paradigm is acquired, feature strength will be determined (strong in the case of rich agreement and weak in the case of impoverished agreement) and both morphological and syntactic variability will cease.

In contrast to Vainikka and Young-Scholten and to Eubank, Clahsen (1988, 1990), Clahsen and Muysken (1989) and Meisel (1991, 1997) take the position that L1 and L2 acquisition differ radically in terms of the relationship between inflectional morphology and syntax, concluding that only L1 acquirers have UG-constrained grammars. Clahsen (1988), for example, examines and compares the acquisition of German by child L1 and adult L2 learners. In the L1 acquisition of German, he reports a close association between the incidence of inflected verb forms in spontaneous production and the acquisition of verb movement. Clahsen argues for a causal connection: the acquisition of certain aspects of the morphological paradigm (in particular, second-person-singular inflection) triggers verb raising. (In other words, although Clahsen's account predates analyses in terms of feature strength, it is a precursor of the Rich Agreement Hypothesis.) In contrast to L1 acquisition, the L2 production data revealed a dissociation between verb movement and inflectional morphology: some L2 learners acquired verb movement before demonstrating accuracy in the verbal inflectional paradigm, while others showed the opposite order. Similarly, Meisel (1991) claims that there is some necessary connection between overt morphology and verb raising in L1 acquisition which is lacking in L2, although he argues that an overt finite versus non-finite distinction in the morphology is the driving factor, rather than the overt realization of distinctions in person or number agreement. According to these researchers, L2 grammars are permanently defective, lacking the triggering relationship between overt morphology and abstract feature strength that is claimed to be a necessary characteristic of L1 grammars. L2 grammars, then, suffer from global impairment (see chapter 4).

To summarize so far, for researchers like Vainikka and Young-Scholten, Eubank, Clahsen, and Meisel, variability in use of tense/agreement morphology, or in free functional morphemes, or absence of such morphology altogether, is a reflection of grammatical competence. For Vainikka and Young-Scholten, this is a purely developmental phenomenon, with grammars of earlier stages differing from grammars of later stages, being in some sense incomplete. In the early grammar, when the relevant overt morphological triggers have not yet been acquired, more abstract syntactic properties, such as functional categories or features, are claimed to be absent. However, morphological paradigms, and their associated syntactic reflexes, are assumed to be acquirable in the longer term. Similarly, in Eubank's earlier work, inertness is taken to be a passing stage: while a grammar with inert features is temporarily defective, L2 grammars are eventually UG-constrained, with abstract morphosyntactic properties ultimately represented. Indeed, L1 and L2 acquisition are considered to be alike in the relevant respects: according to Vainikka and Young-Scholten, L1 acquirers go through similar stages (though with different triggers for the various functional projections), while Eubank maintains that there are parallels between inertness and the kind of underspecification proposed for L1 grammars by Wexler (1994).

In contrast, for Clahsen (1988, 1990) and Meisel (1991, 1997) the observed dissociation in L2 acquisition between overt morphology and certain syntactic phenomena reflects the unavailability of UG, resulting in a permanent impairment to the interlanguage grammar. In other words, the dissociation reported for early stages of L2 acquisition (namely, the failure of a purported triggering relationship) is claimed to have long-term effects on the interlanguage grammar. Since properties of word order cannot, by hypothesis, be attributed to strong features (because feature strength cannot be triggered in the absence of the surface morphology on this kind of account), interlanguage word order must be the result of something quite different. Meisel (1997) suggests some form of linear sequencing strategies, i.e. a kind of pattern matching not constrained by UG (cf. Bley-Vroman 1996, 1997).

The above accounts crucially depend on the claim that acquisition of overt morphology (bound or free) is a necessary precursor to the acquisition of functional syntax. If, as discussed in chapter 5, the Rich Agreement Hypothesis is misconceived on grounds of descriptive adequacy (see Bobaljik, to appear; Lardiere 2000; Sprouse 1998), then there is no reason to expect that overt morphological paradigms drive acquisition of syntax, in either L1 or L2.

Nevertheless, one still has to account for the relative inaccuracy in use of inflectional morphology which is frequently observed in L2 acquisition. If this does not reflect a syntactic deficit, what is the explanation? After all, L1 acquirers of languages with strong features and rich surface morphology successfully acquire both. In the next sections, we consider alternative approaches, according to which abstract agreement is present in the interlanguage grammar from the beginning. Following the Separation Hypothesis, absence of overt morphology is not taken to reflect a lack of morphosyntactic features. In other words, problems with surface morphology are not indicative of temporary lack of acquisition or of more radical defects in interlanguage grammars.

6.4.2 *Syntax-before-morphology: the data*

A number of L2 researchers have (implicitly or explicitly) adopted versions of the Separation Hypothesis, arguing that the crucial issue is not whether L2 learners get the surface morphology right but whether abstract morphosyntactic features are represented in the interlanguage grammar, with their associated syntactic consequences (Epstein et al. 1996; Haznedar and Schwartz 1997; Ionin and Wexler 2002; Lardiere 1998a, b, 2000; Lardiere and Schwartz 1997; Prévost and White 2000a, b; Schwartz 1991).

There have been several studies examining morphological variability in production data drawn from child and adult L2 learners, which look for evidence of abstract syntactic knowledge associated with morphosyntactic features. Results from three relevant studies focusing on L2 English are summarized in table 6.2, in terms of the percentage of suppliance, in obligatory contexts, of inflection and associated syntactic properties.

Haznedar and Schwartz (1997) and Haznedar (2001) report a dissociation between verbal inflection and various syntactic phenomena in production data from a Turkish-speaking child learning L2 English, named Erdem (see chapter 3, section 3.2.1.1). Incidence of inflected and uninflected verb forms, copula and auxiliary *be*, null subjects, and case on subject pronouns is examined over an eighteen-month period. Collapsed over the whole period of observation, Erdem's production data show the following characteristics (see table 6.2): (i) lexical verbs often lack regular past-tense and third-person-singular inflection; (ii) null subjects are almost non-existent; (iii) subject pronouns are almost invariably nominative (*I* rather than *me*, etc.). Furthermore, while suppliance of some properties is high from the earliest recordings (the copula, overt subjects, nominative subjects), inflection for agreement and tense on lexical verbs remains variable throughout the entire period of observation. Haznedar and Schwartz (1997) contrast Erdem's linguistic behaviour with the L1 optional infinitive stage, where, as described in section 6.3.2, L1 acquirers of English: (i) continue to use null subjects during the whole of the optional infinitive period, and (ii) produce accusative pronoun subjects with non-finite verbs. Erdem, then, seems to have unconscious knowledge of certain syntactic requirements of English (subjects must be overt; subject pronouns must be marked nominative) well in advance of consistent suppliance of overt morphology. There is no evidence that abstract Tense is in any sense underspecified (in Wexler's terms) or inert (in Eubank's terms). These results suggest that interlanguage syntax cannot be driven by surface morphology.

Ionin and Wexler (2002) report on production data from twenty children (age range 3,9–13,10) acquiring L2 English, their L1 being Russian. Omission of morphology is quite high, especially third-person-singular agreement on lexical verbs (see table 6.2).[9] At the same time, null subjects are practically non-existent, inappropriate (or faulty) use of inflection is very low, and there are no errors in verb placement: lexical verbs remain in the VP. Such results are inconsistent with Eubank's Valueless Features Hypothesis: while there is variability in suppliance of verbal morphology, there is no variability in verb placement, suggesting that Infl features are present and that they are, appropriately, weak.

Table 6.2 *L2 English: suppliance in obligatory contexts (in %)*

	3SG agreement on lexical verbs	Past tense	Suppletive forms: *Be* (aux/cop)	Overt subjects	Nominative case	V in VP (no raising)
Haznedar 2001	46.5	25.5	89	99	99.9	—
Ionin and Wexler 2002	22	42	80.5	98	—	100
Lardiere 1998a, b	4.5	34.5	90	98	100	100

The above studies focus on learners still in the course of L2 acquisition. Does this mean that divergence between morphology and syntax is purely a developmental phenomenon, which can be expected to disappear? In fact, one of the first researchers to investigate this kind of divergence was Lardiere (1998a, b) who shows that it characterizes at least some endstate grammars as well. Lardiere provides a detailed case study of an adult Chinese speaker's L2 English. The subject, Patty, can no longer be described as a learner of English, her interlanguage grammar being clearly at its endstate. Patty was recorded after she had lived in the USA for ten years and then again almost nine years later. There was little change in the data over this time period. Patty is a fluent user of the language but her production reveals a number of non-native characteristics. Lardiere examines Patty's use of tense and agreement inflection in spontaneous production, as well as a variety of syntactic phenomena associated with abstract Tense and Agreement. Incidence of inflected verbs is low (see table 6.2). Patty's third-person-singular morphology is particularly impoverished, often totally absent; clearly, she has not hit on the correct surface manifestation of weak I in English. Nevertheless, Patty has full command of a variety of syntactic phenomena which implicate Tense and Agreement, consistent with the claim that Infl is represented in her grammar. For example, like the L2 children in the studies described above, Patty shows 100% correct incidence of nominative case assignment, as well as appropriate accusative pronouns in non-nominative contexts, and hardly any null subjects. In addition, she shows no variability in verb placement; verbs are positioned appropriately with respect to adverbs and negation, that is, they do not raise, suggesting, that Infl is weak.

One question that is raised by Patty's relatively low use of tense and agreement morphology is the role of the L1 grammar. Chinese has no overt tense or agreement morphology. Thus, it is possible that the problems exemplified by Patty are, at least in part, a consequence of the total absence of overt inflection in the L1. In another study of a steady-state L2 grammar, White (2002) reports on a speaker of L2 English whose L1 is Turkish, a language with rich tense and agreement morphology but lacking articles (Kornfilt 1997; Underhill 1976). This L2 speaker shows greater inconsistency in suppliance of English determiners than in tense or agreement morphology, suggesting that properties of the L1 grammar do have effects on realization of L2 morphology.

The results reported so far are relatively consistent: learners of English of different ages and at different stages of development supply inflectional morphology rather inconsistently, while nevertheless showing evidence of abstract syntactic knowledge, particularly certain requirements on subjects, as well as verb placement. A number of characteristics of the production data from L2 learners and L2 speakers in these studies implicate Infl. Nominative case is checked in

Infl; consistent suppliance of nominative case to subject pronouns, as well as accusative case to pronouns otherwise, suggests that this functional category and its associated case features is indeed present. Furthermore, as subjects are almost invariably overt, this again implicates Infl, with subjects raising to Spec IP to check their features. Another characteristic reported by Haznedar, by Ionin and Wexler and by Lardiere concerns suppletion. Suppletive forms of auxiliaries and the copula are supplied to a much greater extent than inflectional morphology on lexical verbs (see table 6.2), and with considerable accuracy (see also Lakshmanan 1993/1994, 2000). Tense and agreement features of suppletive forms are checked in Infl – indeed, the only function of the copula is to carry such features – suggesting, again, that the abstract features are indeed represented in the grammar, with feature-checking mechanisms in place. Finally, the evidence from verb placement, in particular, lack of raising of lexical verbs, suggests that feature strength (weak in the case of English) is present.

As for languages other than English, Prévost and White (2000a, b) examine production data from adult L2 acquisition of French and German, languages with richer surface morphology and with strong features in Comp and/or Infl. Since these languages have distinct non-finite morphology, one can distinguish between absence of inflection and non-finite inflection, which it is not possible to do in the case of English, where non-finite forms are uninflected, as are most present-tense finite forms. As with the studies of English discussed above, Prévost and White report morphological variability: finite and non-finite verb forms co-occur. At the same time, when finite forms are supplied, usage is largely accurate, incidence of faulty agreement being quite low.

As mentioned above, several studies of L2 English have shown that verb placement is accurate, with lexical verbs remaining in the VP, consistent with weak feature strength. If L2 learners of French and German have acquired the appropriate [+strong] feature values, one expects the opposite pattern: finite lexical verbs should consistently appear in raised positions (in I or in C), as they do in the grammars of native speakers. Prévost and White examine the issue of verb raising, looking not only at the position of the verb but also at the form (finite versus non-finite).

As mentioned in section 6.3.2, in the L1 acquisition of languages like French and German, there is a contingency between verb position and verb form: during the optional infinitive stage finite verbs consistently appear in raised positions, while non-finite forms do not raise. In the case of adult L2 French and German, on the other hand, this contingency does not hold. When lexical verbs raise, their form is not necessarily finite. Prévost and White show that non-finite forms sometimes appear in positions where a finite verb would be required in the grammar of a native speaker, as shown in (1a) for French and (1b) for German (examples from Prévost

1997). (Vainikka and Young-Scholten (1998: 101) make similar observations.) In (1a), the infinitive, *entrer*, appears to the left of the negative *pas*, suggesting that it has raised out of the VP. Furthermore, it appears with a clitic pronoun subject (*j'*); clitic subjects are restricted to finite verbs. In the question in (1b), the infinitive, *möchten*, has been fronted in a question, again suggesting that it has raised out of the VP.

(1)	a. J'	entrer	pas,	moi.	
	I	enter-INF	not,	me	
	b. Möchten	mal	du	ein	Kaffee?
	want-INF	then	you	a	coffee?

At the same time, Prévost and White report that finite forms are significantly less likely to occur in positions where non-finite forms are expected. In other words, the distribution of overt verbal inflection is not random: finite lexical verbs raise, as required by the L2s in question; non-finite forms appear in both raised and unraised positions. Non-finite forms, then, substitute for finite verbs but not vice versa, suggesting that a form that happens to be superficially non-finite is not inevitably non-finite at an abstract level (in contrast to non-finite forms in L1 acquisition, which are claimed by most researchers to be truly non-finite). We return to implications of this finding below.

In summary, divergence between surface inflection and more abstract syntactic properties is characteristic of L2 acquisition. L2 learners of various languages show relatively inconsistent, though by no means random, use of certain kinds of morphology while being very accurate on related syntactic properties which depend on properties of Infl, such as nominative case, the requirement for overt subjects, and presence or absence of verb raising. These characteristics appear to be true of initial and endstate grammars, as well as grammars undergoing development. Such results are consistent with the Separation Hypothesis and inconsistent with the Rich Agreement Hypothesis, since syntactic knowledge does not depend on overt morphology in any way.

Morphological variability in L2 acquisition is clearly different from L1. In L1 acquisition, while finite and non-finite forms co-occur during the optional infinitive stage, they show distinct distributions: in verb-raising languages, optional infinitives do not raise, whereas finite verbs do. At the same time, incidence of non-finite forms coincides with null subjects and with pronouns marked with default accusative case. When the optional infinitive stage comes to an end, these properties disappear. The situation in L2 acquisition is rather different, as we have seen, difficulties with inflectional morphology being more extensive and longer lasting, without concomitant syntactic effects. These differences are summarized in table 6.3.

Table 6.3 *L1 and L2 acquisition compared*

	L1	L2
Finiteness	Finite and non-finite forms co-occur. Non-finite forms are indeed non-finite, being restricted to non-finite positions (OIs). Inflection when used is accurate.	Finite and non-finite forms co-occur Non-finite forms occur in both finite and non-finite positions. Inflection when used is accurate.
Subjects	Null subjects found during the OI stage. Null subjects disappear when OIs disappear.	Incidence of null subjects is low (unless L1 is prodrop). No relationship between loss of null subjects and loss of non-finite forms.
Case on subject pronouns	Nominative when the verb is finite; accusative when the verb is non-finite.	Nominative with both finite and non-finite verb forms.
Verb placement (L2 French and German)	Raised when the verb is finite; not raised when the verb is non-finite.	Raised when the verb is finite; non-finite forms found in both raised and unraised positions.

In the next section, we turn to accounts which attribute L2 morphological variability not to deficits in linguistic competence but to difficulties in retrieving or accessing particular forms from the lexicon.

6.4.3 Missing surface inflection: explanations

As discussed in the preceding section, several recent studies have demonstrated that L2 learners have syntactic knowledge, such as appropriate verb placement and the requirement for overt subjects bearing nominative case, even in the absence of consistent suppliance of inflection. These studies also show that morphological variability in L2 acquisition is a different phenomenon from optionality in L1 acquisition, requiring a different kind of explanation. Haznedar and Schwartz (1997) argue for *missing inflection*: the absence of verbal morphology indicates nothing more than the absence of surface manifestation of inflection. Prévost and White (2000a, b) emend the term to *missing surface inflection*, to emphasize the point that abstract morphosyntactic features are not lacking.

If abstract syntax is in place prior to the acquisition of surface morphology, rather than the other way round, the failure of syntactic and morphological properties to go hand-in-hand is not surprising. Much of the evidence described above is consistent with the claim that L2 learners have underlying syntactic representations where functional categories like Det, Infl and Comp are represented, as well as their features and feature strength. Even in the absence of consistent or appropriate inflectional morphology, functional categories and features are fully specified in the grammar, with certain 'visible' syntactic consequences. This may be an effect of having a mature L1 grammar. As Lardiere (2000: 121) puts it:

> The most coherent explanation for the L2 data is that . . . learners already have knowledge of functional categories and features via prior language knowledge . . .; the problem lies in figuring out how (and whether) to spell out morphologically the categories they already represent syntactically, i.e. the 'mapping problem'.

In other words, a learner may fail to link an abstract [+past] feature to the particular form /*-ed*/ in English, for example. Although the form has been learned, the learner may be unable to retrieve it on a consistent basis.

6.4.3.1 Learning the forms

Even if abstract features like Tense are present in the grammar, this does not mean that the relevant morphology will be acquired immediately and without difficulty. In discussing similar issues in L1 acquisition, Hyams (1994: 45) points out that:

> The premise that missing functional items = missing functional categories is difficult to maintain given the fact that children have syntactic operations involving functional categories at the point at which they fail to reliably produce functional elements. A simpler explanation for the missing lexical items is just that the lexical items are missing, essentially because they have properties which make them difficult to learn, for example, lack of referentiality or meaning, etc.

As far as L2 is concerned, Herschensohn (2000) and Gess and Herschensohn (2001) make essentially the same point: morphology must be learned. That is, morphological paradigms must gradually be added to the lexicon, just like words. More abstract syntactic properties, on the other hand, derive from UG and do not require learning.

If missing inflection is to be accounted for solely in terms of learning, the problem with overt morphology might be expected to be temporary – as learning proceeds, accuracy should improve. As described in chapter 4, Gess and Herschensohn (2001) find that beginner-level English-speaking learners of French are very accurate on adjective placement, suggesting that they have acquired the strong value of French Num, but are quite inaccurate on gender and number agreement. With increasing L2 proficiency, accuracy on syntactic properties remains high while accuracy on morphology increases, reaching 98% accuracy at the most advanced levels. This looks like a learning problem that is eventually overcome, just as it is overcome in L1 acquisition.

6.4.3.2 Access

The observation that morphology must be learned is entirely plausible. However, it is not so clear that learning can explain the problem of variability in L2 production: if a form has been learned, why is it not used consistently? In addition, an explanation couched solely in terms of learning presumably predicts eventual success; after all, L2 learners appear to be quite successful in learning vocabulary in general, so the same might be expected of inflection. In L1 acquisition such learning takes place over a relatively short period of time, after which there are few problems in the morphological domain. While many L2 learners also achieve considerable accuracy in inflectional morphology and associated function words, this is by no means inevitable. In some cases, as described in section 6.4.2, problems with the realization of morphology can last for years, and may even prove to be permanent (Lardiere 1998a, b; White 2002). This makes it unlikely that the only problem L2 learners face is a learning problem. There must be something else going on as well.

Indeed, learning may not constitute the sole source of difficulty in L1 acquisition either. Even if certain morphological forms have been acquired (that is, entered in a mental lexicon), there may nevertheless be occasions when these are not accessible, for processing reasons.[10] In other words, there is some kind of temporary breakdown between the syntax and the lexicon. As Phillips (1995: 360) puts it:

> In sentence production the advantage of spelling-out inflectional features . . . must be weighed against the cost involved in accessing the morphological spell-out of the inflectional features. For adults [*i.e. native speakers, LW*], accessing inflectional paradigms is a heavily overlearned process, and hence bears minimal or zero cost . . . For young children, on the other hand, accessing morphological form is presumably not an automatic process to begin with, and as a result the cost of accessing a given form may outweigh the cost of failing to realize it . . . The transition . . . to adult-like performance can thus be seen as a transition from controlled to automatic processing of the task of accessing morphological knowledge.

Such observations are just as relevant in the L2 context. In this vein, Lardiere (1998a, b, 2000) and Lardiere and Schwartz (1997) argue that the observed divergence between surface morphology and abstract morphosyntactic features reflects a problem in mapping from abstract categories and features to their particular surface morphological manifestations, a position also assumed by Haznedar and Schwartz (1997) and Prévost and White (2000a, b). In other words, even when learners have acquired the surface morphological manifestations of more abstract features, such that these forms are entered in the mental lexicon, they may not always be able to retrieve the appropriate form for lexical insertion into a syntactic representation. When the form is retrieved, overt inflection is used; when there is a retrieval failure, inflection is missing. Hence, variability is observed.

Up to now, such explanations of morphological variation have largely been post hoc. It might reasonably be objected that attributing inaccuracy with inflectional morphology to mapping or retrieval problems fails to provide a true explanation but rather offers a way to avoid admitting a breakdown in interlanguage syntax. So let us try to make this position more precise. If the effect of mapping failure were simply random incidence of inflectional morphology, there would be no way to distinguish between this claim and claims for more radical breakdown in the grammar itself, of the type proposed by Clahsen (1988) and by Meisel (1997). Thus, it is important to understand that explanations in terms of access do in fact differ from accounts that argue for a more radical breakdown, making different predictions for the data.

There are a number of phenomena relating to inaccuracy in L2 morphology which support some kind of mapping problem account. Firstly, as we have seen, several researchers have reported that when L2 learners are inaccurate in their suppliance of inflectional morphology, the problem is missing inflection rather than faulty inflection. That is, by and large, learners fail to inflect, rather than freely substituting one inflection for another. When agreement morphology is present, it is appropriate (Grondin and White 1996; Haznedar and Schwartz 1997; Ionin and Wexler 2002; Prévost and White 2000b; White 2002), similar to what is reported in L1 acquisition (e.g. Poeppel and Wexler 1993). For instance, given a second-person-singular inflection on the verb in L2 German (*/-st/*), the subject will indeed be second person and not first or third. (Clahsen (1988: 63) observes this same phenomenon, although drawing rather different conclusions.) Suppletive forms are used extensively (see table 6.2) and are used accurately. In other words, the issue is the *degree* to which learners supply agreement rather than the *accuracy* of agreement.

Substitutions are of a specific and limited type, for example, non-finite forms in place of finite. Furthermore, substitutions are often unidirectional: non-finite verb forms are used in place of finite but not vice versa (Prévost and White 2000b); masculine gender is used in place of feminine but not vice versa (Bruhn de Garavito and White, in press; White et al. 2001); indefinite articles are used in place of definite but not vice versa (Leung 2001). Such results suggest that certain forms can act as 'defaults', being able to substitute for others.[11] Hence, the distribution of morphological forms, both accurate and inaccurate, suggests that variability is not indicative of randomness, as might be expected if the problem stemmed from a total breakdown of the grammar.

How can all these facts be reconciled? Recent explanations centre on lexical underspecification (Lardiere and Schwartz 1997; Müller 1998; Prévost and White 2000b), differing substantially from accounts of L1 acquisition in terms of underspecification of functional categories or features as proposed, for example, by Hoekstra and Hyams (1998), Hoekstra, Hyams and Becker (1999) or Wexler (1994). Following Distributed Morphology, the idea is that vocabulary items can be underspecified in the interlanguage lexicon in precisely the same way that they are underspecified in the lexicons of adult native speakers (Halle and Marantz 1993; Harris 1991; Lumsden 1992). In particular, some forms are defaults whose featural content does not need to be fully specified. These defaults can substitute for more fully specified forms, under certain conditions.

Let us consider an example, adapted from Müller (1998), who provides a detailed case study of the L2 German of Bruno, a native speaker of Italian who moved to Germany as a young adult and was studied as part of the ZISA project (Clahsen, Meisel and Pienemann 1983). In studying agreement inflection in Bruno's spontaneous production data (amongst many other properties), Müller observes the following: the suffixes */-st/* (2SG) and */-t/* (3SG) are indeed restricted to second- and third-person contexts, respectively. In other words, if used, these suffixes are used accurately. In contrast, the suffixes */-e/* and */-en/* are overgeneralized, and bare forms also occur. (It should be noted that */-en/* is the suffix marking infinitives, as well as first- and third-person plural; */-e/* indicates first-person singular but also occurs as the infinitival suffix in informal speech in certain German dialects.) In an analysis of two other subjects from the ZISA project, Prévost and White (2000b) report similar results, as does Clahsen (1988).

Müller proposes that the interlanguage syntactic representation for a correctly inflected sentence like *du verstehst* ('you understand'), as well as an incorrectly inflected sentence like *du verstehen*, will be as shown in (2) (adapted from her (28b)). In particular, the head, I, is fully specified for person and number, as is the specifier position.

(2)

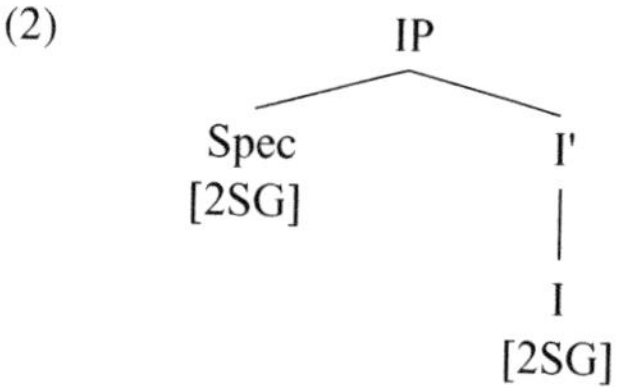

The lexical entries for *verstehen*, *vertehst* and for *versteht* are given in (3) (adapted from Müller's (28a)), where α means that the entry is not specified (or is underspecified) with respect to the features in question.

(3) a. verstehen: [α person, α number]
b. verstehst: [2SG]
c. versteht: [3SG][12]

How does this work? Prévost and White (2000b) offer an account in terms of Distributed Morphology. (See also Lardiere and Schwartz 1997.) Inflected forms in the lexicon are associated with a bundle of features, such as tense, person, number and gender. In (3), the relevant features are person and number. In order for a lexical item to be inserted from the lexicon into the syntactic tree, the features of the vocabulary item must be consistent with the features of the syntactic node in question, that is, there must be no clash between the features of the lexical item and the abstract morphosyntactic features. Features of the syntactic node will be fully specified, as shown in (2). However, features of a lexical item may be underspecified, as is the case for (3a). It is not necessary for the features of the lexical item to provide an exact match with all the features of the hosting node: it is sufficient that they form a proper subset of the feature bundle of that node. In the case of the above examples, the lexical form *verstehst* (3b) does exactly match the abstract features in the tree in (2) and so it can be inserted. In contrast, *versteht* (3c) could not be inserted, since its features are not a proper subset of those under I; rather, there would be a clash between the number features: second person in the syntactic representation, third person on the lexical item. Now consider *verstehen* (3a), which is underspecified with respect to both person and number. Because of this lack of specification, there will be no clash and this form can be inserted into the fully specified syntactic node.

Note how the assumption of underspecified lexical entries can account for at least two of the data observations described above. Firstly, it has been noted that agreement, when present, is largely accurate (i.e. the problem in many cases is missing inflection rather than faulty inflection). This is because the insertion of an incorrectly agreeing form would result in a feature clash, as would be the case of *versteht* in the above example. The only possibilities for insertion, according to Distributed Morphology, are (i) lexical items which are fully and appropriately specified, hence not resulting in features clashes, or (ii) underspecified lexical items. Secondly, we have observed unidirectionality in error patterns. Extending the above example, let us assume that in addition to agreement features, the I node in the tree and the lexical entries of verb forms would include a finiteness feature. An infinitive form like *verstehen* might be underspecified for finiteness in the interlanguage lexicon (Prévost and White 2000b), in contrast to finite forms, as shown in (4):

(4) a. verstehen: [αfinite; αperson, α number]
b. verstehst: [+finite; 2SG]
c. versteht: [+finite; 3SG]

In that case, the underspecified form *verstehen* can be inserted into positions specified as [+finite] or as [−finite], whereas *verstehst* and *versteht* can only be inserted into [+finite] positions, since otherwise a feature clash would result in cases where the syntax specifies [−finite]. The effect, then, is unidirectionality: apparently non-finite forms in finite contexts but not vice versa. Underspecified forms serve as defaults and can surface in a variety of contexts, whereas fully specified forms cannot. (See Ferdinand (1996) for similar proposals for L1 acquisition.)

If this kind of account is on the right lines, we might ask why it is that adult native speakers do not constantly make similar errors, inserting underspecified forms in place of more fully specified ones. (In fact, they do make such mistakes on occasion.) According to Distributed Morphology, the form in the lexicon that corresponds most closely to the syntactic feature specification gets inserted. In the absence of an exact match, there is a competition between potential candidates for insertion, the winner being the form with the most features that match those of the terminal node. The difference between adult native speakers and L2 learners, then, is that in the former case, the most detailed form that fits the feature specification in the tree is almost invariably inserted. In the case of L2 speakers, on the other hand, even when more fully specified forms have been acquired, they do not necessarily 'win' in the competition for lexical insertion. For some reason, less specified forms continue to surface, suggesting that access to the more fully specified lexical entries is sometimes blocked.

6.5 Methodological considerations

Much of the debate discussed in this chapter centres on analyses of spontaneous production data, often involving individual case studies. As we have seen, there is considerable disagreement as to how such data should be interpreted. Most proponents of the morphology-before-syntax position take production data at its face value: if certain forms are absent in production, the relevant property is absent from the grammar; if forms are consistently present in production, the property in question is present in the grammar. According to the syntax-before-morphology position, on the other hand, failure to produce certain inflections or function words, or inconsistency in production, does not preclude an intact and appropriate underlying representation.

We have also seen that when agreement morphology is present in production data it is largely accurate. Yet this claim depends on how the relationship between subject and verb is established. Examining agreement in L1 acquisition, Poeppel and Wexler (1993) argue that one should start from the form of the verb and then look at the nature of its subject. Other researchers, including Clahsen (1988), have taken the opposite approach, starting with the subject and then looking at the form of the corresponding verb. These methods of analysing the data yield quite different results. As Poeppel and Wexler demonstrate for third-person-singular (3SG) agreement in L1 German, if one starts with 3SG verb forms and looks at the nature of the subject, it turns out that there is a very high conditional probability that the subject will indeed be 3SG. However, if one starts with 3SG subjects and looks at corresponding verb forms, the probability that these will be inflected for 3SG is much lower, since many verbs are non-finite or consist of uninflected bare stems. Thus, accuracy rates are quite different, depending on how one treats the data. If the issue is whether the learner has in fact established that a particular form, in this case German 3SG /-t/, provides the overt morphological realization of certain abstract morphosyntactic features, then Poeppel and Wexler's method of analysis is the more appropriate (see also Wexler 1999). If a learner, L1 or L2, only uses /-t/ in 3SG contexts, this strongly suggests that the abstract morphosyntactic features have been acquired, as well as the corresponding features in the lexical entry of the verb.

The morphology-before-syntax and the syntax-before-morphology accounts make different predictions concerning other kinds of data. According to the former, in the absence of surface inflection, functional categories, features or feature strength are not represented in the grammar. Thus, there should be effects on performance in a variety of different tasks. In other words, data from other tasks (grammaticality judgments, comprehension tasks, sentence matching, etc.) should parallel production data: in the absence of consistent overt inflection in production, learners should perform inaccurately on other tasks testing inflectional morphology. According to the syntax-before-morphology view, on the other hand, task differences are conceivable. If problems with surface morphology are attributable to difficulties accessing underlying knowledge (rather than to lack of knowledge), one might expect the problem to affect different kinds of language use differentially. For example, L2 learners might perform more accurately on tasks where they do not themselves have to retrieve forms from the mental lexicon as they speak. Hence, accuracy in spontaneous production might be lower than in other kinds of tasks. In support of this claim, Ionin and Wexler (2002) show that L2 learners do not judge non-finite forms as being fully grammatical even when they are producing them quite extensively. White (2002) found that the Turkish speaker who often failed to supply determiners in spontaneous production was highly accurate in her use of determiners in other tasks. There is clearly a need for further investigation of situations where there is a potential mismatch between what L2 speakers unconsciously know and what they do, and this needs to be established with a wider range of methodologies and by comparison across different tasks.

6.6 The morphology/syntax interface: conclusion

It has been proposed in this chapter that discrepancies in L2 performance with respect to syntax and morphology reflect a problem in mapping from abstract categories to their particular surface morphological manifestations. It has been suggested that the problem is the result of lexical underspecification, rather than syntactic underspecification.

The hypothesis that problems at the morphology/syntax interface can be attributed to mapping problems does not predict that such problems are inevitable, nor that they are permanent. It is nevertheless clear that, for some L2 speakers at least, this is a lasting problem. Fossilization occurs which is attributable not to a breakdown in the grammar as such but, rather, to some kind of unreliability in the interface between the syntax and other areas of the grammar. There is, as yet, no adequate explanation of why some people should be more affected than others in this respect. A more precise characterization is required of these so-called mapping problems, in order to reach a better understanding of what might be going on.

Topics for discussion

- If L2 learners showed evidence of faulty inflection in addition to missing inflection, to what extent would this cast doubt on the claim that a mapping problem, as opposed to a syntactic deficit, is involved?
- Why are L2 speakers better at suppletion than affixation? Lardiere (1999) speculates that the very fact that verbal affixation is relatively uncommon in English may be a contributing factor. Ionin and Wexler (2002) suggest that the fact that auxiliaries in English appear overtly in Infl may explain why learners are more accurate with suppletive forms. Somewhat problematic for these proposals is the fact that adult learners of French and German are also more accurate on suppletive forms than on verbal inflection (Prévost and White 2000b). As French and German have relatively rich overt inflection and as lexical verbs (with inflection) raise overtly in these languages, the explanation must lie elsewhere.
- Explanations of variability in terms of mapping problems raise the question of whether variability is a performance effect or a competence effect, as well as the status (vis-à-vis UG) of grammars exemplifying mapping problems. Is a permanent mapping problem a performance problem or is it a different kind of competence deficit? There is a rather fuzzy line between competence and performance here. (See Lardiere (2000) for discussion.)

Suggestions for additional reading

- Zobl and Liceras (1994) and Hawkins (2001a) provide a useful integration of earlier approaches to the L2 acquisition of morphology with more recent generative approaches.
- For more detailed arguments against morphological paradigms acting as triggers for syntax see Bobaljik (to appear), Lardiere (2000) and Sprouse (1998). All three authors provide arguments, drawn from a variety of domains, against the Rich Agreement Hypothesis in its various manifestations.
- See Prévost (1997) and Prévost and White (2000a) for arguments that child L2 may be different from adult L2, and amenable to an analysis in terms of truncation (Rizzi 1993/1994).
- Beck (1998b) provides a collection of papers, many of them experimental, on L2 morphology and its relationship to syntax in the UG framework.
- There has been some research on L2 word formation and derivational morphology, particularly on compounding, much of it relevant to the syntax/morphology interface (Lardiere 1998c; Lardiere and Schwartz 1997; Liceras and Díaz 2000; Murphy 1997).

7

Argument structure

7.1 Argument structure

In the previous chapter, the interface between morphology and syntax was considered, including the relationship between features of items drawn from the lexicon and abstract features in the syntactic representation. The present chapter explores other properties of the L2 lexicon, particularly the relationship between lexical semantics, argument structure and syntax. The concern is with how certain aspects of meaning (the semantic primitives by which word meanings can be expressed, the event types expressed by verbs, the thematic roles of arguments) are realized in syntax, as well as the morphological forms by which such meanings are expressed.

Detailed investigation of L2 argument structure in the generative framework is relatively recent. In this chapter, the following issues will be discussed: (i) semantic constraints on argument-structure alternations; (ii) crosslinguistic differences in how semantic primitives may combine or conflate; (iii) thematic properties of arguments and how they are realized syntactically; (iv) the effects of morphology which adds or suppresses arguments. We begin with a consideration of the kind of information that is encoded in a lexical entry and how this information is mapped to the syntax.

7.2 Lexical entries

Lexical entries include distinct types of information, semantic and syntactic (e.g. Baker 1997; Grimshaw 1990; Hale and Keyser 1993; Jackendoff 1990; Levin and Rappaport-Hovav 1995; Pinker 1989).[1] At one level, sometimes referred to as lexical conceptual structure (LCS) (Jackendoff 1983, 1990) or the thematic core (Pinker 1989), meaning is represented, particularly aspects of meaning that have consequences for other areas of the grammar. On a number of accounts, meaning is compositional, that is, the meaning of a lexical item can be broken down into semantic primitives or conceptual categories, such as: THING, EVENT, STATE,

PATH, PLACE, PROPERTY, MANNER (Jackendoff 1990; Pinker 1989: 208).[2] These primitives can be combined by various functions (ACT, GO, CAUSE, BE, HAVE, etc.). Semantic primitives are drawn from relatively small sets and are universal. However, languages differ in their conflation patterns, that is, in precisely how the different primitives may combine into words (Talmy 1985). As we shall see, these differences have syntactic consequences, and they have implications for interlanguage grammars.

In addition, the lexical entries of certain categories (verbs, prepositions, adjectives and derived nominals) encode information about argument structure, that is, about the constituents which enter into a relationship with them. Verbs typically take one (*John sneezed*), two (*Mary saw John*) or three (*Mary gave John a book*) arguments. The arguments of a verb are usually, but not necessarily, obligatory (*Mary kicked the ball*; **Mary kicked*; *John ate an apple; John ate*). Arguments of verbs are often referred to in terms of their thematic (theta) roles, including *agent* (animate being initiating and performing an action), *patient/theme* (person or thing undergoing some action or event), and *goal* (endpoint towards which something moves) (Fillmore 1968; Gruber 1965; Jackendoff 1972). Theories differ as to whether thematic roles are represented in conceptual structure or in argument structure, in both or in neither. According to some accounts, thematic roles are simply convenient labels for relationships between arguments (Grimshaw 1990; Hale and Keyser 1993; Jackendoff 1990; Williams 1981). For convenience of exposition, terminology like *agent* and *theme* will be adopted, regardless of whether such concepts are primitives within linguistic theory.

There is a distinction between the external argument of the verb and its internal arguments. Internal arguments are the subcategorized complements of the verb (such as the direct object) and are realized within the same maximal projection as the verb, namely the VP, in contrast to the external argument (Williams 1981, 1994, 1995). The lexical entry of a verb includes information about the number of arguments it takes, which arguments are obligatory, which argument is the external argument, etc. Adjuncts (typically, adverbs and PPs expressing manner, place, time, etc.) are optional constituents, which are not so closely associated with the verb. They do not form part of a verb's argument structure, and do not appear in its lexical entry.[3] The lexical entry also includes subcategorization information about the syntactic categories by which arguments are typically realized.[4]

There are many different theories as to the nature of argument structure. For some researchers, a verb's argument structure consists of a simple listing of the set of its arguments (Levin and Rappaport-Hovav 1995). For others, argument structure is itself structured (Grimshaw 1990; Hale and Keyser 1993). For example, Hale and Keyser (1992, 1993) propose a level within the lexicon (*l-syntax*), which is subject to the same kinds of syntactic constraints as syntax proper.

To illustrate some of these properties, consider the sentences in (1).

(1) a. Mary put the book on the table.
b. *Mary put the book.
c. *Mary put on the table.
d. Mary put the book on the table at 3pm.

As shown in (1a), the verb *put* takes two obligatory internal arguments, a DP theme (*the book*) and a PP location (*on the table*). Neither of these arguments can be omitted, as shown by the ungrammaticality of (1b) and (1c). The subject, *Mary*, is the external argument of *put*, taking the thematic role of agent. The verb *put*, like other verbs, can also take optional adjuncts (such as *at 3pm*), as illustrated in (1d).

The lexical entry of a verb like *put* will be something like (2):[5]

(2) put [+V]
LCS: X CAUSE [y BECOME AT z]
argument structure: x, y, z
(agent, theme, location)
subcategorization: _ NP PP

This entry represents the fact that this verb means that someone causes something to end up at a particular location. The verb *put* has an external argument (the agent), which is represented by underlining (following Williams 1981), as well as two internal arguments, theme and location, which are realized as an NP and a PP, respectively.

7.3 Mapping from lexicon to syntax: the logical problem of argument-structure acquisition

Verbs and their arguments eventually have to fit into particular positions in a syntactic representation, the arguments realized as DPs, PPs or clauses, exhibiting particular structural relationships within the sentence. That is, there must be a mapping from the lexicon to the syntax. It has long been recognized that there is no one-to-one relationship between meaning and form: the same meaning can be expressed in different ways; the same form can express different meanings (e.g. Grimshaw 1981). Nevertheless, there clearly are regularities in how meanings are expressed in the syntax, and there have been many proposals for linking rules or mapping principles to capture these regularities.

The language learner, in addition to having to acquire the phonological form and the meaning of a verb like *put*, must determine that it is a three-argument verb, that these arguments bear particular theta-roles, and that the theme is realized as a DP, while the location generally takes the form of a PP. Such learning might seem to be a relatively straightforward matter: presumably, the input will contain examples with the verb *put* used in contexts where things are placed in particular locations. Thus, it might appear that there is no real acquisition problem as far as verb argument structure is concerned. If everything lines up in a straightforward manner (agent = external argument = subject; theme = internal argument = direct object), then mapping from lexicon to syntax should be a relatively trivial task.

However, the situation is more complex than so far described. There are argument-structure alternations within and across languages which make the solution to the mapping problem less than transparent. There are many cases where the same verb allows its arguments to be realized in terms of different phrasal categories and/or by differences in word order, yet identical theta roles appear to be involved. For example, as will be discussed in more detail in the next section, in English one can say *Mary gave John a book* or *Mary gave a book to John.* In other words, the same set of arguments with the same theta roles may show up in different syntactic structures; arguments are not uniquely and consistently realized in the same way, making the acquisition task particularly difficult. To complicate matters further, such alternations are subject to exceptions.

Not only do alternations show up within the same language but there is crosslinguistic variation in how languages realize arguments morphologically and syntactically, such that differences between the L1 and the L2 may be expected to cause difficulties in L2 acquisition. The L2 learner must arrive at a representation for lexical items in the second language and must map from argument structure to syntax. Since there are crosslinguistic differences in argument structures, there will be cases where the L1 and L2 realize argument structure somewhat differently. In some cases, there is a potential for overgeneralization from the L1 to the L2, for example, where the L1 permits more ways of realizing a particular argument structure in the syntax than the L2. In other cases, there may be undergeneralization, with the L2 learner failing to acquire aspects of L2 argument structure which are nevertheless exemplified in the L2 input. Hence, interlanguage lexical representations may not correspond to argument structures encoded in the lexicons of native speakers of the L2.

7.4 Semantic constraints on argument-structure alternations

Argument-structure alternations have long been identified as a major potential source of acquisition difficulty, largely because of the issue of overgeneralization (Baker 1979; Pinker 1989). One of the first alternations to be considered in this context was the English dative alternation. Dative verbs are those taking theme and goal arguments (*to*-datives) or theme and benefactive arguments (*for*-datives). Common dative verbs (such as *give, sell*, and *buy*) typically alternate: one form is the prepositional dative, where the theme argument is realized as a DP and the goal or benefactive is realized as a PP (introduced by *to* or *for*); the other is the double-object construction, where both internal arguments are DPs. This alternation is shown in (3), where it can also be seen that the order of the internal arguments varies. In the prepositional dative (3a), the theme precedes the goal; in the double-object dative (3b) the goal must precede the theme, as shown by the ungrammaticality of (3c).

(3) a. Mary passed the book to John.
b. Mary passed John the book.
c. *Mary passed the book John.

There is a potential learnability problem for the L1 acquirer of English, because it is not the case that all dative verbs alternate, or that they alternate in all circumstances. Thus, the possibility of overgeneralization arises. Sometimes, the prepositional dative has no double-object equivalent. As shown in (4), a verb like *send* can appear in both the prepositional form (4a) and the double-object form (4b). However, the double-object version is not permitted in the case of (4d), even though there is a corresponding prepositional dative (4c).

(4) a. Mary sent a book to John.
b. Mary sent John a book.
c. Mary sent a book to France.
d. *Mary sent France a book.

Furthermore, it is not the case that every dative verb can alternate. For example, the verb *push*, like *pass*, takes a theme and a goal argument, and occurs in the prepositional dative form. However, it has no double-object equivalent, as shown in (5b).

(5) a. Mary pushed the book to John.
b. *Mary pushed John the book.

It would not be unreasonable for a child to note the alternation with verbs like *pass*, to note the semantic parallel between *pass* and *push*, and then to assume that sentences like (5b) are possible in English.

Many researchers working on L1 acquisition have argued that the lack of direct, consistent and unique mappings between lexical conceptual structure, argument structure and syntax implies that there is a logical problem of language acquisition in the lexical domain. Universal principles (semantic and syntactic) must constrain the child's acquisition of argument structure, limiting the ways in which arguments are realized (Gleitman 1990; Grimshaw 1981; Landau and Gleitman 1985; Pinker 1989). Without such constraints, the acquisition problem appears intractable: the child would require negative evidence in order to learn the impossibility of sentences like (4d) and (5b).

Pinker (1989) and Gropen, Pinker, Hollander, Goldberg and Wilson (1989) argue that there are semantic constraints on the dative alternation which the child discovers. In particular, in the double-object form, the goal argument must be the prospective possessor of the theme argument (Green 1974; Mazurkewich and White 1984; Pinker 1989).[6] It is this possession constraint that explains the ungrammaticality of (4d): France does not possess the book as a result of the sending. In Pinker's account, the two forms of the dative have different conceptual structures: only the double-object dative is represented with a HAVE function, as shown in (6):

(6) a. X CAUSE Y GO to Z (prepositional dative)
b. X CAUSE Z HAVE Y (double-object dative)

L1 acquirers must isolate the HAVE function as common to double-object datives. They must then formulate a broad-range rule which relates one LCS to the other (that is, (6a) to (6b)), provided that the possession constraint is observed (Gropen et al. 1989; Pinker 1989). Even if there is initial overgeneralization of double-object datives, once the broad-range semantic constraint comes into play, overgeneralization will cease.

However, while the broad-range possession constraint is a necessary condition for double-object datives in English, it is not sufficient. There are narrow-range semantic constraints on the alternation as well. In (5b), John would possess the book as a result of Mary's pushing and yet the sentence is ungrammatical. It appears that the dative alternation is restricted to semantically defined subclasses, manner of motion and/or direction being crucially involved (amongst other factors). For example, verbs of 'instantaneous causation of ballistic motion', such as *throw*, can alternate, whereas verbs like *pull* or *push* expressing 'continuous causation of accompanied motion in some manner' cannot (Gropen et al. 1989; Pinker 1989). Unlike the broad-range constraint, which is directly associated with a universal semantic primitive (HAVE), as well as universal linking rules for mapping conceptual structures to syntax, the source of the narrow-range constraints is not clear. Gropen et al. (1989) suggest that there is a (presumably universal) set of grammatically relevant semantic features, on which the narrow-range constraints are based. For the sake of the argument, this claim will be accepted. However, since narrow-range constraints are language specific or even dialect specific (Gropen et al. 1989) and semi-arbitrary (Pinker 1989), sometimes picking out very small classes of verbs with characteristics that do not seem to be generalizable, it is not at all clear that universality is really involved. (See Juffs (1996a) for discussion and arguments against narrow-range rules.)

There have been numerous studies on the dative alternation in L2 acquisition (Bley-Vroman and Yoshinaga 1992; Inagaki 1997; Mazurkewich 1984b; White 1987b; Whong-Barr and Schwartz 2002). (See White (1989: ch. 5) for an overview.) Although these studies were not explicitly couched in terms of argument structure, results suggest a strong influence of the L1 argument structure on the interlanguage lexicon. For example, French-speaking learners of English initially reject double-object forms like (4b), which are ungrammatical in the L1 and grammatical in the L2 (Mazurkewich 1984b), while English-speaking learners of French allow double-object forms, which are grammatical in the L1 but not in the L2 (White 1987b, 1991b).

More recent L2 studies specifically consider argument-structure issues associated with dative verbs, especially the role of broad and narrow semantic constraints. Bley-Vroman and Yoshinaga (1992) investigate the acquisition of the English dative alternation by native speakers of Japanese. Dative verbs in Japanese have only one way of realizing their arguments as far as case marking is concerned: the theme is case marked with accusative *-o*, while the goal is marked with *-ni* (which is either a dative case marker or a postposition, depending on one's analysis), as shown in (7a). (Due to the possibility of scrambling in Japanese, the word order of the arguments is not fixed.) Double accusatives are ungrammatical (Whong-Barr and Schwartz 2002), as can be seen in (7b). (Examples from Whong-Barr and Schwartz.)

(7) a. Hanako ga Taro ni hagaki o oku-tta
Hanako NOM Taro DAT postcard ACC send-PAST
'Hanako sent a postcard to Taro'/'Hanako sent Taro a postcard'
b. *Hanako ga Taro o hagaki o oku-tta
Hanako NOM Taro ACC postcard ACC send-PAST

There is some disagreement as to whether grammatical forms like (7a) are equivalent to the English double-object dative (Bley-Vroman and Yoshinaga 1992; Inagaki 1997) or the English prepositional dative (Whong-Barr and Schwartz 2002).

Bley-Vroman and Yoshinaga are proponents of the Fundamental Difference Hypothesis (Bley-Vroman 1990), which holds that adult L2 acquisition is very different from child L1 acquisition. Specifically, grammatical properties which depend on UG are claimed to be available only via the L1 grammar. As far as the dative alternation is concerned, these researchers argue that Japanese has a possession constraint, so that a broad-range rule can be formulated for L2 datives.

(However, it is not entirely clear how the possession constraint in the L1 Japanese could form the basis for a broad-range rule relating two conceptual structures in the L2, since there is only one dative argument structure in Japanese. See also Whong-Barr and Schwartz (2002).)

At the same time, Bley-Vroman and Yoshinaga assume that Japanese lacks equivalents of the narrow-range rules found in English and that adult learners no longer have access to the universal list of semantic properties that the narrow-range rules draw on. The prediction, then, is that, while Japanese-speaking learners of English will acquire the possibility of the English dative alternation (and restrict the double-object form to contexts involving possession), they will fail to distinguish between subclasses permitted or prohibited by the narrow-range rules.

The prediction that narrow-range rules would not be acquired was tested by means of an experiment involving real and novel (i.e. invented) verbs (following Gropen et al. 1989). The rationale for the use of novel verbs is that learners may well have heard real verbs in relevant contexts; hence, if they get real verbs right in an experimental setting (permitting the double-object form with some verbs but not with others), this may show nothing more than that they have been paying close attention to the input. Novel verbs, on the other hand, will, by definition, not have been encountered before. Hence, the way they are treated is more revealing of unconscious knowledge of underlying generalizations (or lack thereof).

The experiment involved an acceptability-judgment task. Subjects had to read short paragraphs, each of which introduced a novel or real dative verb, followed by two sentences using this verb in the prepositional dative and double-object forms. Subjects had to judge the acceptability of the sentences. (See the example in box 7.1.) Several different narrow-range constraints were investigated, and there were real and novel verbs observing (+NRR) (e.g. *throw*; *gomp*) or not observing (−NRR) (e.g. *push*; *tonk*) the narrow-range rules. Native speakers are expected to permit the double-object structure in the former case and reject it in the latter.

In the case of real verbs, native speakers and L2 learners showed significant differences between dativizable verbs (which observe the narrow-range constraints and are able to occur in the double-object form) and non-dativizable verbs (which fail to observe the narrow range constraints, and hence are disallowed in the double-object form). They accepted double-object versions of the former and rejected the latter. (See table 7.1.1.) The results revealed differences between the native speakers and L2 learners as far as the novel verbs were concerned. The native speakers observed the same distinction in the case of the novel verbs (though not as strongly), while the L2 learners failed to do so: there is no significant difference between their responses to the dativizable and non-dativizable novel verbs. Bley-Vroman and Yoshinaga take this as support for the Fundamental Difference Hypothesis: the Japanese speakers cannot work out the narrow-range constraints because these

Box 7.1 Constraints on the dative alternation (Bley-Vroman and Yoshinaga 1992)

Languages: L1 = Japanese, L2 = English
Task: Acceptability judgments. Paragraphs containing real and novel dative verbs, followed by two sentences to be judged for acceptability on a scale of −3 to +3.
Sample stimulus: (novel verb, −NRR):

Joe invented a robot, which he named Spot, which only responds to high-pitched voices, so he had to learn to speak in a special way, which he called **feening**. Therefore, when Joe needs to communicate to his robot, he would always **feen** the command to the robot.

−3	−2	−1	0	1	2	3	Joe is feening a message to Spot.
−3	−2	−1	0	1	2	3	Joe is feening him a message.

Results:

Table 7.1.1 *Mean acceptances of double-object datives (from −3 to +3)*

	Real verbs		Novel verbs	
	+NRR (# = 3)	−NRR (# = 3)	+NRR (# = 3)	−NRR (# = 3)
L2 learners (n = 84)	1.26	−1.59	−0.19	−0.99
Native speakers (n = 85)	2.29	−1.69	1.14	−0.56

are not available in the L1 and cannot be acquired in the L2, UG no longer being available.

However, there is a problem with this interpretation of the results. Crucially, in the case of the novel verbs, the Japanese speakers *reject* the dative alternation altogether, regardless of presence or absence of narrow-range constraints, as can be seen in table 7.1.1. In other words, they are conservative about accepting double objects (Juffs 1996a). The proposal for narrow-range constraints was made by Pinker (1989) in order to account for why some English dative verbs alternate and others do not. The constraints are intended to account for the lack, or eventual loss, of overgeneralization. In the absence of narrow-range constraints, learners, whether L1 or L2, should *accept* any and all dative verbs in the double-object form (provided that the possession constraint is observed). But the L2 learners in this study do not overgeneralize at all – they simply reject novel double-object forms.

If double-object forms are rejected, then the issue of observing, or failing to observe, the narrow constraints simply does not arise. Inagaki (1997) also found that Japanese-speaking learners of English generally rejected double-object versions of novel verbs (and some real verbs as well). It appears, then, that the Japanese-speaking learners of English are being conservative, rejecting novel double-object datives which they have not seen or heard before. Unfortunately, the stories in the experimental task presented the novel verbs in the prepositional form, so learners may simply have been accepting the version they had read. This problem could have been avoided by omitting the prepositional phrase from the story.

As Whong-Barr and Schwartz (2002) point out, these results are in fact consistent with the claim that L2 learners adopt L1 argument structure, on the assumption that the Japanese dative is equivalent to the English prepositional dative. Whatever the explanation, the results say nothing about presence or absence of narrow-range constraints in the interlanguage lexicon, hence nothing about presence or absence of UG-derived properties or the correctness or incorrectness of the Fundamental Difference Hypothesis. It is noteworthy that Sawyer (1996), using a production task based on Gropen et al. (1989), found that Japanese-speaking learners of English did produce double-object datives with real and novel verbs and that they were more likely to do this in the case of verbs that observed the narrow-range constraints.

7.5 Crosslinguistic differences in conflation patterns

We turn now to L2 research which looks in more detail at semantic primitives, how they combine into words and their consequences for interlanguage syntax. Talmy (1985) points out that there are crosslinguistic differences in conflation patterns, that is, possible combinations of semantic primitives into a single word, such as a verb or preposition. In recent years, L2 researchers have begun to explore the potential effects on interlanguage argument structure of such crosslinguistic differences. Different conflation patterns lead to differences in the surface expression of meaning from language to language, raising the issue of whether or not L2 learners acquire conflation patterns appropriate for the L2.

Talmy identifies several basic conflation patterns in the world's languages as far as motion verbs are concerned. Here, two conflation patterns will be discussed, relating to verbs which occur in expressions that describe movement towards a goal. In languages like English, verbs such as *dance, roll* or *float* can conflate motion with MANNER to express movement in a particular direction. Hence, one can say things like (8), where the meaning is that the bottle moved into the cave in a floating manner. (Examples are drawn from Talmy.)

(8) The bottle floated into the cave.

In languages like Spanish, on the other hand, motion does not conflate with manner in this way. Instead, it conflates with PATH, while manner of motion must be expressed independently, as shown in (9).

(9) La botella entró a la cave flotando.
the bottle moved-in to the cave floating

This pattern is also possible in English, although it is not the most basic or frequent one; that is, there is nothing that says that manner must conflate with motion in English, only that it may do so. Thus, (10) is also possible in English:

(10) The bottle entered the cave (by) floating.

It is important to note that in both language types it is possible to say the equivalent of *the bottle floated (in the sea)*. That is, there is a locational reading of *float* in both languages, as well as a directional one in English.

7.5.1 Conflation patterns in L2 motion verbs

Inagaki (2001; 2002) investigates the effects of crosslinguistic differences in conflation patterns on interlanguage representation of argument structure. Japanese patterns with Spanish in disallowing conflation of MANNER with motion. As Inagaki shows, in the case of expressions involving directional PPs (expressing the goal of the motion), Japanese must use a verb of directed motion like *go* and express manner by means of a gerund, marked with /*-te*/, as shown in (11a). The use of a motion verb like *walk* with a directional PP is ungrammatical, as shown in (11b).

(11) a. John ga gakkoo ni aruite itta.
John NOM school at walk-GER go-PAST
'John went to school walking/John walked to school.'
b. ?*John ga gakkoo ni aruita.
John NOM school at walk-PAST
'John walked to school.'

Inagaki assumes that argument structure is itself structured, along the lines proposed by Hale and Keyser (1992, 1993). He develops an analysis of English and Japanese motion expressions, arguing that they differ as to how the semantic primitives PLACE and PATH are realized. In English, a PLACE preposition incorporates with a PATH preposition in l-syntax (resulting in prepositions like *into, onto*). This allows a verb including MANNER in its meaning to be inserted into the structure. In Japanese, on the other hand, the PATH preposition incorporates into the verb;

as a result, a verb expressing manner can no longer be inserted. (In other words, a verb can incorporate either MANNER or PATH but not both.) The trees in (12) and (13) illustrate these differences in incorporation (from Inagaki 2001).

(12) Incorporation of Place P into Path P in English

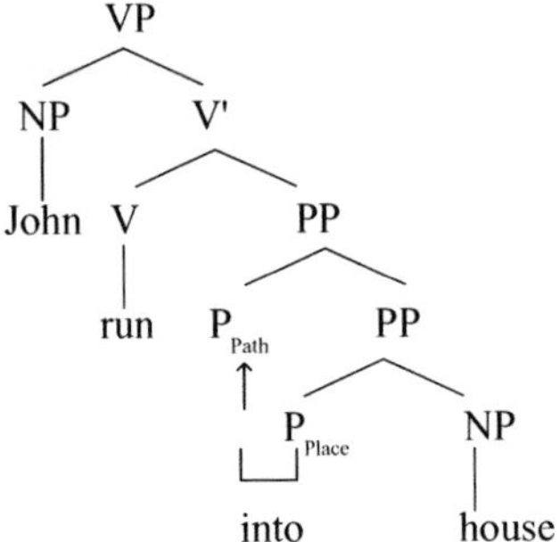

(13) Incorporation of Path P into V in Japanese

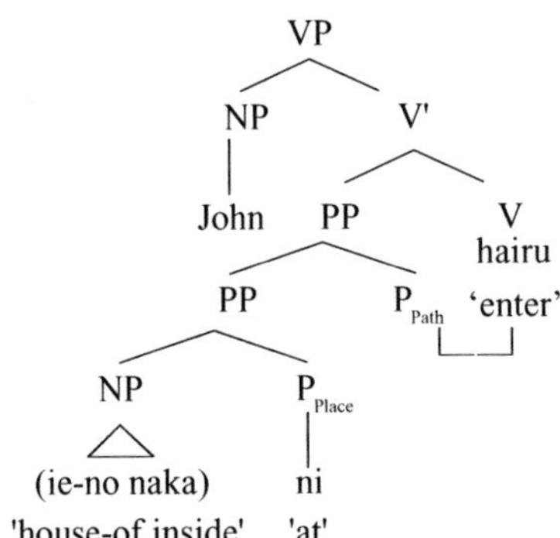

A Japanese-speaking learner of English will presumably hear sentences like (12) (*John ran into the house*), thus receiving positive input that English allows manner of motion verbs to appear with directional/goal PPs. Hence, acquiring the English conflation possibilities should be relatively unproblematic. The situation is less straightforward in the case of English-speaking learners of Japanese, who will receive positive evidence of the existence of manner of motion verbs equivalent to *walk* and *run* (occurring in locational contexts, for example), as well as evidence that motion towards a goal is expressed as in (11a). Crucially, however, there will be no positive evidence to show that the combination of a manner of motion verb with a directional PP is disallowed, that is, no evidence as to the ungrammaticality of (11b). Here, the conflation/incorporation patterns in the L1 English yield a superset of the possibilities in the L2 Japanese. That is, English allows sentence types with and without conflation (compare (8) and (10)), whereas Japanese disallows conflation.

If L2 learners adopt L1 conflation patterns and associated argument structures, there may be directional differences in eventual success in acquiring L2 argument structures. Inagaki (2001) predicts that the Japanese-speaking learner of English will acquire the possibility of conflating manner with motion in the verb's meaning, on the basis of positive L2 input. On the other hand, it may be impossible for the English-speaking learner of Japanese to lose the English-based conflation pattern.

Inagaki conducted a bidirectional study on motion verbs with goal PPs, testing Japanese-speaking learners of English and English-speaking learners of Japanese on the same structures, using the same task. (See box 7.2.) The central sentence types that he considers are Japanese and English versions of the sentences in (11). In (11a), there is a verb of directed motion together with a gerund expressing manner of motion, which is possible in Japanese and also possible (though odd with some verbs) in English. In (11b), there is a manner of motion verb with a goal PP, which is possible in English but not in Japanese.

Inagaki's task made use of pictures followed by sentences (including but not restricted to the types discussed above), which had to be judged for naturalness in the context of the picture. The results show clearly (see table 7.2.1) that there are directional differences in success in acquiring L2 conflation patterns. The learners of English (who are intermediate level) behave similarly to the native speakers of English: they accept manner verbs with goal PP (V+PP) (e.g. *John walked into the house*). They tend to reject sentences which use a verb of motion and a gerund (V+PP+ing) (e.g. *John went into the house walking*), even though equivalents of these sentences are possible in the L1 Japanese; such sentences are accepted, though not very strongly, by the native speakers of English. Both groups, then, prefer the V+PP forms. The learners of Japanese (who are of advanced proficiency), on the other hand, contrast with the native speakers of Japanese. They accept the English-like manner of motion verbs preceded by PPs (PP+V), whereas the Japanese controls reject them. Both groups accept the sentences with directed motion verbs and gerunds (PP+te+V).

The results from Inagaki's experiment support the claim for directional differences in acquirability of L2 conflation patterns: English-speaking learners of Japanese overgeneralize the English conflation pattern, while Japanese-speaking learners of English appear to have no difficulty acquiring a pattern not present in the L1. The results are consistent with theories, such as Full Transfer Full Access, whereby the L1 representation is implicated in the interlanguage lexicon; lexical entries can be restructured on the basis of L2 input. The Japanese-speaking learners of English are exposed to sentences like (12), indicating the need to revise

Box 7.2 Motion verbs with goal PPs (Inagaki 2001)

Languages: L1 = English, L2 = Japanese and L1 = Japanese, L2 = English.
Task: Pictures followed by sentences, to be judged for naturalness in the context of the picture, on a scale of −2 to +2.
Sample stimulus (L2 English study):

Sam walked into the house.	−2	−1	0	1	2
Sam went into the house walking.	−2	−1	0	1	2

Results:

Table 7.2.1 *Mean acceptances of motion verbs with goal PPs (from −2 to +2)*

		L2 English study		L2 Japanese study	
		V+PP	V+PP+ing	PP+V	PP+te+V
L2 groups	L1 Japanese (n = 42)	1.24	−0.22		
	L1 English (n = 21)			0.78	1.32
Native speakers	English (n = 22)	1.92	0.36		
	Japanese (n = 43)			−0.8	1.47

the argument structure accordingly. The English-speaking learners of Japanese, on the other hand, receive no relevant primary linguistic data (no data about the ungrammaticality of sentences like (11b)). Accordingly, the L1 representation is retained.

Nevertheless, there are also cases of undergeneralization, that is, failure to acquire an L2 conflation pattern even when positive evidence is available. Inagaki (2002) investigated another aspect of conflation which is relevant in this context. In English, some directional prepositions that incorporate PLACE into PATH (see (12) above) have a clear morphological reflex of the incorporation: *into* is composed of *in+to* and the meaning can only be directional, not locational. However, many English prepositions do not show such explicit morphology, even when incorporation has taken place, and are ambiguous as to whether they are directional (PATH) or locational (PLACE), as can be seen in (14):

(14) The children jumped behind the wall.
Meaning 1: the children jumped from somewhere to behind the wall (PATH)
Meaning 2: the children were behind the wall, where they were jumping (PLACE)

Similarly, for many native speakers, a preposition like *in* has both interpretations, although a locational reading may be preferred in the absence of context. In (15), the meaning can be that the children were already in the water where they were engaged in jumping activities (PLACE) or it can mean that they were on the edge of the pool and jumped into it (PATH).

(15) The children jumped in the water.

In Japanese, on the other hand, PLACE cannot incorporate to PATH in this way, as discussed above. Rather, PATH incorporates into the verb. In consequence, prepositions which are ambiguous between location and direction in English are unambiguously locational in Japanese. If L2 learners assume the L1 incorporation pattern, they may fail to realize that such PPs are ambiguous in English.

Inagaki explores whether Japanese-speaking learners of English are able to discover the ambiguity of prepositions like *in, under, behind*, occurring with manner of motion verbs. The task involved pairs of pictures, one showing a directional reading and one a locational one. Each pair was accompanied by one sentence and subjects had to indicate which picture the sentence corresponded to, or whether it was true of both of them. The results show that native speakers of English recognize sentences like (15) as being ambiguous; 75% of their responses were that both pictures were possible for any given sentence. The predominant response (70%) of the Japanese-speaking learners of English, on the other hand, was to choose the picture that corresponded to the locational reading. Inagaki suggests

Table 7.1 *Conflation parameter*

	English: CAUS+STATE	Chinese: *CAUS+STATE
Psych verbs	The book disappointed Mary.	*Nei ben shu shiwang le Zhang San. that CL book disappoint PERF Zhang San
Causatives	The sun melted the snow.	*Taiyang hua xue le Sun melt snow ASP
Locatives	John covered the bed with a blanket.	??Zhang San yong tanzi gai le chuang. Zhang San use blanket cover ASP bed

that the directional interpretation of English prepositions is not sufficiently robust in the input to lead to a reanalysis of the L1-based conflation class in such cases, so Japanese-speaking learners of English fail to conflate PLACE and PATH. Since acquisition crucially depends on input as well as on internal factors, lack of restructuring is not surprising in such cases.

7.5.2 Lexical parameters and conflation

The above differences between English and Japanese raise the question of whether parameters are implicated in the lexical domain. Talmy (1985) observed that languages fall into distinct types with respect to the conflation patterns permitted with motion verbs. This suggests that there may indeed be lexical parameters. Juffs (1996a, b, 2000) proposes one such parameter, which divides languages according to whether or not the semantic primitive STATE can conflate into a verbal root which includes the functions CAUSE and GO. In other words, the issue is whether a verb's meaning can include CAUSE and CHANGE OF STATE, or whether one or other of these has to be expressed by means of a separate morpheme. In languages like Chinese, such conflation is not possible, whereas in languages like English, it is. Juffs investigates whether L2 learners can reset this parameter and whether the various structures subsumed under the parameter cluster together in the interlanguage grammar.

The parameter brings together several apparently unrelated argument structures, including those associated with psych verbs, causatives and the locative alternation. In all three cases, CAUSE and STATE can be conflated into a single English verb, whereas this particular conflation is impossible in Chinese. In consequence, certain sentences that are possible in English are not possible in Chinese. These differences are summarized in table 7.1 and described in more detail below.

The first example of this crosslinguistic difference is provided by so-called *psych verbs*, that is, verbs which express psychological states, such as *anger, disappoint* and *frighten*. In (16a), the verb *disappoint* means that something caused the teacher to get into a state of being disappointed; here CAUSE and STATE are conflated within one verb. It is also possible to express the causative separately, using the periphrastic verb *make*, as in (16b). (Examples in this section come from Juffs (1996a, 2000).)

(16) a. The students' behaviour disappointed the teacher.
X CAUSE [Y GO [STATE]]
b. The students' behaviour made the teacher disappointed.

In Chinese, equivalents of (16a) are not possible, whereas the periphrastic causative is grammatical, as shown in (17).

(17) a. *Nei ben shu shiwang le Zhang San.
that CL book disappoint PERF Zhang San
'That book disappointed Zhang San.'
b. Nei ben shu shi Zhang San hen shiwang.
that CL book make Zhang San very disappoint
'That book made Zhang San very disappointed.'

The second crosslinguistic difference relates to the *causative/inchoative alternation*, an alternation which is found with unaccusative change of state verbs. *Unaccusatives* are intransitive verbs whose subject is a theme argument; we will consider these in greater detail in section 7.6.2. Some unaccusatives alternate with a transitive variant, whose meaning includes CAUSE. In (18a), the unaccusative verb *melt* appears with only one argument, the theme, in subject position; this form is called the inchoative. In (18b), the verb appears in a causative variant, taking two arguments. The verb's meaning now includes CAUSE and CHANGE OF STATE (the snow is now melted whereas before it was not). In (18c), the causative is expressed by means of the verb *make*, similar to the situation with psych verbs in (16b).

(18) a. The snow melted.
b. The sun melted the snow.
c. The sun made the snow melt.

Once again, Chinese differs from English, in that the equivalent of (18b) is not possible, as shown in (19).

(19) a. Xue hua le.
Snow melt ASP
b. *Taiyang hua xue le.
Sun melt snow ASP
c. Taiyang shi xue (rong)hua le.
Sun make snow melt ASP

To summarize so far, in English it is possible to express CAUSE in the verb root itself and a CHANGE OF STATE is understood, as seen in (16a) and (18b). In Chinese, on the other hand, CAUSE and STATE may not conflate; instead CAUSE must be expressed separately, by means of a periphrastic verb. Hence, (17b) and (19b) illustrate the appropriate means of conveying the relevant meaning.

Finally, Juffs includes *locative* verbs in the proposed parameter. Locative verbs describe the transfer of some object (the content) to some location (a container or a surface), as illustrated in (20). In the case of verbs like *pour*, the moving object is realized as the direct object, while the location is expressed in a PP, as in (20a). These are *content* verbs, also known as *theme-object, content-oriented* or *figure-oriented*. With verbs like *cover*, the location appears as the direct object, as in (20c). These are *container* verbs, also known as *goal-object, container-oriented* or *ground-oriented*. There are also verbs like *load* which alternate, appearing in content-oriented and container-oriented versions, as shown in (20e) and (20f).

(20) a. Mary poured water into the glass. (content)
X CAUSE [Y GO [PATH]]
b. *Mary poured the glass with water.
c. John covered the bed with a blanket (container)
X CAUSE [Y GO [STATE]]
d. *John covered a blanket onto the bed.
e. The farmer loaded hay onto the wagon (content)
X CAUSE [Y GO [PATH]]
f. The farmer loaded the wagon with hay. (container)
X CAUSE [Y GO [STATE]]

As Juffs discusses, the situation is different in Chinese. Chinese has content verbs like *pour* (involving conflation of CAUSE and PATH), as well as verbs like *load* occurring only in the content version equivalent to (20e). In contrast, container verbs like *cover* cannot be expressed in terms of a single verbal root, as shown in (21a). This follows from the proposed parameter: *cover* means 'cause to become covered', i.e. it conflates CAUSE and STATE. Instead, such verbs in Chinese either behave like content verbs (conflating CAUSE and PATH), as in (21b), or they require the formation of a resultative verb compound by the addition of an explicit morpheme, *-zhu*, denoting STATE, as in (21c).

(21) a. ??Zhang San yong tanzi gai le chuang.
Zhang San use blanket cover ASP bed
'Zhang San covered the bed with a blanket.'
b. Zhang San wang chuang shang gai le tanzi.
Zhang San to bed on cover ASP blanket
'Zhang San covered the blanket onto the bed.'

c. Zhang San yong tanzi gai-zhu le chuang.
Zhang San use blanket cover-complete ASP bed
'Zhang San covered the bed with a blanket.'

Assuming that a parameter is indeed implicated here, what are its effects in L2 acquisition? Is it the case that learners initially adopt the L1 parameter setting and are able to restructure lexical entries in the light of L2 input? Is it the case that all three structures are treated as a cluster? Juffs (1996a, b) investigated such questions by means of an experiment testing Chinese speakers learning English (in China). (See box 7.3.)

The crucial structures are transitive psych verbs, causative versions of inchoative verbs, and container locatives, all of which are ungrammatical in Chinese and grammatical in English. (Juffs claims that the ungrammaticality of sentences like (20d) is also a consequence of the parameter. However, this cannot be correct: although English, in contrast to Chinese, allows conflation of CAUSE and STATE, it does not disallow conflation of CAUSE and PATH (see (20a) and (20e). The ungrammaticality of (20d) depends on an additional semantic restriction and is orthogonal to the proposed parameter.)

As can be seen in table 7.3.1, results from a grammaticality judgment task show native speakers of English behaving as expected, accepting transitive psych verbs, transitive variants of inchoatives (i.e. causatives) and container-oriented locatives (non-alternating). In other words, they accept verbs conflating CAUSE and STATE. The native speakers of Chinese are predicted to show the reverse judgments when judging Chinese. While they reject psych verbs and causatives, they accept the container-oriented locatives, which is unexpected.

As for the L2 learners, by and large the results suggest that they have acquired the possibility of conflation of CAUSE and STATE in English, since they accept sentences that are grammatical in English and ungrammatical in Chinese. Indeed, the psych verbs and the causatives pattern together, with the more advanced groups accepting the grammatical sentences to a greater extent than the groups of lower proficiency. Juffs interprets this difference to mean that the lower-proficiency groups have not yet reset the parameter. However, the results from the container-oriented locatives do not support this interpretation. The judgments on the container verbs show a high degree of acceptance of the grammatical sentences at all levels of proficiency. The judgment data, then, suggest that these learners, regardless of proficiency level, have acquired the English conflation pattern.

Production data from a picture-description task largely support this account. Subjects were asked to describe pictures, using vocabulary (which was supplied) likely to elicit use of the relevant verb classes. They were asked to describe each picture in three different ways. The data presented in table 7.3.2, show the percentage

Box 7.3 A lexical parameter (Juffs 1996)

Languages: L1 = Chinese, L2 = English.
Tasks:

i. Grammaticality judgments, on a scale of −3 to +3.
ii. Elicited production.

Sample stimuli (grammaticality-judgment task):

Psych verb (transitive):	The slow progress frustrated the leaders.
Causative:	Tom rolled the ball down the hill.
Locative:	John loaded the apples onto the truck.

Results:

Table 7.3.1 *Grammaticality-judgment task: mean acceptances (from −3 to +3)*

		Psych verbs	Causatives	Container locatives
L2 groups	Low (n = 56)	0.78	1.35	2.25
	Intermediate (n = 27)	0.73	1.02	2.39
	High (n = 22)	1.45	2.01	2.77
	Advanced (n = 15)	2.16	2.22	2.88
Native speakers	English (n = 19)	2.38	2.66	2.95
	Chinese (n = 22)	−0.88	−1.04	1.34

Table 7.3.2 *Production task. First responses conflating* CAUSE *and* STATE *(in %)*

		Psych verbs	Causatives	Container locatives
L2 groups	Low (n = 56)	21.1	93.8	66.7
	Intermediate (n = 27)	6.8	96.9	59.7
	High (n = 22)	25.7	94.6	88.4
	Advanced (n = 15)	34.5	93.3	81.8
Native speakers	English (n = 19)	32.6	92.1	100

of first responses which used the pattern conflating CAUSE and STATE. Since subjects are under no obligation to use any particular syntactic structure, use of a particular structure provides evidence for its presence in the grammar, even if incidence of the structure is not high, as is the case with transitive versions of psych verbs. Even the native speakers produce these only about 33% of the time.

The incidence of causative versions of inchoatives is much higher. Furthermore, the predominant response of the L2 learners for container locative verbs was the grammatical version which conflates CAUSE and STATE (*John covered the bed with a blanket*).

Both tasks, then, suggest that L2 learners are sensitive to the conflation possibilities in English; they acquire structures which are ungrammatical in the L1 and grammatical in the L2. There is evidence for clustering but not much evidence for the L1 parameter value at the lower levels (contra Juffs's interpretation). However, there are some problems with the proposed parameter. If CAUSE and STATE may not combine in a Chinese root verb, there should be no alternating locative verbs in Chinese, yet alternators do exist (namely, equivalents of verbs like *spray*) (Juffs 1996a). Furthermore, sentences like (21a) are not fully ungrammatical; indeed Juffs's native-speaker control group judged them to be grammatical in Chinese, though not to the same extent as (21b). It may be that the range of phenomena that cluster together is somewhat different from Juffs's original proposal.[7]

7.6 Thematic properties of arguments and their syntactic consequences

Experiments described in the previous sections were concerned with crosslinguistic differences in conflation patterns, that is, the ways in which semantic primitives can combine, as well as their effects on interlanguage lexical representations and corresponding syntax. The following sections discuss L2 research which explores how theta roles and internal or external arguments map to syntactic positions. The question of concern is whether learners acquire L2 argument structures and how they map from argument structure to syntax. Some of the structures that were considered from the point of view of conflation will now be considered from the point of view of realization of arguments (psych verbs, unaccusatives and the causative/inchoative alternation).

We have already seen that there are a variety of argument-structure alternations, such as the dative alternation and the locative alternation. Such alternations have been treated in two different ways in the literature as far as lexical entries and syntactic derivations are concerned. On the one hand, there are accounts that adopt distinct lexical entries for alternating verbs, each version having its own conceptual and argument structures. Lexical redundancy rules relate the two entries to each other (Jackendoff 1975). This, for example, was Pinker's (1989) approach to the dative alternation: the broad-range rules are seen as establishing a relationship between the different conceptual structures underlying the prepositional dative and the double-object dative. Another approach is to maintain that, in the case of at least some alternations (including the dative), there is one lexical entry for any particular verb, hence only one argument structure. This argument structure projects to the syntax, the other variant being derived by movement of arguments in the syntax (Baker 1988). In the L2 research discussed in the next section, it is assumed that certain classes of verbs have one lexical entry, with one underlying argument structure, alternative word orders being derived syntactically.

7.6.1 Thematic hierarchies, UTAH and psych verbs

The syntactic representation of a sentence includes a subject position (Spec IP) and various VP-internal positions. The external argument of the verb maps to subject position, the internal arguments to DPs and PPs within the VP. Subjects are typically agents. Some verbs, however, lack an agent argument. An important question is what argument surfaces in the subject position when there is no agent. We will consider two different kinds of situation: (i) different surface forms, attributable to the same argument structure; (ii) the same surface forms, attributable to different argument structures. Psych verbs exemplify the former, unaccusatives the latter.

Psych verbs express psychological states, as previously mentioned (section 7.5.2). Psych verbs have an experiencer argument (the person experiencing the psychological state) and a theme argument (whatever brings about the psychological state). However, these verbs do not consistently map experiencer to one position and theme to another. Rather, there are two classes of psych verbs in English, some verbs allowing the experiencer to appear in subject position, as in (22a), while others have the experiencer occurring in object position, as in (22b).[8] The mapping of arguments to syntax appears to be arbitrary.

(22) a. The children fear ghosts. (experiencer = subject)
b. Ghosts frighten the children. (experiencer = object)

Note, first, that no agent is involved in either sentence, so a linking rule mapping agent to subject position will not help here. One solution has been to propose a universal hierarchy of thematic roles, as in (23), with the most prominent role on the hierarchy mapping to the highest syntactic position (Belletti and Rizzi 1988; Grimshaw 1990; Jackendoff 1972).[9]

(23) Agent > Experiencer > Goal > Theme

Even assuming a thematic hierarchy, this can only explain (22a), where the experiencer appears in a higher syntactic position (namely, subject) than the theme (the object). (22b) shows the reverse ordering, where the theme surfaces in subject position and the experiencer in object position. Baker's (1988: 46) Uniformity of Theta Assignment Hypothesis (UTAH) was proposed, in part, to account for such alternations in a systematic way, the idea being that one form is basic and the other derived.

(24) UTAH: Identical thematic relationships between items are represented by identical structural relationships between those items at the level of D-structure.

Assuming that alternations like the one in (22) involve identical theta roles (theme and experiencer), UTAH necessitates: (i) that the argument structure for both verbs is identical; and (ii) that the theme at D-structure is an internal argument, with movement to subject position occurring in the syntax (rather like passives, in other words).[10]

Belletti and Rizzi (1988) propose such an analysis of psych verbs in Italian, involving a thematic hierarchy, NP movement and UTAH. According to their proposal, experiencer-subject verbs are straightforward: a verb like *temere* ('fear') has two arguments; the experiencer is higher than theme on the thematic hierarchy, projecting to Spec IP. In the case of experiencer-object verbs like *preoccupare* ('worry'), on the other hand, the theme originates in VP-internal object position and the experiencer in a postverbal VP-internal subject position; thus, UTAH is observed, since the experiencer is underlyingly higher than the theme. The theme then undergoes NP movement to subject position (Spec IP).

7.6.1.1 Psych verbs in L2 acquisition

White, Brown, Bruhn de Garavito, Chen, Hirakawa and Montrul (1999) explore how the argument structure of psych verbs is realized in interlanguage syntax. There is a potential learnability problem in this domain. It is not obvious how to map thematic roles to syntactic positions: the English input will provide evidence that experiencers are subjects in some cases (e.g. (22a)), but objects in others (e.g. (22b)). If learners do not have recourse to UTAH or the thematic hierarchy, one might expect arbitrary mappings and random errors, with both classes of psych verbs causing equal difficulties.

White et al. hypothesize that, in the event that L2 learners have difficulties with psych verbs, they will resort to UTAH and the thematic hierarchy in order to determine how to map thematic roles to syntactic positions. In other words, they will not resort to arbitrary mappings. Instead, given a psych verb with experiencer and theme arguments, learners may resort to a default mapping strategy, whereby the theme is projected to object position and remains there, even when it should have raised to subject position at S-structure. Errors, then, are predicted to be unidirectional: experiencer-object verbs may incorrectly surface with the experiencer in subject position, as in (25a), but experiencer subject verbs should not occur with the theme in subject position, as in (25b).

(25) a. *The students frighten exams.
b. *Exams fear John.

In a series of experiments, White et al. investigated the above hypotheses. In most cases, L2 psych verbs turned out to be relatively unproblematic. That is, L2 learners of English (from a variety of different mother tongues) correctly distinguished between the two types of psych verbs and had few problems with either class. However, where there were problems, these were as predicted. In one experiment (see box 7.4), White et al. found that Japanese-speaking learners of English had considerable problems with experiencer object psych verbs. In a picture-identification task, where they had to indicate which of two pictures best depicted a particular sentence, Japanese speakers as a group performed randomly on experiencer object verbs (such as *frighten, disappoint, surprise, annoy*). (See table 7.4.1.) Analysis of data from individual subjects showed that 7 of the 11 subjects had particular problems with experiencer-object verbs, most of the time picking the picture that had an experiencer-subject interpretation. In the case of experiencer-subject verbs (such as *hate, enjoy, like, admire*), on the other hand, they hardly ever picked the picture that matched the experiencer-object interpretation. Performance on experiencer-object verbs was significantly worse than performance on experiencer subjects, and significantly worse than French-speaking learners of English (at the same level of proficiency) and native-speaker controls. Performance on agentive verbs (such as *lift, spray, hit*) in the active and passive was very accurate, establishing that learners knew that, as a result of NP movement, themes can, in principle, surface as subjects in English.

One possible explanation is that learners might simply be confused about the verb meanings; for example, they may think that the English word *frighten* is the correct way to express the meaning *fear*. (Across several experiments, White et al. in fact found the opposite problem, that is, learners had problems with *fear*, suggesting that they might have thought it was the form to express the meaning *frighten*. This was the only experiencer subject verb to cause consistent difficulties.) While confusion of this type would provide a plausible account in the event that only one verb was problematic, in the experiment described here, the Japanese speakers had problems with almost all the experiencer-object verbs and few problems with any of the experiencer-subject verbs, suggesting that something else is involved. If difficulties simply reflect problems of verb meaning, one would not expect errors to be so pervasive, nor would one expect them to occur in only one of the two verb classes.

Box 7.4 Psych verbs (White et al. 1999)

Languages: L1s = French/Japanese, L2 = English.
Task: Picture identification. Pairs of pictures, accompanied by a sentence. Subjects indicate which picture matches the sentence.
Sample stimulus (experiencer object verb):

The man frightens the dog.

Results:

Table 7.4.1 *Accuracy by sentence type (in %)*

		Active (# = 5)	Passive (# = 5)	ExpSubj (# = 10)	ExpObj (# = 10)
L2 groups	L1 Japanese (n = 11)	98	96.5	91	53.5
	L1 French (n = 15)	98.5	98.5	88	90
Native speakers (n = 14)		98.5	96	95.5	93

There appears to be an L1 effect here. The French-speaking and Japanese-speaking students were at the same proficiency level and in the same intensive programme but their performance on English psych verbs was quite different. There is an important difference between Japanese and English or French in morphology associated with psych verbs: Japanese has an explicit and productive causative morpheme, which is required in the case of experiencer-object psych verbs. In the absence of an overt morpheme in the L2, the Japanese speakers had considerable difficulties. In section 7.7, we will consider in more detail the consequences for the interlanguage grammar of differences between the L1 and the L2 relating to explicit morphology signalling argument-structure alternations.

In summary, errors with experiencer-object psych verbs suggest a failure to raise the theme to subject position. Such errors are nevertheless indicative of an interlanguage system that recognizes the mapping of themes to VP-internal direct-object position. As we shall see in the next section, errors with unaccusatives similarly suggest that verbs whose argument structure includes only a theme are recognized as such and are distinguished from verbs which include an agent argument.

7.6.2 The Unaccusative Hypothesis

Verbs that take a single argument are classified as intransitive. In surface syntax, this argument is realized as the subject. However, it has long been recognized that there are, in fact, two classes of intransitive verbs, so-called unaccusatives (or ergatives) and so-called unergatives (Burzio 1986; Levin and Rappaport-Hovav 1995; Perlmutter 1978). The sole argument of unaccusative verbs is a theme, whereas the sole argument of unergative verbs is agentive/volitional. As can be seen in (26a), although *the door* is the subject of the verb *open*, it is not the agent. Rather, it is the theme, the thing that is affected by the action of the verb. This is confirmed by the transitive use of *open* in (26b), where *the door* appears as the direct object of the verb and another NP, *Mary*, is both agent and subject. The example in (26c) also has an intransitive verb, *bark*, but here the subject (*the dog*) is performing the action of barking.

(26) a. The door opened. (intransitive: unaccusative)
b. Mary opened the door. (transitive)
c. The dog barked. (intransitive: unergative)

The implication of UTAH (see (24)) is that the argument structures of unaccusatives and unergatives must be distinct; such verbs must project differently in the syntax. Unaccusatives take an internal-theme argument, whereas unergatives take an external-agent argument. In the case of unaccusatives, the theme argument is projected to the VP-internal direct-object position, subsequently moving to subject position to receive case. This is because unaccusatives, like passives, are deemed to be unable to assign case to their internal argument (hence the name). Sentences like (26a), then, are derived via NP movement of *the door*, as in (27)

(Burzio 1986). There is no such movement in the case of unergatives; rather, the agent argument is projected to subject position.

(27) The $door_i$ opened t_i

So far, the differences between unaccusatives and unergatives appear to be largely semantic, relating to the theta roles that their arguments take. In fact, there are other differences between them as well. In many languages, there are a variety of syntactic and morphological reflexes of unaccusativity, which have been used by L2 researchers as diagnostics for determining how unaccusativity is played out in interlanguage grammars. An example is a morphological difference between unaccusatives and unergatives found in Italian (Burzio 1986; Sorace 1993a, b). The perfective form of the verb in Italian requires the use of an auxiliary verb followed by the past participle. In the case of transitive verbs and unergatives, the auxiliary in question is *avere* ('have'), as shown in (28a). In the case of unaccusatives, on the other hand, the auxiliary is *essere* ('be'), as shown in (28b).

(28) a. Giovanni ha telefonato.
Giovanni has telephoned
b. Giovanni è arrivato.
Giovanni is arrived

7.6.2.1 Unaccusatives in L2 English

If the distinction between unaccusatives and unergatives is related to universal mapping principles, such as UTAH, the argument structure of the two verb classes should be represented differently in the interlanguage lexicon. There has been considerable research on unaccusatives in L2 acquisition, much of it devoted to L2 English. Most of this research has focused, in one way or another, on incorrect morphology. Unlike Italian, English does not show a distinction between unaccusatives and unergatives as far as auxiliary choice is concerned. Nevertheless, L2 learners (of a variety of L1 backgrounds) sporadically treat English as if it did observe such a distinction. In particular, passive morphology is occasionally overused in unaccusative contexts. That is, unaccusative verbs appear with the auxiliary *be* and the past participle in interlanguage English.

Zobl (1989) was one of the first people to draw attention to production errors like those in (29) (in this case from written compositions) and to propose that unaccusativity was the key to what was going on.

(29) a. The most memorable experience of my life was happened fifteen years ago.
b. My mother was died when I was just a baby.

Here, unaccusative verbs appear with passive morphology (*was happened*; *was died*), even though these verbs could not be passivized by native speakers.

Since Zobl's original observations, other researchers have described similar errors in both spoken and written production (Oshita 1997; Yip 1995). A number of accounts of the phenomenon have been offered, which agree that use of passive morphology with unaccusative verbs is an indication of NP movement in the interlanguage grammar. (See Oshita (2000) and Hirakawa (2000) for recent overviews of the data and theories in this area.) In the English passive, there is NP movement of the theme argument from object position to subject position, for reasons of case assignment, as shown in (30). This movement is indicated by passive morphology.

(30) The apples$_i$ were eaten t$_i$ by the children

The account proposed for passivization errors with interlanguage unaccusatives is that learners of English note (unconsciously) the parallel with true passives: the theme originates as the internal argument of the verb and raises to subject position for reasons of case. The problem is that they take passive morphology as a means of indicating NP movement, even when passivization has not taken place.

Additional support for the claim that learners are sensitive to the underlying argument structure of unaccusatives comes from another kind of error reported by Zobl. In the examples in (31), the subject of an unaccusative verb appears in postverbal position, with or without an expletive subject. Zobl found that such inversions only occurred with unaccusative verbs.

(31) a. It is so changing everything.
'Everything is changing so much.'
b. I was just patient until dried my clothes.
'I was just patient until my clothes dried.'
c. Sometimes comes a good regular wave.
'Sometimes a good regular wave comes.'

In these examples, the verb is not passivized. Indeed, this observation further supports the NP-movement analysis of cases like (29). When the internal argument appears in postverbal position, it has not moved, so no special morphology is required.

One problem with relying on spontaneous production data is that these errors are quite infrequent and may in some sense be accidental. The passivization error is only of interest if it is confined to unaccusative verbs. If unergatives are also passivized, then it cannot be the case that learners are sensitive to the fact that the argument of an unaccusative is a theme and/or undergoes NP-movement. Oshita (2000) presents data from the Longman Learners' Corpus, a database of written English produced by learners with a variety of L1s. The corpus was searched for ten preselected unaccusative verbs and ten unergative verbs. Out of 941 tokens of unaccusatives, there were 38 sentences involving passivized unaccusatives like those in (29). Such passivization errors were not at all frequent (only 4%); however, they were the most common kind of error with unaccusatives that Oshita found. Out of 640 tokens involving unergatives, there was only one error of this type (0.15%). Mistaken passivization of unergatives, then, is practically non-existent. These results, from a large corpus, confirm Zobl's original observations.

To sum up, such errors as are found with unaccusatives (whether involving passivization or postverbal subjects) support two claims: (i) unergatives and unaccusatives are represented as distinct verb classes in interlanguage grammars – if it were not for this distinction, we would expect similar errors to occur with unergative verbs, contrary to fact; (ii) learners are sensitive to the fact that the sole argument of an unaccusative verb is an internal theme.

So far, it appears that L2 learners of English have relatively few problems with unaccusatives. Errors are relatively infrequent; where they occur, they suggest that learners are sensitive to the underlying argument structure of unaccusatives and to differences between unaccusatives and unergatives. By and large, incorrect usage does not appear to be an L1-based effect: it has been reported from speakers of a variety of languages: Chinese (Balcom 1997; Yip 1995); Japanese (Hirakawa 1995, 2000); Italian/Spanish/Korean/Japanese (Oshita 2000). (Some long-term L1 effects on unaccusatives will be considered in chapter 8, where we examine Sorace's (1993a, b) research on ultimate attainment.)

Given the paucity of production errors even when a large corpus is examined, some researchers have chosen to take a more experimental approach, devising elicited production tasks and grammaticality-judgment tasks to investigate whether or not the production errors described above indeed reflect underlying interlanguage competence. Several studies report much higher incidence, in elicited production, of passivization errors with unaccusatives than with other verbs, as well as acceptance of passivized unaccusatives in grammaticality-judgment tasks (Balcom 1997; Hirakawa 1995; Oshita 1997). In some cases, there is a corresponding failure to accept grammatical unaccusatives (Oshita 1997; Yip 1995). In general, then, it seems reasonable to conclude that L2 learners represent the argument structure of unaccusative verbs as having an internal theme argument. Furthermore, they map this argument appropriately, to a position within the VP. Their problems, which are not extensive, relate to movement of this argument to subject position in the syntax, and particularly to morphology associated with NP movement.

7.6.2.2 Unaccusatives in L2 Japanese

Because there are relatively few structural reflexes of unaccusativity in English, it is of considerable interest to investigate languages where subtle consequences of the distinction between unaccusatives and unergatives reveal themselves in a wider variety of constructions. Investigation of the L2 acquisition of such languages is potentially more revealing of interlanguage knowledge of unaccusativity than is L2 English. If interlanguage grammars are constrained by universal mapping principles like UTAH, L2 learners should eventually show sensitivity to how the two verb classes behave in a range of constructions.

Hirakawa (1999, 2001) investigates whether L2 learners of Japanese observe the distinction between the two classes of intransitive verbs. To illustrate the main issues, only one construction will be discussed here, involving the adverb, *takusan* ('a lot'). *Takusan* can modify an underlying object but not a subject. The sentences in (32) illustrate the relevant properties.

(32) a. Takusan kaita.
a lot write-PAST
'Somebody wrote a lot.'
b. Takusan oti-masi-ta.
a lot fall-POL-PAST
'A lot (of things) fell.'
c. Takusan hashitta.
a lot run-PAST
'Somebody ran a lot.'

In (32a), the verb is transitive, with a null subject and a null object. This sentence is unambiguous: it means that some person(s) wrote a lot of things (modifying the null object), not that a lot of people wrote something (modifying the null subject). *Takusan* can modify the subject of an unaccusative (because this is an underlying object) but not the subject of an unergative (because this is an underlying subject), hence (32b), with an unaccusative verb, is grammatical. The unergative (32c) is also grammatical but it has only one interpretation: the sentence cannot mean that a lot of people ran.

Hirakawa (1999) tested English-speaking and Chinese-speaking learners of Japanese, using a truth-value-judgment task, in which subjects had to indicate whether a sentence matched a picture. The sentences were all grammatical but not necessarily appropriate for a particular picture; for example, a sentence like (32c) would appear twice in the test, once below a picture of someone running hard (true description) and once below a picture of a lot of people running (false description).

It was necessary first to establish that the learners are making the relevant distinction in the case of transitive verbs; if they do not realize that *takusan* can modify the object of a transitive verb but not the subject, then one cannot expect them to distinguish between unaccusatives and unergatives in this respect. The results show that both L2 groups make the distinction with respect to transitive verbs (table 7.5.1). Crucially, as far as the main test items are concerned (namely, the unaccusative versus unergative verbs), L2 learners distinguish between false

Box 7.5 Unaccusativity (Hirakawa 1999)

Languages: L1s = Chinese/English, L2 = Japanese.
Task: Truth-value judgments. Contexts provided by pictures.
Sample stimuli:

True sentence–picture pairing
(Unaccusative: *A lot fell.*)

たくさん 落ちました。

False sentence–picture pairing
(Unergative: *A lot swam.*)

たくさん 泳ぎました。

Results:

Table 7.5.1 *Mean acceptances of sentence–picture pairings*

		Transitive – true (# = 5)	Transitive – false (# = 5)	Unaccusative – true (# = 5)	Unergative – false (# = 5)
L2 groups	L1 Chinese (n = 16)	4.61	1.31	4.31	2.38
	L1 English (n = 13)	4.31	1.23	4.23	2.38
Native speakers (n = 20)		4.7	0.55	4.55	0.9

unergatives and true unaccusatives: that is, they were significantly more likely to accept an unaccusative than an unergative verb paired with a picture showing a number of instances of the subject NP doing something. Hirakawa (2001) reports essentially similar results from intermediate-level English-speaking learners of Japanese. In general, then, Hirakawa's results suggest that L2 learners of Japanese are distinguishing between unaccusative and unergative verbs.

To summarize, L2 learners of English and Japanese show sensitivity to the distinction between the two classes of intransitive verbs, supporting the claim that the argument structures of unaccusatives and of unergatives are represented differently in the interlanguage lexicon, with the single argument projecting to different positions in the syntax. At the same time, in the course of L2 acquisition, learners have occasional difficulties with the unaccusative class: they show inappropriate morphology in L2 English, as well as failure to make a clear-cut distinction in some of the relevant structures in L2 Japanese. Problems with unaccusativity do not go away. In chapter 8, we will revisit this topic when we look at Sorace's (1993a, b) research on how unaccusatives are represented in the endstate grammars of near-native speakers of the L2.

7.7 Transitivity alternations and effects of argument-changing morphology

Results on unaccusativity suggest that L2 learners are indeed sensitive to the presence of two intransitive verb classes, and that these are represented with distinct argument structures in the interlanguage lexicon. Where errors occur, these support the claim that the learner correctly represents the argument structure of unaccusatives as taking an internal theme argument. The study by White et al. (1999) suggests that the same is true of psych verbs: problems that occur are consistent with an appropriate argument structure for psych verbs but difficulties in determining where the theme argument should surface.

In this section, we consider whether explicit morphology impinges on the realization of arguments. Morphology that signals changes in argument structure is not uncommon and there is considerable crosslinguistic variation in this area, raising the question of whether it is an advantage or disadvantage (or neither) if the L1 and L2 differ in the type of morphology they employ. In the case of psych verbs (section 7.6.1.1), presence of overt causative morphology in L1 Japanese and absence of such morphology in L2 English may have contributed to the problem L2 learners had in working out the mapping of English experiencer-object verbs, since French speakers had no such difficulties and French, like English, lacks overt morphology associated with psych verbs.

In this section, the reverse is examined in the context of the causative/inchoative alternation, namely, a situation where overt morphology is absent in the L1 and present in the L2. A subclass of unaccusative verbs participates in this alternation, hence members of this class are sometimes referred to as *alternating unaccusatives*. The same verb can be used transitively (the causative) or intransitively (the inchoative). The examples (18) and (26), repeated here as (33) and (34), illustrate the alternation.

(33) a. The snow melted.
b. The sun melted the snow.

(34) a. The door opened.
b. Mary opened the door.

Each of the (a) examples includes an intransitive unaccusative verb, or inchoative. In the (b) examples, the verb is used transitively, an external cause having been added. In the case of (33b), for example, the meaning is that the sun caused the ice to melt. In the inchoatives in (33a) and (34a), there is no particular implication of cause. (In fact, there is considerable disagreement on this issue; Levin and Rappaport-Hovav (1995) argue that cause is implicated in inchoatives.)

Transitivity alternations are often marked by explicit morphology. In some languages, there is an overt causative morpheme which marks the transitive use of the verb, as shown in the Turkish examples in (35) (adapted from Montrul 2000).

(35) a. Gemi bat-tı. (inchoative)
ship sink-PAST
'The ship sank.'
b. Asker-ler gemi-yi bat-ır-dı. (causative)
Soldier-PL ship-ACC sink-CAUS-PAST
'The soldiers sank the ship.'

In other languages, an overt morpheme is found in the intransitive variant. For example, in Spanish, the inchoative must be marked by means of the reflexive clitic *se*, as shown in (36). This pattern is often referred to as *anticausative*, since it is the noncausative variant that is overtly marked.

(36) a. María rompió los vasos. (causative)
Mary broke the glasses
b. Los vasos se rompieron. (inchoative)
the glasses CLI broke
c. *Los vasos rompieron.
the glasses broke

Causative morphology adds an argument (an external cause); anticausative morphology indicates that a cause argument has been suppressed.

Some languages have both causative and anticausative morphology. As discussed by Montrul (2000), certain verbs in Turkish require a causative morpheme when they occur in the transitive form, as shown in (35b). The causative morpheme does not occur on the intransitive version (35a). With other verbs in Turkish, however, it is the noncausative, inchoative form that gets the overt morphology, as shown in (37), similar to the situation in Spanish. The anticausative morpheme takes the same form as the passive, namely the suffix */-ıl/*.

(37) a. Adam pencere-yi kır-dı. (causative)
man window-ACC break-PAST
'The man broke the window.'

b. Pencere kır-ıl-dı. (inchoative)
window break-PASS-PAST
'The window broke.'

In a complex set of experiments, Montrul (2000, 2001a, b) investigates a number of issues relating to the L2 acquisition of argument structure, including differences between the L1 and the L2 in causative or anticausative morphology. Here, we will consider her studies involving L2s with overt argument-changing morphology, namely L2 Spanish (L1s English and Turkish) and L2 Turkish (L1s English and Spanish). (See box 7.6.)

The main task involved rating the appropriateness of sentences as descriptions of particular pictures. This task, unfortunately, confounds grammaticality and appropriateness. As discussed in chapter 3 (section 3.2.3.1), in tasks involving matching sentences to contexts (including pictures) it is desirable that test items should be grammatical in some context. In Montrul's experiment, some of the sentences were ungrammatical rather than inappropriate for the context. As can be seen in the example in box 7.6, the sentence *La ventana rompió* is ungrammatical (since it lacks the clitic *se* that obligatorily marks an inchoative) but nevertheless true. To get round this problem, subjects were asked to attend both to form and to meaning.

Montrul reports L1 effects that relate to whether or not there is overt morphological marking for the inchoative, which is marked with the reflexive *se* in Spanish, with the suffix */-ıl/* in Turkish, and with no morphology in English. In the case of both L2s, it can be seen that the learners whose L1 overtly marks the inchoative perform like native speakers in accepting forms with the inchoative morpheme and rejecting those that lack it (table 7.6.1). In other words, the Spanish-speaking learners of Turkish and the Turkish-speaking learners of Spanish seem to benefit from the fact that the L1 has an overt inchoative morpheme, even though this morphology is quite different in the two languages (a suffix in Turkish, a clitic in Spanish). The English speakers, on the other hand, behave somewhat differently. In the case of L2 Turkish, they recognize the grammaticality of inchoative verbs with */-ıl/* (though they do not accept them to the same extent as the Spanish speakers or the controls). At the same time, they fail to reject sentences lacking obligatory inchoative morphology. Their performance in L2 Spanish is even more striking: they fail to accept sentences with *se*, while accepting those without.

In conclusion, results from Montrul's studies suggest that if there is morphology in the L1 which signals argument-structure properties (particularly suppression

Box 7.6 Transitivity alternations (Montrul 2000)

Languages: L1s = English/Spanish, L2 = Turkish and L1s = English/Turkish, L2 = Spanish.
Task: Pictures followed by two sentences to be judged for appropriateness and grammaticality on a scale of −3 to +3.
Sample stimulus (L2 Spanish study):

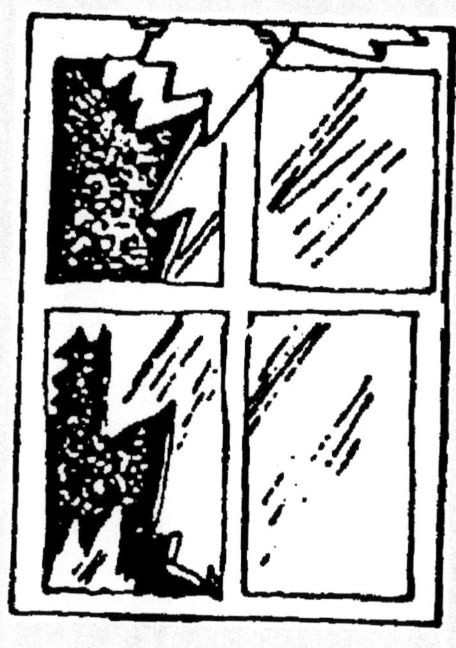

La ventana se rompió (*The window broke*)	−3	−2	−1	0	1	2	3
La ventana rompió (*The window broke*)	−3	−2	−1	0	1	2	3

Results:

Table 7.6.1 *Mean responses to inchoatives (from −3 to +3)*

		L2 Turkish study		L2 Spanish study	
		+ *ıl*	*−*ıl*	+ *se*	*−*se*
L2 groups	L1 English(n = 18 and n = 15)	1.44	−0.16	0.07	1.82
	L1 Spanish (n = 14)	2.71	−1.9		
	L1 Turkish (n = 19)			2.37	−2.03
Native speakers	Turkish (n = 18)	3	−2.96		
	Spanish (n = 20)			2.85	−2.81

of arguments), the learner is sensitized to such morphology in the L2. Montrul proposes that Full Transfer Full Access holds at the level of morphology in this case.

7.8 Methodological considerations

Some of the studies described in this chapter are bidirectional, comparing English-speaking learners of Japanese and Japanese-speaking learners of English (Inagaki 2001, 2002) or Spanish-speaking learners of Turkish and Turkish-speaking learners of Spanish (Montrul 2000, 2001b) with respect to the same properties by means of the same tasks. (See also chapter 4, section 4.3.2.) Bidirectional studies are particularly useful in cases where the learnability situation may differ depending on which language is the L1 and which the L2. That is, the potential for overgeneralization (failure to abandon L1 argument structure) or undergeneralization (failure to acquire L2 argument structure) depends on properties of the L2 input interacting with the interlanguage representation. If the interlanguage representation draws on the L1 representation, we expect differences depending on which language is the L1 and which the L2. If the L1 is not implicated in interlanguage lexical representations, no such differences are predicted.

Several of the experiments ask learners to make judgments on a scale, the rationale being that some sentences may sound better or worse than others (see Birdsong 1992; Chaudron 1983). Use of scalar judgments is not by any means unique to experiments on argument structure. However, there is something of a problem with scales which have positive and negative values (for example, +3 to −3), as is the case for many of the experiments described here (Bley-Vroman and Yoshinaga 1992; Inagaki 2001; Juffs 1996a; Montrul 2000). In particular, difficulties of interpretation arise with respect to judgments of 0: does 0 mean *don't know* or does it mean *neither good nor bad*? If scalar judgments are used, it is desirable to use scales that are entirely on the positive side (1 to 5, for example). In any case, a separate response category should be included for *not sure*. Another problem relates to interpreting differences on the same side of the scale. What does it mean if learners' mean responses are at around +1, say, whereas native speakers opt for +3? Does this indicate degrees of certainty or degrees of grammaticality? One simply cannot tell. (See chapter 8, section 8.8, for further discussion.)

7.9 Argument structure: conclusion

In this chapter, properties of interlanguage lexical entries have been considered, including semantic constraints on argument structures, conflation patterns for semantic primitives, the mapping of thematic roles to syntax, and argument-changing morphology. The results from the various studies described here provide evidence of L1 influence, as well as successful acquisition of L2 properties.

Assuming that such properties derive from UG and that at least some of them are parameterized, the hypotheses that we have been considering throughout this book are relevant in this context. On No Parameter Resetting accounts, the L2 learner will presumably be restricted to L1 semantic constraints, L1 conflation patterns and L1 argument structures. We have seen evidence that this is not the case. For example, Juffs (1996a,b) shows that Chinese-speaking learners of English acquire the English value of the parameter that allows conflation of CAUSE and STATE, with consequences for a range of argument structures. According to Full Access without Transfer, the L2 learner should not face any particular problems in domain of argument structure: properties of L1 lexical entries will not form part of the initial representation, so the L2 argument structure should be acquirable without transfer. Again, we have seen that properties of L1 lexical entries do in fact influence interlanguage lexical entries in a variety of respects. For example, Montrul (2000) shows that presence or absence of overt argument-changing morphology in the L1 affects sensitivity to such morphology in the L2. As far as Full Transfer Full Access is concerned, the L1 forms the basis of the L2 learner's initial interlanguage representation, including the representation of argument structure. Given suitable positive evidence, lexical entries can be restructured, along lines consistent with UG. In support of this account, we have seen evidence of successful acquisition of L2 lexical properties. However, we have also seen cases where the L1 argument structure is maintained, even in the grammars of advanced L2 speakers. In the interlanguage grammars of advanced English-speaking learners of Japanese, the English conflation pattern for motion verbs with goal PPs is maintained (Inagaki 2001, 2002). This failure to lose L1 argument structure arises in situations where the L1 grammar yields a superset of the possibilities permitted in the L2. That is, positive L2 input for restructuring the lexical entry is lacking. In conclusion, interlanguage lexical entries are UG-constrained but acquisition of L2-like argument structure is not inevitable, depending on which language is the L1 and which the L2.

Topics for discussion

- Many researchers have suggested that there is a family of related constructions involving complex predicates, including double-object datives, verb-particle constructions, resultatives and perception verbs. According to Snyder and Stromswold (1997), a parameter is implicated; in L1 acquisition, these constructions are acquired concurrently. If datives are part of such a parameter, to what extent would this affect claims about L2 acquisition of constraints on the English dative alternation?

- As we have seen, errors involving unaccusatives in L2 English spontaneous production are relatively infrequent. At the same time, several experimental studies report that learners have problems with unaccusatives on grammaticality-judgment tasks, as well as in elicited production tasks. What are the implications of such discrepancies as far as establishing the L2 learner's underlying linguistic competence is concerned?

Suggestions for additional reading

- The learnability issue with respect to argument-structure alternations was originally raised by Baker (1979), in the context of L1 acquisition. Pinker (1989) provides extensive discussion of the problem, and some solutions.
- Juffs (2000) provides a useful overview of research on L2 argument structure.
- A special issue of *Studies in Second Language Acquisition* (vol. 23: 2, 2001), edited by Montrul, is devoted to argument structure and the lexico-syntactic interface.

8

Ultimate attainment: the nature of the steady state

8.1 Introduction

The research discussed so far has explored the nature of interlanguage representations during the course of L2 development, investigating the extent to which interlanguage grammars are constrained by UG, from the initial state onwards. As we have seen, according to some accounts, adult interlanguage grammars fail to conform to principles or parameters of UG (e.g. Clahsen and Hong 1995; Neeleman and Weerman 1997), whereas on other accounts they are UG-constrained (e.g. Schwartz and Sprouse 1994, 1996; White 1989, 1996b, 2000). We have also seen that there are transition problems: parameter resetting in interlanguage grammars is not inevitable and when it does occur, the parameter settings achieved do not invariably correspond to those of the L2 grammar. In consequence, even if interlanguage grammars conform to UG, they may differ in various respects from the grammars of native speakers. In the present chapter, the focus is on ultimate attainment, that is, the steady-state grammar of people who have completed their L2 acquisition. In other words, they are no longer L2 learners but, rather, bilingual (or multilingual) speakers or users of the L2.

In L1 acquisition, it is presupposed that all acquirers of the same language or dialect achieve essentially the same steady state (barring 'pathological' exceptions). Indeed, much research in current linguistic theory is addressed towards discovering and describing that endstate, in other words, the nature of linguistic competence. In contrast, relatively little is known about the steady-state grammars of L2 speakers. Intuitively, it might seem obvious: (i) that L2 speakers differ from each other in their ultimate attainment, even in the case of speakers with the same L1 who have acquired the same L2; and (ii) that the endstate grammars of L2 speakers differ from the native-speaker steady state.

In fact, it should not be taken for granted that non-native performance by L2 speakers necessarily indicates basic qualitative differences between the grammars of L2 speakers and native speakers. In recent years, considerable research has been directed towards discovering the nature of the ultimate attainment of L2 learners, with particular reference to linguistic properties which have their origins in UG.

In this chapter, we consider: (i) whether or not endstate non-native grammars differ qualitatively from native-speaker grammars; and (ii) whether differences, if found, reflect absence of UG constraints. As we shall see, research results suggest that steady-state interlanguage grammars often (though not inevitably) diverge from native-speaker grammars. In many cases, it can be demonstrated that the endstate grammar is a UG-sanctioned grammar, although not equivalent to the L2 grammar.

In this chapter, the steady-state grammars of L2 speakers will frequently be compared with the grammars of native speakers. This might seem at odds with the position taken earlier (see chapter 2, section 2.4) that interlanguage grammars should be considered as systems in their own right, avoiding the *comparative fallacy* (Bley-Vroman 1983). The aim of much of the research described in this book has been to discover the essential characteristics of the L2 learner's or L2 speaker's representation of the L2 input, the central issue being whether interlanguage grammars are of the type sanctioned by UG, not whether they are identical to native-speaker grammars. Nevertheless, in order to understand the nature of interlanguage representations, it is sometimes fruitful to consider whether or not the grammar has the same properties as the native-speaker grammar. If there turns out to be divergence, then the divergent grammar must be carefully investigated, in order to fully understand the linguistic system under investigation.

8.2 Convergence versus divergence

It is important to recognize that the ultimate attainment of the L2 speaker might be fully native-like, near-native, or non-native (in varying degrees). In other words, the endstate grammar of an L2 speaker might converge on the grammar of a native speaker, being identical in all relevant respects, or it might diverge, to a greater or lesser extent. While convergence would constitute evidence that UG constrains the steady-state grammar, the opposite conclusion cannot be drawn from failure to converge. Indeed, as mentioned above, the central issue is not whether an interlanguage grammar is native-like but whether it is UG-constrained, whether it falls within the range sanctioned by UG (Cook 1997; Schwartz 1990; White 1996b). White (1996b) considers three scenarios with respect to endstate L2 competence:

i. Convergence. The steady-state grammar is effectively identical to the grammar of native speakers of the L2, subject to the same constraints of UG and the same parameter settings. That is, representations generated by the grammars of L2 speakers are the same as native-speaker representations, in all significant respects. (This does not mean that L2 speakers must acquire a vocabulary identical to native speakers, nor that language-specific peripheral rules will necessarily have been acquired. Native speakers, after all, often differ from one another in these respects.)

ii. UG-constrained divergence. The endstate grammar is different from the grammar of native speakers of the L2 but nevertheless subject to UG constraints. In other words, it is a *possible* grammar which happens not to correspond to the grammar of a native speaker. It may combine properties of the L1 grammar and the L2 grammar, as well as grammars of other languages.

iii. Unconstrained divergence. The endstate grammar not only fails to converge on the grammar of native speakers of the L2, but it is also not subject to UG constraints, being qualitatively different from the linguistic systems of native speakers. In terms of the discussion in chapter 2, endstate grammars of this type would be wild.

In the past, lack of total success (where success is defined as acquiring a grammar like that of a native speaker) has been interpreted as implying absence of UG (e.g. Bley-Vroman 1990; Schachter 1989, 1990). L2 speakers and native speakers have been compared with respect to UG properties, the native speaker providing a reference point for assessing UG availability. If L2 speakers render judgments or otherwise behave like native speakers with respect to some principle or parameter of UG, then they are deemed to have access to UG; on the other hand, if they differ from native speakers, then their grammars are assumed not to be constrained by UG. In other words, if the interlanguage grammar (during the course of L2 acquisition or in the endstate) is not equivalent to the grammar of a native speaker of the L2 with respect to some UG-derived property, this is taken as evidence that interlanguage grammars are not UG-constrained.

The problem with this line of argumentation is that it presupposes that the only UG-sanctioned outcome of the L2 acquisition process is convergence. In fact, non-attainment of native-like competence is fully compatible with the claim that interlanguage grammars are UG-constrained. An interlanguage grammar which diverges from the native grammar can nevertheless fall within the bounds laid down by UG. For example, as discussed in chapter 4 (section 4.8.1), MacLaughlin (1996, 1998) shows that some L2 learners arrive at values for binding parameters which are those of neither the L1 nor the L2 but, rather, some other language. Of particular significance in this context is Lightfoot's (1999b) claim that divergence is not uncommon in L1 acquisition either: linguistic change is brought about when the grammars of L1 acquirers fail to converge on the grammars of their parents. (See chapter 5.)

It is quite consistent with the UG approach to assume that L2 speakers will in fact end up with different competences, especially if they start out from different initial states, based on the L1 grammar. As noted by White (1996b), native speakers of different languages end up with different UG-constrained competences (a representation for English, a representation for Chinese, a representation for Turkish, etc.). What is different in the L2 context is that, even looking at only one L2, say English, we are entertaining the possibility that L2 speakers might arrive at different grammars (English 1, English 2, English *n*).

8.3 How to identify an endstate grammar

An important methodological issue in the investigation of steady-state competence is how to determine that an L2 speaker is indeed at the end of the acquisition process, unlikely to progress beyond whatever point he or she has reached. (See Long (2003) for relevant discussion.) A number of different criteria have been used, including length of residence in a country where the L2 is spoken, frequency of use of the L2, proficiency level, or degree of native-like performance (often assessed impressionistically). In many cases, it is taken for granted that a steady state will have been reached if an L2 speaker is sufficiently advanced and/or has lived for a long time in a country where the L2 is spoken. Such criteria are somewhat misleading: a person might be at a low level of L2 proficiency with an interlanguage grammar already at the steady state; a learner might be at a high level of proficiency and yet not at the endstate; someone might have lived in an L2 community for a long time and still be in the process of learning the language.

Perhaps the most satisfactory method of determining whether an interlanguage grammar is indeed a steady-state grammar is by means of longitudinal data, a method adopted by Lardiere (1998a, b). As discussed in chapter 6 (section 6.4.2), Lardiere reports on a speaker of L2 English, named Patty, whose mother tongue is Chinese. Patty was initially recorded after ten years in the USA and then again almost nine years later. There was no change in her use of tense and agreement morphology over this extended time period, nor in her performance on any of the syntactic structures that Lardiere investigated. This lack of change over time strongly suggests that Patty's grammar would undergo no further development. While the data from Patty were production data, longitudinal data involving testing and retesting on a variety of experimental tasks would provide another means of determining whether or not a steady state has been achieved. But, of course, for practical reasons, it is not always possible to gather longitudinal data, hence the adoption of the somewhat less satisfactory criteria described above.

8.4 Age effects on ultimate attainment

Ultimate attainment has frequently been examined from the perspective of critical or sensitive periods, the proposal being that there is a time period which is optimal for language acquisition, with a maturational decline with increasing age. Based on an extensive survey of the literature on maturational constraints in language acquisition, Long (1990: 255) argues that:

> There are sensitive periods governing the ultimate level of first or second language attainment possible in different linguistic domains, not just phonology, with cumulative declines in learning capacity, not a catastrophic one-time loss, and beginning as early as age 6 in many individuals, not at puberty, as is often claimed.

In other words, it is not simply the case that language-learning abilities decline; this decline is claimed (by some researchers at least) to affect the eventual outcome of the acquisition process. In the case of morphology and syntax, Long suggests that the sensitive period comes to an end before the age of 15.

Although many critical period studies refer to level of ultimate attainment in various areas of grammar, this is rarely defined in terms of a particular grammatical system or theory of grammar.[1] Instead, ultimate attainment is described fairly generally – for example, in terms of whether L2 proficiency is native-like or not – and tested by means of rather global criteria (e.g. Patkowski 1980). Such studies are not strictly relevant for determining the exact nature of ultimate attainment, particularly whether endstate L2 grammars fall within the class sanctioned by UG.

8.4.1 Violations of Subjacency

One study that is exceptional in this respect is Johnson and Newport (1991), who investigated whether there are maturational effects on Subjacency, a principle of UG. Johnson and Newport specifically address the issue of non UG-constrained grammars:

> Poor performance on . . . subjacency would suggest that maturation may lead learners to violate language universals, entertaining hypotheses about English which are thought to be outside the possible class of human grammars. (1991: 226)

Johnson and Newport, then, entertain the possibility that the grammars of adult L2 speakers might be wild (see chapter 2).

As discussed in chapter 4 (section 4.6.1), Subjacency is a principle which places constraints on movement, determining how far a phrase can move from its underlying position. Fronted *wh*-phrases may not cross more than one bounding node (or barrier) at a time. In chapter 4, Hawkins and Chan's (1996) investigation of Subjacency effects within relative clauses was discussed. In Johnson and Newport's study, the issue is how Subjacency restricts *wh*-extraction in questions. The example in (1a) illustrates this point: the *wh*-phrase, *who*, has been extracted out of a relative clause to form a question, crossing two contiguous bounding nodes (NP, IP); the resulting question is ungrammatical. This contrasts with (1b), where extraction is possible from the embedded clause because the *wh*-phrase can pass through the intermediate Spec of CP, since it is not already occupied by a *wh*-phrase.

(1) a. *Who did Mary meet the man who saw?
[$_{CP}$ Who$_i$ [$_{IP}$ did Mary meet [$_{NP}$ the man [$_{CP}$ who [$_{IP}$ saw t$_i$]]]]]
b. Who did Mary believe that the man saw?
[$_{CP}$ Who$_i$ [$_{IP}$ did Mary believe [$_{CP}$ t$_i$ that [$_{IP}$ the man saw t$_i$]]]]

In a language with syntactic *wh*-movement, such as English, the Subjacency principle prevents various kinds of illicit long-distance *wh*-extraction. On the other hand, in languages which lack syntactic *wh*-movement, such as Chinese, the principle is vacuous, at least in syntax, because *wh*-phrases do not move; rather, they remain *in situ*, as shown in (2).

(2) Zhang San xihuan shei?
Zhang San like who
'Who does Zhang San like?'

Thus, if Subjacency constrains L2 grammars, and provided that *wh*-movement has been acquired, L2 speakers of English whose L1 is Chinese should observe restrictions on *wh*-extraction, even though such restrictions are not exemplified in the L1.

Subjects in Johnson and Newport's study were native speakers of Chinese, adults at the time of testing, who were first exposed to the L2 at different ages, ranging from age 4 to adulthood. (See box 8.1.) The group whose first extensive contact with the L2 was as adults had resided in the USA for at least five years, with substantial day-to-day exposure to the L2.[2] They are assumed to have achieved a steady state, based on length of residence and the extent of their contact with – and use of – English (in a university context); however, there was no independent measure of proficiency or assessment of endstate competence.

Subjects were tested on a grammaticality judgment task (presented aurally) involving declarative statements, grammatical *wh*-questions, ungrammatical *wh*-questions without subject–auxiliary inversion, and ungrammatical Subjacency violations. The group who arrived in the USA as adults performed significantly

Box 8.1 Age effects and Subjacency (Johnson and Newport 1991)

Languages: L1 = Chinese, L2 = English.
Task: Grammaticality judgments.
Sample stimuli:

Declarative (grammatical): The policeman who found Cathy should get a reward.
Wh-question (grammatical): What should the policeman who found Cathy get?
No inversion (ungrammatical): What the policeman who found Cathy should get?
Subjacency violation (ungrammatical): Who should the policeman who found get a reward?

Results:

Table 8.1.1 *Adult learners: mean acceptances by sentence type*

	Declaratives (# = 36)	*Wh*-questions (# = 36)	*No inversion (# = 36)	*Subjacency violations (# = 36)
L2 learners (n = 23)	31	24	10	14
Native speakers (n = 11)	34	32	1.5	1

Table 8.1.2 *Mean rejections of Subjacency violations by age of arrival*

Age of arrival	Rejections of Subjacency violations (# = 36)
4–7 years (n = 6)	33
8–13 years (n = 9)	32
14–16 years (n = 6)	28
Adults (n = 23)	22
Native speakers (n = 11)	35

below native controls on Subjacency violations, incorrectly accepting more than a third of them. (See table 8.1.1.) When this group is compared with subjects whose age of arrival was younger (table 8.1.2), results show a continuous decline in accurate rejections of Subjacency violations and a correlation between performance and age of arrival in the USA, leading Johnson and Newport to conclude that constraints like Subjacency are subject to a maturational decline and that the ultimate attainment of adult learners is different in essence from that of child learners, with grammars that tolerate violations of universal constraints in the former case.

8.4.2 Subjacency violations: a reanalysis

However, this conclusion may be premature, for two reasons, relating to the syntactic analysis and to some of the test sentences. Not unreasonably, Johnson and Newport presuppose that failure to reject Subjacency violations indicates a grammar which is not constrained by UG: learners have grammatical *wh*-movement but do not observe constraints on this movement. Nevertheless, an alternative analysis is possible. As discussed in chapter 4 (section 4.6.1), it is not necessarily the case that movement is implicated (Hawkins and Chan 1997; Martohardjono and Gair 1993; White 1992c). Instead, learners may represent questions without movement, base-generating the *wh*-phrase in topic position, with a corresponding *pro* in the lower clause, as in (3a), rather than a variable or trace, as in (3b). Since movement is not involved, Subjacency is irrelevant, placing no constraint on the structures in question.

(3) a. Which test$_i$ don't you know who failed *pro*$_i$?
b. *Which test$_i$ don't you know who failed t$_i$?

There is some evidence from Johnson and Newport's results that favours such an analysis. The issue centres on whether or not the L2 speakers treat *wh*-questions as involving movement. Johnson and Newport assume that the answer is in the affirmative, based on some simple *wh*-questions included in their test, on which subjects performed very accurately. But performance on other sentences casts doubt on this conclusion. In particular, it is crucial to know whether subjects permit licit cases of long-distance extraction, such as (1b). Johnson and Newport include complex grammatical *wh*-questions, which are, presumably, intended to control for this point. But it turns out that many of these sentences do not involve extraction from an embedded clause at all.

Consider the example of a grammatical *wh*-question in box 8.1 (*What should the policeman who found Cathy get*?). While this sentence includes a relative clause (*. . . who found Cathy*), the *wh*-phrase *what* is the object of the main verb *get*. In other words, the *wh*-phrase has *not* been extracted from an embedded clause. In consequence, one simply cannot tell whether or not grammatical long-distance extraction is permitted in principle; if it is not, then acceptance of Subjacency violations is consistent with a non-movement analysis of at least some of these structures.[3] It is noteworthy that the adult group's performance on the grammatical *wh*-questions is somewhat depressed; these sentences are accepted only about two thirds of the time (see table 8.1.1), again favouring the supposition that *wh*-movement is not robustly represented. Additional support comes from performance on the ungrammatical no-inversion sentences, which the L2 speakers accept to a significantly greater extent than the native speakers. This is not unexpected if *wh*-phrases are base-generated topics, since there is no reason to invert the subject and verb in the absence of movement.

Clearly, the subjects who acquired English as adults have arrived at a grammar which diverges from the L2. According to Johnson and Newport, this grammar is not only divergent but also violates UG. However, an interpretation of the results consistent with the data is that the adult group have adopted a possible grammar (based on the L1, Chinese). This is a grammar constrained by UG, where Subjacency is irrelevant because *wh*-structures do not invariably involve *wh*-movement. Even so, Johnson and Newport's results are consistent with the claim for age effects in L2 acquisition. Only the group that arrived in the USA as adults ends up with a non-movement analysis of *wh*-questions, based on properties of the L1.

It is not, however, inevitable that adult learners will end up with non-native competence with respect to *wh*-movement and Subjacency. White and Juffs (1998) administered a grammaticality judgment task, focusing on Subjacency, to very proficient Chinese speakers who had acquired English in China, as adults. (This task was the same as the one used by White and Genesee (1996) – see section 8.5 and box 8.2 for details.) Subjects did not differ significantly from native speakers on ungrammatical Subjacency violations, rejecting them with a high degree of accuracy, suggesting that native-like competence is attainable even where the L1 and L2 differ in the relevant respects.[4] It remains to be explained why this group should have been able to abandon an analysis in terms of base-generated *wh*-phrases and *pro*, whereas the adult subjects studied by Johnson and Newport were unable to do so.

To summarize so far, results on age effects on UG properties are mixed. While age effects have been reported, these are not inevitable, nor are they necessarily indicative of grammars tolerating violations of UG principles.

8.5 Age effects in near-native speakers

As mentioned above, the ultimate attainment of the L2 speaker might be native-like, near-native or non-native. While the adult group in Johnson and Newport's study ended up with non-native (but, arguably, UG-constrained) competence, the youngest subjects achieved fully native-like success, in the sense that their judgments did not differ from native speakers. Hence, presumably, their grammars of English permit *wh*-movement, constrained by Subjacency.

In the next few sections, we explore the issue of near-nativeness, looking at the linguistic competence of L2 speakers who can, for the most part, pass as native speakers of the L2. As White and Genesee (1996) point out, such people are

Box 8.2 More on age effects and Subjacency (White and Genesee 1996)

Languages: L1 = French (+various others), L2 = English.
Task: Timed grammaticality judgments.
Sample stimuli (ungrammatical items):

Extraction from noun complement: *What did you hear the announcement that Ann had received?
Extraction from relative clause: *Who does Tom love the woman who married?
Extraction from adjunct island: *Who did you meet Tom after you saw?
Extraction from subject island: *What was a dish of cooked by Ann?

Results:

Table 8.2.1 *Mean accuracy and response times, by age of acquisition*

	Grammatical sentences		Ungrammatical sentences	
Age of L2 acquisition	Accuracy (# = 30)	Response time (in secs)	Accuracy (# = 30)	Response time (in secs)
0–7 years (n = 22)	27.46	3.85	26.68	4.82
8–13 years (n = 7)	27.29	3.5	27.86	4.4
14–16 years (n = 7)	27	3.43	26.11	4.19
Adults (n = 9)	26.11	3.92	27.78	4.43
Native speakers (n = 19)	27	3.19	27.21	3.74

presumably likely to have attained a stable, steady-state linguistic competence. Nevertheless, several researchers have argued that they fail to achieve representations similar or identical to native speakers.

It is important to distinguish between native-like performance and native-like competence in this context. According to some versions of the critical periods hypothesis, L2 speakers whose *performance* is native-like should nevertheless have an underlying linguistic *competence* which differs in significant respects from native speakers, if they acquired the L2 after the sensitive period (Lee and Schachter 1997; Schachter 1996). Lee and Schachter, for example, argue for maturational effects on UG access, adopting the strong position that principles of UG become inaccessible after the sensitive period is over. On this kind of account, although certain L2 speakers may superficially pass as native speakers, their underlying representations will be radically different from those of native speakers, failing to conform to the requirements of UG.

In contrast, White and Genesee (1996) hypothesize that near-native competence can be native-like, the grammar generating representations in conformity with UG. They investigate the Subjacency Principle in the grammars of adult L2 speakers of English (the majority being native speakers of French), who started learning English at different ages. Whereas Johnson and Newport (1991) took years of residence and quality of exposure to English as sufficient indication that L2 speakers were at the endstate as far as grammar acquisition was concerned, White and Genesee selected subjects who, according to independent criteria, appear to have achieved native-like proficiency. Subjects were interviewed and then assessed by independent judges according to several rating criteria.

The task involved grammaticality judgments administered on a computer, which recorded both judgments and response times. Test sentences included ungrammatical Subjacency violations, as well as grammatical sentences to ascertain whether *wh*-extraction out of complex sentences was accepted, thus avoiding the problem that Johnson and Newport ran into. The near-native speakers performed with a high level of accuracy on grammatical and ungrammatical sentences. (See table 8.2.1.) There were no significant differences between near-native speakers and native speakers on any sentence type, no differences in response times, and, crucially, no evidence of a maturational decline with age: the group that learned English as adults was just as accurate as the groups who had learned at younger ages. On the basis of the grammaticality-judgment results, White and Genesee conclude that the competence of these near-native speakers was native-like. In addition, on the basis of the response-time data, they conclude that there were no processing differences between these L2 speakers and native speakers either, both groups accessing their linguistic competence in a similar way.

Lee and Schachter (1997: 335, note 1) claim that near-native speakers are atypical. If they are successful in spite of having learned the L2 as adults, this should not count as evidence against sensitive periods or in favour of access to UG after the sensitive period. However, this objection is misconceived. If the focus of enquiry is on the nature of the interlanguage grammar, then there are good reasons to pick subjects whose performance, at least, is native-like. One can then concentrate on exploring their linguistic competence. In the study by White and Genesee, subjects not only exhibited near-native performance but also native-like competence with respect to the Subjacency principle. However, it might reasonably be objected that the native-like representation of *wh*-movement and Subjacency, as well as the lack of age effects, is attributable to the fact that the L1 of many of the subjects was French, another language with *wh*-movement. In subsequent sections, we turn to situations where the L1 and L2 differ with respect to the properties under investigation.

8.6 Convergence or not: more on near-native speakers

Other researchers argue for qualitative differences between the endstate grammars of native speakers and near-native speakers. One of the first people to investigate the possibility that native-like proficiency might not imply native-like competence was Coppieters (1987). He identified the importance of investigating steady-state grammars in L2 acquisition, and pointed out that performance and competence must be distinguished.

Coppieters studied adult L2 speakers of French (with a variety of L1s) who were living in France and who passed as near-native by a variety of informal criteria, as well as on the basis of an in-depth interview with the researcher. A questionnaire was constructed, consisting of sentences illustrating a range of structures, including some that Coppieters assumes not to be relevant to UG, as well as others that are. Subjects were interviewed individually and their intuitions and interpretations of the sentences were elicited and discussed. Coppieters reports quantitative and qualitative differences between native and near-native speakers. Native speakers showed considerable agreement in their responses, whereas the near-natives showed considerable variation. No near-natives performed like natives. Where differences in morphological or syntactic form reflected differences in meaning, the near-natives had different intuitions from the native speakers about the meaning contrasts. Divergence between natives and near-natives was not uniform across the various structures tested: they diverged least on what Coppieters characterizes as formal (UG-related) properties. (Coppieters looked at the *A-over-A Constraint*, a constraint that has since been subsumed under Subjacency. L2 French speakers rejected A-over-A violations, as did native speakers.)

As discussed by Birdsong (1992), there are a number of methodological and conceptual flaws with Coppieters's study. The task was very metalinguistic, requiring conscious reflection about the sentences, tapping L2 speakers' ability to talk about the language rather than reflecting their unconscious knowledge of the language. Furthermore, the numbers of sentences testing each structure varied enormously (from only 2 sentences on one structure to 28 sentences on another) and sentences were not controlled for grammaticality, in the sense of having equivalent numbers of grammatical and ungrammatical versions. Based on his findings, Coppieters claims that there are competence differences between near-native speakers of an L2 and native speakers, across a variety of structures. However, because of the problems described above, this conclusion is premature.

Coppieters also suggests that there are fewer differences between native speakers and near-native speakers in the UG domain. As Birdsong points out, the basis on which Coppieters distinguishes between UG-related and non-UG structures is unclear. In addition, the questionnaire included some sentences where subjects were given a choice between possible forms and others where they had to make outright judgments. The supposedly non-UG structures were tested by the former means and the structures relevant to UG by the latter. This means that the results are not strictly comparable; rather than indicating superior performance on UG-related structures, the results might simply indicate superior performance on outright judgments.

Birdsong (1992) sought to remedy some of the shortcomings of Coppieters's study, also considering the ultimate attainment of L2 French speakers. In Birdsong's study, all subjects had the same L1, namely English. Although Birdsong criticizes Coppieters for not having an adequate method of subject selection, he fails somewhat in this area himself. Subjects were chosen who had resided for at least three years in France (arriving there as adults) and who spoke French fluently, a subjective judgment on the part of the experimenter.

Birdsong devised several tasks, including a grammaticality judgment task exemplifying various structural features of French, some of which were the same as those tested by Coppieters. Birdsong provides a better balance in terms of numbers and types of sentences. In contrast to Coppieters, Birdsong found few indications of major competence differences between native speakers and near-native speakers of French, reporting a much lower incidence of divergence between natives and near-natives, even for structures where Coppieters did find differences. Furthermore, several of the near-natives achieved scores comparable to the native speakers. There was no discernible +/– UG pattern in the results.

In addition to the already mentioned problems with the task developed by Coppieters, there are other peculiarities in the test construction, which raise some general issues. Coppieters deliberately included what he terms *controversial* sentences, that is, sentences where he expected variation or inconsistency in native-speaker judgments. Similarly, Birdsong included items of questionable grammatical status. But in the absence of a theory to account for native-speaker variability (predicting and explaining when and why it happens), it is not at all obvious what such sentences can reveal about underlying linguistic competence, nor is it clear how to interpret L2 performance on such sentences. (See Schütze (1996) for problems that arise in interpreting inconsistent judgments from native speakers.) In constructing grammaticality judgment tasks, it is more appropriate to concentrate on sentences that unambiguously exemplify a particular structure, establishing this in advance by means of pilot testing. An additional concern is that both Coppieters and Birdsong included sentences in their tests which they drew directly from the linguistic literature, a practice which is potentially problematic, since sentences invented by linguists to illustrate theoretical points are not necessarily appropriate as test items in experiments, given that vocabulary choice, sentence length and sentence complexity are not controlled for.

To sum up, Coppieters claims to have found substantial differences between native speakers and near-native speakers in several areas of the grammar. Nevertheless, given the methodological problems with his study, as well as Birdsong's failure to replicate his results, the nature of near-native linguistic competence remains to be determined.

8.7 Non-UG structures revisited

As mentioned in the preceding section, it is not obvious what criteria Coppieters used to determine whether or not a construction falls within the domain of UG. In any case, as linguistic analyses change, the relevance of certain structures to the UG debate also changes. One of the properties investigated by Coppieters was the distinction between the French *imparfait* and the *passé composé*, particularly differences in interpretation associated with these two forms, as shown in (4).

(4)

a.

Est-ce que	tu	savais	conduire	dans	la	neige?
Q	you	knew-IMP	drive-INF	in	the	snow

'Did you know how to drive in the snow?'

b.

Est-ce que	tu	as	su	conduire	dans	la	neige?
Q	you	have	known	drive-INF	in	the	snow

'Did you manage to drive in the snow?'

When Coppieters defined certain linguistic phenomena as being + or – UG, he argued that tense/aspect distinctions are semantic and outside the scope of UG. (Why semantics should be excluded from UG is unclear.) The distinction between *imparfait* and the *passé composé* was the one which led to the greatest degree of divergence between native speakers and near-native speakers in his study. Coppieters established a *prototypical norm* for responses.[5] In the case of the *imparfait/passé composé* contrast, native speakers hardly deviated from this norm, whereas the near-native speakers showed considerable deviance.

On many current analyses, both tense and aspect are represented in functional categories, hence such distinctions are worth revisiting in the context of current research on the nature of interlanguage grammars. A recent study which explores the nature of ultimate attainment with respect to aspectual interpretation is presented by Montrul and Slabakova (2001, 2003), who look at the Spanish imperfect versus preterite distinction, a contrast similar to the *imparfait/passé composé* contrast in French. Subjects are native speakers of English, a language which does not differentiate between verb forms on the basis of these aspectual distinctions.

In Spanish, aspect is expressed morphologically on the verb: the preterite is used to mark perfective aspect [+perfective], indicating that an event is bounded, with a beginning and an end point. The imperfect [–perfective] is used to indicate that an event is unbounded. This is illustrated in (5) (from Montrul and Slabakova).

(5) a. Laura construyó una casa.
Laura build-PRET a house
'Laura built a house.'
b. Laura construía una casa.
Laura build-IMP a house
'Laura was building a house.'

In English, past-tense eventive verbs are inherently perfective; this is not something that is supplied by overt morphology. English lacks simplex past-tense forms corresponding to the Spanish imperfect. Instead, unboundedness is expressed via the progressive, as can be seen in the gloss to (5b). (The English progressive is not equivalent to the Spanish imperfective: both the preterite and the imperfect can occur in the progressive in Spanish.)

Following Giorgi and Pianesi (1997), Montrul and Slabakova adopt an analysis whereby aspect is represented in a functional category, Asp, as shown in (6). There is a parametric difference between languages like Spanish and languages like English with respect to Aspect. In Spanish, preterite and imperfect morphology are checked against the features [±perfect], located in Aspect. Oversimplifying somewhat, in the absence of a morphologically realized contrast [±perfective], English lacks this functional category (see Montrul and Slabakova 2002: note 3).

(6)

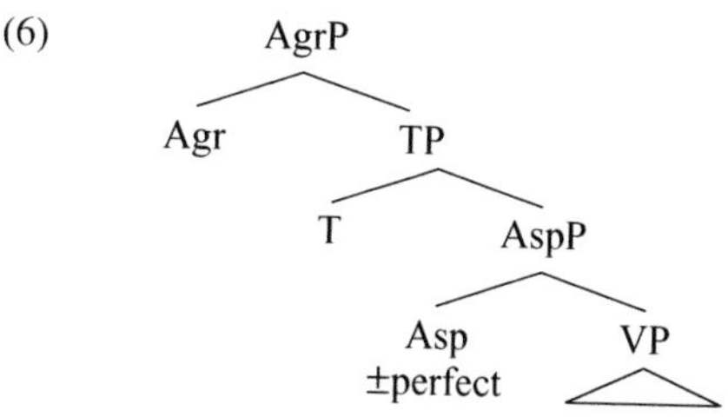

Montrul and Slabakova consider ultimate attainment in the context of the Failed Functional Features Hypothesis (see chapter 4, section 4.6), namely, the claim that the L2 learner is permanently restricted to the functional categories and features realized in the L1 grammar (Hawkins and Chan 1997; Smith and Tsimpli 1995). On this account, the steady-state grammar of L2 speakers must necessarily diverge from native-speaker grammars whenever the L1 and L2 differ as to the categories and features that they instantiate. In the case of aspectual features, near-native speakers of Spanish whose mother tongue is English should be unable to represent the [±perfective] distinction, given the lack of this featural contrast in English. In opposition to the Failed Functional Features Hypothesis, Montrul and Slabakova hypothesize that the steady-state grammar of near-native speakers of Spanish will represent the relevant aspectual distinctions.

The hypothesis is tested by investigating morphological and semantic differences between the Spanish imperfect and preterite. Like Coppieters (1987), Montrul and Slabakova argue that there is a poverty-of-the-stimulus problem in determining, from naturalistic input, the precise meanings of the two aspects. At the same time, some distinctions between imperfect and preterite are taught; hence, if differences in meaning and form are acquired, this could be attributed to classroom input. For this reason, it is essential to investigate some subtle contrast in the use of the imperfect and preterite that is not taught, and where L2 input alone would be unlikely to yield knowledge of the contrast.

Montrul and Slabakova identify the following contrast as meeting this criterion: the form of the verb in impersonal constructions with null subjects determines the interpretation of the subject as generic or specific. When the verb occurs in the imperfect, as in (7a), there are two possible interpretations of the sentence: it can mean that people in general (*one*) used to eat well or that specific people (*we*) ate well. However, when the preterite is used, the generic interpretation is unavailable, as in (7b).

(7) a. Se comía bien en ese restaurante.
CLI eat-IMP well in that restaurant
'One/we ate well in that restaurant.'
b. Se comió bien en ese restaurante.
CLI eat-PRET well in that restaurant
'We/*one ate well in that restaurant.'

Details aside, the possibility of a generic interpretation interacts with the [–perfective] feature value. Montrul and Slabakova suggest that there is a poverty-of-the-stimulus problem in this case: the learner has to discover that a particular interpretation (generic) is ruled out in impersonals with one of the verb forms (preterite) but not the other (imperfect). If L2 speakers demonstrate unconscious knowledge of these interpretive differences, this would support the claim for a functional category Aspect in the interlanguage grammar, with features [±perfective], even though the category and features in question do not form part of the L1 representation.

Subjects were adult speakers of L2 Spanish, classified as near-native speakers by means of a proficiency test and an assessment procedure similar to that used by White and Genesee (1996) (see section 8.5). The contrast between the two verb forms with respect to specific and generic interpretations was tested by means of a truth-value judgment task. (See box 8.3.) (Other contrasts typically taught in the classroom were also tested; these will not be discussed here.) Results show

Box 8.3 Aspectual contrasts in Spanish (Montrul and Slabakova 2001)

Languages: L1 = English, L2 = Spanish.
Task: Truth-value judgments.
Sample stimuli:

Specific (true)	Generic (false)
Según la mayoría de la gente, el restaurante de la calle Jefferson era muy bueno y el servicio era exelente. Fuimos a celebrar el cumpleaños de Carlos y todos nos gustó mucho. Qué lástima que lo cerraron! Se comió bien en ese restaurante.	Según el periódico, el restaurante de la calle Jefferson era muy bueno y el servicio era exelente. Lamentablemente el restaurante cerró el verano pasado y nunca tuvimos la oportunidad de ir. Se comió bien en ese restaurante.
According to most people, the restaurant on Jefferson Street was very good and the service was excellent. We went there to celebrate Carlos's birthday and we all liked it a lot. It's a pity that it closed. *(We) ate (*PRET*) well in that restaurant.*	*According to the newspaper the restaurant on Jefferson Street was very good and customers were always happy with the service. Unfortunately the restaurant closed last summer and we never got to go.* *(We) ate (*PRET*) well in that restaurant.*

Results:

Table 8.3.1 *Mean responses of true*

	Specific contexts		Generic contexts	
	Preterite – true (# = 6)	Imperfect – true (# = 6)	Preterite – false (# = 6)	Imperfect – true (# = 6)
L2 speakers (n = 17)	5.05	4.82	0.65	5.11
Native speakers (n = 20)	5.2	4.8	0.8	5.55

no differences between native speaker and near-native speakers. In particular, L2 speakers and native speakers denied the truth of statements with the verb in the preterite where the context forced a generic reading for the null subject (*one*) but accepted the preterite where the context allowed a specific reading (*we*). At the same time, the imperfect was accepted by both groups in both contexts. (See table 8.3.1.) Furthermore, analysis of the data from individual subjects shows that individual performance is accurately reflected by the group results. Thus, the L2 speakers showed sensitivity to a subtle kind of ungrammaticality, despite lack of positive input or instruction.

When investigating interpretations of sentences involving the Spanish preterite and imperfect, it is not possible to use a straightforward grammaticality-judgment task, because sentences with either form of the verb will usually be grammatical in the absence of context. When Coppieters wanted to probe interpretations associated with different verb forms in French, he presented a sentence with contrasting verb forms and asked subjects to indicate whether or not both forms were possible and to explain any meaning differences between them. As mentioned above, this is a very metalinguistic approach, not suitable for investigating the unconscious grammatical knowledge. In contrast, Montrul and Slabakova investigated L2 speakers' interpretations without eliciting any kind of metalinguistic commentary. Subjects were not expected to make any kind of judgment on the verb form, concentrating, rather, on the meaning of test items.

Montrul and Slabakova's results contrast with those of Coppieters, suggesting that subtle interpretive properties are acquired by L2 speakers, even when the L1 and L2 differ in the relevant respects. In addition, assuming an analysis of aspect in terms of functional categories and features, their results argue against the Failed Functional Features Hypothesis, since the L1, English, lacks the [±perfective] distinction and yet L2 speakers of Spanish are highly sensitive to it.

In the next section, we consider L2 speakers who pass as near-native but who nevertheless fail to achieve native-like competence. Instead, the L1 appears to be a major determinant of the grammar, even in the steady state.

8.8 Divergence: L1 influence

Some of the studies discussed so far report relatively few competence differences between native speakers and near-native speakers, even when the L1 and L2 differ in significant respects. However, it is not inconceivable that the endstate competence of L2 speakers, including those who pass as near-native, might diverge from the grammar of a native speaker precisely because of properties of the L1. Indeed, according to the reconsideration of Johnson and Newport's (1991) data proposed above (section 8.4.1), the analysis of *wh*-constructions in L2 English interlanguage grammars crucially depends on the possibility of base-generated topics and null objects in the L1 Chinese.

Given that the L1 is a natural language, it might seem obvious that interlanguage grammars which incorporate aspects of the L1 will be UG-constrained. However, Sorace (1993a) suggests that the L1 can have rather different effects. She distinguishes between two different kinds of near-native grammars, both qualitatively different from native speakers, namely *divergent* grammars and *incomplete* grammars. While the former are UG-constrained, the status of the latter is less obvious.

Sorace hypothesizes that adults cannot attain native-like competence, even if they pass as near-native speakers. She examines steady-state knowledge of unaccusativity in L2 Italian. As discussed in chapter 7 (section 7.6.2), unaccusative verbs (such as *arrive* and *fall*) take only one argument, a theme, which is the underlying object of the verb, surfacing in subject position. In Italian, there are a number of morphological and syntactic phenomena which are restricted to unaccusatives and which can be used as diagnostics to determine whether a verb is unaccusative or not (Burzio 1986). Sorace uses some of these diagnostics to investigate how unaccusativity is represented in the steady-state grammars of near-native speakers of Italian whose L1s are French and English. In particular, Sorace examines the behaviour of unaccusative verbs in so-called *restructuring* contexts, namely biclausal sentences involving a modal or aspectual verb (such as *potere* 'can', *volere* 'want' or *cominciare* 'begin') in the higher clause.

All unaccusative verbs in Italian take the auxiliary *essere* ('to be') to form the perfective, in contrast to unergatives and transitives, which require *avere* ('to have') (Burzio 1986; Sorace 1993a,b), as shown in (8) (repeated from chapter 7, example (28)).

(8) a. Giovanni ha telefonato.
Giovanni has telephoned
b. Giovanni è arrivato.
Giovanni is arrived

In Italian restructuring contexts, if the lower verb is unaccusative, hence normally requiring *essere*, and the higher verb is a modal, normally requiring *avere*, the choice of auxiliary with the higher verb is optional, as shown in the minimal pair in (9). (Examples are drawn from Sorace.)

(9) a. Maria non ha potuto venire alla mia festa.
Maria not have can come to my party
'Maria couldn't come to my party.'
b. Maria non è potuta venire alla mia festa.
Maria not be can come to my party
'Maria couldn't come to my party.'

In cases of restructuring, auxiliary choice interacts with the position of clitics. A clitic pronoun associated with the lower verb can, optionally, appear in the higher clause; this is known as *clitic climbing*. If the clitic remains attached to the embedded verb, either auxiliary is permitted. This is illustrated in (10).

(10) a. Alla mia festa, Maria non ha potuto andarci.
To my party Maria not have can come-CLI
b. Alla mia festa, Maria non è potuta venirci.
To my party Maria not is can come-CLI

However, when the clitic has climbed to the main verb, the auxiliary *essere* becomes obligatory, as shown in (11).

(11) a. *Alla mia festa, Maria non ci ha potuto andare.
To my party Maria not CLI have can come
b. Alla mia festa, Maria non ci è potuta venire.
To my party Maria not CLI is can come

Italian contrasts with French with respect to auxiliary choice with unaccusative verbs, as well as clitic climbing in restructuring contexts. In French, a subset of unaccusative verbs take *être* ('to be'), while others take *avoir* ('to have'). There is no optional auxiliary change with modal or aspectual verbs; in structures involving a higher modal verb and a lower unaccusative, the required auxiliary is always *avoir*. Although French, like Italian, has clitics, there is no clitic climbing in these contexts. In English, all verbs (transitive, unergative and unaccusative) form the perfect with the auxiliary *have* and there are no clitics.

Sorace investigates how near-native speakers of Italian whose mother tongues are French and English treat auxiliaries in restructuring contexts. Subjects started learning Italian after the age of 15; assessment of near-nativeness was impressionistic. Test items focused on auxiliary choice with unaccusative verbs in three different contexts: (i) basic restructuring constructions without clitics (as in (9)); restructuring with clitics but without climbing (as in (10)); (iii) restructuring with clitic climbing (as in (11)).

The task was an acceptability-judgment task, making use of a procedure known as *magnitude estimation*, in which subjects make comparative judgments on sentences, inventing their own rating scale (Bard, Robertson and Sorace 1996; Sorace 1996). Subjects are asked to assign a numerical rating to the first sentence that they hear and to assign ratings to subsequent sentences based on whether they seem more or less acceptable than the original sentence. Thus, for example, if a rating of 15 is assigned to the first sentence and the subject feels that the next sentence is twice as good, it should be assigned a rating of 30. For subsequent analysis of the results, ratings are transformed to log-scores for purposes of comparability.

Results show considerable differences between the two near-native groups, as well as between both near-native groups and the native speakers. (See box 8.4.) In the case of basic restructuring sentences without clitics where either auxiliary is in principle possible, the native speakers of Italian indeed give high ratings to both auxiliaries. The French speakers, in contrast, give high ratings to *avere*

Box 8.4 Unaccusativity (Sorace 1993a)

Languages: L1s = English/French, L2 = Italian.
Task: Grammaticality judgments (magnitude estimation).
Results:

Table 8.4.1 *Mean log scores on auxiliary choice in restructuring contexts*

		Basic sentences		Clitic low		Clitic climbing	
		essere	*avere*	*essere*	*avere*	*essere*	**avere*
L2 groups	L1 French (n = 20)	3.824	9.420	4.065	7.841	8.525	4.285
	L1 English (n = 24)	7.231	6.977	6.784	6.211	6.286	6.623
Native speakers (n = 36)		9.260	9.749	8.159	8.779	8.587	3.143

but find *essere* relatively unacceptable. The English speakers do not distinguish between the two, rating them equally, with scores in the middle range. In the case of sentences without clitic climbing, the native speakers, once again, give both auxiliaries a high rating, while the French speakers distinguish between *avere* and *essere*, showing significantly higher ratings for the former. As before, the English speakers do not distinguish between the two, rating them in the mid range. So far, the behaviour of the French speakers is consistent with an analysis of Italian based on French, where *avoir* would be required and *être* prohibited in these contexts.

In the case of clitic climbing (not permitted in Modern French), the Italian native speakers and French-speaking near-native speakers of Italian behave alike, showing significant differences in ratings of the two auxiliaries, in favour of *essere*. Once again, the English speakers show no difference in their ratings of the two auxiliaries, their acceptance level again being in the mid range.

Sorace draws two conclusions from these results. Firstly, the French speakers show representations of unaccusativity which diverge from Italian native speakers in so far as basic restructuring sentences are concerned, as well as sentences involving an unraised clitic. In these cases, L2 speakers distinguish between the possibility of *essere* and *avere*, strongly preferring the latter. In the case of clitic climbing, on the other hand, they behave like Italian native speakers, strongly preferring *essere*. As White (1996b) points out, their grammars appear to be UG-constrained, their problem being with optional auxiliary choice, which they reject. Accepting only *avere* in basic restructuring contexts and in contexts not involving clitic climbing is entirely consistent with how similar structures are analysed in French. However, faced with a possibility that is not found in French (namely, clitic climbing in restructuring contexts), L2 speakers successfully acquire *essere* as the obligatory auxiliary. Thus, as Sorace points out, their behaviour cannot be accounted for simply in terms of surface transfer. Sorace argues that the judgments of the French speakers are *determinate*; in other words, unaccusativity is represented in the grammar and L2 speakers have clear intuitions about associated reflexes, in this case auxiliary selection in restructuring contexts.

Secondly, as far as the English speakers are concerned, Sorace concludes that their interlanguage grammars are in some sense incomplete. In other words, they have no representation of how auxiliaries interact with unaccusatives in restructuring contexts, leading them to make judgments which presumably constitute guesses. She claims that their judgments are *indeterminate*, as evidenced by the fact that their acceptance of auxiliaries mostly fall in the 6–7 range, in contrast to the controls (8–10 range). (As Sorace does not provide individual subject analyses, one cannot in fact tell whether the judgments of all the English speakers fall in the mid range like this.) This difference in range of acceptability rating is the only difference between the English speakers and the native speakers as far as basic constructions and restructuring without clitic climbing are concerned. As Papp (2000) points out, Sorace does not provide clear criteria for distinguishing complete from incomplete grammars. It seems somewhat arbitrary to say that ratings around 6–7 indicate indeterminacy (hence, incompleteness) and yet at the same time to say that ratings round 3–4 constitute outright rejection (as is implied in the discussion of the controls and the French speakers when they reject one or other auxiliary).

As Sorace (1996: 397) herself points out in her discussion and rejection of the use of fixed numerical scales in grammaticality-judgment tasks, there is a problem with interpreting results that fall into the middle category on a scale. (See also, chapter 7, section 7.8.) Subjects might use the middle of the scale either to indicate uncertainty or to indicate that a sentence is neither acceptable nor unacceptable. (For relevant discussion, see Schütze 1996.) Certainty and grammaticality are orthogonal to each other; the middle of a scale ought to be used to indicate something about grammaticality (i.e. that a sentence is neither grammatical nor ungrammatical). In fact, in the absence of explicit instruction as to what to do when uncertain, subjects may use the middle of the scale to indicate uncertainty.

Contrary to Sorace's assumptions, there seems to be just as much of a problem in interpreting middle-ranking ratings in the case of magnitude estimation data as there is with fixed scales. Thus, it is hard to draw firm conclusions about the grammars of the English speakers, in particular with respect to incompleteness. At least two interpretations of Sorace's data are possible: (i) the English speakers might have representations permitting optional auxiliary selection (including in contexts where native speakers do not permit this) but at the same time be somewhat uncertain of their judgments, leading them to rate these sentences lower than others; lack of certainty, however, does not logically imply lack of representation; or (ii) they may feel that the sentences are neither acceptable nor unacceptable. Sorace interprets the English speakers' judgments in the range of around 6–7 more or less in the second sense. That is, she takes the rankings to indicate that the sentences are of indeterminate status, with unaccusatives with either auxiliary being neither fully acceptable nor fully unacceptable. She concludes from this that the English speakers do not in fact have a representation for this domain of grammatical knowledge, the grammar being incomplete.

To sum up, what Sorace describes as divergence is UG-constrained, in that the near-native speaker represents some linguistic phenomenon in a manner which is consistent with a natural language grammar, the L1. The speaker with a divergent grammar renders grammaticality judgments which are determinate (i.e. consistent rather than variable) but which happen to be inappropriate for the L2. Incomplete grammars, on the other hand, are potentially more problematic. Sorace appears to be claiming that there are some properties that a near-native speaker is unable to represent at all, that these are simply absent from the grammar; this lack of knowledge is reflected in indeterminate judgments. As a result, the near-native speaker will be unable to analyse certain L2 phenomena.

This raises the question of whether UG tolerates incomplete grammars. Presumably, grammars in L1 acquisition are sometimes incomplete, if certain properties have not yet emerged. For example, as discussed in chapter 6 (section 6.3.2), the L1 grammar during the optional infinitive stage is in some sense incomplete with respect to representation of Tense. Thus, one might argue that an incomplete grammar is simply another kind of divergent grammar. This is an issue which requires considerably more investigation.

8.9 Non-native ultimate attainment: optionality revisited

Near-native speakers might be expected to provide the 'best-case scenario', in terms of convergence on native-like competence. While some of the research discussed above supports convergence, this is by no means inevitable. Sorace's results suggest that the grammars of near-natives differ from those of native speakers, with divergence attributable to properties of the L1. Nevertheless, the steady-state interlanguage grammar is UG-constrained (at least in the case of the French speakers).

By no means all endstate L2 speakers pass as near-native; indeed, the majority do not. Native-like performance is the exception rather than the rule. One case of an L2 speaker whose performance is clearly non-native even though her grammar is at a steady state was considered in chapter 6 (section 6.4.2), where Lardiere's (1998a, b) case study of Patty was discussed. Recall that Patty, a fluent speaker of L2 English, shows relatively low incidence of inflection for tense and agreement in spontaneous production (see chapter 6, table 6.2). Lardiere (2000) suggests that Patty has *fossilized*, which would seem to imply that it is her grammar which diverges from native-speaker grammars. However, as Lardiere shows, this divergence is only true in the morphological domain; syntactically, Patty exhibits reflexes of tense and agreement appropriate to English, such as nominative case assignment and correct verb placement. Furthermore, as discussed in chapter 6, divergence may be attributable not so much to the underlying grammar itself but to differences in how morphological forms are accessed from the lexicon.

The morphological variability identified by Lardiere is quite extensive: more often than not, Patty omits tense and agreement affixes. Sorace (1999) points to a different form of optionality found in endstate grammars, a kind of optionality that is much more restricted. Sorace terms this *residual* optionality. As she puts it:

> In the typical L2 endstate characterized by optionality, optional variants are not in free variation: a steady state is reached, in which the target option is strongly but not categorically preferred, and the non-target option surfaces in some circumstances. (1999: 666)

As we shall see, the non-target option is attributable to characteristics of the L1 grammar.

The examples of residual optionality cited by Sorace are syntactic rather than morphological. A particular case is presented by Robertson and Sorace (1999), who look at L2 speakers of English whose mother tongue is German. As described in chapter 1 (section 1.4.1), German is a V2 language, the finite verb in main clauses always appearing in second position. The verb cannot be the third constituent in German (V3), as shown in (12).

(12) *Kaffee Maria trinkt.
coffee Maria drinks
'Maria drinks coffee.'

In English, on the other hand, V2 is disallowed in affirmatives (*V2),[6] while V3 is grammatical, as shown in (13a, b).

(13) a. *At breakfast does Maria drink coffee.
b. At breakfast, Maria drinks coffee.

Robertson and Sorace hypothesize that there will be residual V2 effects in the interlanguage grammars of German-speaking learners of English and that these effects will persist even in the endstate. That is, due to the influence of German,

L2 speakers will allow V2 where it is ungrammatical in English. Contrary to their prediction, in a study which included very proficient L2 speakers whose grammars Sorace (1999) describes as being in the steady state, group results from an acceptability-judgment task (using magnitude estimation) show that L2 speakers are generally aware of the ungrammaticality of V2 and the grammaticality of V3 in English, preferring the latter over the former. Individual subject analyses, however, show that there is a minority whose judgments are consistent with a V2 analysis of English, preferring *V2 to V3 (i.e. sentences like (13a) are more highly rated than sentences like (13b)): there was one such individual, out of a total of 23, but others occasionally accepted *V2. Furthermore, in a corpus of written essays, very occasional ungrammatical V2 sentences were found. In general, the results suggest that there are some individuals who will accept or produce *V2, though not frequently or consistently, while the majority of their judgments and productions are appropriately V3. This, then, is what Sorace terms residual optionality.

One might reasonably object that such behaviour is so marginal that it is not relevant to endstate linguistic competence at all. However, Robertson and Sorace propose that residual optionality sheds light on interlanguage lexical entries. The V2 effect is a consequence of a strong feature in C, which causes the verb to raise for feature checking (see chapter 1, section 1.4.1). According to Robertson and Sorace, strong features are represented in the lexicon as abstract lexical entries. In the case of L2 acquisition, the learner may copy such abstract entries from the L1 lexicon to the interlanguage lexicon. Thus, simplifying somewhat, the interlanguage lexicon of a German-speaking learner of English will include an entry [+strong C], required for German but not for English. If this feature is selected from the lexicon, it enters the derivation and overt movement of the verb to C is forced. If the feature is not selected, there is no motivation for overt verb raising. The optionality is due to the fact that the lexical item is present but not necessarily selected. As the L2 speaker becomes more proficient in the L2, the strong feature is selected less and less often. Occasionally, the strong feature is selected, enters the numeration and leads to residual V2 effects. Robertson and Sorace suggest that these L1-derived entries are subject to attrition, though it is not entirely clear what would cause them to be lost.

Thus, Robertson and Sorace (1999), like Lardiere (2000) and Prévost and White (2000b), explain optionality in terms of the relationship between two different parts of the grammar, the interlanguage lexicon and interlanguage syntax. There are similarities and differences between the various accounts of optionality that we have considered so far. Lardiere (1998a, b, 2000) points to a fairly extensive underuse of L2 morphology, in other words, variability in suppliance of inflection, with no concomitant problems in the syntactic domain. As discussed in chapter 6 (section 6.4.2), this variability is attributed to problems of mapping between the syntax and the morphology, in particular, to difficulties in determining which morphological forms are appropriate for spelling out certain syntactic features. Although they do not deal with endstate grammars, Prévost and White (2000b) share Lardiere's assumption that features are fully specified in the syntax; they propose that lexical entries may be underspecified for features (or, if fully specified, that the fully specified entry is not always accessible), hence allowing certain default forms to be inserted. In both cases, the effects of optionality are confined to inflection. In contrast, Robertson and Sorace (1999) and Sorace (1999) point to optionality whose effects are visible in the syntax (inappropriate V2, in this case), resulting from inappropriate lexical entries (namely abstract strong features) entering the derivation.

8.10 Summary: endstate competence

In the present chapter, the ultimate attainment of L2 speakers has been considered, concentrating on the question whether or not the grammars of L2 speakers converge on the grammars of native speakers. Clearly, convergence is by no means inevitable. Rather, the data are often compatible with UG-constrained divergence. The L1 representation appears to be a major determinant of the final outcome of L2 acquisition. For example, in the case of the failure of Chinese speakers to reject Subjacency violations in English, as reported by Johnson and Newport (1991), it has been proposed that the representation of *wh*-structures does not involve movement at all, but, rather, a base-generated *pro*, as in Chinese. In the case of optional auxiliary selection with restructuring verbs and unaccusatives, near-native speakers of Italian assume obligatory auxiliary selection, along the lines of what is required in the L1 French. Even though complete success is not inevitable, if this is interpreted as the achievement of a grammar indistinguishable from native speakers, steady-state interlanguage grammars are not wild.

8.11 Conclusion: initial to steady state

This book has examined different perspectives on the grammars of L2 learners and L2 speakers, concentrating in particular on the status of UG and its relationship to interlanguage grammars. As we have seen, two main positions have been identified. On the one hand, interlanguage grammars are claimed to be defective, differing from native-speaker grammars in fundamental respects. Such claims contrast with proposals that interlanguage grammars are UG-constrained at all stages. Within these two broad perspectives, we have considered a variety of competing hypotheses as to the nature of the initial state in L2 acquisition, the kinds of changes that can be expected in developing grammars, and the final outcome, or steady-state grammar. Table 8.1 presents a revised summary of predictions of the various hypotheses examined in this book (see also chapter 3, table 3.1).

Considering, first, the position that argues for defective interlanguage grammars, on this kind of account, interlanguage grammars are not (fully) constrained by UG; rather, they suffer from global or local impairment. Clahsen and Hong (1995) and Neeleman and Weerman (1997) argue for a radical breakdown in interlanguage representations (see chapter 4, section 4.3). This has implications for grammars at any point in development. These researchers do not explicitly discuss the initial state. Possibly, the L1 grammar might be implicated. However, as the main thrust of these proposals is that there is a breakdown in the parametric system, such that interlanguage grammars treat constructions separately, with no properties being grouped together under some parameter value, it appears that the possibility of L1 parameter settings is being denied altogether. On the assumption of global impairment, endstate grammars will necessarily be radically different from the grammars of native speakers; indeed, they will not be like natural language grammars at all.

The results reported by Johnson and Newport (1991) (see section 8.4) at first sight support claims for global impairment in the steady state. The interlanguage grammars of L2 speakers whose L1 lacks syntactic *wh*-movement appear to tolerate representations of *wh*-questions which include violations of Subjacency; in other words, L2 speakers have a wild grammar. However, on the proposed reanalysis of *wh*-structures in terms of properties of the L1 Chinese (base-generated topics and null *pro*) (see section 8.4.1), a UG-constrained grammar is in fact implicated.

The other proposal for defective grammars is provided by the Local Impairment Hypothesis (chapter 4, section 4.4), an extension of the Valueless Features Hypothesis (chapter 3, section 3.2.3). This hypothesis stipulates that there is a local breakdown in interlanguage grammars, relating to feature values, which are claimed to be inert. The implication of this claim is that interlanguage grammars are not fully UG-constrained, since inertness is not characteristic of natural language in general. According to the Local Impairment Hypothesis, inertness is expected not only in the initial state but also during the course of development and even in the steady state. Lardiere's (1998a,b) results (see chapter 6, section 6.4.2) show that this prediction is false: Patty's endstate L2 grammar shows no evidence whatsoever of variable verb placement, this being one of the purported consequences of inert features.

In opposition to claims for defective grammars are the various approaches that maintain that interlanguage grammars are UG-constrained from the initial to the steady state. Hypotheses differ over the extent to which the L1 grammar is implicated in interlanguage representations. At one extreme is the No Parameter Resetting Hypothesis (chapter 4, section 4.6), according to which interlanguage grammars have recourse *only* to those parameter settings realized in the L1, subsequent parameter resetting being impossible. In other words, new parameter values cannot be acquired, the interlanguage system being permanently restricted to representations based on the L1 grammar. Some research on the steady state is consistent with this hypothesis. As discussed in section 8.8, Sorace (1993a) reports L1-based differences in the endstate grammars of near-native speakers of Italian whose L1s are French and English. On the other hand, results reported by Montrul and Slabakova (2003) (see section 8.7) suggest that the steady-state grammar of L2 Spanish speakers represents aspectual contrasts not realized in the L1, in which case L2 speakers cannot be restricted to L1 features.

Finally, there are two perspectives which attribute a more dominant role to UG, claiming full access. In other words, not only are interlanguage grammars UG-constrained but L2 learners and L2 speakers are not restricted to representations based on the L1 grammar. Parameters can be set or reset to L2 values. The first of these hypotheses, Full Access (without Transfer) (see chapter 3, section 3.3), in fact denies a role to the L1 grammar in interlanguage representations, initially or subsequently. Convergence on the L2 linguistic system is expected. According to Flynn (1996: 150), full access to UG implies ultimate attainment of L2-like competence: 'the developing language abilities of the learners do not always appear to converge on an adult NS . . . However, because there is a mismatch in linguistic *abilities* does not necessarily mean that there are differences in linguistic *competences*.' Since the L1 grammar is not implicated in the initial state on this view, no L1 effects are expected in endstate L2 grammars (or in interlanguage grammars at any stage). However, as we have seen, there are in fact several cases where steady-state representations exhibit properties attributable to the L1 grammar (see sections 8.4.1 and 8.8).

The Full Transfer Full Access Hypothesis (chapter 3, section 3.2.1) captures the insight that both UG and the L1 grammar are major influences on the form and functioning of the interlanguage grammar. According to this hypothesis, the interlanguage initial state is entirely based on the L1 grammar. Restructuring takes place in response to L2 input, within the bounds sanctioned by UG. Thus, convergence on grammars like those of native speakers is in principle possible. However, convergence is not guaranteed. Where L2 input is available to disconfirm an inappropriate L1-based analysis, restructuring takes place. In some cases, however, the current grammar may appear to accommodate the L2 input adequately. Change will not be motivated because of an absence of suitable triggers. An example of this kind was discussed in chapter 7 (section 7.5.1). Inagaki (2001) showed that, with respect to verbs expressing manner of motion, Japanese-speaking learners of English attain the relevant L2 argument structure (not present in the L1 but exemplified in the L2 input), whereas English-speaking learners of Japanese overgeneralize the English conflation pattern and appear to be unable to lose it because the L2 Japanese data are partially consistent with the L1 based analysis. In such cases, the interlanguage endstate will necessarily diverge from grammars of native speakers.

In this chapter we have considered studies reporting that endstate L2 grammars are native-like (Birdsong 1992; Montrul and Slabakova 2003; White and Genesee 1996), as well as studies reporting L1 effects on ultimate attainment (Sorace 1993a), or reinterpretable in that way (Johnson and Newport 1991). While absence of L1 effects in the steady state is consistent both with Full Access without Transfer and with Full Transfer Full Access, L1 effects in endstate grammars are problematic for the Full Access without Transfer Hypothesis. Only Full Transfer Full Access, which allows a role for both the L1 and UG, has the potential to account for native-like ultimate attainment or lack thereof.

While the Full Transfer Full Access Hypothesis allows for the possibility of either convergent or divergent UG-constrained outcomes, we are still far from having achieved an adequate explanation of why some aspects of the L1 representation persist even into the endstate while others do not. Conversely, we do not know why in some cases the effects of the L1 are so fleeting as to be barely noticeable even in early stages. It is likely that a deeper understanding of the relationship between grammars and input will help to answer at least some of these questions. Other puzzles remain. As discussed in chapter 6 (section 6.4.3), even on the hypothesis that interlanguage grammars are UG-constrained, it is nevertheless the case that L2 speakers have considerable difficulties in mapping from abstract categories to their particular surface manifestations. We do not yet understand why this should be the case.

In conclusion, there has been progress in recent years in our understanding of the nature of interlanguage grammars, the influence of the L1 and the role of UG. There is a now considerable body of research whose results are consistent with the claim that learners arrive at mental representations for the L2 input which are systematic and UG-constrained. At the same time, it is clear that L2 acquisition differs in a variety of respects from L1 acquisition and that interlanguage grammars diverge from native-speaker grammars more often than not. It is easy to underestimate linguistic competence in L2 acquisition because of issues relating to linguistic performance. In addition, there are cases where the distinction between competence and performance is obscured. As Lardiere (2000: 124) points out:

Table 8.1 *L2 acquisition and UG: initial to steady state*

	UG-impaired		UG-constrained		
	Global Impairment	Local Impairment	No Parameter Resetting	Full Access (without Transfer)	Full Transfer Full Access
Initial state	?	L1 grammar + inert features	L1 grammar	UG	L1 grammar
Development	Pattern matching; separate constructions	Some L2 properties acquirable. Features remain inert.	No parameter resetting	Parameter setting, directly to L2 values	Parameter resetting (L1 to L*n*)
Final outcome	Grammar essentially different from native-speaker grammars. L2-like grammar not attainable.	Features still inert. L2-like grammar not attainable.	L1-like grammar L2-like grammar not attainable.	L2-like grammar.	L2-like grammar possible but not inevitable.

> Ultimately, the issue of whether (adult) second language acquisition is constrained by UG or not will only be resolvable if we are able to clarify for ourselves whether by 'UG' we mean only the syntactic computational component (as is often traditionally assumed), or also the mapping procedures that get us from the syntax to PF, and which seem to be the source of much of the divergence between adult and child acquisition outcomes.

In other words, and not surprisingly, theories as to the form and content of UG have direct implications for UG-based approaches to L2 acquisition. Our perspective on what it means for a grammar to be UG-constrained will inevitably shift as definitions of UG change and develop.

Topics for discussion

- Is it conceivable that L2 learners might achieve the same endstate as native speakers but by totally different means, without UG acting as a system of constraints? What would the implications be as far as the logical problem of language acquisition is concerned?
- Is it necessarily the case that a sensitive period for language acquisition, with a maturational decline in language-learning abilities, implies that the outcome of adult L2 acquisition will be different from child L1 acquisition?
- Native speakers can have 'indeterminate' judgments on certain sentence types. What does this say for the concept of incomplete grammars in L2 speakers?
- Sorace (1993a: 22–3) comments: 'If interlanguage development was constrained by UG in its entirety, there would be no cognitive obstacle to complete success.' Is this necessarily the case? What other factors might impinge on L2 performance, such that 'complete success' is not inevitable?

Suggestions for additional reading

- The question of whether or not there is a critical period (or periods) for language acquisition is much debated. Much of the debate is not directly concerned with the issue of UG availability. There is a vast literature on the Critical Period Hypothesis and on maturational effects in L2 acquisition. See Long (1990) and Hyltenstam and Abrahamsson (2003) for overviews, as well as papers in Birdsong (1999) for contributions from a variety of perspectives. An important question is the extent to which age is the critical factor or whether supposed age-related differences between younger and older learners can at least partly be accounted for in terms of other factors, such as amount and type of L2 input, level of education, degree of use of the L1 or the L2, etc. See, for example, Bialystok (1997) and papers by Flege and colleagues (e.g. Flege and Liu 2001; Flege, Yeni-Komshian and Liu 1999; Meador, Flege and Mackay 2000).

- Long (2003) discusses problems and inconsistencies in the use of the term *fossilization* in the L2 field and provides a useful critique of research on this topic.
- For an account of endstate optionality couched in terms of ranking and reranking the constraints of Optimality Theory, see Sorace (2003).

Glossary

Adjunct Island Constraint: see **Subjacency**.

agent: a **theta role** characterizing an animate being that, intentionally, performs the action expressed by the verb.

allophones: variants of a phoneme whose occurrence is phonetically determined, usually occurring in complementary distribution.

anaphor: a pronoun such as a reflexive (e.g. *himself/herself*) or a reciprocal (e.g. *each other*) which requires an **antecedent**, since it does not have independent reference.

antecedent: an expression to which a pronoun or an anaphor refers. For example, in the sentence *Mary introduced herself*, *Mary* is the antecedent of the reflexive *herself*.

argument: a constituent (typically a DP) that enters into a relationship with a predicate (typically a verb). For example, in the sentence *John saw Mary*, *John* and *Mary* are arguments of the verb *see*.

Binding Theory: a set of UG principles which determine the conditions under which anaphors, pronouns, or referential expressions may refer to an antecedent.

Principle A: an **anaphor** must be bound in its **governing category**. In other words, the **antecedent** of an anaphor must **c-command** it within a local domain.

Principle B: a pronoun must be free in its **governing category**. In other words, the **antecedent** of the pronoun may not **c-command** it within a local domain.

Principle C: referential expressions must be free. That is, the antecedent of an NP must not **c-command** it at all.

bound variable: a pronoun or **trace** whose antecedent is a **quantifier** or ***wh*-phrase** and whose interpretation is not fixed (i.e. it does not denote a particular individual).

bounding nodes: see **Subjacency**.

broad-range rules: see **dative alternation**.

case: different morphological forms taken by NPs serving different syntactic functions (e.g. nominative case for subjects, accusative case for objects, genitive case for possessors, etc.). Case is overtly marked in some languages and not in others. At an abstract level, all NPs must have case (the Case Filter).

case drop: the possibility of omitting overt case markers in informal speech in languages like Japanese.

causatives: verbs whose meaning expresses causation, for example *drop* (meaning *cause to fall*). Many languages have overt causative morphemes, which turn non-causative verbs into causatives.

causative/inchoative alternation: an alternation between a transitive **causative** verb and an intransitive counterpart. The **theme** argument appears as the direct object in the causative version and as the subject of the intransitive (inchoative) version, e.g. *The child broke the plate* (causative); *the plate broke* (inchoative).

c-command: a structural relationship between categories within a sentence. A category α c-commands a category β if the first branching node (in a syntactic tree) dominating α also dominates β.

clitic pronouns: pronouns which cannot occur alone but must be found in close proximity to a verb. Often referred to as *weak* pronouns. Such pronouns are characteristic of Romance languages.

clitic climbing: in complex sentences in some Romance languages, an object clitic which is an **argument** of a lower verb can appear associated with a higher verb. This is observed in so-called **restructuring** contexts, where the higher verb is modal or aspectual, as well as with **periphrastic causatives**. For example, in the Spanish sentence, *Pedro lo quiere comprar* ('Pedro wants to buy it'), the clitic *lo* ('it') appears next to the higher verb *quiere*, rather than the lower verb *comprar*.

coindexing: a convention involving subscripting with the same index, to indicate when two expressions are coreferential. Contraindexing (subscripting with different indices) indicates disjoint reference; subscripting with a * indicates that a particular interpretation is impossible. For example, in the sentence: *Mary*$_i$ *said that John*$_j$ *hates her*$_{i/*j}$, *Mary* and *her* share the same index (*i*), indicating that they refer to the same person, *Mary* and *John* have different indices (*i* versus *j*) indicating that they are not the same person, while *her* has the index **j*, indicating that it cannot be interpreted as coreferential with *John*.

comparative fallacy: failure to consider the interlanguage system in its own right, instead comparing it to the 'target' language (i.e. the L2).

complement: a constituent closely associated with a **head** and selected by it. Heads and complements combine to form an intermediate **projection** (**X′**). In English, complements follow heads. For example, in the sentence *Mary read a very long book*, the DP *a very long book* is the complement of the verb *read*.

Complex Noun Phrase Constraint: see **Subjacency**.

continuant: a phonetic feature indicating whether the airflow through the oral cavity is free or obstructed.

coreference: two expressions are said to be coreferential if they refer to the same entity. Two expressions are disjoint in reference when they refer to different entities. See **coindexing**.

coronal: a phonetic feature characterizing sounds made by raising the tip or blade of the tongue.

covert movement: see **LF movement**.

cue: see **trigger**.

dative alternation: dative verbs in English (such as *give*, *sell*, and *buy*) typically allow two forms. One is the prepositional dative, e.g. *Mary sent a book to John* and the other is the double object dative, e.g. *Mary sent John a book*. There is a broad-range constraint (relating to possession) on the dative alternation, as well as narrow-range rules, relating to manner of motion, etc. If these constraints are observed, a verb can alternate. If not, it occurs only in the prepositional form.

D-structure: a level where the underlying (or deep) structure of the sentence is represented. In Minimalism, D-structure no longer constitutes a distinct level of representation.

domain: the area (defined syntactically) within which some syntactic operation takes place. For example, the **governing category** is the domain within which an **anaphor** must have an **antecedent**. A checking domain is a domain within which features must be checked.

economy principles: principles which ensure that a derivation will involve as few steps as possible and that a representation will involve as few symbols as possible.

Exceptional Case Marking (ECM): the assignment of objective (accusative) case to the subject of an embedded non-finite clause by a preceding verb in a higher clause. For example, in the sentence *Mary believes him to be a fool*, the verb *believe* assigns case to *him*, which is the subject of the infinitive *to be*.

Empty Category Principle (ECP): a principle of UG which states that a non-pronominal **empty category** must be properly governed (i.e. the ECP does not apply to *pro* and PRO). See **Government**.

empty category: there are four kinds of empty category, with rather different properties. Two are **traces**: trace of NP movement, trace of *wh*-movement, and two are pronouns: **PRO** and ***pro***.

experiencer: a **theta role** assigned to an **argument** of a **psych verb** (such as *fear* or *frighten*), namely, to the person experiencing the psychological state expressed by the meaning of the verb.

expletive: a pronoun, such as English *it* and *there*, which has no semantic content but serves the requirement that sentences must have subjects.

Failed Functional Features Hypothesis: the claim that adult L2 learners are unable to acquire features of functional categories which differ from those realized in the L1.

features: the smallest structural unit expressing grammatical properties. There are phonetic features (e.g. ±**voice**), (morpho)syntactic features (e.g. ±past) and semantic features (e.g. ±animate).

feature strength (strong vs. weak): a property of syntactic **features** which determines whether overt movement (e.g. verb movement to I) takes place. Strong feature values motivate movement.

feature geometry: a theory of the representation of phonological segments in terms of hierarchical relationships between their features.

fossilization: a phenomenon whereby the L2 speaker's grammar is permanently non-native.

Full Access Hypothesis: the proposal that the grammars of L2 learners are constrained by UG and that L2 learners are not restricted to the L1 grammar.

Full Transfer Full Access Hypothesis: the hypothesis that the initial state of interlanguage is the L1 grammar and that subsequent UG-constrained restructuring takes place.

functional categories: categories such as Det, Infl, Comp, which convey grammatical information. These contrast with **lexical categories**.

Fundamental Difference Hypothesis: the claim that L2 acquisition is radically different from L1 acquisition in terms of the processes involved, as well as the outcome. In particular, UG is only weakly accessible, via the L1 grammar.

goal: a **theta role** expressing the endpoint towards which something moves.

governing category: the **domain** in which an **anaphor** must be bound and a pronoun must be free. (See **Binding Theory**.) In English, the governing category is typically a finite clause. Thus, reflexives must refer to an antecedent within the same clause, whereas pronouns may not do so. In the sentence *Mary introduced herself*, *herself* refers to *Mary* whereas in the sentence *Mary introduced her*, *her* cannot refer to Mary.

Governing Category Parameter: a parameter accounting for crosslinguistic differences in the domains within which anaphors must be bound and pronouns free. This parameter was argued to have five values, which were in subset/superset relationships to each other.

Government: α governs β if α c-commands β, both are within the same maximal **projection** and no maximal projection intervenes between them. Proper government requires that α is a lexical category or that α and β are coindexed.

grammaticality-judgment task: a task where the learner has to decide whether sentences are grammatical or ungrammatical. This is parallel to the use by linguists of intuitional data to determine the grammaticality of sentences.

head: a lexical or functional category that heads a phrase. Thus, N is the head of NP, I is the head of IP, etc. Heads have **specifiers** and **complements**.

Head–Complement Parameter: a parameter which determines the relative ordering of **heads** and their **complements**, for example, VO versus OV. (Also known as the Head Parameter, the Head-Initial/Head-Final Parameter, etc.)

identification: see **Null-Subject Parameter**.

inchoative verbs: see **causative/inchoative alternation**.

incorporation: the movement of a head from some underlying position to combine with another head, forming a complex head.

indirect negative evidence: the possibility of inferring ungrammaticality on the basis of absence of certain forms in the input.

inertness: see **Valueless Features Hypothesis**.

interlanguage: a term describing the language of L2 learners.

interlanguage grammar: the unconscious underlying linguistic system of an L2 learner.

L1: first language, mother tongue.

L2: second language, non-native language.

lexical categories: categories such as N, V, P, Adj, Adv, which have semantic content. Also known as *content words*.

licensing: see **Null-Subject Parameter**.

Logical Form (LF): level of representation at which certain aspects of meaning are represented, in particular, the structural meaning or interpretive properties of sentences (as opposed to word meaning). In Minimalism, LF is one of two *interfaces*, the other being Phonetic Form (PF).

LF movement: movement that takes place covertly, after syntactic operations have taken place. For example, in **wh-in-situ** languages like Chinese, *wh*-phrases do not undergo syntactic movement. Neverthless, they must be interpreted in the same way as *wh*-phrases in languages with *wh*-movement, taking scope over the clause at LF; this is represented in terms of LF movement.

local anaphor: an **anaphor** which requires its **antecedent** to be within a local **domain**, usually the same clause as the anaphor, e.g. English *himself/herself*.

locative verbs: verbs which describe the transfer of some object (the content) to some location (a container or a surface), e.g., *Mary poured the water into the glass* (content locative) or *John covered the bed with a blanket* (container locative). A number of verbs participate in the locative alternation, allowing both argument structures: *The farmer loaded hay into the wagon/The farmer loaded the wagon with hay*.

logophor: an anaphor which is exempt from binding principles and which can be bound non-locally within the discourse, e.g. *A picture of myself would be nice on that wall*.

long-distance anaphor: see **non-local anaphor**.

merge: a computational operation which combines two categories to form a new category. For example, a V and a DP may merge to form a VP.

Minimal Trees Hypothesis: the claim that the grammars of L2 acquirers initially represent no functional categories and features, these being gradually added in response to input. (See **Weak Continuity**.)

Move α/Move: a computational operation which moves a constituent from one position to another.

narrow-range rules: see **dative alternation**.

negative evidence: information about ungrammaticality, which may be explicit, such as correction or grammar teaching.

non-local anaphor: an **anaphor** whose **antecedent** does not have to be within the same local **domain**, hence the anaphor and antecedent may appear in different clauses, e.g. Japanese *zibun*. Also known as *long-distance anaphors*.

No Parameter Resetting Hypothesis: the hypothesis that interlanguage grammars have recourse only to those parameter settings realized in the L1. Parameter resetting in L2 acquisition is claimed to be impossible.

null prep: the omission of an obligatory preposition in questions or relative clauses, e.g. *Which exam is the student worrying*? (Compare: *The student is worrying about the exam.*)

null subject/object: a subject or object pronoun which is not phonetically realized, referred to as ***pro*** or *small pro*.

Null Subject Parameter: a parameter which distinguishes between languages that permit null subjects as well as overt subjects (e.g. Spanish, Japanese) from those that require overt subjects (e.g. English). Also known as the Prodrop Parameter.

licensing: the abstract property that permits null subjects in principle.

identification: the means by which the content of a null subject is recovered, for example, by rich verbal agreement or identification with a topic in the previous discourse.

optional infinitives: a phenomenon reported for early stages of L1 acquisition of many languages, where the main verb in the child's utterance is sometimes finite and sometimes non-finite.

orientation: used to distinguish between **anaphors** that require their antecedents to be subjects (subject-oriented) and those that do not have such a requirement.

Overt Pronoun Constraint: a principle of UG which states that overt pronouns in null-subject languages cannot receive a **bound variable** interpretation.

parameter: a principle of UG which is not invariant. Parameters have built in options/settings/values (usually binary) and are proposed as an account of crosslinguistic variation. Most parameters are currently formulated in terms of variation in feature strength.

parsing: the assignment of structural representations to utterances as they are heard.

periphrastic causative: an expression which makes use of a verb such as *make* (or its equivalent) in order to express causation, e.g. *Mary made her children do their homework.*

phi (ϕ)-features: features involved in agreement, such as number, person and gender.

pied-piping: a situation (in a question or relative clause) where the whole prepositional phrase, including the preposition, undergoes ***wh*-movement**, e.g. *Up which hill did she climb?*

positive evidence: the input (utterances) that the language learner is exposed to. Also referred to as *primary linguistic data.*

primary linguistic data (PLD): see **positive evidence**.

preposition stranding: a situation (in a question or relative clause) where a preposition is 'left behind' when part of the prepositional phrase undergoes ***wh*-movement**, e.g. *Which hill did she climb up?*

***pro*:** a null pronoun (often referred to as *small pro*), occurring as the subject of finite clauses in null-subject languages. Some languages also permit a null-object *pro*.

PRO: an empty category (often referred to as *big PRO*) which is typically found as the subject of non-finite clauses, e.g. *The children want _ to win.*

process nominal: a nominal which describes an event or something ongoing, e.g. *destruction* in *The enemy's destruction of the city was awful to watch.*

prodrop: see **null subject**.

projection: the expansion of some head into another constituent, for example, NP is a projection of N, VP is a projection of V, etc. A maximal projection is the topmost expansion of a head. There can also be intermediate projections between the head and the maximal projection.

Proper Antecedent Parameter: a parameter accounting for crosslinguistic differences in the **orientation** of anaphors. Some anaphors require their antecedents to be subjects (e.g. Japanese *zibun*), whereas others permit both subject and object antecedents (e.g. English *himself/herself*).

Proper Government: see **Government**.

psych verbs: verbs which express psychological states, such as *anger*, *disappoint*, and *frighten*. Some psych verbs take **experiencer** subjects and **theme** objects (e.g. *fear*), while others take theme subjects and experiencer objects (e.g. *frighten*).

quantifier: an expression which does not denote particular individuals but a quantity of individuals, e.g. *everyone, nothing, many books, some people*, etc.

reflexive: a pronoun whose form includes the equivalent of *-self* (e.g. *himself/herself*) and whose reference is determined on the basis of some antecedent within the same domain. See also **anaphor**.

relativized SUBJECT: a phrasal anaphor must be bound within a domain containing a subject XP, whereas a head anaphor must be bound within a domain of a head (namely, Agr).

representation: the structural description (syntactic, semantic, phonological or morphological) of a sentence, as shown, for example, by means of a syntactic tree or labelled bracketing. The term is also used to refer to different *levels of representation* (LF, PF, D-structure, S-structure), as well as sometimes being used in a more general sense, more or less equivalent to the term *grammar*.

restructuring verbs: Romance modal/aspectual verbs, such as Spanish *querer* ('wish') and Italian *volere* ('want') which permit **clitic climbing**, amongst other properties.

result nominal: a nominal which describes the outcome of an event or process, e.g. *destruction* in *The destruction was awful to see*.

resultative: a construction expressing the effect on the direct object of the event or action described by the verb, e.g. *The students painted the house orange*. Here, the house became orange as a result of the painting.

Rich Agreement Hypothesis: the assumption that the acquisition of rich overt morphological paradigms is a necessary precursor to the acquisition of functional categories, features or feature strength.

root infinitives: see **optional infinitives**.

S-structure: a level where the surface structure of the sentence is represented. In Minimalism, S-structure no longer constitutes a distinct level of representation.

scrambling: the possibility of relatively free word-order variation within a language.

specifier: a constituent which combines with a **head** and its **complement** (i.e. an X′ projection) to form a maximal **projection** (**XP**). In English, specifiers precede heads.

Spec–head agreement: a relationship between a head and a phrase in its specifier, such that they agree in features. For example, in English *wh*-questions, there is a [+wh] feature in the head C; the ***wh*-phrase** raises to Spec of CP, where its features can be checked by Spec–head agreement.

Strong Continuity Hypothesis: the claim that the grammars of L1 acquirers represent all functional categories and features from the outset. (Also known as Full Competence. The nearest L2 equivalents are the **Full Access Hypothesis** and the **Full Transfer Full Access Hypothesis**.)

Subjacency: a principle of UG which places limitations on how far expressions such as ***wh*-phrases** can move. A phrase may not cross more than one bounding node at a time, where DP and IP are bounding nodes in English. Various *island* constraints originally proposed as independent principles of UG were subsequently subsumed under Subjacency, e.g. the Adjunct Island Constraint, the Complex Noun Phrase Constraint, the *Wh*-Island Constraint. The idea is that certain domains are islands from which constituents cannot be extracted.

Subset Principle: a learning principle formulated to ensure that acquisition can proceed on the basis of **positive evidence** only. Given input which is consistent with more than one grammar, the learner must adopt the most restrictive grammar consistent with that input (the grammar generating a subset of the possibilities allowed by alternative grammars). If this turns out to be too restrictive, there will be positive input to motivate restructuring of the grammar.

thematic hierarchy: a universal hierarchy, determining relative prominence of theta roles (Agent > Experiencer > Goal > Theme).

theme: a **theta role** for the argument which characterizes the person or thing undergoing some action, event or state. Also referred to as *patient*, in the case of animate themes.

theta/thematic roles: the semantic role of an argument, such as *agent* (animate being initiating and performing an action), *theme/patient* (person or thing undergoing some action or event), and *goal* (endpoint towards which something moves).

trace (t): an empty category left behind as a result of movement, marking the underlying position of the moved phrase, e.g. *[Which movie]$_i$ did you see t_i?*

trigger: partially or fully analysed input that determines which parameter setting is adopted.

truth-value-judgment task: a task which requires the learner to assess the appropriateness of a sentence in relation to some context, such as a story or picture. The learner concentrates on the meaning but the researcher is able to draw inferences about the grammaticality of certain sentence types in the interlanguage grammar.

unaccusative verbs: intransitive verbs whose sole argument, a **theme**, is the underlying object, e.g. *arrive*, *fall*.

underspecification: a situation where a representation is not fully determined with respect to a potential set of features. Used particularly of functional categories, some of whose features are omitted some of the time.

unergative verbs: intransitive verbs whose sole argument, an **agent**, is the underlying subject, e.g. *jump*, *telephone*.

Uniformity of Theta Assignment Hypothesis (UTAH): the hypothesis that identical thematic relationships between items are represented by identical structural relationships between those items at D-structure.

Valueless Features Hypothesis: the proposal that the strength of features in Infl is inert or valueless in early interlanguage grammars, rather than being strong or weak.

verb movement/verb raising: movement of the verb out of the VP, into a higher functional category such as I or C.

Verb Movement Parameter: a parameter whose settings are attributable to the strength of features in Infl, which may be strong (as in French) or weak (as in English). Each setting has a range of consequences for verb placement. (Also known as the Verb Raising Parameter.)

voice: a phonetic feature indicating whether or not the vocal cords are vibrating.

Weak Continuity Hypothesis: The claim that the grammars of L1 acquirers initially represent few or no functional categories and features, these being gradually added in response to input. (The nearest L2 equivalent is the **Minimal Trees Hypothesis**.)

***Wh*-in-situ:** in some languages, such as Chinese, ***wh*-movement** does not take place overtly. Rather, the ***wh*-phrase** remains in its underlying position. Thus, a question equivalent to *Which book did Mary read?* would be expressed as *Mary read which book?*

***wh*-movement:** movement of a ***wh*-phrase** to Spec of CP, either overtly or covertly. For example, in the English sentence, *Which book did Mary read?*, the phrase *which book* has moved from its underlying position as object of the verb *read*.

***wh*-phrase:** a word or phrase, such as *who* or *which book*, containing an interrogative or relative pronoun.

Notes

1 Universal Grammar and language acquisition

1. The term *mental representation* is used in two somewhat different ways in the field. On the one hand, it is used to refer to the particular structural representations (syntactic, semantic, phonological or morphological) underlying particular sentences. In this sense, the grammar generates representations. On the other hand, the term is also sometimes used in a more general sense, equivalent to the term *grammar*.
2. There are additional complications and subtleties, related to contrastive focus, which will not be considered here. See Pérez-Leroux and Glass (1997) for discussion.
3. Many speakers, nevertheless, show a preference for the null pronoun to take the matrix subject as antecedent, rather than an antecedent from elsewhere in the discourse (Montalbetti 1984).
4. The Overt Pronoun Constraint covers two different eventualities: (a) [±null subject] languages in general; (b) within null subject languages, alternations between null and overt pronouns. There are syntactic positions where only an overt pronoun could occur (for example, Spanish does not have null objects); in such cases, an overt pronoun can serve as a bound variable (Montalbetti 1984). There have been other proposals to account for the facts. See Noguchi (1997) for a recent treatment. Noguchi shows that overt object pronouns in languages with null objects show Overt Pronoun Constraint effects.
5. On some analyses of German, IP is head initial (Travis 1984; Zwart 1993). We do not consider here the possibility that all languages are head initial at some level (Kayne 1994).

2 Principles of Universal Grammar in L2 acquisition

1. A small proportion of the translations involved other responses, such as full NPs instead of pronouns. This explains why the totals do not add up to 100%.
2. According to Grimshaw (1990), process nominals denote complex events; as such, they are like verbs in having an argument structure, and are subject to constraints on argument structure with respect to realization of obligatory arguments, etc. Result nominals, on the other hand, do not take true arguments; rather, NPs that occur in construction with result nominals are modifiers.
3. In L1 acquisition, it has been argued that certain UG principles are delayed and emerge according to a maturational schedule (Borer and Wexler 1987) or that principles of UG can exist in an immature form (Wexler 1998). Even if such proposals are correct for L1 (and there is considerable debate on this issue), they will hardly apply to adult L2 acquisition, where maturation has already taken place.
4. I thank Mikinari Matsuoka for this example.
5. Unaccusatives are intransitive verbs whose sole argument is underlyingly a theme (e.g. *The glass broke*). Unaccusative subjects have a number of properties in common with the objects of transitive verbs. See chapters 7 and 8 for further discussion.
6. If the object 'scrambles', that is, moves so that it is no longer adjacent to the verb, the particle cannot be dropped. See Yoo, Kayama, Mazzotta and White (2001) for evidence that L2 learners of Japanese are sensitive to the adjacency requirement on case drop.

7. Kellerman et al. acknowledge that their testing phase might have encouraged problem-solving rather than unconscious linguistic knowledge, but they do not seem to recognize that the same is true of their teaching phase.
8. On the other hand, there are researchers who argue that UG constraints are no longer operative in interlanguage grammars at all, even through the L1 (Clahsen and Muysken 1986; Meisel 1997). To counter these suggestions, it is sufficient to show that interlanguage grammars are subject to UG constraints when the L1 and L2 do not differ with respect to some principle. (See White and Genesee 1996.)
9. Christie and Lantolf also look at L2 Spanish, which we will not consider here.
10. Christie and Lantolf are well aware of the problem of preferences in this context; the truth-value-judgment methodology was adopted to try and avoid the preference problem. See White, Bruhn-Garavito, Kawasaki, Pater and Prévost (1997) for relevant findings and discussion.
11. It is in fact impossible to tell from Christie and Lantolf (1998) how many test items are involved, or what type they are, since this paper lacks methodological details. The relevant information is to be found in Christie (1992).
12. Four items may in fact be insufficient to allow such an analysis.
13. *Zibun* does have a number of pronominal properties (see Aikawa 1999), so this would not be an unreasonable analysis.
14. For other arguments in favour of null resumptive pronouns in L2, see White (1992c).

3 The initial state

1. The Fundamental Difference Hypothesis does not, however, depend on whether or not UG turns into a specific grammar: even if UG is distinct from any particular grammar it could be argued to become inaccessible in later life.
2. Schwartz and Sprouse's original (1994) argument for Full Transfer Full Access was also based on word order data from a case study of an adult Turkish-speaking learner of German. Since both Turkish and German are head final, this muddied the waters somewhat: correct headedness in L2 German could have come from the L1 grammar or the L2 input.
3. English progressive forms are atelic but non-progressive forms are not necessarily telic.
4. This, of course, results in an apparent contradiction. The same learners appear to have acquired the weak L2 value when negatives are involved but still have the strong L1 value when adverbs are involved. As discussed by White (1992a), this contradiction can be resolved under the split Infl hypothesis of Pollock (1989). See chapter 4.
5. Eubank et al. (1997: note 11) consider and reject this possibility.
6. Indeed, their position on the L1 is inconsistent. Epstein et al., as well as Flynn (1987, 1996) and Flynn and Martohardjono (1994), argue that L2 acquisition involves the assignment of 'additional' parameter values where L1 and L2 do not match in parameter settings. Notice, however, that it is only if the initial representation includes parameter settings exemplified in the L1 that the issue of 'additional' parameter settings arises. If the initial state is not the L1, all settings are 'new'.

4 Grammars beyond the initial state: parameters and functional categories

1. However Epstein et al. (1996) argue for delay when the L1 and L2 settings differ. The logic of this claim is not clear, given their assumption that the L1 is not involved in the initial representation.
2. Presumably, before this, when German children have null subjects and no agreement, they have a Korean-type grammar, with topic identification of null subjects. See Jaeggli and Hyams (1988).
3. Neeleman and Weerman account for the parametric differences in terms of the domain within

which case is checked; details of this proposal need not concern us here. There have been several proposals for such word-order parameters over the years (the Head-Initial/Head-Final Parameter; the Head Parameter; the Head-Direction Parameter; Principal Branching Direction; etc.). Under Kayne's (1994) proposal for a universal underlying SVO order, there is no such parameter.

4. Beck is in fact neutral as to whether I in German is head-initial rather than head-final. Her test sentences do not allow one to distinguish between these two options or to establish where I is in the interlanguage grammar. If German is SIOV, then it is I rather than C that is impaired. Variable verb placement is predicted in either case.
5. The research described here was part of a larger project looking at the effects of instruction, which will be discussed in chapter 5. Here, we consider data gathered prior to any special instructional intervention.
6. Subsequent accounts place Agr higher than T (Belletti 1991).
7. Alternatively, a number of researchers (e.g. Iatridou 1990; Travis 1988) have proposed that the position of adverbs in the clause is independent of the Verb Movement Parameter. If this is correct, then these French speakers have in fact successfully reset the parameter, as shown by their treatment of negatives and questions. They continue to have problems with adverb placement, an independent property.
8. There is a class of Romance adjectives which precede the head noun; these will not be discussed here.
9. This is an oversimplification on my part, for ease of exposition. In fact, Agr is argued to be 'anaphoric' (Borer 1989; MacLaughlin 1998; Progovac 1993).
10. This is defined technically. It is not identical to the intuitive notion of a subject.

5 The transition problem, triggering and input

1. It is nevertheless the case that Japanese-speaking learners of English are often instructed on the /l/ vs. /r/ distinction and can be trained to pronounce them differently and appropriately. Thus, for example, if asked to read *lake* and *rake*, as opposed to listening to these words, many Japanese speakers are able to pronounce /r/ and /l/ as two distinct sounds.
2. See Gibson and Wexler (1994) and Fodor (1998, 1999) for examples.
3. This is considerable disagreement on this issue. On some accounts, parameters in L1 acquisition can be set inappropriately and then have to be reset (e.g. Gibson and Wexler 1994).
4. Alternatively, Lightfoot suggests that the cue is that any constituent can appear in the Spec CP position. In (6), then, the cue would be the presence of the adverb *heute* in Spec CP.
5. Unfortunately, sentences like (12e) are in fact ambiguous as to where the adverb is located, so that they cannot serve as truly unambiguous triggers. As well as VP-initial adverbs, which are crucial for determining whether or not verb movement has taken place, English allows certain adverbs to be generated in a higher position, between the subject (in Spec IP) and I, as in *Mary probably will take the bus*, a position that is not available in French. In (12e), it is not in fact possible to determine which position the adverb is in.
6. A number of acquisition researchers have argued against the efficacy of indirect negative evidence, on the grounds that it is too vague (see White 1989: 15).
7. It should be noted that there is considerable disagreement as to when parameter resetting took place historically and what precisely motivated it. The threshold concept may be required independently, in order to prevent parameters from being inappropriately set on the basis of degenerate data. Valian (1990) proposes that children entertain competing parameter settings at the same time and that they must be able to weigh the evidence, in order to come down in favour of one setting over another.
8. Both French and English allow clause-initial and clause-final adverb placement. This is not relevant to the Verb Movement Parameter and will be ignored here. Also, as discussed in section 5.5, the

languages are alike with respect to adverb placement in the context of auxiliary verbs.

9. But see Wexler (1998) for arguments that parameter setting is extremely early. In consequence, Wexler has to resort to various maturational explanations to account for the fact that L1 acquisition is not instantaneous and error-free.

6 Morphological variability and the morphology/syntax interface

1. Alternatively, in accordance with the tenets of Distributed Morphology (Halle and Marantz 1993), we can consider *sing* to be an underspecified form lacking certain features; in the absence of a more specified form, the underspecified one is inserted into the tree. See section 6.4.3.2.
2. For Radford (1990), there is no causal connection. The acquisition of morphology does not drive the acquisition of functional syntax. Rather, maturation explains the emergence of functional syntax and associated overt morphology.
3. Earlier proposals tried to relate richness of verbal morphological paradigms to presence/absence of null subjects (Jaeggli and Hyams 1988; Jaeggli and Safir 1989). However, in this L1 literature, it was usually recognized that the issue was rich morphology in some abstract sense which would not necessarily correspond to how the morphology happens to be realized at surface. For relevant discussion, see Hyams and Safir (1991).
4. The stand taken by Rohrbacher elsewhere (1994, 1999) with respect to the Rich Agreement Hypothesis is inconsistent with the Separation approach advocated by Borer and Rohrbacher (1997).
5. There does not appear to be an OI stage in the acquisition of null subject languages (e.g. Guasti 1994).
6. In fact, it is not the case that null subjects occur exclusively in non-finite clauses in the optional infinitive stage. See Rizzi (2000) for an alternative account, involving truncation.
7. Underspecification is also proposed by proponents of the morphology-before-syntax position, e.g. Clahsen (1990), who argues for an underspecified FP.
8. Vainikka and Young-Scholten (1994), however, suggest that FP may be triggered by word order rather than morphology. In other words, the trigger is syntactic.
9. Gavruseva and Lardiere (1996) also report low incidence of agreement in a Russian-speaking child learning English.
10. In addition, as pointed out by Demuth (1994), there may be phonological reasons why the L1 acquirer does always access certain morphological forms.
11. The choice of default may vary from person to person. For example, Hawkins (1998) suggests that some subjects use masculine gender as a default, while others use feminine.
12. This is also the form for second-person plural. For the sake of the example, only the singular is discussed here.

7 Argument structure

1. Lexical entries also include information as to how words are pronounced. This will not be discussed here.
2. This view of meaning as compositional is somewhat controversial (e.g. Fodor, Fodor and Garrett 1975).
3. There are many cases where the status of a constituent as argument or adjunct is not entirely clear. For example, a constituent that seems to be adjunct-like may nevertheless be obligatory, e.g. *John sat on the table*/?**John sat*.
4. As many researchers have pointed out (e.g. Stowell 1981; Williams 1995), this leads to considerable redundancy. For example, the theme argument in English is typically a DP, goal and location arguments are typically PPs, propositions are typically CPs, etc.
5. There are many different conventions for representing argument structure. The precise formalisms

need not concern us. See Grimshaw (1990: 2) for discussion.

6. In addition, there is a morphological constraint on the English dative alternation: verbs that alternate are (mostly) monosyllabic and Germanic in origin rather than polysyllabic and Latinate. *Give* alternates, while *donate* does not. This morphological constraint will not be discussed here.
7. For example, Kim, Landau and Phillips (1999) also identify two language types as far as the locative alternation is concerned but they propose a slightly different account, where the crucial difference relates to whether or not languages allow serial-verb constructions, rather than to the conflation of CAUSE and STATE.
8. Many languages, such as Italian, have a third class of psych verbs, where the experiencer is expressed with dative case (Belletti and Rizzi 1988).
9. A variety of hierarchies have been proposed in the literature, which vary as to the precise theta roles that are included as well as to whether the theme argument is more or less prominent than the goal. For example, Baker (1988, 1997) places the theme above the goal. There are also proposals for several different hierarchies, operating in parallel (e.g. Grimshaw 1990).
10. An alternative account, which nevertheless preserves UTAH, says that different theta roles are involved (Pesetsky 1995), i.e. that the two classes of psych verbs have different argument structures.

8 Ultimate attainment: the nature of the steady state

1. There is also considerable discussion of age effects on rate of acquisition, with some researchers claiming that older learners have an advantage over younger (e.g. Snow and Hoefnagel-Hohle 1978). Rate of acquisition is an orthogonal issue which will not be discussed.
2. Prior foreign language instruction in English during high school in China is discounted.
3. As White (1992c) discusses, the interlanguage grammar in such cases must permit both a movement and a non-movement analysis, since it is not the case that all Subjacency violations are accepted. Cole (1987) and Saito (1985) argue that such dual analyses are in fact characteristic of Japanese and Korean.
4. In the case of the grammatical sentences, White and Juffs found that native speakers and L2 speakers alike showed interesting differences between accuracy on extracted objects versus extracted subjects, with greater acceptance of the former. White and Juffs attribute this difference to processing difficulties in the case of subjects. See also Schachter and Yip (1990).
5. This was calculated as follows. Each sentence was assigned an *evaluation index* corresponding to the majority opinion of the native speakers. This provides the prototypical norm. Coppieters then calculated the extent to which subjects (native or near-native) deviated from the norm, either by accepting sentences that the majority rejected or by rejecting sentences that the majority accepted. In determining deviations from the norm for particular sentence types, grammatical and ungrammatical sentences are, unfortunately, grouped together.
6. English requires V2 in negative contexts, e.g. *Never have I ever seen such a beautiful sight.*

References

Adjémian, C. (1976). On the nature of interlanguage systems. *Language Learning* 26: 297–320.

Aikawa, T. (1999). Reflexives. In N. Tsujimura (ed.), *The handbook of Japanese linguistics* (pp. 154–90). Oxford: Blackwell.

Aitchison, J. (1976). *The articulate mammal*. New York: Routledge.

Archangeli, D. and T. Langendoen (eds.). (1997). *Optimality Theory: an overview*. Oxford: Blackwell.

Bailey, N., C. Madden and S. Krashen. (1974). Is there a 'natural sequence' in adult second language learning? *Language Learning* 24: 235–43.

Baker, C. L. (1979). Syntactic theory and the projection problem. *Linguistic Inquiry* 10: 533–81.

Baker, C. L. and J. McCarthy (eds.). (1981). *The logical problem of language acquisition*. Cambridge, MA: MIT Press.

Baker, M. (1988). *Incorporation: a theory of grammatical function changing*. Chicago: University of Chicago Press.

Baker, M. (1997). Thematic roles and syntactic structure. In L. Haegeman (ed.), *Elements of grammar: handbook in generative syntax* (pp. 73–137). Dordrecht: Kluwer.

Balcom, P. (1997). Why is this happened? Passive morphology and unaccusativity. *Second Language Research* 13: 1–9.

Baptista, M. (1997). The morpho-syntax of nominal and verbal categories in Capeverdean Creole. Unpublished PhD thesis, Harvard University.

Bard, E. G., D. Robertson and A. Sorace. (1996). Magnitude estimation of linguistic acceptability. *Language* 72: 32–68.

Bardovi-Harlig, K. (1987). Markedness and salience in second-language acquisition. *Language Learning* 37: 385–407.

Bates, E. and B. MacWhinney. (1987). Competition, variation and language learning. In B. MacWhinney (ed.), *Mechanisms of language acquisition* (pp. 157–93). Hillsdale, NJ: Lawrence Erlbaum.

Beard, R. (1987). Morpheme order in a lexeme/morpheme-base morphology. *Lingua* 72: 1–44.

Beard, R. (1995). *Lexeme-morpheme base morphology*. Albany: SUNY Press.

Beck, M.-L. (1997). Viruses, parasites and optionality in L2 performance. Paper presented at the Second Language Research Forum, Michigan State University.

Beck, M.-L. (1998a). L2 acquisition and obligatory head movement: English-speaking learners of German and the local impairment hypothesis. *Studies in Second Language Acquisition* 20: 311–48.

Beck, M.-L. (ed.). (1998b). *Morphology and its interfaces in second language knowledge.* Amsterdam: John Benjamins.

Belletti, A. (1991). *Generalized verb movement: aspects of verb syntax.* Turin: Rosenberg and Sellier.

Belletti, A. and L. Rizzi. (1988). Psych-verbs and θ-theory. *Natural Language and Linguistic Theory* 6: 291–352.

Bennett, S. (1994). Interpretation of English reflexives by adolescent speakers of Serbo-Croatian. *Second Language Research* 10: 125–56.

Bennett, S. and L. Progovac. (1998). Morphological status of reflexives in second language acquisition. In S. Flynn, G. Martohardjono and W. O'Neil (eds.), *The generative study of second language acquisition* (pp. 187–214). Mahwah, NJ: Lawrence Erlbaum.

Bernstein, J. (1993). Topics in the syntax of nominal structure across Romance. Unpublished PhD thesis, City University of New York.

Berwick, R. and A. Weinberg. (1984). *The grammatical basis of linguistic performance: language use and acquisition.* Cambridge, MA: MIT Press.

Bialystok, E. (1997). The structure of age: in search of barriers to second language acquisition. *Second Language Research* 13: 116–37.

Birdsong, D. (1989). *Metalinguistic performance and interlinguistic competence.* New York: Springer Verlag.

Birdsong, D. (1992). Ultimate attainment in second language acquisition. *Language* 68: 706–55.

Birdsong, D. (ed.). (1999). *Second language acquisition and the critical period hypothesis.* Hillsdale, NJ: Lawrence Erlbaum.

Bley-Vroman, R. (1983). The comparative fallacy in interlanguage studies: the case of systematicity. *Language Learning* 33: 1–17.

Bley-Vroman, R. (1990). The logical problem of foreign language learning. *Linguistic Analysis* 20: 3–49.

Bley-Vroman, R. (1996). Conservative pattern accumulation in foreign language learning. Paper presented at the European Second Language Association, Nijmegen.

Bley-Vroman, R. (1997). Features and patterns in foreign language learning. Paper presented at the Second Language Research Forum, Michigan State University.

Bley-Vroman, R. and C. Chaudron. (1994). Elicited imitation as a measure of second-language competence. In E. Tarone, S. Gass and A. Cohen (eds.), *Research methodology in second-language acquisition* (pp. 245–61). Hillsdale, NJ: Lawrence Erlbaum.

Bley-Vroman, R., S. Felix and G. Ioup. (1988). The accessibility of universal grammar in adult language learning. *Second Language Research* 4: 1–32.

Bley-Vroman, R. and D. Masterson. (1989). Reaction time as a supplement to grammaticality judgements in the investigation of second language competence. *University of Hawai'i Working Papers in ESL* 8.2: 207–37.

Bley-Vroman, R. and N. Yoshinaga. (1992). Broad and narrow constraints on the English dative alternation: some fundamental differences between native speakers and foreign language learners. *University of Hawai'i Working Papers in ESL.* 11: 157–99.

Bloom, P. (ed.). (1994). *Language acquisition: core readings.* Cambridge, MA: MIT Press.

Bobaljik, J. (To appear). Realizing Germanic inflection: why morphology does not drive syntax. *Journal of Comparative Germanic Linguistics.*

Bobaljik, J. and H. Thráinsson. (1998). Two heads aren't always better than one. *Syntax* 1: 37–71.

Borer, H. (1984). *Parametric syntax*. Dordrecht: Foris.

Borer, H. (1989). Anaphoric Agr. In O. Jaeggli and K. Safir (eds.), *The null subject parameter* (pp. 69–109). Dordrecht: Kluwer.

Borer, H. (1996). Access to Universal Grammar: the real issues. *Brain and Behavioral Sciences* 19: 718–20.

Borer, H. and B. Rohrbacher. (1997). Features and projections: arguments for the full competence hypothesis. In E. Hughes, M. Hughes and A. Greenhill (eds.), *Proceedings of the 21st Annual Boston University Conference on Language Development* (pp. 24–35). Somerville, MA: Cascadilla Press.

Borer, H. and K. Wexler. (1987). The maturation of syntax. In T. Roeper and E. Williams (eds.), *Parameter setting* (pp. 123–72). Dordrecht: Reidel.

Brown, C. (1998). The role of the L1 grammar in the L2 acquisition of segmental structure. *Second Language Research* 14: 136–93.

Brown, C. (2000). The interrelation between speech perception and phonological acquisition from infant to adult. In J. Archibald (ed.), *Second language acquisition and linguistic theory* (pp. 4–63). Oxford: Blackwell.

Brown, R. (1973). *A first language: the early stages*. Cambridge, MA: Harvard University Press.

Bruhn-Garavito, J. (1995). L2 acquisition of verb complementation and Binding Principle B. In F. Eckman, D. Highland, P. Lee, J. Mileman and R. Rutkowski Weber (eds.), *Second language acquisition theory and pedagogy* (pp. 79–99). Hillsdale, NJ: Lawrence Erlbaum.

Bruhn de Garavito, J. and L. White. (2000). L2 Acquisition of Spanish DPs: the status of grammatical features. In C. Howell, S. Fish and T. Keith-Lucas (eds.), *Proceedings of the 24th Annual Boston University Conference on Language Development* (pp. 164–75). Somerville, MA: Cascadilla Press.

Bruhn de Garavito, J. and L. White. (2002). L2 acquisition of Spanish DPs: the status of grammatical features. In A. T. Pérez-Leroux and J. Liceras (eds.), *The acquisition of Spanish morphosyntax: the L1/L2 connection* (pp. 151–76). Dordrecht: Kluwer.

Burzio, L. (1986). *Italian syntax: a government-binding approach*. Dordrecht: Reidel.

Carroll, S. (1996). Parameter-setting in second language acquisition: explanans and explanandum. *Brain and Behavioral Sciences* 19: 720–1.

Carroll, S. (1999). Input and SLA: adults' sensitivity to different sorts of cues to French gender. *Language Learning* 49: 37–92.

Carroll, S. (2001). *Input and evidence: the raw material of second language acquisition*. Amsterdam: John Benjamins.

Carroll, S. and J. Meisel. (1990). Universals and second language acquisition: some comments on the state of current theory. *Studies in Second Language Acquisition* 12: 201–8.

Carstens, V. M. (1991). The morphology and syntax of determiner phrases in Kiswahili. Unpublished PhD thesis, UCLA.

Carstens, V. M. (2000). Concord in Minimalist Theory. *Linguistic Inquiry* 31: 319–55.

Chaudron, C. (1983). Research on metalinguistic judgements: a review of theory, methods and results. *Language Learning* 33: 343–77.

Cheng, L. and R. Sybesma. (1999). Bare and not-so-bare nouns and the structure of NP. *Linguistic Inquiry* 30: 509–42.

Chomsky, N. (1959). A review of B. F. Skinner's *Verbal Behaviour*. *Language* 35: 26–58.

Chomsky, N. (1965). *Aspects of the theory of syntax*. Cambridge, MA: MIT Press.

Chomsky, N. (1975). *Reflections on language*. New York: Pantheon Books.

Chomsky, N. (1977). On wh-movement. In P. Culicover, T. Wasow and A. Akmajian (eds.), *Formal syntax*. New York: Academic Press.

Chomsky, N. (1980). *Rules and representations*. Oxford: Blackwell.

Chomsky, N. (1981a). *Lectures on government and binding*. Dordrecht: Foris.

Chomsky, N. (1981b). Principles and parameters in syntactic theory. In N. Hornstein and D. Lightfoot (eds.), *Explanation in linguistics: the logical problem of language acquisition* (pp. 32–75). London: Longman.

Chomsky, N. (1986a). *Barriers*. Cambridge, MA: MIT Press.

Chomsky, N. (1986b). *Knowledge of language: its nature, origin, and use*. New York: Praeger.

Chomsky, N. (1991). Some notes on economy of derivation and representation. In R. Freidin (ed.), *Principles and parameters in comparative grammar* (pp. 417–54). Cambridge, MA: MIT Press.

Chomsky, N. (1993). A minimalist program for linguistic theory. In K. Hale and S. J. Keyser (eds.), *The view from building 20: essays in linguistics in honor of Sylvain Bromberger* (pp. 1–52). Cambridge, MA: MIT Press.

Chomsky, N. (1995). *The minimalist program*. Cambridge, MA: MIT Press.

Chomsky, N. (1999). On the nature, use and acquisition of language. In T. Bhatia and W. Ritchie (eds.), *Handbook of child language acquisition* (pp. 33–54). San Diego: Academic Press.

Christie, K. (1992). Universal Grammar in the second language: an experimental study of the cross-linguistic properties of reflexives in English, Chinese and Spanish. Unpublished PhD thesis, University of Delaware.

Christie, K. and J. Lantolf. (1998). Bind me up bind me down: reflexives in L2. In S. Flynn, G. Martohardjono and W. O'Neil (eds.), *The generative study of second language acquisition* (pp. 239–60). Mahwah, NJ: Lawrence Erlbaum.

Cinque, G. (1990). *Types of A′ -Dependencies*. Cambridge, MA: MIT Press.

Cinque, G. (1999). *Adverbs and functional heads: a crosslinguistic perspective*. Oxford: Oxford University Press.

Clahsen, H. (1988). Parameterized grammatical theory and language acquisition: a study of the acquisition of verb placement and inflection by children and adults. In S. Flynn and W. O'Neil (eds.), *Linguistic theory in second language acquisition* (pp. 47–75). Dordrecht: Kluwer.

Clahsen, H. (1990). The comparative study of first and second language development. *Studies in Second Language Acquisition* 12: 135–53.

Clahsen, H. (1990/1991). Constraints on parameter setting: a grammatical analysis of some acquisition stages in German child language. *Language Acquisition* 1: 361–91.

Clahsen, H., S. Eisenbeiss and M. Penke. (1996). Lexical learning in early syntactic development. In H. Clahsen (ed.), *Generative perspectives on language acquisition: empirical findings, theoretical considerations, crosslinguistic comparisons* (pp. 129–59). Amsterdam: John Benjamins.

Clahsen, H., S. Eisenbeiss and A. Vainikka. (1994). The seeds of structure: a syntactic analysis of the acquisition of Case marking. In T. Hoekstra and B. D. Schwartz (eds.),

Language acquisition studies in generative grammar (pp. 85–118). Amsterdam: John Benjamins.

Clahsen, H. and U. Hong. (1995). Agreement and null subjects in German L2 development: new evidence from reaction-time experiments. *Second Language Research* 11: 57–87.

Clahsen, H., J. Meisel and M. Pienemann. (1983). *Deutsch als Zweitsprache: der Spracherwerb ausländischer Arbeiter*. Tübingen: Gunther Narr Verlag.

Clahsen, H. and P. Muysken. (1986). The availability of universal grammar to adult and child learners: a study of the acquisition of German word order. *Second Language Research* 2: 93–119.

Clahsen, H. and P. Muysken. (1989). The UG paradox in L2 acquisition. *Second Language Research* 5: 1–29.

Clahsen, H. and M. Penke. (1992). The acquisition of agreement morphology and its syntactic consequences: new evidence on German child language from the Simone-corpus. In J. Meisel (ed.), *The acquisition of verb placement* (pp. 181–224). Dordrecht: Kluwer.

Clahsen, H., M. Penke and T. Parodi. (1993/1994). Functional categories in early child German. *Language Acquisition* 3: 395–429.

Clark, R. and I. Roberts. (1993). A computational approach to language learnability and language change. *Linguistic Inquiry* 24: 299–345.

Cole, P. (1987). Null objects in Universal Grammar. *Linguistic Inquiry* 18: 597–612.

Cole, P., G. Hermon and L.-M. Sung. (1990). Principles and parameters of long-distance reflexives. *Linguistic Inquiry* 21: 1–22.

Cook, V. (1988). *Chomsky's Universal Grammar: an introduction*. Oxford: Blackwell.

Cook, V. (1990). Timed comprehension of binding in advanced L2 learners of English. *Language Learning* 40: 557–99.

Cook, V. (1991). The poverty-of-the-stimulus argument and multicompetence. *Second Language Research* 7: 103–17.

Cook, V. (1997). Monolingual bias in second language acquisition research. *Revista Canaria de Estudios Ingleses* 34: 35–49.

Cook, V. and M. Newson. (1996). *Chomsky's Universal Grammar: an introduction*. Oxford: Blackwell.

Coppieters, R. (1987). Competence differences between native and near-native speakers. *Language* 63: 544–73.

Corbett, G. (1991). *Gender*. Cambridge: Cambridge University Press.

Corder, S. P. (1967). The significance of learners' errors. *International Review of Applied Linguistics* 5: 161–70.

Crain, S. and R. Thornton. (1998). *Investigations in Universal Grammar: a guide to experiments on the acquisition of syntax*. Cambridge, MA: MIT Press.

Davies, W. and T. Kaplan. (1998). Native speaker vs. L2 learner grammaticality judgements. *Applied Linguistics* 19: 183–203.

DeGraff, M. (1999). Creolization, language change, and language acquisition: a prolegomenon. In M. DeGraff (ed.), *Language creation and language change: creolization, diachrony and development* (pp. 1–46). Cambridge, MA: MIT Press.

Dekydtspotter, L., R. Sprouse and B. Anderson. (1997). The interpretive interface in L2 acquisition: the process-result distinction in English-French interlanguage grammars. *Language Acquisition* 6: 297–332.

Dekydtspotter, L., R. Sprouse and B. Anderson. (1998). Interlanguage A-bar dependencies: binding construals, null prepositions and Universal Grammar. *Second Language Research* 14: 341–58.

Demuth, K. (1994). On the 'underspecification' of functional categories. In B. Lust, M. Suñer and J. Whitman (eds.), *Syntactic theory and first language acquisition: Cross-linguistic perspectives.* Vol. 1: *Heads, projections and learnability* (pp. 119–34). Hillsdale, NJ: Lawrence Erlbaum.

Dresher, E. (1999). Charting the learning path: cues to parameter setting. *Linguistic Inquiry* 30: 27–67.

Dresher, E. and J. Kaye. (1990). A computational learning model for metrical phonology. *Cognition* 34: 137–95.

du Plessis, J., D. Solin, L. Travis and L. White. (1987). UG or not UG, that is the question: a reply to Clahsen and Muysken. *Second Language Research* 3: 56–75.

Duffield, N. and L. White. (1999). Assessing L2 knowledge of Spanish clitic placement: converging methodologies. *Second Language Research* 15: 133–60.

Duffield, N., L. White, J. Bruhn de Garavito, S. Montrul and P. Prévost. (2002). Clitic placement in L2 French: evidence from sentence matching. *Journal of Linguistics* 38.3.

Dulay, H. and M. Burt. (1974). Natural sequences in child second language acquisition. *Language Learning* 24: 37–53.

Eckman, F. (1994). Local and long-distance anaphora in second-language acquisition. In E. Tarone, S. Gass and A. Cohen (eds.), *Research methodology in second-language acquisition* (pp. 207–25). Hillsdale, NJ: Lawrence Erlbaum.

Ellis, R. (1990). Grammaticality judgments and learner variability. In H. Burmeister and P. Rounds (eds.), *Proceedings of the 10th Second Language Research Forum* (pp. 25–60). American English Institute, University of Oregon.

Emonds, J. (1978). The verbal complex V′ – V in French. *Linguistic Inquiry* 9: 151–75.

Epstein, S., S. Flynn and G. Martohardjono. (1996). Second language acquisition: theoretical and experimental issues in contemporary research. *Brain and Behavioral Sciences* 19: 677–758.

Epstein, S., S. Flynn and G. Martohardjono. (1998). The strong continuity hypothesis: some evidence concerning functional categories in adult L2 acquisition. In S. Flynn, G. Martohardjono and W. O'Neil (eds.), *The generative study of second language acquisition* (pp. 61–77). Mahwah, NJ: Lawrence Erlbaum.

Eubank, L. (1993). Sentence matching and processing in L2 development. *Second Language Research* 9: 253–80.

Eubank, L. (1993/1994). On the transfer of parametric values in L2 development. *Language Acquisition* 3: 183–208.

Eubank, L. (1994). Optionality and the initial state in L2 development. In T. Hoekstra and B. D. Schwartz (eds.), *Language acquisition studies in generative grammar* (pp. 369–88). Amsterdam: John Benjamins.

Eubank, L. (1996). Negation in early German-English interlanguage: more valueless features in the L2 initial state. *Second Language Research* 12: 73–106.

Eubank, L., J. Bischof, A. Huffstutler, P. Leek and C. West. (1997). 'Tom eats slowly cooked eggs': thematic-verb raising in L2 knowledge. *Language Acquisition* 6: 171–99.

Eubank, L. and S. Grace. (1998). V-to-I and inflection in non-native grammars. In M.-L. Beck (ed.), *Morphology and its interfaces in L2 knowledge* (pp. 69–88). Amsterdam: John Benjamins.

Felix, S. (1986). *Cognition and language growth.* Dordrecht: Foris.

Felix, S. (1988). UG-generated knowledge in adult second language acquisition. In S. Flynn and W. O'Neil (eds.), *Linguistic theory in second language acquisition* (pp. 277–94). Dordrecht: Kluwer.

Felix, S. and W. Weigl. (1991). Universal Grammar in the classroom: the effects of formal instruction on second language acquisition. *Second Language Research* 7: 162–80.

Ferdinand, A. (1996). *The development of functional categories: the acquisition of the subject in French.* The Hague: Holland Academic Graphics.

Fernández, E. (1999). Processing strategies in second language acquisition. In E. Klein and G. Martohardjono (eds.), *The development of second language grammars: a generative approach* (pp. 217–39). Amsterdam: John Benjamins.

Fernández, E. (To appear). *Bilingual sentence processing: relative clause attachment in English and Spanish.* Amsterdam: John Benjamins.

Fillmore, C. (1968). A case for case. In E. Bach and R. Harms (eds.), *Universals in linguistic theory* (pp. 1–88). New York: Holt Rinehart and Winston.

Finer, D. (1991). Binding parameters in second language acquisition. In L. Eubank (ed.), *Point counterpoint: Universal Grammar in the second language* (pp. 351–74). Amsterdam: John Benjamins.

Finer, D. and E. Broselow. (1986). Second language acquisition of reflexive-binding. In S. Berman, J.-W. Choe and J. McDonough (eds.), *Proceedings of NELS 16* (pp. 154–68). University of Massachusetts at Amherst: Graduate Linguistics Students Association.

Flege, J. E. and S. Liu. (2001). The effect of experience on adults' acquisition of a second language. *Studies in Second Language Acquisition* 23: 527–52.

Flege, J. E., G. Yeni-Komshian and S. Liu. (1999). Age constraints on second-language acquisition. *Journal of Memory and Language* 41: 78–104.

Flynn, S. (1987). *A parameter-setting model of L2 acquisition.* Dordrecht: Reidel.

Flynn, S. (1996). A parameter-setting approach to second language acquisition. In W. Ritchie and T. Bhatia (eds.), *Handbook of language acquisition* (pp. 121–58). San Diego: Academic Press.

Flynn, S. and G. Martohardjono. (1994). Mapping from the initial state to the final state: the separation of universal principles and language-specific principles. In B. Lust, M. Suñer and J. Whitman (eds.), *Syntactic theory and first language acquisition: cross-linguistic perspectives.* Vol. 1: *Heads, projections and learnability* (pp. 319–35). Hillsdale, NJ: Lawrence Erlbaum.

Fodor, J. D. (1994). How to obey the Subset Principle: binding and locality. In B. Lust, G. Hermon and J. Kornfilt (eds.), *Syntactic theory and first language acquisition: cross-linguistic perspectives.* Vol. 2: *Binding, dependencies and learnability* (pp. 429–51). Hillsdale, NJ: Lawrence Erlbaum.

Fodor, J. D. (1998). Unambiguous triggers. *Linguistic Inquiry* 29: 1–36.

Fodor, J. D. (1999). Learnability theory: triggers for parsing with. In E. Klein and G. Martohardjono (eds.), *The development of second language grammars: a generative approach* (pp. 363–403). Amsterdam: John Benjamins.

Fodor, J., J. D. Fodor and M. Garrett. (1975). The psychological unreality of semantic representations. *Linguistic Inquiry* 6: 515–31.

Franceschina, F. (2001). Morphological or syntactic deficits in near-native speakers? An assessment of some current proposals. *Second Language Research* 17: 213–47.

Freedman, S. and K. Forster. (1985). The psychological status of overgenerated sentences. *Cognition* 19: 101–31.

Fukuda, M. (1993). Head government and case marker drop in Japanese. *Linguistic Inquiry* 24: 168–72.

Fukui, N. and M. Speas. (1986). Specifiers and projection. *MIT Working Papers in Linguistics* 8: 128–72.

Gass, S. (2001). Sentence matching: a reexamination. *Second Language Research* 17: 421–41.

Gavruseva, L. and D. Lardiere. (1996). The emergence of extended phrase structure in child L1 acquisition. In A. Stringfellow, D. Cahana-Amitay, E. Hughes and A. Zukowski (eds.), *Proceedings of the 20th Annual Boston University Conference on Language Development* (pp. 225–36). Somerville, MA: Cascadilla Press.

Gerbault, J. (1978). The acquisition of English by a five year old French speaker. Unpublished MA thesis, UCLA.

Gess, R. and J. Herschensohn. (2001). Shifting the DP parameter: a study of anglophone French L2ers. In C. R. Wiltshire and J. Camps (eds.), *Romance syntax, semantics and their L2 acquisition* (pp. 105–19). Amsterdam: John Benjamins.

Gibson, E. and K. Wexler. (1994). Triggers. *Linguistic Inquiry* 25: 407–54.

Giorgi, A. and F. Pianesi. (1997). *Tense and aspect: from semantics to morphosyntax*. Oxford: Oxford University Press.

Gleitman, L. (1990). The structural sources of verb meaning. *Language Acquisition* 1: 3–55.

Goodluck, H. (1991). *Language acquisition: a linguistic introduction*. Oxford: Blackwell.

Green, G. (1974). *Semantics and syntactic regularity*. Bloomington: Indiana University Press.

Gregg, K. (1996). The logical and developmental problems of second language acquisition. In W. Ritchie and T. Bhatia (eds.), *Handbook of second language acquisition* (pp. 49–81). San Diego: Academic Press.

Gregg, K. (2003). SLA theory construction and assessment. In C. Doughty and M. Long (eds.), *Handbook of second language acquisition*. Oxford: Blackwell.

Grimshaw, J. (1981). Form, function and the language acquisition device. In C. L. Baker and J. McCarthy (eds.), *The logical problem of language acquisition*. Cambridge, MA: MIT Press.

Grimshaw, J. (1990). *Argument structure*. Cambridge, MA: MIT Press.

Grimshaw, J. and S. T. Rosen. (1990). Knowledge and obedience: the developmental status of the binding theory. *Linguistic Inquiry* 21: 187–222.

Grondin, N. and L. White. (1996). Functional categories in child L2 acquisition of French. *Language Acquisition* 5: 1–34.

Gropen, J., S. Pinker, M. Hollander, R. Goldberg and R. Wilson. (1989). The learnability and acquisition of the dative alternation in English. *Language* 65: 205–57.

Gruber, J. (1965). *Lexical structures in syntax and semantics*. Amsterdam: North Holland.

Guasti, M. T. (1994). Verb syntax in Italian child grammar: finite and non-finite verbs. *Language Acquisition* 3: 1–40.

Haegeman, L. (1991). *Introduction to government and binding theory*. Oxford: Blackwell.

Haegeman, L. (1995). Root infinitives, tense and truncated structures. *Language Acquisition* 4: 205–55.

Hale, K. (1996). Can UG and the L1 be distinguished in L2 acquisition? *Brain and Behavioral Sciences* 19: 728–30.

Hale, K. and S. J. Keyser. (1992). The syntactic character of thematic structure. In I. Roca (ed.), *Thematic structure: its role in grammar* (pp. 107–44). Dordrecht: Foris.

Hale, K. and S. J. Keyser. (1993). On argument structure and the lexical expression of syntactic relations. In K. Hale and S. J. Keyser (eds.), *The view from building 20* (pp. 53–109). Cambridge, MA: MIT Press.

Halle, M. and A. Marantz. (1993). Distributed morphology and the pieces of inflection. In K. Hale and S. J. Keyser (eds.), *The view from building 20* (pp. 111–76). Cambridge, MA: MIT Press.

Hamilton, R. (1998). Underdetermined binding of reflexives by adult Japanese-speaking learners of English. *Second Language Research* 14: 292–320.

Harris, J. (1991). The exponence of gender in Spanish. *Linguistic Inquiry* 22: 27–62.

Hawkins, R. (1998). The inaccessibility of formal features of functional categories in second language acquisition. Paper presented at the Pacific Second Language Research Forum, Tokyo.

Hawkins, R. (2000). Persistent selective fossilisation in second language acquisition and the optimal design of the language faculty. *Essex Research Reports in Linguistics* 34: 75–90.

Hawkins, R. (2001a). *Second language syntax: a generative introduction.* Oxford: Blackwell.

Hawkins, R. (2001b). The theoretical significance of Universal Grammar in second language acquisition. *Second Language Research* 17: 345–67.

Hawkins, R. and Y.-H. C. Chan. (1997). The partial availability of Universal Grammar in second language acquisition: the 'failed functional features hypothesis'. *Second Language Research* 13: 187–226.

Haznedar, B. (1997). L2 acquisition by a Turkish-speaking child: evidence for L1 influence. In E. Hughes, M. Hughes and A. Greenhill (eds.), *Proceedings of the 21st Annual Boston University Conference on Language Development* (pp. 245–56). Somerville, MA: Cascadilla Press.

Haznedar, B. (2001). The acquisition of the IP system in child L2 English. *Studies in Second Language Acquisition* 23: 1–39.

Haznedar, B. and B. D. Schwartz. (1997). Are there optional infinitives in child L2 acquisition? In E. Hughes, M. Hughes and A. Greenhill (eds.), *Proceedings of the 21st Annual Boston University Conference on Language Development* (pp. 257–68). Somerville, MA: Cascadilla Press.

Herschensohn, J. (2000). *The second time round: Minimalism and L2 acquisition.* Amsterdam: John Benjamins.

Hilles, S. (1991). Access to Universal Grammar in second language acquisition. In L. Eubank (ed.), *Point counterpoint: Universal Grammar in the second language* (pp. 305–38). Amsterdam: John Benjamins.

Hirakawa, M. (1990). A study of the L2 acquisition of English reflexives. *Second Language Research* 6: 60–85.

Hirakawa, M. (1995). L2 acquisition of English unaccusative constructions. In D. MacLaughlin and S. McEwen (eds.), *Proceedings of the 19th Boston University Conference on Language Development* (pp. 291–302). Somerville, MA: Cascadilla Press.

Hirakawa, M. (1999). L2 acquisition of Japanese unaccusative verbs by speakers of English and Chinese. In K. Kanno (ed.), *The acquisition of Japanese as a second language* (pp. 89–113). Amsterdam: John Benjamins.

Hirakawa, M. (2000). Unaccusativity in second language Japanese and English. Unpublished PhD thesis, McGill University.

Hirakawa, M. (2001). L2 acquisition of Japanese unaccusative verbs. *Studies in Second Language Acquisition* 23: 221–45.

Hirsh-Pasek, K., R. Treiman and M. Schneiderman. (1984). Brown and Hanlon revisited: mothers' sensitivity to ungrammatical forms. *Journal of Child Language* 11: 81–8.

Hoekstra, T. and N. Hyams. (1998). Aspects of root infinitives. *Lingua* 106: 81–112.

Hoekstra, T., N. Hyams and M. Becker. (1999). The role of the specifier and finiteness in early grammar. In D. Adger, S. Pintzuk, B. Plunkett and G. Tsoulas (eds.), *Specifiers: minimalist approaches* (pp. 251–70). Oxford: Oxford University Press.

Hornstein, N. and D. Lightfoot (eds.). (1981). *Explanation in linguistics: the logical problem of language acquisition*. London: Longman.

Huang, C.-T. J. (1984). On the distribution and reference of empty pronouns. *Linguistic Inquiry* 15: 531–74.

Hulk, A. (1991). Parameter setting and the acquisition of word order in L2 French. *Second Language Research* 7: 1–34.

Hyams, N. (1986). *Language acquisition and the theory of parameters*. Dordrecht: Reidel.

Hyams, N. (1992). The genesis of clausal structure. In J. Meisel (ed.), *The acquisition of verb placement* (pp. 371–400). Dordrecht: Kluwer.

Hyams, N. (1994). V2, null arguments and COMP projections. In T. Hoekstra and B. D. Schwartz (eds.), *Language acquisition studies in generative grammar* (pp. 21–55). Amsterdam: John Benjamins.

Hyams, N. (1996). The underspecification of functional categories in early grammar. In H. Clahsen (ed.), *Generative perspectives on language acquisition: empirical findings, theoretical considerations, crosslinguistic comparisons* (pp. 91–127). Amsterdam: John Benjamins.

Hyams, N. and K. Safir. (1991). Evidence, analogy and passive knowledge: comments on Lakshmanan. In L. Eubank (ed.), *Point Counterpoint: Universal Grammar in the second language* (pp. 411–18). Amsterdam: John Benjamins.

Hyams, N. and S. Sigurjonsdottir. (1990). The development of 'long-distance anaphora': a cross-linguistic comparison with special reference to Icelandic. *Language Acquisition* 1: 57–93.

Hyltenstam, K. and N. Abrahamsson. (2003). Maturational constraints in SLA. In C. Doughty and M. Long (eds.), *Handbook of second language acquisition*. Oxford: Blackwell.

Iatridou, S. (1990). About AgrP. *Linguistic Inquiry* 21: 551–7.

Inagaki, S. (1997). Japanese and Chinese learners' acquisition of the narrow-range rules for the dative alternation in English. *Language Learning* 47: 637–69.

Inagaki, S. (2001). Motion verbs with goal PPs in the L2 acquisition of English and Japanese. *Studies in Second Language Acquisition* 23: 153–70.

Inagaki, S. (2002). Japanese learners' acquisition of English manner-of-motion verbs with locational/directional PPs. *Second Language Research* 18: 3–27.

Ionin, T. and K. Wexler. (2002). Why is 'is' easier than '-s'?: acquisition of tense/agreement morphology by child second language learners of English. *Second Language Research* 18: 95–136.

Izumi, S. and U. Lakshmanan. (1998). Learnability, negative evidence, and the L2 acquisition of the English passive. *Second Language Research* 14: 62–101.

Jackendoff, R. (1972). *Semantic interpretation in generative grammar*. Cambridge, MA: MIT Press.

Jackendoff, R. (1975). Morphological and semantic regularities in the lexicon. *Language* 51: 639–71.

Jackendoff, R. (1983). *Semantics and cognition*. Cambridge, MA: MIT Press.

Jackendoff, R. (1990). *Semantic structures*. Cambridge, MA: MIT Press.

Jaeggli, O. (1982). *Topics in Romance syntax*. Dordrecht: Foris.

Jaeggli, O. and N. Hyams. (1988). Morphological uniformity and the setting of the null subject parameter. *Proceedings of NELS 18* (pp. 238–53). University of Massachusetts at Amherst: Graduate Linguistics Students Association.

Jaeggli, O. and K. Safir. (1989). The null subject parameter and parametric theory. In O. Jaeggli and K. Safir (eds.), *The null subject parameter* (pp. 1–44). Dordrecht: Kluwer.

Johnson, J. and E. Newport. (1991). Critical period effects on universal properties of language: the status of subjacency in the acquisition of a second language. *Cognition* 39: 215–58.

Juffs, A. (1996a). *Learnability and the lexicon: theories and second language acquisition research*. Amsterdam: John Benjamins.

Juffs, A. (1996b). Semantics-syntax correspondences in second language acquisition. *Second Language Research* 12: 177–221.

Juffs, A. (2000). An overview of the second language acquisition of links between verb semantics and morpho-syntax. In J. Archibald (ed.), *Second language acquisition and linguistic theory* (pp. 187–227). Oxford: Blackwell.

Juffs, A. and M. Harrington. (1995). Parsing effects in second language sentence processing: subject and object asymmetries in wh-extraction. *Studies in Second Language Acquisition* 17: 483–516.

Juffs, A. and M. Harrington. (1996). Garden path sentences and error data in second language sentence processing. *Language Learning* 46: 283–326.

Kanno, K. (1996). The status of a nonparameterized principle in the L2 initial state. *Language Acquisition* 5: 317–32.

Kanno, K. (1997). The acquisition of null and overt pronominals in Japanese by English speakers. *Second Language Research* 13: 265–87.

Kanno, K. (1998a). Consistency and variation in second language acquisition. *Second Language Research* 14: 376–88.

Kanno, K. (1998b). The stability of UG principles in second language acquisition. *Linguistics* 36: 1125–46.

Kanno, K. (1999). Case and the ECP revisited: reply to Kellerman and Yoshioka (1999). *Second Language Research* 16: 267–80.

Katada, F. (1991). The LF representation of anaphors. *Linguistic Inquiry* 22: 287–313.

Kayne, R. (1994). *The antisymmetry of syntax*. Cambridge, MA: MIT Press.

Kellerman, E., J. van Ijzendoorn and H. Takashima. (1999). Retesting a universal: the Empty Category Principle and learners of (pseudo)Japanese. In K. Kanno (ed.), *The acquisition of Japanese as a second language* (pp. 71–87). Amsterdam: John Benjamins.

Kellerman, E. and K. Yoshioka. (1999). Inter- and intra-population consistency: a comment on Kanno (1998). *Second Language Research* 15: 101–9.

Kim, M., B. Landau and C. Phillips. (1999). Cross-linguistic differences in children's syntax for locative verbs. In A. Greenhill, H. Littlefield and C. Tano (eds.), *Proceedings of the 23rd Annual Boston University Conference on Language Development* (pp. 337–48). Somerville, MA: Cascadilla Press.

Klein, E. (1993a). A problem for UG in L2 acquisition. *Issues in Applied Linguistics* 4: 33–56.

Klein, E. (1993b). *Toward second language acquisition: a study of null-prep*. Dordrecht: Kluwer.

Klein, E. (1995a). Evidence for a 'wild' L2 grammar: when PPs rear their empty heads. *Applied Linguistics* 16: 87–117.

Klein, E. (1995b). Second versus third language acquisition: is there a difference? *Language Learning* 45: 419–65.

Klein, E. (2001). (Mis)construing null prepositions in L2 intergrammars: a commentary and proposal. *Second Language Research* 17: 37–70.

Klein, E. and G. Martohardjono. (1999). Investigating second language grammars: some conceptual and methodological issues in generative SLA research. In E. Klein and G. Martohardjono (eds.), *The development of second language grammars: a generative perspective* (pp. 3–34). Amsterdam: John Benjamins.

Kornfilt, J. (1997). *Turkish*. London: Routledge.

Kuno, S. (1973). *The structure of the Japanese language*. Cambridge, MA: MIT Press.

Lakshmanan, U. (1993/1994). 'The boy for the cookie' – some evidence for the nonviolation of the case filter in child second language acquisition. *Language Acquisition* 3: 55–91.

Lakshmanan, U. (2000). Clause structure in child second language grammars. In A. Juffs, T. Talpas, G. Mizera and B. Burtt (eds.), *Proceedings of GASLA IV* (pp. 15–39). University of Pittsburgh Working Papers in Linguistics.

Lakshmanan, U. and L. Selinker. (1994). The status of CP and the tensed complementizer *that* in the developing L2 grammars of English. *Second Language Research* 10: 25–48.

Lakshmanan, U. and L. Selinker. (2001). Analysing interlanguage: how do we know what learners know? *Second Language Research* 17: 393–420.

Landau, B. and L. Gleitman. (1985). *Language and experience: evidence from the blind child*. Cambridge, MA: Harvard University Press.

Lantolf, J. (1990). Reassessing the null-subject parameter in second language acquisition. In H. Burmeister and P. Rounds (eds.), *Proceedings of the 10th Second Language Research Forum* (pp. 429–52). American English Institute, University of Oregon.

Lardiere, D. (1998a). Case and tense in the 'fossilized' steady state. *Second Language Research* 14: 1–26.

Lardiere, D. (1998b). Dissociating syntax from morphology in a divergent end-state grammar. *Second Language Research* 14: 359–75.

Lardiere, D. (1998c). Parameter-resetting in morphology: evidence from compounding. In M.-L. Beck (ed.), *Morphology and its interfaces in second language knowledge* (pp. 283–305). Amsterdam: John Benjamins.

Lardiere, D. (1999). Suppletive agreement in second language acquisition. In A. Greenhill, H. Littlefield and C. Tano (eds.), *Proceedings of the 23rd Annual Boston University Conference on Language Development* (pp. 386–96). Somerville, MA: Cascadilla Press.

Lardiere, D. (2000). Mapping features to forms in second language acquisition. In J. Archibald (ed.), *Second language acquisition and linguistic theory* (pp. 102–29). Oxford: Blackwell.

Lardiere, D. and B. D. Schwartz. (1997). Feature-marking in the L2 development of deverbal compounds. *Journal of Linguistics* 33: 327–53.

Lee, D. and J. Schachter. (1997). Sensitive period effects in binding theory. *Language Acquisition* 6: 333–62.

Leung, Y.-K. I. (2001). The initial state of L3A: full transfer and failed features? In X. Bonch-Bruevich, W. Crawford, J. Hellerman, C. Higgins and H. Nguyen (eds.), *The past, present and future of second language research: selected proceedings of the 2000 Second Language Research Forum* (pp. 55–75). Somerville, MA: Cascadilla Press.

Levin, B. and M. Rappaport-Hovav. (1995). *Unaccusativity: at the syntax-lexical semantics interface*. Cambridge, MA: MIT Press.

Liceras, J. (1986). *Linguistic theory and second language acquisition*. Tübingen: Gunter Narr Verlag.

Liceras, J. (1997). The then and now of L2 growing pains. In L. Díaz and C. Pérez (eds.), *Views on the acquisition and use of a second language* (pp. 65–85). Barcelona: Universitat Pompeu Fabra.

Liceras, J. and L. Díaz. (2000). Triggers in L2 acquisition: the case of Spanish N-N compounds. *Studia Linguistica* 54: 197–211.

Lightfoot, D. (1989). The child's trigger experience: Degree-0 learnability. *Brain and Behavioral Sciences* 12: 321–75.

Lightfoot, D. (1999a). Creoles and cues. In M. DeGraff (ed.), *Language creation and language change: creolization, diachrony and development* (pp. 431–52). Cambridge, MA: MIT Press.

Lightfoot, D. (1999b). *The development of language: acquisition, change and evolution*. Oxford: Blackwell.

Long, M. (1990). Maturational constraints on language development. *Studies in Second Language Acquisition* 12: 251–85.

Long, M. (2003). Stabilization and fossilization in interlanguage development. In C. Doughty and M. Long (eds.), *Handbook of second language acquisition*. Oxford: Blackwell.

Lumsden, J. (1992). Underspecification in grammatical and natural gender. *Linguistic Inquiry* 22: 469–86.

Lust, B. (1994). Functional projection of CP and phrase structure parameterization: an argument for the strong continuity hypothesis. In B. Lust, M. Suñer and J. Whitman (eds.), *Syntactic theory and first language acquisition: cross-linguistic perspectives*. Vol. 1: *Heads, projections and learnability* (pp. 85–118). Hillsdale, NJ: Lawrence Erlbaum.

Lust, B., S. Flynn and C. Foley. (1996). What children know about what they say: elicited imitation as a research tool for assessing children's syntax. In D. McDaniel, C. McKee and H. S. Cairns (eds.), *Methods for assessing children's syntax* (pp. 55–102). Cambridge, MA: MIT Press.

MacLaughlin, D. (1996). Second language acquisition of English reflexives: is there hope beyond transfer. In A. Stringfellow, D. Cahana-Amitay, E. Hughes and A. Zukowski (eds.), *Proceedings of the 20th Annual Boston University Conference on Language Development* (pp. 453–64). Somerville, MA: Cascadilla Press.

MacLaughlin, D. (1998). The acquisition of the morphosyntax of English reflexives by non-native speakers. In M.-L. Beck (ed.), *Morphology and its interfaces in second language knowledge* (pp. 195–226). Amsterdam: John Benjamins.

MacWhinney, B. (1995). *The CHILDES project: tools for analyzing talk*. Hillsdale, NJ: Lawrence Erlbaum.

Manzini, R. and K. Wexler. (1987). Parameters, binding theory, and learnability. *Linguistic Inquiry* 18: 413–44.

Marantz, A. (1995). The minimalist program. In G. Webelhuth (ed.), *Government and binding theory and the minimalist program* (pp. 349–82). Oxford: Blackwell.

Martohardjono, G. (1993). Wh-movement in the acquisition of a second language: a crosslinguistic study of three languages with and without movement. Unpublished PhD thesis, Cornell University.

Martohardjono, G. (1998). Measuring competence in L2 acquisition: commentary on Part II. In S. Flynn, G. Martohardjono and W. O'Neil (eds.), *The generative study of second language acquisition* (pp. 151–7). Mahwah, NJ: Lawrence Erlbaum.

Martohardjono, G. and J. Gair. (1993). Apparent UG inaccessibility in second language acquisition: misapplied principles or principled misapplications? In F. Eckman (ed.), *Confluence: linguistics, L2 acquisition and speech pathology* (pp. 79–103). Amsterdam: John Benjamins.

Mazurkewich, I. (1984a). Dative questions and markedness. In F. Eckman, L. Bell and D. Nelson (eds.), *Universals of second language acquisition* (pp. 119–31). Rowley, MA: Newbury House.

Mazurkewich, I. (1984b). The acquisition of the dative alternation by second language learners and linguistic theory. *Language Learning* 34: 91–109.

Mazurkewich, I. and L. White. (1984). The acquisition of the dative alternation: unlearning overgeneralizations. *Cognition* 16: 261–83.

McDaniel, D., H. S. Cairns and J. R. Hsu. (1990). Binding principle in the grammars of young children. *Language Acquisition* 1: 121–39.

McDaniel, D., C. McKee and H. S. Cairns. (1996). *Methods for assessing children's syntax*. Cambridge, MA: MIT Press.

Meador, D., J. E. Flege and I. MacKay. (2000). Factors affecting the recognition of words in a second language. *Bilingualism: Language and Cognition* 3: 55–67.

Meisel, J. (1989). Early differentiation of languages in bilingual children. In K. Hyltenstam and L. Obler (eds.), *Bilingualism across the lifespan: aspects of acquisition, maturity and loss* (pp. 13–40). Cambridge: Cambridge University Press.

Meisel, J. (1991). Principles of Universal Grammar and strategies of language learning: some similarities and differences between first and second language acquisition. In L. Eubank (ed.), *Point counterpoint: Universal Grammar in the second language* (pp. 231–76). Amsterdam: John Benjamins.

Meisel, J. (1997). The acquisition of the syntax of negation in French and German: contrasting first and second language acquisition. *Second Language Research* 13: 227–63.

Meisel, J., H. Clahsen and M. Pienemann. (1981). On determining developmental stages in natural language acquisition. *Studies in Second Language Acquisition* 3: 109–35.

Montalbetti, M. (1984). After binding: on the interpretation of pronouns. Unpublished PhD thesis, MIT.

Montrul, S. (2000). Transitivity alternations in L2 acquisition: toward a modular view of transfer. *Studies in Second Language Acquisition* 22: 229–73.

Montrul, S. (2001a). Agentive verbs of manner of motion in Spanish and English as second languages. *Studies in Second Language Acquisition* 23: 171–206.

Montrul, S. (2001b). First-language-constrained variability in the second-language acquisition of argument-structure-changing morphology with causative verbs. *Second Language Research* 17: 144–94.

Montrul, S. and R. Slabakova. (2001). Is native-like competence possible in L2 acquisition? *Proceedings of the 25th Annual Boston University Conference on Language Development*. Somerville, MA: Cascadilla Press.

Montrul, S. and R. Slabakova. (2002). Acquiring morphosyntactic and semantic properties of aspectual tenses in L2 Spanish. In A. T. Pérez-Leroux and J. Liceras (eds.), *The acquisition of Spanish morphosyntax: the L1/L2 connection* (pp. 113–49). Dordrecht: Kluwer.

Montrul, S. and R. Slabakova. (2003). Competence similarities between native and near-native speakers: an investigation of the preterite/imperfect contrast in Spanish. *Studies in Second Language Acquisition* 25.3.

Müller, N. (1998). UG access without parameter setting: a longitudinal study of (L1 Italian) German as a second language. In M.-L. Beck (ed.), *Morphology and its interfaces in L2 knowledge* (pp. 115–63). Amsterdam: John Benjamins.

Müller, N. and A. Hulk. (2000). Bilingual first language acquisition at the interface between syntax and pragmatics. *Bilingualism: Language and Cognition* 3: 227–44.

Murphy, V. (1997). Level-ordering and dual-mechanisms as explanations of L2 grammars. In M. Hughes and A. Greenhill (eds.), *Proceedings of the 21st Annual Boston University Conference on Language Development* (pp. 410–21). Somerville, MA: Cascadilla Press.

Neeleman, A. and F. Weerman. (1997). L1 and L2 word order acquisition. *Language Acquisition* 6: 125–70.

Nemser, W. (1971). Approximative systems of foreign language learners. *International Review of Applied Linguistics* 9: 115–23.

Newport, E. and R. Aslin. (2000). Innately constrained learning: blending old and new approaches to language acquisition. In C. Howell, S. Fish and T. Keith-Lucas (eds.), *Proceedings of the 24th Annual Boston University Conference on Language Development* (pp. 1–21). Somerville, MA: Cascadilla Press.

Noguchi, T. (1997). Two types of pronouns and variable binding. *Language* 73: 770–97.

O'Grady, W. (1987). *Principles of grammar and learning*. Chicago: Chicago University Press.

O'Grady, W. (1996). Language acquisition without Universal Grammar: a general nativist proposal for L2 learning. *Second Language Research* 12: 374–97.

O'Grady, W. (1997). *Syntactic development*. Chicago: University of Chicago Press.

O'Grady, W. (2003). The radical middle: nativism without Universal Grammar. In C. Doughty and M. Long (eds.), *Handbook of second language acquisition*. Oxford: Blackwell.

Oshita, H. (1997). The unaccusative trap: L2 acquisition of English intransitive verbs. Unpublished PhD thesis, University of Southern California.

Oshita, H. (2000). *What is happened* may not be what appears to be happening: a corpus study of 'passive' unaccusatives in L2 English. *Second Language Research* 16: 293–324.

Ouhalla, J. (1991). *Functional categories and parametric variation*. London: Routledge.

Papp, S. (2000). Stable and developmental optionality in native and non-native Hungarian grammars. *Second Language Research* 16: 173–200.

Paradis, J. and F. Genesee. (1996). Syntactic acquisition in bilingual children: autonomous or interdependent. *Studies in Second Language Acquisition* 18: 1–25.

Parodi, T., B. D. Schwartz and H. Clahsen. (1997). On the L2 acquisition of the morphosyntax of German nominals. *Essex Research Reports in Linguistics* 15: 1–43.

Patkowski, M. (1980). The sensitive period for the acquisition of syntax in a second language. *Language Learning* 30: 440–72.

Pérez-Leroux, A. T. and W. Glass. (1997). OPC effects in the L2 acquisition of Spanish. In A. T. Pérez-Leroux and W. Glass (eds.), *Contemporary perspectives on the acquisition of Spanish*. Vol. 1: *Developing grammars* (pp. 149–65). Somerville, MA: Cascadilla Press.

Pérez-Leroux, A. T. and W. Glass. (1999). Null anaphora in Spanish second language acquisition: probabilistic versus generative approaches. *Second Language Research* 15: 220–49.

Pérez-Leroux, A. T. and X. Li. (1998). Selectivity in the acquisition of complex NP islands. In E. Klein and G. Martohardjono (eds.), *The development of second language grammars: a generative approach* (pp. 148–68). Amsterdam: John Benjamins.

Perlmutter, D. (1978). Impersonal passives and the unaccusative hypothesis. *Berkeley Linguistics Society* 4: 157–89.

Pesetsky, D. (1995). *Zero syntax: experiencers and cascades*. Cambridge, MA: MIT Press.

Peters, A. (1985). Language segmentation: operating principles for the perception and analysis of language. In D. Slobin (ed.), *The crosslinguistic study of language acquisition*. Vol. 2: *The theoretical issues* (pp. 1029–67). Hillsdale, NJ: Lawrence Erlbaum.

Phillips, C. (1995). Syntax at age two: cross-linguistic differences. In C. Schütze, J. Ganger and K. Broihier (eds.), *Papers on language processing and acquisition. MIT Working Papers in Linguistics* 26: 325–82.

Phillips, C. (1996). Root infinitives are finite. In A. Stringfellow, D. Cahana-Arnitay, E. Hughes and A. Zukowski (eds.), *Proceedings of the 20th Annual Boston University Conference on Language Development* (pp. 588–99). Somerville, MA: Cascadilla Press.

Pica, P. (1987). On the nature of the reflexivization cycle. In J. McDonough and B. Plunkett (eds.), *Proceedings of the North Eastern Linguistics Society* (pp. 483–500). University of Massachusetts, Amherst: GLSA.

Pinker, S. (1984). *Language learnability and language development*. Cambridge, MA: Harvard University Press.

Pinker, S. (1989). *Learnability and cognition: the acquisition of argument structure*. Cambridge, MA: MIT Press.

Pinker, S. (1994). *The language instinct*. New York: William Morrow and Co.

Platzack, C. (1986). The position of the finite verb in Swedish. In H. Haider and M. Prinzhorn (eds.), *Verb second phenomena in Germanic languages* (pp. 27–47). Dordrecht: Foris.

Platzack, C. (1996). The initial hypothesis of syntax: a minimalist perspective on language acquisition and attrition. In H. Clahsen (ed.), *Generative perspectives on language acquisition: empirical findings, theoretical considerations, crosslinguistic comparisons* (pp. 369–414). Amsterdam: John Benjamins.

Platzack, C. and A. Holmberg. (1989). The role of AGR and finiteness. *Working Papers in Scandinavian Syntax* 43: 51–76.

Poeppel, D. and K. Wexler. (1993). The full competence hypothesis of clause structure in early German. *Language* 69: 1–33.

Pollock, J.-Y. (1989). Verb movement, Universal Grammar, and the structure of IP. *Linguistic Inquiry* 20: 365–424.

Pollock, J.-Y. (1997). Notes on clause structure. In L. Haegeman (ed.), *Elements of grammar: handbook in generative syntax* (pp. 237–79). Dordrecht: Kluwer.

Prévost, P. (1997). Truncation in second language acquisition. Unpublished PhD thesis, McGill University.

Prévost, P. and L. White. (2000a). Accounting for morphological variation in L2 acquisition: truncation or missing inflection? In M.-A. Friedemann and L. Rizzi (eds.), *The acquisition of syntax* (pp. 202–35). London: Longman.

Prévost, P. and L. White. (2000b). Missing surface inflection or impairment in second language acquisition? Evidence from tense and agreement. *Second Language Research* 16: 103–33.

Progovac, L. (1992). Relativized SUBJECT: long-distance reflexives without movement. *Linguistic Inquiry* 23: 671–80.

Progovac, L. (1993). Long-distance reflexives: movement-to-Infl vs. relativized subject. *Linguistic Inquiry* 24: 755–72.

Progovac, L. and P. Connell. (1991). Long-distance reflexives, Agr-subjects, and acquisition. Paper presented at the Formal Linguistics Society of Mid-America, University of Michigan, Ann Arbor.

Radford, A. (1990). *Syntactic theory and the acquisition of English syntax*. Oxford: Blackwell.

Radford, A. (1997). *Syntactic theory and the structure of English: a minimalist approach*. Cambridge: Cambridge University Press.

Reinhart, T. and E. Reuland. (1993). Reflexivity. *Linguistic Inquiry* 24: 657–720.

Rice, K. and P. Avery. (1995). Variability in a deterministic model of language acquisition: a theory of segmental acquisition. In J. Archibald (ed.), *Phonological acquisition and phonological theory* (pp. 23–42). Hillsdale, NJ: Lawrence Erlbaum.

Ritchie, W. and T. Bhatia (eds.). (1999). *Handbook of child language acquisition*. San Diego: Academic Press.

Ritter, E. (1991). Two functional categories in noun phrases: evidence from Modern Hebrew. In S. Rothstein (ed.), *Syntax and Semantics* (pp. 37–62). San Diego: Academic Press.

Ritter, E. (1992). Cross-linguistic evidence for number phrase. *Canadian Journal of Linguistics* 37: 197–218.

Ritter, E. (1993). Where's gender? *Linguistic Inquiry* 24: 795–803.

Rizzi, L. (1982). *Issues in Italian syntax*. Dordrecht: Foris.

Rizzi, L. (1986). Null objects in Italian and the theory of pro. *Linguistic Inquiry* 17: 501–57.

Rizzi, L. (1990). *Relativized minimality*. Cambridge: MIT Press.

Rizzi, L. (1993/1994). Some notes on linguistic theory and language development: the case of root infinitives. *Language Acquisition* 3: 371–93.

Rizzi, L. (1994). Early null subjects and root null subjects. In T. Hoekstra and B. D. Schwartz (eds.), *Language acquisition studies in generative grammar* (pp. 151–76). Amsterdam: John Benjamins.

Rizzi, L. (1997). The fine structure of the left periphery. In L. Haegeman (ed.), *Elements of grammar: handbook in generative syntax* (pp. 281–337). Dordrecht: Kluwer.

Rizzi, L. (2000). Remarks on early null subjects. In M.-A. Friedemann and L. Rizzi (eds.), *The acquisition of syntax: studies in comparative developmental linguistics* (pp. 269–92). London: Longman.

Rizzi, L. and I. Roberts. (1989). Complex inversion in French. *Probus* 1: 1–30.

Robertson, D. (2000). Variability in the use of the English article system by Chinese learners of English. *Second Language Research* 16: 135–72.

Robertson, D. and A. Sorace. (1999). Losing the V2 constraint. In E. Klein and G. Martohardjono (eds.), *The development of second language grammars: a generative approach* (pp. 317–61). Amsterdam: John Benjamins.

Rochette, A. (1988). Semantic and syntactic aspects of Romance sentential complementation. Unpublished PhD thesis, MIT.

Roeper, T. and J. de Villiers. (1992). Ordered decisions in the acquisition of wh-questions. In J. Weissenborn, H. Goodluck and T. Roeper (eds.), *Theoretical issues in language acquisition: continuity and change in development* (pp. 191–236). Hillsdale, NJ: Lawrence Erlbaum.

Roeper, T. and J. Weissenborn. (1990). How to make parameters work: comment on Valian. In L. Frazier and J. de Villiers (eds.), *Language processing and language acquisition* (pp. 147–62). Dordrecht: Kluwer.

Rohrbacher, B. (1994). The Germanic VO languages and the full paradigm: a theory of V to I raising. Unpublished PhD thesis, University of Massachusetts at Amherst.

Rohrbacher, B. (1999). *Morphology-driven syntax : a theory of V to I raising and pro-drop*. Amsterdam: John Benjamins.

Ross, J. (1967). Constraints on variables in syntax. Unpublished PhD thesis, MIT.

Rumelhart, D. E. and M. J. L. (1987). Learning the past tenses of English verbs: implicit rules or parallel distributed processing? In B. MacWhinney (ed.), *Mechanisms of language acquisition* (pp. 195–248). Hillsdale, NJ: Lawrence Erlbaum.

Saito, M. (1985). Some asymmetries in Japanese and their theoretical implications. Unpublished PhD thesis, MIT.

Sawyer, M. (1996). L1 and L2 sensitivity to semantic constraints on argument structure. In A. Stringfellow, D. Cahana-Amitay, E. Hughes and A. Zukowski (eds.), *Proceedings of the 20th Annual Boston University Conference on Language Development* (pp. 646–57). Somerville, MA: Cascadilla Press.

Schachter, J. (1988). Second language acquisition and its relationship to Universal Grammar. *Applied Linguistics* 9: 219–35.

Schachter, J. (1989). Testing a proposed universal. In S. Gass and J. Schachter (eds.), *Linguistic perspectives on second language acquisition* (pp. 73–88). Cambridge: Cambridge University Press.

Schachter, J. (1990). On the issue of completeness in second language acquisition. *Second Language Research* 6: 93–124.

Schachter, J. (1996). Maturation and the issue of Universal Grammar in L2 acquisition. In W. Ritchie and T. Bhatia (eds.), *Handbook of language acquisition* (pp. 159–93). New York: Academic Press.

Schachter, J. and V. Yip. (1990). Grammaticality judgments: why does anyone object to subject extraction? *Studies in Second Language Acquisition* 12: 379–92.

Schaeffer, J. (2000). *Direct object scrambling and clitic placement: syntax and pragmatics*. Amsterdam: John Benjamins.

Schütze, C. (1996). *The empirical base of linguistics: grammaticality judgments and linguistic methodology*. Chicago: University of Chicago Press.

Schütze, C. and K. Wexler. (1996). Subject case-licensing and English root infinitives. In A. Stringfellow, D. Cahana-Amitay, E. Hughes and A. Zukowski (eds.), *Proceedings of the 20th Annual Boston University Conference on Language Development* (pp. 670–81). Somerville, MA: Cascadilla Press.

Schwartz, B. D. (1987). The modular basis of second language acquisition. Unpublished PhD thesis, University of Southern California.

Schwartz, B. D. (1990). Un-motivating the motivation for the fundamental difference hypothesis. In H. Burmeister and P. Rounds (eds.), *Proceedings of the 10th Second Language Research Forum* (pp. 667–84). American English Institute, University of Oregon.

Schwartz, B. D. (1991). Conceptual and empirical evidence: a response to Meisel. In L. Eubank (ed.), *Point Counterpoint: Universal Grammar in the second language* (pp. 277–304). Amsterdam: John Benjamins.

Schwartz, B. D. (1993). On explicit and negative data effecting and affecting competence and 'linguistic behavior'. *Studies in Second Language Acquisition* 15: 147–63.

Schwartz, B. D. (1997). On the basis of the Basic Variety. *Second Language Research* 13: 386–402.

Schwartz, B. D. (1998a). On two hypotheses of 'Transfer' in L2A: minimal trees and absolute L1 influence. In S. Flynn, G. Martohardjono and W. O'Neil (eds.), *The generative study of second language acquisition* (pp. 35–59). Mahwah, NJ: Lawrence Erlbaum.

Schwartz, B. D. (1998b). The second language instinct. *Lingua* 106: 133–60.

Schwartz, B. D. and L. Eubank. (1996). What is the 'L2 initial state'? *Second Language Research* 12: 1–5.

Schwartz, B. D. and M. Gubala-Ryzak. (1992). Learnability and grammar reorganization in L2A: against negative evidence causing unlearning of verb movement. *Second Language Research* 8: 1–38.

Schwartz, B. D. and R. Sprouse. (1994). Word order and nominative case in nonnative language acquisition: a longitudinal study of (L1 Turkish) German interlanguage. In T. Hoekstra and B. D. Schwartz (eds.), *Language acquisition studies in generative grammar* (pp. 317–68). Amsterdam: John Benjamins.

Schwartz, B. D. and R. Sprouse. (1996). L2 cognitive states and the full transfer/full access model. *Second Language Research* 12: 40–72.

Schwartz, B. D. and R. Sprouse. (2000a). The use and abuse of linguistic theory in L2 acquisition research. In A. Juffs, T. Talpas, G. Mizera and B. Burtt (eds.), *Proceedings of GASLA IV* (pp. 176–87). University of Pittsburgh Working Papers in Linguistics.

Schwartz, B. D. and R. Sprouse. (2000b). When syntactic theories evolve: consequences for L2 acquisition research. In J. Archibald (ed.), *Second language acquisition and linguistic theory* (pp. 156–86). Oxford: Blackwell.

Schwartz, B. D. and A. Tomaselli. (1990). Some implications from an analysis of German word order. In W. Abraham, W. Kosmeijer and E. Reuland (eds.), *Issues in Germanic syntax* (pp. 251–74). Berlin: Walter de Gruyter.

Schwartz, B. D. and S. Vikner. (1996). The verb always leaves IP in V2 clauses. In A. Belletti and L. Rizzi (eds.), *Parameters and functional heads: essays in comparative syntax* (pp. 11–62). Oxford: Oxford University Press.

Selinker, L. (1972). Interlanguage. *International Review of Applied Linguistics* 10: 209–31.

Sells, P. (1984). The syntax and semantics of resumptive pronouns. Unpublished PhD thesis, University of Massachusetts at Amherst.

Slabakova, R. (2000). L1 transfer revisited: the L2 acquisition of telicity marking in English by Spanish and Bulgarian native speakers. *Linguistics* 38: 739–70.

Slabakova, R. (2001). *Telicity in the second language*. Amsterdam: John Benjamins.

Smith, C. (1991). *The parameter of aspect*. Amsterdam: John Benjamins.

Smith, N. and I.-M. Tsimpli. (1995). *The mind of a savant*. Oxford: Blackwell.

Snow, C. and M. Hoefnagel-Hohle. (1978). Age differences in second language acquisition. In E. Hatch (ed.), *Second language acquisition: a book of readings*. Rowley, MA: Newbury House.

Snyder, W. (1995a). Language acquisition and language variation: the role of morphology. Unpublished PhD thesis, MIT.

Snyder, W. (1995b). A neo-Davidsonian approach to resultatives, particles and datives. In J. Beckman (ed.) *Proceedings of NELS 25* (pp. 457–71). University of Massachusetts at Amherst, GLSA.

Snyder, W., A. Senghas and K. Inman. (2002). Agreement morphology and the acquisition of noun-drop in Spanish. *Language Acquisition* 9: 157–73.

Snyder, W. and K. Stromswold. (1997). The structure and acquisition of English dative constructions. *Linguistic Inquiry* 28: 281–317.

Sorace, A. (1993a). Incomplete and divergent representations of unaccusativity in non-native grammars of Italian. *Second Language Research* 9: 22–48.

Sorace, A. (1993b). Unaccusativity and auxiliary choice in non-native grammars of Italian and French: asymmetries and predictable indeterminacy. *Journal of French Language Studies* 3: 71–93.

Sorace, A. (1996). The use of acceptability judgments in second language acquisition research. In T. Bhatia and W. Ritchie (eds.), *Handbook of language acquisition*. New York: Academic Press.

Sorace, A. (1999). Initial states, end-states and residual optionality in L2 acquisition. In A. Greenhill, H. Littlefield and C. Tano (eds.), *Proceedings of the 23rd Annual Boston University Conference on Language Development* (pp. 666–74). Somerville, MA: Cascadilla Press.

Sorace, A. (2000). Differential effects of attrition in the L1 syntax of near-native L2 speakers. In C. Howell, S. Fish and T. Keith-Lucas (eds.), *Proceedings of the 24th Annual Boston University Conference on Language Development* (pp. 719–25). Somerville, MA: Cascadilla Press.

Sorace, A. (2003). Optimality as a feature of L2 end-state grammars. In C. Doughty and M. Long (eds.), *Handbook of second language acquisition*. Oxford: Blackwell.

Sprouse, R. (1997). The acquisition of German and the 'Initial Hypothesis of Syntax': a reply to Platzack. In W. Abraham and E. van Gelderen (eds.), *German: syntactic problems – problematic syntax* (pp. 307–17). Tübingen: Max Niemeyer Verlag.

Sprouse, R. (1998). Some notes on the relationship between inflectional morphology and parameter setting in first and second language acquisition. In M.-L. Beck (ed.), *Morphology and its interfaces in second language knowledge* (pp. 41–67). Amsterdam: John Benjamins.

Stowell, T. (1981). Origins of phrase-structure. Unpublished PhD thesis, MIT.

Stromswold, K. (1996). Analyzing children's spontaneous speech. In D. McDaniel, C. McKee and H. S. Cairns (eds.), *Methods for assessing children's syntax* (pp. 23–53). Cambridge, MA: MIT Press.

Talmy, L. (1985). Lexicalization patterns: semantic structure in lexical forms. In T. Shopen (ed.), *Language typology and syntactic description* (pp. 57–149). Cambridge: Cambridge University Press.

Thiersch, C. (1978). Topics in German syntax. Unpublished PhD thesis, MIT.

Thomas, M. (1991a). Do second language learners have 'rogue' grammars of anaphora. In L. Eubank (ed.), *Point counterpoint: Universal Grammar in the second language* (pp. 375–88). Amsterdam: John Benjamins.

Thomas, M. (1991b). Universal Grammar and the interpretation of reflexives in a second language. *Language* 67: 211–39.

Thomas, M. (1993). *Knowledge of reflexives in a second language.* Amsterdam: John Benjamins.

Thomas, M. (1994). Young children's hypotheses about English reflexives. In J. Sokolov and C. Snow (eds.), *Handbook of research in language development using CHILDES* (pp. 254–85). Hillsdale, NJ: Lawrence Erlbaum.

Thomas, M. (1995). Acquisition of the Japanese reflexive *zibun* and movement of anaphors in Logical Form. *Second Language Research* 11: 206–34.

Thomas, M. (1998). Binding and related issues in second language acquisition: commentary on Part III. In S. Flynn, G. Martohardjono and W. O'Neil (eds.), *The generative study of second language acquisition* (pp. 261–76). Mahwah, NJ: Lawrence Erlbaum.

Thráinsson, H. (1996). On the (non-) universality of functional categories. In W. Abraham, S. Epstein, H. Thráinsson and J.-W. Zwart (eds.), *Minimal ideas: syntactic studies in the minimalist framework* (pp. 253–81). Amsterdam: John Benjamins.

Tiphine, U. (undated). The acquisition of English negation by four French children. University of Kiel.

Trahey, M. (1996). Positive evidence in second language acquisition: some long term effects. *Second Language Research* 12: 111–39.

Trahey, M. and L. White. (1993). Positive evidence and preemption in the second language classroom. *Studies in Second Language Acquisition* 15: 181–204.

Travis, L. (1984). Parameters and effects of word order variation. Unpublished PhD thesis, MIT.

Travis, L. (1988). The syntax of adverbs. *Special Issue on Comparative German Syntax. McGill Working Papers in Linguistics*: 280–310.

Tsimpli, I.-M. and A. Roussou. (1991). Parameter resetting in L2?, *UCL Working Papers in Linguistics* 3: 149–69.

Underhill, R. (1976). *Turkish Grammar*. Cambridge, MA: MIT Press.

Vainikka, A. (1993/1994). Case in the development of English syntax. *Language Acquisition* 3: 257–325.

Vainikka, A. and M. Young-Scholten. (1994). Direct access to X'-theory: evidence from Korean and Turkish adults learning German. In T. Hoekstra and B. D. Schwartz (eds.), *Language acquisition studies in generative grammar* (pp. 265–316). Amsterdam: John Benjamins.

Vainikka, A. and M. Young-Scholten. (1996a). The early stages of adult L2 syntax: additional evidence from Romance speakers. *Second Language Research* 12: 140–76.

Vainikka, A. and M. Young-Scholten. (1996b). Gradual development of L2 phrase structure. *Second Language Research* 12: 7–39.

Vainikka, A. and M. Young-Scholten. (1998). Morphosyntactic triggers in adult SLA. In M.-L. Beck (ed.), *Morphology and its interfaces in second language knowledge* (pp. 89–113). Amsterdam: John Benjamins.

Valian, V. (1990). Null subjects: a problem for parameter-setting models of language acquisition. *Cognition* 35: 105–22.

Valois, D. (1991). The internal syntax of DP. Unpublished PhD thesis, UCLA.

Verrips, M. and J. Weissenborn. (1992). Verb placement in early German and French: the independence of finiteness and agreement. In J. Meisel (ed.), *The acquisition of verb placement: functional categories and V2 phenomena in language acquisition* (pp. 283–331). Dordrecht: Kluwer.

Vikner, S. (1995). *Verb movement and expletive subjects in the Germanic languages*. Oxford: Oxford University Press.

Vikner, S. (1997). V-to-I movement and inflection for person in all tenses. In L. Haegeman (ed.), *The new comparative syntax* (pp. 189–213). London: Longman.

Webelhuth, G. (1995). X-bar theory and case theory. *Government and binding theory and the minimalist program* (pp. 15–95). Oxford: Blackwell.

Weissenborn, J. and B. Höhle (eds.). (2001). *Approaches to bootstrapping: phonological, lexical, syntactic and neurophysiological aspects of early language acquisition*. Amsterdam: John Benjamins.

Werker, J. and R. Tees. (1984). Cross-language speech perception: evidence for perceptual reorganization during the first year of life. *Infant Behaviour and Development* 7: 49–63.

Wexler, K. (1994). Optional infinitives, head movement and the economy of derivations. In D. Lightfoot and N. Hornstein (eds.), *Verb movement* (pp. 305–50). Cambridge: Cambridge University Press.

Wexler, K. (1998). Very early parameter setting and the unique checking constraint: a new explanation of the optional infinitive stage. *Lingua* 106: 23–79.

Wexler, K. (1999). Maturation and growth of grammar. In W. Ritchie and T. Bhatia (eds.), *Handbook of child language acquisition* (pp. 55–109). San Diego: Academic Press.

Wexler, K. and R. Manzini. (1987). Parameters and learnability in binding theory. In T. Roeper and E. Williams (eds.), *Parameter setting* (pp. 41–76). Dordrecht: Reidel.

White, L. (1982). *Grammatical theory and language acquisition*. Dordrecht: Foris.

White, L. (1985a). Is there a logical problem of second language acquisition? *TESL Canada* 2: 29–41.

White, L. (1985b). The pro-drop parameter in adult second language acquisition. *Language Learning* 35: 47–62.

White, L. (1986). Implications of parametric variation for adult second language acquisition: an investigation of the 'pro-drop' parameter. In V. Cook (ed.), *Experimental approaches to second language acquisition* (pp. 55–72). Oxford: Pergamon Press.

White, L. (1987a). Against comprehensible input: the input hypothesis and the development of L2 competence. *Applied Linguistics* 8: 95–110.

White, L. (1987b). Markedness and second language acquisition: the question of transfer. *Studies in Second Language Acquisition* 9: 261–86.

White, L. (1988). Island effects in second language acquisition. In S. Flynn and W. O'Neil (eds.), *Linguistic theory in second language acquisition* (pp. 144–72). Dordrecht: Kluwer.

White, L. (1989). *Universal grammar and second language acquisition*. Amsterdam: John Benjamins.

White, L. (1990). Second language acquisition and universal grammar. *Studies in Second Language Acquisition* 12: 121–33.

White, L. (1990/1991). The verb-movement parameter in second language acquisition. *Language Acquisition* 1: 337–60.

White, L. (1991a). Adverb placement in second language acquisition: some effects of positive and negative evidence in the classroom. *Second Language Research* 7: 133–61.

White, L. (1991b). Argument structure in second language acquisition. *Journal of French Language Studies* 1: 189–207.

White, L. (1992a). Long and short verb movement in second language acquisition. *Canadian Journal of Linguistics* 37: 273–86.

White, L. (1992b). On triggering data in L2 acquisition: a reply to Schwartz and Gubala-Ryzak. *Second Language Research* 8: 120–37.

White, L. (1992c). Subjacency violations and empty categories in L2 acquisition. In H. Goodluck and M. Rochemont (eds.), *Island Constraints* (pp. 445–64). Dordrecht: Kluwer.

White, L. (1995a). Chasing after linguistic theory: how minimal should we be? In L. Eubank, L. Selinker and M. Sharwood Smith (eds.), *The current state of interlanguage: studies in honor of William E. Rutherford* (pp. 63–71). Amsterdam: John Benjamins.

White, L. (1995b). Input, triggers and second language acquisition: can binding be taught? In F. Eckman, D. Highland, P. Lee, J. Mileman and R. Rutkowski Weber (eds.), *Second language acquisition theory and pedagogy* (pp. 63–78). Mahwah, NJ: Lawrence Erlbaum.

White, L. (1996a). Clitics in L2 French. In H. Clahsen (ed.), *Generative perspectives on language acquisition: empirical findings, theoretical considerations, crosslinguistic comparisons* (pp. 335–68). Amsterdam: John Benjamins.

White, L. (1996b). Universal grammar and second language acquisition: current trends and new directions. In W. Ritchie and T. Bhatia (eds.), *Handbook of language acquisition* (pp. 85–120). New York: Academic Press.

White, L. (2000). Second language acquisition: from initial to final state. In J. Archibald (ed.), *Second language acquisition and linguistic theory* (pp. 130–55): Blackwell.

White, L. (2002). Morphological variability in endstate L2 grammars: the question of L1 influence. In A. Do, S. Fish, and B. Skarabela (eds.), *Proceedings of the 26th Annual Boston University Conference on Language Development* (pp. 758–68). Somerville, MA: Cascadilla Press.

White, L., C. Brown, J. Bruhn de Garavito, D. Chen, M. Hirakawa and S. Montrul. (1999). Psych verbs in second language acquisition. In G. Martohardjono and E. Klein (eds.), *The development of second language grammars: a generative approach* (pp. 173–99). Amsterdam: John Benjamins.

White, L., J. Bruhn-Garavito, T. Kawasaki, J. Pater and P. Prévost. (1997). The researcher gave the subject a test about himself: problems of ambiguity and preference in the investigation of reflexive binding. *Language Learning* 47: 145–72.

White, L. and F. Genesee. (1996). How native is near-native? The issue of ultimate attainment in adult second language acquisition. *Second Language Research* 11: 233–65.

White, L., M. Hirakawa and T. Kawasaki. (1996). Effects of instruction on second language acquisition of the Japanese long distance reflexive *zibun*. *Canadian Journal of Linguistics* 41: 235–54.

White, L. and A. Juffs. (1998). Constraints on wh-movement in two different contexts of non-native language acquisition: competence and processing. In S. Flynn, G. Martohardjono and W. O'Neil (eds.), *The generative study of second language acquisition* (pp. 111–29). Mahwah, NJ: Lawrence Erlbaum.

White, L., N. Spada, P. Lightbown and L. Ranta. (1991). Input enhancement and L2 question formation. *Applied Linguistics* 12: 416–32.

White, L., E. Valenzuela, M. Macgregor, Y.-K. I. Leung and H. Ben-Ayed. (2001). The status of abstract features in interlanguage grammars: gender and number in L2 Spanish. In A. H.-J. Do, L. Domínguez and A. Johansen (eds.), *Proceedings of the 25th Annual Boston University Conference on Language Development* (pp. 792–802). Somerville, MA: Cascadilla Press.

Whong-Barr, M. and B. D. Schwartz. (2002). Morphological and syntactic transfer in child L2 acquisition of the English dative alternation. *Studies in Second Language Acquisition* 24: 579–616.

Williams, E. (1981). Argument structure and morphology. *The Linguistic Review* 1: 81–114.

Williams, E. (1994). *Thematic structure in syntax*. Cambridge, MA: MIT Press.

Williams, E. (1995). Theta theory. In G. Webelhuth (ed.), *Government and binding theory and the minimalist program* (pp. 99–124). Oxford: Blackwell.

Yip, V. (1995). *Interlanguage and learnability: from Chinese to English*. Amsterdam: John Benjamins.

Yoo, M., Y. Kayama, M. Mazzotta and L. White. (2001). Case drop in L2 Japanese. In A. H.-J. Do, L. Domínguez and A. Johansen (eds.), *Proceedings of the 25th Annual Boston University Conference on Language Development* (pp. 825–34). Somerville, MA: Cascadilla Press.

Yuan, B. (1998). Interpretation of binding and orientation of the Chinese reflexive *ziji* by English and Japanese speakers. *Second Language Research* 14: 324–40.

Yuan, B. (2001). The status of thematic verbs in the second language acquisition of Chinese. *Second Language Research* 17: 248–72.

Xu, L. and T. Langendoen. (1985). Topic structures in Chinese. *Language* 61: 1–27.

Zobl, H. (1989). Canonical typological structures and ergativity in English L2 acquisition. In S. Gass and J. Schachter (eds.), *Linguistic perspectives on second language acquisition* (pp. 203–21). Cambridge: Cambridge University Press.

Zobl, H. and J. Liceras. (1994). Functional categories and acquisition orders. *Language Learning* 44: 159–80.

Zwart, J.-W. (1993). Dutch syntax: a minimalist approach. Unpublished PhD thesis, University of Groningen.

Index